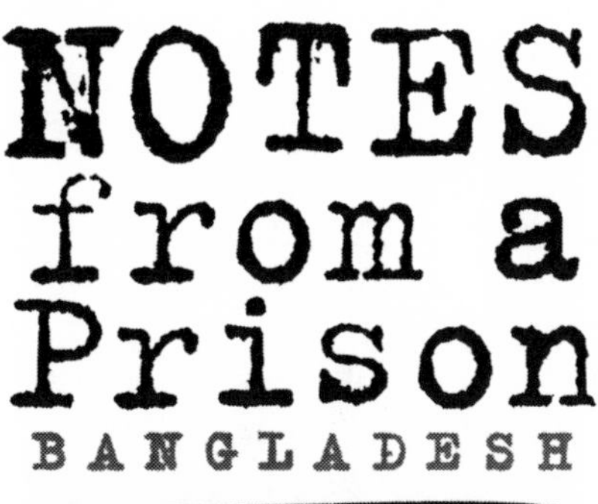

MUHIUDDIN KHAN
ALAMGIR

Foreword by William Christensen, S.M., Ph.D.

Social Justice Publishers

Published by Social Justice Publishers, an imprint of CESJ
P.O. Box 40711, Washington, D.C. 20016, USA
www.cesj.org

International Standard Book Number: 978-0-944997-04-8

Library of Congress Control Number: 2009942874

Cover design by Rowland L. Brohawn

For my wife Sitara

and my sons Shuvo and Joy

Table of Contents

Foreword

One of the inspiring symbols for our Bangladeshi people is the Royal Bengal Tiger. These animals, noted for their courage, strength and ferocity, are indigenous to the Sunderbans mangrove forest area in southwestern Bangladesh. Unfortunately, the courage and strength represented by the tiger is in too short supply among the Bangladesh population today, as it is perhaps worldwide. The majority people of Bangladesh cower before tyranny and oppression, even with the marvelous history of the successful 1971 independence struggle against Pakistan, whose army is estimated to have massacred three million people during those nine months, but who could not get the people to give up their struggle for freedom.

I am most honored to have been invited to write the foreword to *Notes from a Prison Bangladesh*, written by Dr. Muhiuddin Khan Alamgir. His friendship over the past two decades and inspirational example of strength and courage in the face of tyranny, oppression and immense personal suffering, are exemplified in this stirring book.

Recently, the Prime Minister was queried by army personnel: "Why doesn't Dr. Alamgir like the army?" Certainly, he has had a reputation over many years of confronting military leaders who misused power and brought the institution into disrepute. I recall well a visit to his residence in Dhaka, while General Ershad was the country's dictator. Dr. Alamgir mentioned to me that Ershad had said to him "Why don't you come over to the other side? The grass is greener here." The effort to corrupt him was the greatest of insults. As the elected General Secretary of the union for the top civil servants, Dr. Alamgir fought successfully to prevent retired military personnel from increasing the percentage of the top positions that would be reserved for them.

While he was a State Minister in the 1996-2001 Awami League government, he was asked by the Prime Minister to negotiate the Ganges water sharing agreement with India and the peace treaty agreement between the government and the tribal insurgents in the southeastern Chittagong Hill Tracts, near the country's border with Myanmar/Burma. He successfully negotiated both of these vital agreements, which were ratified by the Cabinet. Dr. Alamgir proposed to the Prime Minister that the Taka 10 million (US$ 147,000) being spent per day by the army for controlling the insurgency — perhaps involving significant corruption — should be transferred to development of the Hill Tracts, in order to make peace there permanent. This brilliant suggestion was obviously a source of further antipathy towards Dr. Alamgir by misguided military personnel.

I know Dr. Alamgir well enough to appreciate his respect for the army as an institution, but likewise his readiness to confront its misuse by power-hungry individuals. In these notes, Dr. Alamgir has indicated his position most clearly when reflecting in 2007 in jail on the country's independence 36 years after it was won by the valiant freedom fighters, with help of the Indian army. He says: ". . . some goons lusting for political power through the barrels of their guns given to them for protecting our freedom and independence have come to corral us into submission and servitude. In my subconscious I resolved this could not be allowed; we were not born in 1971 for defeat in 2007."

This book gives in great detail the distortion of the military's purpose — from protecting freedom and independence to becoming a tool of oppression and tyranny in the hands of military leaders promoting their personal ambition. Their use of the methodology developed by the Pakistani dictator Pervez Musharraf to discredit politicians and others who would not cower down to them, by sponsoring a so-called anti-corruption campaign, is fully exposed in this book. The "shoeshine boys" who provided a civilian front for the military leaders were symbolic of many other "sunshine patriots" throughout society, who succumbed to intimidation and fear, thereby strengthening the hands of the tyrants.

The book is replete with references to others who have stood for justice in their personal lives or promoted it through their literary efforts. These others served as a source of inspiration to help Dr. Alamgir overcome the ever-present threat of depression and despair. He realized that ". . . if not confronted at the place where injustice was hewed in by the demon, it would encompass everywhere our people and our children would also live with it." "I remembered that Martin Luther King in 1963 had written from Birmingham jail where he was incarcerated, that oppressed people could not remain oppressed forever. . . ."

"I recalled Robert Frost: 'And I have promises to keep,/And miles to go before I sleep.' That reinforced my will to fight the evil and injustice with dignity." "I also thought of the need for raising the collective conscience of the society recognizing what Dr. Martin Luther King recognized as early as 1963 in the U.S.: that injustice anywhere was a threat to justice everywhere."

As you read this personal testimony of a courageous individual battling defiantly against seemingly overwhelming power, two lessons will blossom forth. Firstly, in spite of all our concern for justice and to protect human rights, humanity is greatly deficient in actually promoting justice and defending human rights. We have ". . . miles to go. . . ." The solution, consistent with the example given by Dr. Alamgir in this book, is to organize to carry out "acts of social justice." The goal of social justice is to restructure our institutions so that the practice of individual virtue once again becomes the natural thing to do in any situation.

Secondly, it is imperative to have persons such as Dr. Muhiuddin Khan Alamgir exemplify for us the way to work for freedom, to defy injustice and to persevere in the struggle to overcome oppression and make the world better for all humankind. In this way we will educate people on the basis of reason enlightened by faith, offer mutual support among small groups organized to improve the common good, identify true "servant leaders" with the prestige and credentials to advocate the new vision and plan for social change and sway public opinion, and develop projects that prove that it is possible for everyone to enjoy equal political, economic, and religious rights.

William Christensen
Founder and Advisor
Institute of Integrated Rural Development (IIRD)
Dhaka, Bangladesh

Preface

From January 11, 2007 till the present, Bangladesh was taken over by a military-controlled government with eleven "shoeshine boys" to give it an image of a civilian regime. During this period hundreds of politicians and businessmen were incarcerated so as to make them bow to those in power and to support the rulers unrepresentative of the citizens. The propaganda machinery of the regime gave the arrestees an image of being corrupt and swindlers of the public fund. I was one of the arrestees incarcerated in jail from February 3, 2007 to October 20, 2008. The military government held out a carrot of discharge if I publicly supported them and, alternatively, a stick of seven criminal charges if I did not succumb to their wishes. After one year and eight months I was posted on bail by the Supreme Court still bearing the burden of false charges and punishment for the drummed-up corruption and criminality.

This is a true story written while I was behind bars — a story that illustrates the de-construction of a dream of freedom in Bangladesh. This is also a tale of how systematically some brutes in the uniformed services riding on the strength of the barrel of the gun, persecuted people and vandalized social, political and administrative institutions developed over decades and violated universally recognized human rights in their drive to perpetuate their illegitimate rule.

For people loving and yearning for freedom everywhere, this journal will provide telltale signs of an undemocratic government and the institutions such a government is bent to manipulate or destroy. The moral of the story and the tale is that it is only through raising universal consciousness against persecution and tyranny that we humankind can give a better account of ourselves as agents and beneficiaries of civilization. It is by fighting injustice anywhere that we can establish justice everywhere.

Muhiuddin Khan Alamgir
Dhaka, Bangladesh
November 2008

1 Background

(1)

It is Sunday, July 13, 2008. I had been arrested by military security forces without warrant or charge in the dead of the night of February 2, 2007. Counting from that night, I have survived till today seventeen months eleven days in prison. Today a petition to post me on bail is being moved before the High Court on the ground that, despite the time limit of ninety days for disposing appeal by the High Court from the date of its filing, it has been pending without hearing for more than eight months. Under the Emergency Powers Rules (a special law in effect after suspension of basic civil rights safeguarded in the Constitution), bail in a graft case in which I have been an accused would not be given, on the grounds that disposal of the case would be quick. The judicial system of the country, reeling under the emergency, has been viewing the time limit in disposal as directory or indicative, but the denial of bail as mandatory.

Since the proclamation of emergency on January 11, 2007 till today, as many as *246 citizens of the country have been killed in the custody of the security forces*; as many as 187 citizens were reported to have been killed in "cross-fire," a sugarcoated version of cold-blooded and deliberate killing without trial or judicial sanction. The proclamation of emergency itself was unconstitutional inasmuch as such a proclamation in accordance with Article 141(a) 2 of the Constitution could be made only on the recommendation of the Prime Minister. Today I am looking forward to a decision by the High Court as to how long a citizen of this independent country could be incarcerated in prison, irrespective of final adjudication of innocence or guilt, in violation of the Constitution and for not submitting to a few men with power flowing through the barrels of their guns and trumpeted by their eleven "shoeshine" supporters.

Today I have arranged the notes that I have mentioned in the prison, in chronological sequence as far as possible. The first two nights following arrest, I was confined in the headquarters of the RAB (the Rapid Action Battalion) of the police in the outskirts of Dhaka city. Then on the night of the 3rd I was taken to the Dhaka

Cantonment Police Station around 9:00 a.m. and kept there till 12 noon next day, and then taken to the court of the Chief Metropolitan Magistrate, Dhaka. While in the Cantonment Police Station, my wife Sitara, nephew Farid and friend Aziz could meet me. Sitara brought me some sandwiches that I ate ravenously.

Upon my reaching the court, without letting me know of the charges against me, the Magistrate somewhat apologetically read out an order, presumably written or handed down previously, interning me into the Dhaka Central Jail under S-16(2) of the Emergency Powers Rules. This law that went into effect from January 11, 2007, empowered the police and the security forces to arrest any citizen of the country without warrant and detain him for an unlimited period; furthermore, the magistracy could not post the arrestee on bail. Completing formalities, I found my way through thousands of party activists, following the cataclysmic paths created by the police in uniform and plainclothes men. With hunger howling in my stomach, I reached the Dhaka Central Jail around 9:00 in the night.

After a thorough search and an abominable process of recognition and registration, I along with thirteen others found a bed each in the Karnaphuli Wing of the jail. We were served morsels of half-cooked rice, overly sparse pulses thrown into disproportionately more water than what was required to constitute the Bangali's *dal* (lentils) and two pieces of almost unbaked *brinjals* (eggplant) for each. Gulping this down, with a glass of water drawn from the jail's tap, I found a makeshift bed with a dirty sheet covering its dilapidated frame as my place for rest for each of four days since I along with the others had been arrested.

Rising next day, I found the prison's yard quite bright in the morning sun. The sky was clear blue with sporadic patches of white clouds passing over. The Karnaphuli Wing, the place of my incarceration, was situated in the southeast corner of the Dhaka Central Jail. The structure with high ceilings was dilapidated, built perhaps during the days of the British Raj.[1] It smelled more of lime and brickbats than of cement. General Ershad, the last military ruler prior to the current regime, was incarcerated in this building when he was thrown out of power in 1991. In deference to his taste and needs, the building was repaired, repainted and provided with a toilet that still worked.

---

[1] The period of British rule, when India, Pakistan, and Bangladesh were all under the same administration.

Strolling in the yard, I found fourteen politicians and businessmen coming out of their makeshift beds in a single long room, where I had slept along with them during the night before. We blinked at the sunlit streaks of freedom from outside the prison-walls that the morning presented us. I saw my friend Salman F. Rahman, who in my assessment was the best entrepreneur of the country (also one of the country's wealthiest businessmen), Mohammad Nasim, the Home Minister in Sheikh Hasina's government, Salahuddin Quader Chowdhury, the Special Advisor to the immediate past Prime Minister Khaleda Zia, Kamal Majumder, a former member of the Parliament and a stalwart of the Dhaka City Awami League, Lotus-Kamal, a chartered accountant and businessman of repute supporting the Awami League, Manzurul Ahsan Munshi, a former member of the Parliament from the Bangladesh Nationalist Party (BNP) and Barrister Nazmul Huda, the Minister of Communication in Khaleda Zia's Cabinet and a few others. All of us were arrested in the night of February 2, kept either in the dungeons of the headquarters of the Rapid Action Battalion of the Police (RAB) or the Bangladesh Rifles (BDR), the country's border security force.

Over a stale cup of tea, a piece of half-baked *ruti* (leavened flat bread) and fried vegetables dispensed by the jail people, we heard each other's accounts: when and how we were arrested and incarcerated in the night, what was the treatment accorded to us by the arrestors, and whether we were given food and water and interrogated. I sighed and said: "If persons who had established their places, if not names, in the society could be arrested and treated the way we were, we would find it difficult to call ourselves a democratic and pluralistic society."

"Don't worry, it will be over soon," said Manjurul Ahsan Munshi with real confidence.

"Not soon, not in at least six months," commented Salman rather dryly.

"Who were behind these arrests? Fakhruddin, (the military-appointed Chief Advisor), or the armed forces attempting a takeover of the government?" Salahuddin Quader Chowdhury wanted to know, dropping ashes from a cigarette held in between two fingers of his left hand.

"Be ready to live in the jail for at least two years," Kamal Majumder, somewhat sick and grim, announced his assessment. He was arrested before us on January 12, immediately after the proclamation of emergency.

"Oh no; the country cannot function this way; they have to release us soon. What crime we have committed that they will keep us in jail just like this?" Lotus-Kamal wanted to know.

"This should not have happened. Both our parties, your Awami League and our BNP, acted foolishly. If we could have gone for election as slated, these people in uniform with Fakhruddin and others as their shoeshine boys, would not have appeared in the scene," Barrister Huda gave his judgment. He forgot to mention that the elaborate arrangements made by their party for rigging the slated election were not only an act of foolishness but also of betrayal.

With the dream in my mind of freedom and democracy (self-evident truths of a free society still unfulfilled in ours), I heard them, walked around them at a slow pace — and kept silent.

(2)

On February 2 in the early morning, I had left Dhaka for my village home and electoral constituency in Chandpur district. When I was ready to leave, I found my wife sleeping peacefully. I decided not to wake her up and skipped my breakfast. It was a beautiful winter morning with very light traffic within the city and on the highway. Taking a circuitous shortcut and looking over green patches of vegetables and potatoes on two sides, I reckoned I would reach my village home in a little over two hours.

As soon as I crossed the Meghna-Gomti Bridge, I had sensed that I was being followed by a jeep with three persons on board. Seeing me taking the circuitous route that would certainly take me to my village, the jeep veered to the right at Narayanpur, a bazaar about four miles to the west of my village, so I thought the jeep was pursuing something else. In my village home, I took my breakfast, talked to my political workers, and walked with them to Debipur, a village lying to the south of mine. I asked everyone to prepare themselves for the election originally slated for January 22 but postponed, and to be orderly and disciplined in the face of obvert provocation from those in power. Then in the evening, I went to village Meghdair, lying to the north of mine, to a religious function. I spoke to a couple of hundred villagers, ate a quick dinner with the organizers and around 8:00 p.m. started back for Dhaka, taking another route to the main Dhaka-Chittagong Highway. I reached Gouripur, a bazaar on the highway about four miles to the east of the Meghna-Gomti Bridge, around 9:00 p.m.

As was usual with me, at Gouripur I stopped at the first filling station, named Chandraban Petrol Pump, to use the restroom.

The manager and other employees were always very respectful and considerate to me; they allowed me to use their owner's restroom upstairs. As I came down from the restroom, my chauffeur pointed at the very jeep, with the very three persons I had observed earlier, stationed on the other side of the highway at a distance of about 30 yards from the Honda CRV I was riding. The three persons though in civvies, with their closely cropped hair and demeanor, looked like personnel of the armed forces.

During the civil unrest centering around the national election slated for January 22, the President on January 11 had proclaimed emergency throughout the country and postponed the election indefinitely. I did not know for certain, at least not at that time, whether in this proclamation he was backed by the armed forces or whether he had asked the armed forces to take all power and responsibility on his behalf,

Seeing those three persons following me, even at night, gave me an ominous feeling. I could not find any cogent reason why I should be shadowed the way I had been. As a member of the Awami League, I was in opposition to the BNP (Bangladesh Nationalist Party, the party in power for five years till November 2006, and those in power could not make any accusation of abuse of office against me.

I asked my chauffeur to drive quickly onto the highway towards Meghna-Gomti Bridge and then, all of a sudden, take a turn to the left along a rural road. Having played a role in negotiations with the Japanese for constructing the bridge, I had occasion to visit the site and surrounding places frequently in 1997 before the bridge was completed and opened to traffic. So I knew these side roads, which were possibly unknown to my followers.

They lost us. I waited for about an hour and sent out Kamal Bhuiyan, a former Chairman of Sachar Union Parishad, in a rickshaw to scout for the jeep. He signaled all clear; we started for Dhaka and drove at a slow pace. I reached my house at Banani around 11:30 p.m., found Sitara my wife waiting for me somewhat cross, and drew a hot bath in preparation for going to bed.

A little after midnight, I closed the door to our bedroom. Sitara put out the light and sat by me, somewhat softened over my late return home. Then came the bang at the door, loud beyond the point of civility. I opened, saw six persons, one in front with a revolver in hand. Sitara came behind me, clutched my wrist with her two hands and looked straight at them as I did.

I demanded their identity. The man with the revolver said he was a Lieutenant Commander of the navy working along with others in the RAB (Rapid Action Battalion of the police) and that they had come to take me out as per orders of their superiors. I asked whether they had a warrant of arrest against me from a court of law. They said it was not necessary; they had come to take me, and they would, warrant or no court warrant.

Sitara shouted at them and said they could not treat me like a criminal. She exclaimed that what we had done for the country, its freedom and development, none of them had ever done. They responded they would give me 30 minutes to prepare, pack a briefcase or small suitcase with nightclothes, a tube of toothpaste and a brush, soap and a towel. I asked them to wait in our living room, went inside the bedroom and packed. Sitara took the bedroom phone and informed my brother Dr. Jahangir at Gulshan and our sons Shuvo and Joy in Boston, USA, before the line was broken from outside.

During the time we took to pack, the group, led by one Colonel Badrul (a short fellow with a goatee), ransacked our living room, library and my personal office down below, throwing around papers, files and books. And then they entered our bedroom with a video camera, searched through wardrobes and the chest of drawers, and below the bed we slept. They threw things here and there, grabbed our cheque books, a few thousand Takas[2] that we had at that time, and seized our mobile phone sets. We looked in silence, did not protest. Silently my wife gave me a cup of coffee; I held her hands for a few seconds and came out after them with my briefcase.

A black SUV quite shiny under the streetlights was waiting for us down below. They made me board. Sitting in the middle in the back seat, I was flanked by the Lieutenant Commander on the right, and a major on the left. They put a black patch over my eyes, despite my protest. Before they tightened the patch, I put my hands over my eyes, pretending I was protecting them against sludge and dust. As a result the patch was loosely set over my eyes and after a while I could make out the surroundings.

The SUV took a turn to the west, made a right turn past Tofail Ahmed's house located on the same street where our house was, and then, keeping the American Center on the right, took the main road leading toward the airport. As a captive, I was traveling along the well-trodden road that I frequently used to go to the northern districts on political tours. Going straight, keeping the airport on the left, the SUV entered the premises of the RAB

[2] "Taka," abbreviated "Tk," is the unit of currency in Bangladesh.

headquarters and stopped in front of a two-storied building at the northwestern corner.

I was made to climb the stairs with the black patches on my eyes and then thrown into a cell, without a window, a bed or a bedcover. I found a single coarse khaki blanket, spewing odor of human excreta and sweat, lying on the cold, damp floor. While clanging shut the cell, a guard told me with a sardonic smile that I would have to make do with that blanket for the wintry night.

Around 3:00 in the night, I shouted to be taken to the toilet. After my continued shouting and banging against the iron cell door, the guards relented and took me to a ramshackle toilet set in between cells. While going out and coming back, I could identify, amongst others, Salahuddin Quader Chowdhury, Lotus-Kamal and Manjurul Ahsan Munshi in other cells. Salahuddin Quader Chowdhury had been the mercurial Advisor to the immediate past Prime Minister Khaleda Zia of the BNP, quite well known for his sharp tongue and support for a very conservative approach to politics. Lotus-Kamal was a well-known businessman, a chartered accountant by training, a suave gentleman by nature and a member of the Awami League's Advisory Council. Munshi was a Member of the Parliament from the BNP, a tough and uncompromising politician from Comilla. All other cells were full with politicians they brought in. I could identify two trade union leaders amongst them. They had, as became evident, incarcerated as many as they could.

The morning came without removing the darkness around me. The darkness made my confinement all the more pronounced. Around 9:00 a.m., the guards threw in a plate with two pieces of *ruti* along with a cup of stale tea, which enabled me to take my pills for diabetes and hypertension. I shouted for a newspaper and was responded to with laughter from the guards. Around 3:00 in the afternoon a plate of half-cooked rice mixed with lentils was thrown in without a glass of water. At about 3:30 p.m., someone wearing a stethoscope around his neck came in, examined me, and told me that my pulse and blood pressure were within tolerable ranges. He looked scared like a wet crow, did not utter any other word and went out without even asking whether I had with me medicines for diabetes and hypertension.

(3)

After he left, I tried to figure out why I had been incarcerated the way I was. I was involved in politics and had taken active part in rallies and demonstrations against the government since I had come out of jail in September 2002. I was Secretary to Prime Minister Sheikh Hasina for about a year in 1996 and 1997, then a State Minister in charge of the Ministry of Planning till the elected government handed over the reins to a caretaker government in July 2001 in order to hold a fair and impartial election.

The caretaker government, in accordance with the Constitution, was headed by Latifur Rahman, the immediate past Chief Justice of the country. As it turned out, neutrality and fairness as matters of principle were unknown to him. The Awami League, which obtained about 42% of the total votes cast (even within the scheme by the opposition party in collaboration with the government to rig the election), could secure only 62 seats in the Parliament. With the BNP's securing 38% of the votes, and with 14% made to cast in favor of the Jamaat-i-Islam, the caretaker government showed that the alliance of the BNP-Jamaat had secured 238 seats in Parliament.

In my constituency, the police and other security forces, won over by money, did not allow our workers and voters even to go to many of the polling stations. The religious minority, the Hindus, were beaten back to their villages and homes on their way to the polling stations. With the connivance of the bribed polling personnel, all their votes were shown to have been cast in favor of the BNP.

I was forced to leave the country a day after the election to save my life. After staying about three months outside, I flew into Dhaka airport from the U.S. and was arrested right at the airport on grounds of "activities prejudicial to the interest of the State." After fighting a series of legal battles, I was released on orders of the Supreme Court (High Court Division) on Sept 17, 2002. I had not been in the government since 2001; I had not had any business or transaction with the government since then. The question of election-rigging, corruption and public misdemeanor could not be raised against me in 2007, as have been raised in the case of those with the government in the last five years, *i.e.*, the BNP leaders.

After some time, I could think of two reasons for my incarceration. Firstly, President Iajuddin — faced with a massive upsurge of discontent and protest against his partisan activities in sync with a similarly partisan Election Commission led by Justice Aziz — was forced to proclaim a state of emergency on January 11 by the armed forces. The three military services chiefs, led by the Chief of Staff of the army, seized Bangabhaban and forced the President to resign as the Chief Advisor to the government. This position the President had assumed unconstitutionally in order to rig the slated election in favor of his party, *i.e.*, the BNP. The military chiefs then proclaimed a state of emergency and postponed the election. This action of the armed forces — though it had postponed an election that the President and his cohorts had rigged — was illegal. It amounted to the armed forces taking over the government, specifically violating Article 141(a) 2 of the Constitution, which requires the Prime Minister to agree to a proclamation of emergency.

In the meeting of the Presidium of the Awami League on the evening of January 11, I protested against the taking over of the government in this way. I suggested that we should not attend the oath-taking ceremony of the new caretaker government backed by the armed forces and, even if it was decided that we as a party should, our Chief Sheikh Hasina should not. This would leave room for dissent in the probable event the caretaker government or the armed forces veered off course in order to settle themselves in power for a long period. In the heat of the moment, I was overruled. Along with Sheikh Hasina, all members of the Awami League Presidium present in Dhaka, including myself, attended the oath taking by Dr. Fakhruddin Ahmed as the Chief Advisor of the caretaker government. This, I suspected, was reported to the powers that be by a quisling[3] mixed up with us.

Dr. Fakhruddin was long known to me. He and I taught Economics in Dhaka University in the early 1960s before we joined the civil service. I found Fakhruddin unusually grim when I greeted him after he was installed as the Chief Advisor. This, I presumed, was the result of what might have been reported by the quisling amongst us. It was, of course, quite well-known before and at the time that I was always against military takeover and rule. In a meeting only a week before this proclamation of emergency and takeover by the military-backed regime, I said that independence for us was not fought and won in order to establish military or autocratic rule in this country.

Secondly, I had publicly opposed, in somewhat vehement terms, sale and handover of the Rupali Bank, a State-owned financial institution, to a Saudi Prince at a price that was actually much less than what was touted by the Privatization Commission. The Commission at the time was led by Enam Ahmed Chowdhury, a brother-in-law of Dr. Fakhruddin. The price offered by the Saudi Prince was touted by the Privatization Commission to be about

---

[3] A traitor, or collaborator with occupying forces.

$536 million. This concealed the fact that from this price, bad debt estimated at $235 million would have to be deducted or taken over by the government.

In a piece that I wrote and published in the *Janakantha*, a leading daily of the country, I brought this out in public and cautioned all concerned to guard against squandering a state commercial bank having 235 branches throughout the country and assets over $1,200 million. Earlier in the same daily, I had focused on an underhand sale of the Rupali Bank's subsidiary in Karachi (which had the status of a full-fledged commercial bank), with the connivance of the Privatization Commission. The representatives of the bank's employees came in hundreds to my house at Banani to express to me their gratitude for revealing the truth and for protecting the employees' interest and publicly created assets.

As a result the sale of the Rupali Bank was stopped. Enam Ahmed Chowdhury and his cohorts became furious. At the Republic Day reception in the residence of the Indian High Commissioner, on January 26, Chowdhury took me aside and told me I did not do a good work by writing those pieces in the *Janakantha*. By that time Dr. Fakhruddin was installed as the Chief Advisor and Chowdhury's younger brother, Iftekhar Ahmed Chowdhury, as the Advisor for Foreign Affairs. Half humorously, I told him at the reception that I had omitted to mention about 34 crores[4] (340 million) of Taka that were spent by the Privatization Commission and its Chairman on road shows to facilitate the bank's sale in the international market.

This made Chowdury all the more furious and he said he would see me at a proper time. I also became somewhat angry. I told him I had yet to write a piece on why and how Dr. Fakhruddin, when he was the Governor of the Bangladesh Bank (*i.e.*, the central bank of the country during Khaleda Zia's regime), appointed another of his brother-in-laws, Masum Ahmed Chowdhury, as the Chairman of the Oriental Bank. (The brother-in-law, to his credit, had his last stint of service as an ambassador). The Oriental Bank had been taken under supervision of the central bank of the country. I said, once so published, Chowdhury might write and publish a rejoinder to prove if he could, that I was wrong.

With these thoughts and observing the indecent and unlawful conduct of the security forces personnel who had arrested me, I found the night falling with its darkness all around. After leftovers from dinner of half-cooked rice, a morsel of vegetables and a

---

[4] A crore is a "unit of account," usually for money, denominating 10 million.

few lentils, I was examined by a doctor who did not give his name. I was then taken out of the cell to an adjacent room. There a very well-behaved officer, presumably from the Army, gave me a form bound by a file cover with "Top Criminal" printed on it.

The officer politely asked me to fill in the form, giving particulars of my education, work, family history, relations working in the government and outside, and a description and valuation of assets I held. I filled in the form, refused to sign it, seeking protection of Article 35 of the Constitution. Article 35 of the Constitution clearly stated that no citizen would be forced to give evidence against himself. The officer seemed to have no knowledge of Article 35. He said that other arrested persons including Salahuddin Quader Chowdhury had already signed it and it would be not taken very kindly by "authorities" if I did not sign the form I had filled in. But I stuck to what I said. He offered me a cup of tea that I politely refused. It was about 3:00 in the night. Then he himself took me to another room where I found six officers sitting around a chair where I was made to sit down.

The officers did not introduce themselves. Only two (presumably one of the National Security Intelligence and the other of the Special Branch of the police) gave their names, which I knew were not real. They interrogated me almost ceaselessly for two hours. The interrogation centered around three main points: (1) why I negotiated the Ganga Water Sharing Treaty with India; (2) how and on whose instructions I wrote the Peace Accord for Chittagong Hill Tracts and (3) what specific development projects were framed, processed and passed on Sheikh Hasina's specific instructions. I told them, from my action and work as the State Minister for Planning or Secretary to the Prime Minister, I was not accountable to them and that I was bound by the oath of secrecy that I took in accordance with the Constitution before entering the office of the State Minister; thus I could not divulge anything to them.

They requested, demanded, threatened, cajoled at times. Two of them even called me names, but I remained firm and smiling most of the time. Like half-baked potatoes, time and again, they wanted me to tell them about Sheikh Hasina's management of the government finances, along with her Finance Minister Kibria who was killed earlier. They told me there would not be anything standing in the way of my going back to my family if I cooperated with them.

A little too sure of themselves, they even produced a paper for me to sign. I refused to look at or sign it. I told them I would not sign anything on a dotted line prepared by others. For them, as it appeared, it was a tepid excuse. I kept my cool, smiled and said time and again that I would not tell a lie; I would not betray the trust Sheikh Hasina deposed on me; and I would not do a thing to harm or hurt her — the daughter of the father of the nation — for anything in the world. And I told them they should not forget what they owed to Bangabandhu for the positions they had been holding in an independent Bangladesh. Then the morning came and I was taken back to the cell. The door clanged shut as soon as I was pushed inside.

My mouth was feeling somewhat foul for I could not brush my teeth or wash my mouth. There was no toothpaste or toothbrush; the water trickling down the tap in the toilet room looked and tasted like something coming out of the sewer. I found that the toothpaste tube and the brush were missing from my briefcase. I knew while I was being interrogated some of the spooks opened my briefcase, along with those of others, and in haste misplaced my paste and brush out of my briefcase.

Around 10:00 in the morning, a Major in uniform appeared. I asked him to let me know whether I was under arrest and if so, as per the law, I should be produced before a Magistrate within 24 hours of when I was brought into this cell and kept captive. He went out with a malignant smile adorning his lips, came back by 11:30 and asked me to board a SUV that would take me to the Cantonment Police Station for producing before a Magistrate. I understood these ruffians wanted to keep their records clean. They wanted to show us as detained by the police and confined in the police station, and to produce before the Magistrate by recording in the relevant forms that I along with others were not detained in the police station for more than 24 hours in violation of our constitutional rights and the law.

When I boarded the SUV they wanted to put those patches over my eyes; I stoutly refused, even shouted. To avoid a scene on the main road they stopped trying. Reaching the Cantonment Police Station, I found another set of eight politicians in addition to ten brought from the RAB Headquarters. I found Salman F. Rahman, Mohammad Nasim, Jahangir Sattar Tinku and even Sheikh Hasina's Private Secretary Dr. Awlad Hossain who was arrested a fortnight[5] earlier than we were. Awlad was in the custody of the joint interrogation cell – a pseudonym for the torture cell of the Directorate General of the Forces Intelligence (DGFI). He was

---

[5] A period of fourteen days, or two weeks.

brought to the Cantonment Police Station to whitewash the record of his unlawful arrest, detention and torture by the DGFI.

I found Barrister Nazmul Huda, Minister of Communication of Khaleda Zia's government, also sitting grimly with Mohammad Nasim and others. Barrister Huda had been avidly against the Awami League, specially my leader Sheikh Hasina. As I had found out, he had been instrumental in arresting me earlier in March 2002. His elder brother was my contemporary and that was how I knew the Barrister for so long.

"So we are in the same boat, brother," I said feigning cheerfulness.

He responded with a quaint smile.

(4)

In the Cantonment Police Station, in contrast to that dungeon in the RAB headquarters, the environment was somewhat lax and relaxed. My wife Sitara could come with a basket of breakfast and a flask of tea after I was able to make a call to her over a mobile phone. I was told Farid, my maternal nephew, was outside and was not being allowed to enter. With an air of defiance, I walked to the gate and asked the sentry to let him in, which surprised him, and he did allow Farid to come in and see me. I brushed my teeth, washed my mouth in the bathroom of the Officer-in-Charge of the Police Station, ate breakfast and drank tea with the others.

From talks with other arrested persons and my wife, I would come to know that all told, fifty politicians and businessmen were arrested the night I was arrested. Arrests were proposed by the DGFI and other intelligence agencies. Dr. Fakhruddin as the Chief Advisor, *i.e.*, the chief executive of the caretaker government, consented. In my case, through the grapevine of the bureaucracy my wife could liaison with, I learned that Dr. Fakhruddin himself made the decision, at the suggestion of Barrister Moinul Hossain, Advisor-in-Charge of Law and Information.

I knew both Dr. Fakhruddin Ahmed and Barrister Moinul Hossain. Moinul Hossain was my contemporary during university days, and Dr. Fakhruddin and I taught Economics in the University after we got our Masters. Moinul was not very well-known for avoiding meanness; values of tolerance, the democratic way and respect for others were not his strong points. Through the grapevine I came to know that when some of our common friends confronted Barrister Moinul about my arrest, he said I had once slapped him hard on the face in the premises of the Supreme

Court Bar Association while having an argument with him. Hearing this, I wished I had done that.

I regarded Dr. Fakhruddin as being above all this, but I thought he was propelled in this process of persecution by that Rupali Bank episode. I joked with Barrister Sigma Huda, Barrister Nazmul Huda's wife. She had flown into Dhaka from London that morning, hearing of the incarceration of her husband. She introduced me to their daughter Antora – a cute, budding barrister coming to the rescue of her father. Borrowing a mobile phone from someone, I talked to my brother Dr. Burhanuddin Khan Jahangir in Gulshan, Dhaka and my two sons in Boston, USA. My friend Aziz sent me a message that Dr. Fakhruddin asked the police to treat us well. On hearing this, I smiled and recalled a saying in Bangla: "some people do not hesitate to present you with a pair of shoes after killing your cattle."

While in the Cantonment Police Station, on and off, the arrestees asked each other why we had been arrested. None could say in definite terms as to what crimes we had committed to draw the wrath of the government of Dr. Fakhruddin, or what power had placed him on the post. I asked the Officer-in-Charge to let us know under what specific law or its sections we would be forwarded to the court. He said he did not know and was awaiting instructions from above. I asked who were the persons living and working above. He pointed his forefinger to the west where the office of the DGFI was located and smiling, did not reply in words.

Around 2:30 in the afternoon, I along with others was asked to board a bus to go to the court of the Metropolitan Magistracy. I took leave of my wife, told her I would not be late in returning home, gave some soothing words that I did not believe myself nor did she, and started towards the abode of justice at the primary level under the law of our land. Peeping through the iron bar crossed holes of the prison van, I could see hundreds of common people and well-wishers lined up on two sides of the road to the court, some showing us "V" signs with their fingers. As we did, they also knew we were being taken to the court so that the powers that be could give us a cover of law to detain us beyond its competent intention.

The court premises were full of lawyers and party activists. I signed some greenish papers at the behest of our lawyers even without looking at them, exchanged greetings with party activists and then was taken before a solemn-looking young man sitting on a platform high above the lawyers and the justice-seekers. I could not say anything nor could others; the lawyers jabbered and at times shouted but the solemn-looking Magistrate waved them into silence and announced without looking at us that we had been arrested under R-16(2) of the Emergency Powers Rules.

This Rule empowered the police and the security forces to arrest anyone, including former Ministers and possibly even the President of the Republic on suspicion of being involved in commission of some specified crimes and, once so arrested, the arrestee could not even apply for being posted on bail. The draconian provision was about the worst possible violation of human rights written into our Constitution. So the Magistrate ordered that all of us should be taken to the Dhaka Central Jail as detainees, in accordance with the Emergency Powers Rules. After completing the paper work and lining up transports, counting of heads, receiving of command certificates by the police and saying goodbyes to our lawyer friends and loyal activists, we started for the jail and reached that namesake for hell around 9:00 in the night, as I said earlier.

We spent three days in the Karnaphuli Wing of the jail. We were locked in that long room of Ershad vintage at sundown. Before the locking in, we were to take our evening meal, rice or *ruti* with half-cooked vegetables (about three tablespoonfuls each) and lentil water (two spoonfuls each out of a bowl made of aluminum). We were locked out at sunup, given an hour to walk and wash, and then a treat of breakfast (two *rutis*, two tablespoonfuls of the cheapest seasonal vegetables, a portion of egg, a smelly concoction going by the name of butter and a mug of stale tea for each).

We exchanged notes: the law under which we were arrested and treated, and the law on the strength of which our residences were searched and ransacked. It seemed, those of us who were residing on the western part of the city were arrested late, taken to the BDR (Border Security Force) headquarters and treated comparatively well. Some amongst us were warned over phone by our leaders that we were being arrested. Sheikh Hasina was reported to have warned Salman and Lotus-Kamal about the impending arrest. No one had warned me. Sheikh Hasina had told both Salman and Lotus-Kamal as they told us, to keep out of their houses to avoid arrest. She had thought the spate of arrests would slow down after a night or two.

Sheikh Hasina had also thought, as she told some later, that a few of the Awami League leaders would be arrested by the armed forces so as to maintain a semblance of treatment equal to what would be meted out in severity to the corrupt leaders of the BNP. I could not find any logic as to why even a single innocent person should be arrested to maintain such a semblance of equal treatment under law and why such arrest should go without protest by our leaders.

It seemed they failed to understand and appreciate that detention of even a single person without a cogent reason or lawful authority was unjust and could not be conceded to as a matter of principle. Injustice, if not stood against right at the start or on its tiniest onslaught, could not be stopped or contained later or in the distant future. The episode of purges by the Nazis in Germany in the 1930s, suppression of the people's rights by Burma's military junta in recent years, bear eloquent testimony to the tragedy that might thwart human values and life, if injustice is not protested and fought against right at the start.

In these three days, I came to know, amongst others, Salahuddin Ahmed, Manzurul Ahsan Munshi, Amanullah Aman, Mufti Shahidul Islam and Mosaddeque Ali Falu, all MPs of the erstwhile Parliament from the BNP. I found Salahuddin Ahmed robust in body and attitude, having a lot of interest in edibles and unabashed liking for profanity. Quite rough at times, he seemed undaunted by his reported misdeeds, especially of his running away from Jatrabari area on the outskirts of Dhaka city when the public rose against him after October 28 — *i.e.*, after the BNP left the government leaving it at the hands of a caretaker outfit.

Manzurul Ahsan Munshi, during the days he was an MP, did not allow his political opponents even to enter his constituency. I found him a happy and jovial person, engaging himself quite often with his lips to a pipe placed on "a hookah" blazing with "misha." He told me "misha" did not have any element of addiction or injury to health. He made me take a puff or two, which I found uninteresting and quite a strain on my lungs.

Amanullah Aman was a State Minister in Khaleda's government. He came from the very locality where the Dhaka Central Jail was located. I found him well-behaved, considerate and quite sedate. He wielded, as it turned out, quite an influence on the jail personnel and through them got through hot snacks, cooked meals and a lot of fruit into the Karnaphuli Wing. He never took anything without offering or giving these to us.

Barrister Huda also seemed to have an easy way to get cooked food and fruit inside. His sharing somewhat favored those with the BNP mintage.

Mufti Shahid was a religious person, always eager to help others and very suave. He could persuade and enthuse all of us to say our prayers five times a day.

Unlike what I heard about him earlier, I found Falu well-behaved and soft-spoken. He was always relaxed and cheerful, bearing a soft smile whenever we met or exchanged glances. He said, "shed your worries; we should be ready to stay in the jail for about two years. In this time the military would come to realize that they would not be able to ride the horse of power and find a way to dismount with our consent."

"Yours is a bizarre fantasy," responded Munshi.

"Ridiculous! How can they hold us that long?" commented Aman.

"How can they do this to us?" wailed Mir Nasir.

I heard them, did not participate in the conversation. Salman kept silent.

Lotus-Kamal whispered, "Did you hear what they (the BNP men) are saying? We have been put in this cesspool because of their misdeeds. They don't realize this even now."

The BNP government had put me in jail in early 2002 on a number of drummed-up charges. At that time I was incarcerated in the so-called "old 20 cell" alone without a bedstead, a pillow or a mosquito net. Compared to that situation our stay at Karnaphuli was somewhat more tolerable. There was a bedstead and mosquito net for everyone; we were each allowed to have a radio, clean bed sheets from our houses and somewhat better food.

In the evening of the second day, when the Deputy Inspector General Prison (DIG) Major Haider Siddiky came to see how we were doing, I suggested that he should show us various areas of the jail. Surprisingly he agreed, took us to cells where four national leaders had been shot and killed in 1975, the gallows where hanging was done, the death-row cells where the killers of Bangabandhu were confined, the two rooms where Bangabandhu had been kept confined for thirteen years out of twenty-three years of the Pakistan regime, symbols that had been erected in 1972 to commemorate Bangabandhu's six-point demand made in 1966 and finally to that dungeon in the old 20 cell where I had been interned in 2002.

I showed everyone the dungeon in which I had been interned about five years back. I touched the iron grills that stood out blacker on that black night, the ramshackle of the latrine I had used and finally the *shefali* flower tree on the corner that sprouted hope in the abyss of darkness. Everyone agreed that compared to that cell in which I had been confined in 2002, the Karnaphuli Wing was better. I recalled the days of my solitary confinement and came back along with others to the Karnaphuli Wing in a pensive mood.

The next evening, without a prior notice, DIG Siddiky and Deputy Jailor Rafiq asked us to have an early meal before sending us to various other jails. Why the jail administration made this decision remained a mystery to me. It was probable that they thought our collective stay in the Karnaphuli might foster some sort of solid fraternity subversive of the interests of the powers that be. It was also probable that they wanted to make room to accommodate others who would be arrested and kept in the Dhaka Central Jail. Mohammad Nasim and Lotus-Kamal were selected to go to the Sylhet Central Jail; Salman and Mufti Shahidul Islam were selected for the Mymansingh Central Jail. Ahsan Munshi and Salahuddin would go to the Comilla Central Jail. I along with Kamal Majumder was paired last and was sent off to the Kashimpur Jail 1 at Gazipur. All the pairs were made to board microbuses with armed jail guards in the front and the police in the rear. Secured as such, Kamal Majumder and I reached the Kashimpur Jail 1 a little after 1:00 a.m. We found both Superintendent Matin and Jailor Enam waiting at the gate to receive us into captivity.

2 Kashimpur Jail

(1)

The Kashimpur Central Jail 1, as a part of the Dhaka Central Jail, was inaugurated in an unfinished state by the then-Chief Advisor, Latifur Rahman in early 2001. The rigging of the election in 2001 was largely his handicraft. The jail, still unfinished, was not yet officially handed over to the Prison Inspectorate by the government's Public Works Department. The peripheral wall on the southeastern corner beyond the second high one was not yet built, the water supply system incomplete, electric supply work largely unfinished and the gallows not fixed-in over the well of death. Kamal and I found our cells on the 3rd floor of the southeastern building designed for the "division" prisoners. The entire 3rd floor consisting of ten rooms or cells had been vacated by other non-division prisoners to yield places for us. They were shoved down to other floors below. These non-division prisoners were not supposed to be in this building, however. We were told that congestion of prisoners in recent days made the Superintendent accommodate non-division or ordinary prisoners in this building also.

As "division" prisoners, we each got a cell with an attached bath. Attachment of the bath was designed more to keep an inmate inside than for comfort. Down below, in each cell of the same size with one bath, 20-22 prisoners were accommodated to live on bare floors. We were treated as division prisoners in accordance with the revised Jail Code. According to this revision, Ministers, State Ministers and MPs were to be accorded division status right from the start. As division prisoners, we each had one bedstead topped with two-inch thick bedspread stuffed with raw cotton, a table, one wooden chair, a mosquito net, a basin, a shower and a commode in the bathroom. Each cell was fitted with two fans and a reasonably wide verandah running west from east the entire length of the floor in front of all cells. Sitting on the verandah on a chair enabled me to see south and east across the jail walls and see the activities of free men outside and to have a feel of the breeze swirling in from the free world. This silhouetted embodiment of freedom remained before my eyes till the dark of the evening weighed heavily on me. Fans worked when there was a power supply, which usually lasted for 6-8 hours a day, especially in the night. There was a generator installed in the jail premises, but it never worked, for the government did not provide diesel to operate it.

In front of our division building there was a one-storied dining-cum-cooking facility designed for cooking food for the division prisoners and for eating their meals. We were provided with cooks and attendants from amongst the convicted prisoners trusted by the jail administration and told that we could, if we so wanted, supervise cooking of our food within the limit of Tk. 88 per day per head. Gas for cooking was plentiful and along with that, cooking utensils were available free of cost to us. We were allowed to buy our own plates, tea cups, flasks, soap, toothpastes, etc. There were some shrubs, a few flower beds with plants sprouting flowers, bordering 2-3 patches of plots growing vegetables on the ground to the south of the building. In the jail these were elements of a relaxing environment, raising memories from deep in the past. The guards, in addition to an attendant given to each of us, were mostly amiable: the Jailor, his Deputies, and above them, the Superintendent, were all reasonably well-behaved. Contrasted with the Dhaka Central Jail, especially with the environment I was thrown into during my incarceration in 2002, Kashimpur appeared to be a much better place for survival, even in chains.

Amongst us, Kamal Majumder was the first person to be arrested. He was arrested by the army on the night of January 12, just 20 hours following the Proclamation of Emergency on January 11, 2007. Kamal was a stalwart amongst the Awami League workers in the Mirpur area of Dhaka City and the army had a score to settle with him. They had suspected that their movement was stopped by mobs organized by Kamal during the days of mass protest and upsurge preceding the Proclamation of Emergency.

Kamal was very hurt and anguished, as his arrest was not protested by Sheikh Hasina or the Awami League. He used to tell me that if the Awami League had protested his arrest by the army immediately, we would not have been arrested subsequently. From an assessment of circumstances, I was inclined to believe him. He was paid no more heed by his colleagues above and below than the yard chickens brought for slaughter without any remorse. History has given us a lesson that we often forget: persecution and violation of human rights, if not protested and stood against by all right from the start, will not stop to spare those who failed to protest and stand against these injustices at the beginning. Dancing between the right and the wrong before the arrayed players of evil, was a hypocrisy that over time did not reward the dancer in any way.

(2)

On October 28, 2007, the BNP Government handed over power to the caretaker government headed by President Iajuddin Ahmed, ostensibly to conduct a free and fair election to the national parliament. Iajuddin Ahmed, violating the constitutional provisions for forming the caretaker government headed by a neutral Chief Advisor, appointed himself the Chief Advisor, *i.e.*, the "neutral" head of the government in addition to his being the President, *i.e.*, the Head of State. He was elected President by the BNP, and he proved himself the epitome of allegiance and loyalty to the party that gave him that position. It seemed he was so drunk with his position of power that he had gone past stupor down to unthinkable senselessness.

Earlier, another BNP loyalist Abdul Aziz, a Justice of the Appellate Division of the Supreme Court, was appointed as the Chief Election Commissioner without making him vacate his position of a Justice of the same Court. The Chief Election Commissioner, aided by two other henchmen — Commissioners Mahfuzur Rahman and Zakaria — fabricated electoral rolls comprising ghost voters, specifically excluding the voters who supported the Awami League. They had previously appointed partisan workers as election officers at sub-district levels, located polling stations in locations under the influence and grip of the BNP stalwarts and in connivance with the Chief Advisor's office (*i.e.*, the executive part of the government), deployed district and sub-district level government officers and other functionaries in accordance with their partisan choices.

Thus a blueprint for rigging the election slated for January 22, 2007 was perfected and put under implementation. The Awami League protested and staged mass demonstrations against this slated rigging. Even a few advisors of the Council of Advisors appointed to run the government as a caretaker outfit resigned. President Iajuddin, loyal as he was to the BNP, remained unnerved and unmoved. Agitation increased and intensified; the economy almost came to a standstill. In fights with the police at various places, killings took place.

The Awami League announced on January 3rd that they would not participate in the election. Law and order deteriorated beyond anticipation. The army was looking for such an opportunity. Keeping unlawful liaison with both the Awami League and the BNP, they proposed to take the role of the saviors. To some leaders of the Awami League they said they would make Iajuddin postpone the election, resign as the Chief Advisor, appoint a neutral Chief and other Advisors, and ensure a fair and free election. To the BNP their message was: only proclamation of an emergency and buying of some time before a proper election could save them from the people's wrath and fate of contempt that they had earned during their misrule. Thus on January 11, deep in the night, the army took over the Bangabhaban (the Presidential Palace), forced President Iajuddin to proclaim an emergency, resign as the Chief Advisor and appoint Dr. Fakhruddin Ahmed (a former Governor of the Bangladesh Bank and before that a Senior Loan Officer of the World Bank) as the Chief Advisor.

People in general welcomed the change. The leaders of the military hoped that as the situation evolved they would be able to take over formally the powers of the government as was done earlier by General Ziaur Rahman (1975) and General Ershad (1981). The army and, on its behalf the new government of Dr. Fakhruddin Ahmed, announced that in order to clear the course for a free and fair election, they would proceed with "zero tolerance" of corruption of the politicians.

And then, in the first installment of heated intolerance, they arrested, on the night of February 2nd, fifty politicians of both the BNP and the Awami League. I was included in this first installment of arrests. Surprisingly the Awami League leadership did not protest; the BNP kept silent. The Awami League leadership was made to understand that a few from the Awami League would be arrested to maintain equilibrium or a semblance of equal treatment of both the major parties. The BNP leadership was made silent in the fear that in the event of protest, arrest of more of their leaders would follow and those who protested would be hauled in.

Thus the undemocratic attitude of the BNP with its lust for power through any means, coupled with the Awami League's staunch opposition to the BNP's scheme of things and their trust in the army's perfume of phony holiness, delivered the government on a platter to the military. It was undoubtedly a failure of the political leadership of the BNP; it made it eloquently evident that at political levels, there was an acute shortage of acumen as well as foresight. For the Awami League, it was the second of the two worst things to happen. In their assessment a rigged election putting the BNP to power again would have been the worst compared to the lesser evil embodied in the indirect and hopefully limited military intervention. But the worst of their conduct was a statement made by General Secretary Abdul Jalil in London that the Awami League supported actions against the corrupt and would expel them. Little did he realize at that time that he would himself be arrested by the military-backed government in a few months on a charge of corruption. While decrying Jalil's statement against the so-called corrupt and arrested leaders of his own party, I predicted to Kamal that as soon as the government was finished using him to make such statements and had wrung out all support from him, he would be hauled up. Kamal agreed.

(3)

Considering that we were in jail, living in Kashimpur was not bad. The day started with the morning prayer a little before sunrise, followed by a bath and a breakfast around 8:00. In between prayer and bath, I would walk on the long verandah or on the ground below for full one hour. The attendant assigned to me, Omar, was a silent worker. Knowing that I liked a bath in hot water, he used to heat up a bucketful in the division kitchen down below and bring it up the first thing in the morning. By the time I came out of the bathroom he was ready with breakfast: cereal in form of *muri* or *khai* or cornflakes and half-cream milk (from powder) brought in by my wife once a week, a piece of banana and a half-boiled egg and one piece of *ruti* supplied from the division kitchen, and a cup of milk-less tea. Breakfast over, I read for about two hours, mostly fiction supplied by my wife and brother Dr. Jahangir. Around 11:00 a.m., two newspapers were supplied to me, the *Daily Star* and the *Sangbad*, as I had selected. The daily *Janakantha* was not allowed in. Kamal got the *Ittefaq* and the *Manab Jamin*. Long and unstoppable time at hand allowed both of us to read the four papers almost from the beginning to the end. Around 12:30 in the noon, finished with the papers, I used to sit with Kamal on the verandah on two plastic chairs (bought by Kamal) and talked over a cup of tea about the news and the views we read in the papers. After the mid-day prayer at 1:30, we ate our lunch, a government issue in its entirety. It consisted of moderately well-cooked rice, two small pieces of fish, neither stale nor fresh, and a tasteless mix of a few pieces of vegetables, usually the cheapest ones available at the time, watery lentils always in want of a pinch of salt, and two pieces of fried pinkish *patal* or blackish eggplants. After lunch, I read and rested on my bed, got up at 5:00 p.m. with a cup of tea brought in by Omar, then went down the stairs to the ground and walked till sundown. After sundown and *Maghreb* prayer, we talked with each other till 7:30 when the BBC Bangla came on with news. We were ardent listeners of the BBC Bangla and found the medium very honest and realistic with news and views. Around 8:00, Superintendent Matin, Jailor Enam or the Jail Doctor Shamsuddin used to come, sit with us for a while and talk about their triumphs and tribulations with the prisoners deserving discipline. Occasionally they also bemoaned outside difficulties: coping with the price spirals and the administration over their heads that held up many of their reformative steps. Around 9:00 p.m. dinner was brought in. It was the usual government issue, at times coupled with specially cooked meat or fish brought in by Kamal with the consent of the Jailor or the Superintendent. Besides, we had a reasonable supply of fruit; all our visitors brought fruit as tokens of their love and affection, and these constituted our dessert for dinner. At the beginning, except for the lack of freedom, we did not have much to complain about at the Kashimpur Jail.

"I administer this jail quite well," at times boasted Superintendent Matin, a short, somewhat hesitant officer soon to retire from service.

"Well, at least better than the Central Jail at Dhaka," I used to tell him.

Kamal did not comment in the course of such a conversation.

At this time in Kashimpur, I came to know two prisoners, one ordinary and the other of division status. The ordinary one was Tonai Mollah, who had been the Chairman of Zazira Union Parishad of Shariatpur. He was convicted of murder by an additional sessions judge named Shahed Nuruddin. Tonai was quite popular in his area and also a man of means. After he was imprisoned, his wife was elected Chairman and has been serving as such since then. I came to know her during one of her visits to Tonai when coincidentally I was present in the office of the Superintendent of the jail. Mrs. Tonai was about 40, quite healthy and good-looking even at this age. More important, she was confident about herself and her supporters, and was convinced of the innocence of her husband. I sat with Tonai on a number of occasions, heard his story of arrest, prosecution and adjudication. Only one witness had told the court that he had heard from someone else that Tonai had been behind the murder in question. From my knowledge of our Evidence Act, this was a hearsay that could not have been a reason enough for conviction. Tonai told me in confidence that Judge Shahed Nuruddin, through a third person, demanded Tk. 5 lacs[6] to adjudicate him innocent and set him free. Tonai, spirited as he was, refused to oblige and the Judge committed him to imprisonment for life. I was stunned.

"Beware of a Judge like Shahed Nuruddin."

"What can I do, Tonai? Can I choose my judge if I am put to trial?" I asked.

"No," responded Tonai. "Even then try as best as you can through your friends and colleagues not to fall into the hand of such a crooked judge," he added.

"Well, the two of us friends will be in jail together," I joked.

Tonai winced but kept mum. Little did I realize at that time that Shahed Nuruddin would be the Special Judge at my trial.

Tonai had filed an appeal with the High Court Division of the Supreme Court against his conviction. He was waiting for about a year and a half for a hearing. Justice delayed in this case was almost amounting to its denial. Tonai, at about 50, seemed to have broken down in health, if not in spirit. Tonai was an unusual name in our country. I found out from someone that "Tonai" in Persian meant someone second to none. Kamal Majumder found in him good company. Occasionally Tonai sent us up shrimp cooked with coconut kernel, a specialty of his area and home-prepared, sugar-free yoghurt. Superintendent Matin came from his area and treated him with courtesy and consideration. Every time I met him, mostly while taking a walk on the ground below, he gave me words of encouragement, affection and respect. Kamal used to treat him to tea whenever he could come up, avoiding the eyes of the spooks the jail administration selected from amongst the convicts and the guards, to chat with us.

Through Tonai, I came to know another prisoner, Alauddin who, with three of his brothers, were all accused and convicted of murder. Alauddin was the youngest of these brothers. All the brothers were associated with distribution of newspapers and periodicals in Dhaka City. About four years back, a person associated with another cooperative distributor of newspapers in the city was found killed. The business rivals implicated Alauddin and his brothers. I was told, as they could not satisfy the investigating Police Officer, the Public Prosecutor and the Judge (all ea-

---

[6] A lac is "money of account" equal to 100,000 units of currency. The judge thus demanded a bribe of 500,000 Taka (Tk.), or approximately US $7,250.

ger to use such accused as beasts and birds of prey), Alauddin and his brothers were convicted and sentenced to imprisonment for life. They filed appeals with the High Court Division, which granted them bail until final disposal of the case. On grounds of an element of incompletion in a sentence in the orders of the High Court Division, the Judge who had convicted them did not post them on bail for more than a year. Fortunately, sometime in late September, 2008, this could be brought to the notice of the Appellate Division of the Supreme Court and they were finally posted on bail. Alauddin was about 30 years old, his three other brothers were within 50. How callousness on the part of a Justice and vindictiveness of a judge below could take away the freedom of as many as four persons for over four years and with impunity, appalled me.

In this period the other prisoner I came to know was one Mr. Raihan, living in a room down below the division jail floor. Raihan came upstairs on our floor one morning and introduced himself. While in the Dhaka Central Jail in 2002, I had heard about him. A former industrialist, he was convicted for murdering his own son, a lecturer-in-law in Dhaka University in the late 1980s. He was sentenced to life imprisonment. I found him well-educated, amiable and a genuine gentleman in his talk and conduct. On many an occasion I had time to sit and talk with him, at times for hours at a stretch. As of then, he did not know where the other members of his family were. About two years back, his youngest daughter who had just married came to meet him at the jail gate. That was the last time he had contact with any member of his family. In silent obstinacy, Raihan represented a will to survive against all depredations of time. He reminded us that, though life at times failed in some respects, success or fulfillment yet did not always elude us.

As he was somewhat introverted, I could get only one answer from him to the question asked by the rest of us: "How could a father kill his own son?"

"Why did not the society investigate at length to find out what actually happened?" he said.

"Why didn't you tell the court or the society your side of the story?"

"It was the society's responsibility to find out the truth instead of making me a lifer on hearsay," he responded without faltering.

Beyond this, our conversation on this did not proceed further. I was pleasantly surprised to find that he had been writing poems in Bangla following *"chowka"* and *"haiku"* styles of the Japanese literature. He read out a few to me. These poems were methodically very good and appealing with more than a whiff of the past. I asked him to publish these and even suggested that I would take them out of the jail to be published if he so wished. He said about two years back he had submitted a manuscript of these poems to the jail authority for permission to print and publish them. Permission was yet to be accorded. I was sure his request had been gathering dust somewhere in the office of the Inspector General of Prison, if not already thrown out into the garbage bin. I recalled while he was in jail, Pandit Nehru wrote the *Discovery of India* which was allowed, protected and permitted for publication even by the British Raj. I had seen the manuscript of the *Discovery of India* in the *Tin Murti Bhaban*[7] in New Delhi when I visited the place leisurely in January, 2002 along with Sitara. In the *Tin Murti Bhaban,* Nehru lived as the Prime Minister of India for two decades after Independence. It seemed that was a world and environment quite different from what we have now created for ourselves in Bangladesh.

From both the Superintendent and the Jailor I came to know that Raihan was an amiable but a strong person. He did not have any grievance against anybody or anything. His wants were simple and limited: he got his clothes and soap from the jail, whenever the jailor pleased to give, did not want even toothpaste or a brush, ate usual jail chow, did not talk much, as a matter of fact talked only when he was spoken to. I found him a great lover of flowers. Every morning he walked down to the ground, collected a bunch of flowers and came up with them to keep in a jar made of a half-empty mineral water bottle. On March 17, I found him fasting on the birthday of Bangabandhu in his memory. I found him fasting later on November 3 and 4 for salvation of souls of the slain four national leaders. I gave him a copy of *Bangabandhu Sarak Grantha,* a 2-volume collection of articles on Bangabandhu edited by Nazrul Islam, a friend of mine now living in Vienna and published in 2007. With great effort, I could give him a *"kurta"* to alternatively wear with the government-issue *kameez* that he wore as a convict. On two or three occasions, I could make him accept some fruit sent by Sitara and he thanked me for this almost every time I met him afterwards. Superintendent Matin told me, he had spent about 20 years in jail as a convict and Matin had written three times for his release on compassionate grounds. This response still remained to be received from the Ministry of

---

[7] "Bhaban" means "building."

Home. I vowed to myself but did not tell him so, lest he would be embarrassed that one of my first acts would be to release him after I would be released from jail.

Raihan's tale in Kashimpur made me recall the fate of one Sukha Ranjan in the Jessore Central Jail sometime in the late 1970s. When I visited the Jessore Central Jail as the Deputy Commissioner, lifer Sukha Ranjan, sitting on a line of applicants, handed me a paper on which he had composed a beautiful poem in appealing handwriting. In its construct, the poem was quite modern and in its theme artfully abstract in exquisite diction, testifying to Sukha Ranjan's good education and affluent mind. He did not have any grievance against anything or anybody, not even against the judge making him a lifer, condemned to live a desolate and meaningless life. There were certainly quite a number of lifers like Raihan and Sukha Ranjan in our jails. Could we devise ways and means to find out whether such lifers were really condemnable or deserved harsh punishments, as they did not care about trials despite their creativity? It would be a proof of the society's loathsome cowardliness if it did not pause and ponder for a while to answer this question. Such cowardliness would contribute to setting us apart from a reality, which could escalate steadily into an error-prone fury in a society incapable of change, preferring to meet the desires of its prideful members.

To the west of the "division" building, beyond a walkway between two walls, was a building accommodating at that time about 50 lifers, including 26 to be taken to the gallows. While going by along the walkway in the afternoon or taking it to and from the jail office in the morning, I sometimes talked, amongst others, to Sweden Aslam and Adnan, standing on the way or sitting at the entrance of the building. There was a garden of roses in front of this building; this was well cared for not by the employees of the jail but by the prisoners doing their time or awaiting the gallows. Over the shrubberies of rose, henna and jasmine we would hear the twittering of birds, ringing of life and song for those destined to dismalness.

I knew "Sweden" Aslam when I was in the Dhaka Central Jail in 2002. Adnan, a handsome young man of a quite fair complexion, introduced himself as a local social worker of the Awami League in western Dhanmondi area of Dhaka. He was arrested by the BNP regime in 2002. Almost always he greeted me with a red rose picked afresh from the garden. Unlike his name and fame as a fearsome terrorist, I found Sweden Aslam quite an amiable and soft-spoken person with a receding hairline. "Sweden" came to be affixed to his name Aslam as he had been to Sweden as a migrant worker about fifteen years back. He was in the jail since 1998 and did not appear to have broken down in spirit. He usually complained about the price spiral and the miscarriage of justice in the country because of dishonest and callous police and the magistracy.

I found the jail employees quite aware of the presence of these two prisoners. They held them in awe as well as in respect. Both Adnan and Sweden Aslam almost never talked or complained about their cases and the judgments they had received. Seeing and talking to them, I felt an acute need for social or correctional service for the inmates instead of shoving them into an abyss of oblivion. Among the other inmates, a person in his mid-40s wearing a clean starched *kurta* and having bright spectacled eyes caught my attention. I was told he was accused of murdering Ahsanullah Master, a very popular Member of the Parliament belonging to the Awami League in Gazipur area. Superintendent Matin told me he used to work in England and was on a vacation in Gazipur when Ahsanullah Master was killed. He was falsely implicated in this murder through connivance of a very powerful minister of the BNP regime sheltering the real culprits. He had filed an appeal with the High Court Division of the Supreme Court. I hoped he would be able to vindicate his position and come through in the impartial adjudication of the High Court Division.

Of the lifers and prisoners condemned to the gallows, the maximum numbers were sent there, I was told, by Additional Judge Shahed Nuruddin. As the impression went, there seemed to be sufficient room for such a judge to improve his knowledge of law, adherence to honesty and dispassionate analysis of cases and events of crimes. Fortunately, most of the lifers and gallows-waiters[8] as dispensed by him were being released by the High Court Division on appeal. This was of some relief to hear but it was also painful to realize that filing appeals cost money and at times made the families of the appellants paupers in the process. The way to justice for most of these people was not a well-paved one. While hearing about these deeds and misdeeds of Judge Shahed Nuruddin, little did I realize at that time that he would be the one to adjudicate charges to be framed soon against me.

In a society left to be kept in order by not-too-honest police, inept magistracy and callous and dishonest lower judiciary, it seemed that by far the majority of the prisoners in the Kashimpur

[8] Prisoners on Death Row.

Jail were innocent victims. While discussing this at length with Superintendent Matin and Jailor Enam, I told them, in my assessment, about 50% of those who were in their jail either as convicts or accused were innocent. They said almost in unison that the number would be more, at least 60% and not only in Kashimpur but in every one of 66 other jails of the country. Superintendent Matin after putting in 34 years of service was retiring in about three months; Jailor Enamul had put in 22 years of service in various jails throughout the country before coming to Kashimpur. I did not have much of a reason to refute their assessment. I thought, a situation like this was indicative not only of savagery and lawlessness but also of a large-scale failure of the administrative-judicial system of the country. This might be summed up as a pre-posthumous obituary of the existing societal fabric.

A manifestation of this observation of the jailors was seen in the presence of a large number of teenage prisoners in Kashimpur. On a sample basis, on my way in and out of the jail office and the in course of my walks on the grounds, I befriended a number of them. From those I came to know, most of these teenagers were half-educated and on the verge of entering productive and adult life. They were caught for petty crimes, interned and, in the absence of adequate legal aid, were inflicted with unreasonably long punishment.

As I recalled, in 2003 the High Court Division had issued a seven-point directive to the government to ensure transfer of all juvenile prisoners from jails to correction centers with utmost expedition. There were at that time five correction centers in the country operating under-capacity while the jails were bursting with the glowering juveniles and the youth. There was no arrangement for education of these inmates within the jail, no permission was given to sit for statutory examinations even if one or two were prepared to sit for those. Nobody bothered to think what would happen to them or the society they would live in after they would be freed from such a predicament. Most certainly they would rage and stumble around seeking retribution.

As in other jails, a few educated teenagers, chosen in consideration of being more docile than their peers, were also employed as helping hands to the regular jail personnel in Kashimpur. In the language of the jail they were known as "writers;" they wrote accounts and details of daily receipts and use of supplies, sat at the feet of the Superintendent and the Jailor when they held "court." In other words, they heard grievances of the inmates and complaints against them by the jail guards, for meting out punishment through application of cane, denial of food periodically, assignment to cleaning jobs, and relocation to unhealthier and overcrowded sleeping quarters. Some carried bags of the jail physician and the pharmacist and served as notice- and letter-carriers and errand boys of the deputy jailors. These personnel of the jail did not have enough competence, which obligated these literate teenagers to do these things.

One morning I was pleasantly surprised when one of these writers carrying the physician's bag asked me whether he could borrow an English novel from the stack I had on my table. These were the latest best-sellers sent to me by my wife and two sons from Boston. I lent him the book he wanted and asked him how he learned English. He said he was a graduate student of the Aligarh University in India. He was studying there on a scholarship given by the government of India. While on vacation in Gazipur near his home village one day, he ventured to calm down and settle a brawl of the local *mastans*[9] in front of the police station and as a reward was hauled up by the police, tried by a Magistrate who did not understand the local area and environment, and sent to the jail, ruining his career for trying to do something good on his own. It seemed the society slammed its door on the very people who wanted to help and keep order. It inserted the fat steel needle of punishment into healthy members instead of giving due attention to the ailing ones.

(4)

February 21 is a memorable day every year in our lives. On this day in 1952, our students and people gave their lives to establish their rights to protect their mother language. I was a student of Class Vl at Dhaka's Armenitola Government High School in that year. Following mostly the elder students, I was at the rear of the very procession when it was fired upon around 4:30 in the afternoon on the road to the north of today's Dhaka Medical College Hospital almost at the front on which the Central Shaheed Minar is now located. My elder brother Dr. Burhanuddin Khan Jahangir was in front of the procession. As I heard later, he saw Abul Barkat hit, falling down right before his eyes. Since then, every year I was in Dhaka on February 21, I took part in processions that went to the Shaheed Minar to remember and respect the martyrs of the language. Even after I was married, my wife and I used to join the commemorating events of the 21st of February every year.

---

[9] Hoodlums, street thugs.

We used to take our two sons to the Shaheed Minar every year as soon as they learned to walk. Our pride went sky-high when February 21 was declared and accepted as the International Mother Language Day in 1999 during Sheikh Hasina's Prime Ministership.

That day dawned in 2007 when I was in the Kashimpur Jail. I was recalling February 21 and its declaration as the International Mother Language Day in the morning, while taking a walk on the grounds of the division building. Suddenly I noticed Nekmat, an old and freckle-faced prisoner with grey beard, now acclaimed and much used as an able electrician in the jail, coming with two fairly large bouquets of flowers in his two hands. He was being followed by 10-15 other prisoners, all younger than him. The bouquets with red roses in the middle and *rajanigandha*, *jaba, kathalchapa* and purple *masandas* around were fresh and beautiful, exuding life and its bounties. When asked, Nekmat told me these were bouquets designed to be taken to the Shaheed Minar located in the nearby school. I wanted to know how they would take the bouquets there. He told me a body of 10-15 prisoners would take the bouquets to the jail gate and then, in collaboration with the jail guards, hand over the same to a group of students who would be waiting outside. They have been presenting bouquets of flowers as tokens of their respect to martyrs every year since the jail was set up in 2001.

I was happy beyond measure, felt proud of and hopeful for the prisoners living with us. What I could not think of, they thought and acted out. Despite their imprisonment and the injustice meted out to most of them by the administrative-judicial system of the country, they proved that they had not forgotten about the contribution of the martyrs of the language movement, the very beginning of the country's liberation. Despite pitfalls, unfulfilled expectations and inordinate delay in suppressing those who used them as targets of oppression, the prisoners showed, beyond all reasonable doubt, and perhaps before the awakening on that misty morning of the very judges who had meted out unjust punishments to most of them, their allegiance to this country and respect to their heroes. Later, I witnessed the same dimension of allegiance and patriotism of these prisoners on Bangabandhu's birthday on March 17 and the Independence Day on March 26.

By mid-February 2007, the Kashimpur 1 Prison's "Division" had grown in its reputation as a better place for living and surviving. As a result, political prisoners sent to other jails from the Dhaka Central started coming to Kashimpur 1. The first two to arrive were Salman F. Rahman and Mufti Shahidul Islam from Mymensingh. They were followed by Kazi Zafarullah, Mohammad Nasim and Lotus-Kamal, and then by Engineer Mosharraf Hossain and Obaidul Kader. All of them were Awami Leaguers. Mohammad Nasim and Lotus-Kamal came from the Comilla Central Jail, Engineer Mosharraf Hossain came from the Chittagong Central Jail while Obaidul Kader made his entry, rather reluctantly and somewhat lately, from the Dhaka Central Jail. From the BNP came Ali Asgar Lobi, Asadul Habib Dulu, Silver Selim and at last, Hashem and Naser.

The eastern-most cell on the top floor was occupied by Kamal Majumder. My cell was next to his, followed by that of Silver Selim. The cell next to Selim was taken by Mosharraf Hossain and Obaidul Kader. Then a cell to the west we kept and fixed up as our common dining place. Next to the dining place to its west was the cell taken by Lotus-Kamal and Kazi Zafarullah. The cell next to them was taken by Mohammad Nasim, who had been the Home Minister during Sheikh Hasina's government. The last one from the east, *i.e.*, the westernmost cell was taken by Salman and Mufti. They wanted to stay in the same cell. When Hashem, Naser and Dulu came, they had to go a floor down and take the two eastern cells, one by Hashem and Naser and the other by Dulu. Hashem and Naser were very close and did not want to take separate cells though available.

With all these people, the community of the "division" building of the Kashimpur Jail was full and somewhat alive in companionship and occasional rosy daydreams, which were sometimes torn apart in rage. Of all of us, Salman, an entrepreneur like Andrew Carnegie of 19th century America, organized our community life. First, he took up earmarking the room for prayer and furnished it with pedestal fans and prayer mats, and made it fit and appropriate for offering of prayers five times a day at appointed hours. With the sounding of the *Azan* at the break of the dawn he walked down to each cell, woke and took us all to the morning prayer, ably led by Mufti Shahidul Islam, our undeclared Imam. At times of other prayers, he used to walk from his cell to the end of the verandah more than 150 feet in length on the top floor and then a half of the verandah on the floor below to tell each of us loudly, clearly and quite often persistently, that times were for assembling and praying in congregation. The *Juma* prayer on Friday was not insisted upon as according to him and Mufti such a prayer was required to be performed in an open space and in freedom.

Salman had turned himself into a deeply religious person since the unfortunate death of his beloved daughter some five years back. With white flowing beard and ankle-up pajama and knee-down *kurta* he had the appearance of a religious leader rather than an astute businessman and a successful entrepreneur of the country. At the same time, he exuded the most confidence and hope amongst all of us. The division building, especially the floors down below where the ordinary prisoners lived, had a short water supply; the overhead tanks were small and less than the required number; the electricity supply running the pumps was both short and erratic. As a result, water for meeting the requirements of 20-22 people in all cells on each of those floors was inadequate and uncertain.

Out of all the persons living on our floor, this attracted Salman's attention. Immediately he persuaded Superintendent Matin to permit him to dig a tube well. Matin was surprised, nodded his permission and in two days, reflecting efficiency of the private enterprise, Salman's people sunk the tube well. Prisoners got unexpected relief and looked up at Salman who was walking the corridor and was identified by a few. One tube well, hand-driven, however, turned out to be inadequate after some days. Undaunted, Salman mobilized his own resources, obtained permission of the Deputy Inspector General of Prisons, Major Shamsul Haider Siddiky and dug a deep tube well down to 120 feet below the surface, fitted in an electrically driven pump and arranged to pump up to their brims an adequate supply of clean water to the overhead tanks. The water problem was solved for us living on top floors as well as for those living down below. Superintendent Matin was asked to include both the hand-driven shallow and the electrically operated deep tube wells as assets or equipment of the jail donated by inmate Salman. Costs of both totaled near about Tk. 2 lacs. It was indeed a generosity, unknown to people outside the jail. Salman himself never talked about it either with us or others.

There were two other vexatious problems at hand. One was our being locked up in each of our cells at 6:00 in the evening. The attendant gave us our food, usually in a hot carrier, brought at our cost around 5:45 p.m., and the jail guards came at 6:00, confirmed with certainty that we were in our respective cells and then locked us up and tallied their books of prisoners. One day at the end of February, DIG Prison, Major Shamsul Haider Siddiky came to see us around 8:00 in the evening and stayed with us till 9:30. At that time, we pointed out that, instead of locking us inside in our respective cells at 6:00 in the evening, they might install a main gate in front of the stairwell at the entrance of the 3rd floor and avoid bothering to lock us individually in our respective cells. That would give us free and association time with each other till 9:00 to see TV, hear news broadcasts and pray in congregation at sundown and at night.

The DIG admitted that it was sensible but the Public Works Department of the government would have to install a central gate at the entrance of the stairwell on the second floor and as the experience had it, it would take not months but years to get it sanctioned, budgeted, constructed and installed. Smilingly he said that by that time all of us would be gone out of the jail. Salman promptly proposed that he would install the gate and leave it memorialized for those who would come and stay later in our places.

"It will be our gift to our captors who would find place here after we leave," I said laughingly.

"Who knows?" responded the DIG.

"The history of our country says unjust captors became just captives as time went by," philosophized Mohammad Nasim.

"The day may come sooner than you may think," Lotus-Kamal added rather prophetically.

"God does not like the persecutors; time and again it is so said in the Quran," I added.

All fell silent to see how the DIG would react. But the DIG to our pleasant surprise asked Superintendent Matin to see it done the way we wanted. Agreed that way, the central gate was installed through Nuru, a jail contractor in seven days and all of us came to enjoy companionship in the night as well as the day. Salman of his own volition paid for the entire cost. He did not even ask anybody to share it with him.

The other vexation was the frequent loadshedding[10] of the Dhaka Electric Supply Company, a government undertaking perennially short of power supply and fully overstocked with an uncaring and indifferent personnel. The results were power outages and unwholesome darkness in the night, especially between 6:00 to 10:00, and stillness of fans between 10:00 a.m. and 5:00 p.m. in the day when they were needed most for respite from the heat. The heat was quite intense, as we were on the top floor and the ceiling above us — as the product of a fiduciary conspiracy be-

---

[10] Referring to an intentionally engineered electrical power outage, caused by insufficient available resources to meet prevailing demand for electricity.

tween the contractor-builders and the engineers of the Public Works Department — was left without the required coating to prevent the seeping in of rainwater and the emission of heat from the sun.

Again Salman came with the rescue plan. He persuaded Superintendent Matin to bring in three IPS or power storage batteries at our cost and lined them up with lights and fans in all the cells of the top floor. The result was somewhat embarrassing for the jail personnel. While in their respective offices, power outage left them either sweating or cursing in the dark, we had our fans moving and giving us relief from the heat and freedom from the darkness around. Of the three IPSs, one was brought and installed by Salman, one by Lotus-Kamal and the third one by Silver Selim. As luck would have it, my cell was connected to Salman's IPS, which turned out to be the best in terms of duration and operation.

Mufti Shahid, amongst us very thorough in his religious duty, took up the responsibility to look after our kitchen and feed us well within the constraints of the jail life. The government issue of food for us was Tk.88 per head per day exclusive of cost of gas, utensils and labor. To this we in a council, decided to contribute Tk.100 each per day. With Tk.188 per day per head, Mufti made arrangements with the contractor who supplied provisions to the jail to bring extras for us. Both the Superintendent and the Jailor, at our behest, asked the contractor to give us fresh provisions as far as possible. Mufti took supervision of the kitchen seriously and chose cooks and assistants from amongst the experienced convict prisoners. We decided to give food to the cooks, their assistants and our attendants chosen from the convicts. All told these extra mouths to be fed figured at 21 or so. Even then we found food aplenty and reasonably well-cooked and served.

At times, Mufti and others, notably Giasuddin, a former Member of the Parliament from Narayangonj, could detect cases of petty theft; pieces of meat and fish, onions and red chilies being carried off to other convicts by cooks and their attendants. Given the need for food, especially something other than the ordinary chow of the jail, we did not mind, but kept watch so that theft would not exceed a reasonable limit. Mufti, in addition took it upon himself to feed our attendants, usually sitting with them after we had taken our meal. Whenever we asked for something extra albeit of "*bharta,*" or a piece of shrimp, Mufti never said no; he arranged a piece or a morsel from somewhere he alone knew. One day while he was eating his meal with the attendants after feeding us all, I found out the secret: he did not have a piece of meat and fried shrimp that we had sitting at the table before him. He gave his share to us without letting us know.

Our meals qualitatively improved over days and on three counts. First, Salman brought a full set of crockery from his factory Shinepukur Ceramics and a microwave. Bringing these in was difficult; in exchange he had to give three more sets with special inscription in golden letters of the Inspectorate General, Prisons, to the jail authorities more or less as gift. The DIG prison was especially pleased to see that henceforth the top brass of the jail would be able to give special dinner to their bosses when occasions so demanded. Through the conduit of pleasure of the immediate boss, Superintendent Matin allowed in the boxes containing the crockery for us along with the box containing a microwave. The box containing the microwave was apparently taken in as another box of crockeries. It was a case of letting a sleeping dog lie, without a whimper from those bent upon beating us in a battle of wits. Third, we could persuade our jailors to let us have fruit and cooked food from our visitors and made it a rule that anything brought into the jail by a visitor of anyone would belong to everyone of the division prisoners.

Lotus-Kamal specialized in bringing mangoes and assorted fruit; Salman liked warm soups brought in flasks and ice creams in cool carriers, and Lobi's liking manifested in *haluwas*[11] and *khicheries*. Mufti's family used to send us *kababs* and especially cooked meats. And Kamal Majumder usually brought in fish specially cooked in the canteen just outside the jail by his own cook, brought from his farm in Savar. And when Hashem joined us later, he saw to it that we got ample supply of well-cooked small fishes of delicacy. In addition, Hashem being the owner of the plant manufacturing "Mum" brand mineral water, we started getting free supply of that. Giasuddin from Narayangonj was the conduit for getting specially made yogurt and curries for all of us, made by his affectionate mother under her own supervision. At times we received fish boastfully reported to have been cooked by his wife herself from Tonai Mollah living on the 2nd floor of the division building. Besides, whoever went to the court in pursuit of justice, which seemed more and more elusive as days went by, brought in fruit and sweets, given by their dear and near ones.

We tried to fix various days of the week for our suppliers of these extras, to avoid duplication and possible waste. But the en-

---

[11] A sweet dish closely resembling pudding.

thusiasm of our visitors and reasonable dispensation of cost for risk involved in taking them inside did not make the scheme work at times without duplication and somewhat expensive waste. Otherwise vacant spaces in three refrigerators, brought in ostensibly for keeping insulin by us old people, were used to prevent waste and ensure continuous fresh supply. Mufti took it to himself to manage the food chain. What we could not consume fresh or that was over-supplied was distributed down below among the common prisoners to their delight.

(5)

Well-cooked food, its supply in reasonable quantities and distribution to the satisfaction of all who worked with us, could not decrease our solitude and longing for dear and near ones. Salman was quite an introvert in respect to his family since the tragic death of his daughter about seven years back. At times, while talking about soup and ice cream, he recalled his wife's making and serving them at home; her religious bent of mind and uprightness in the face of all odds; his son Shaihan's intelligence and enterprise and his brother Sohel's contribution to the building up of their enterprise and providing employment to about 40,000 people in Beximco's various mills and factories. Till November 2007, despite search and investigation day and night by a contingent of joint force, nothing could be found against him or his brother. To keep him still incarcerated the government took recourse to detention under the Special Powers Act and two ludicrous cases of alleged extortion of a few lacs of Taka and default in payment of loans to the commercial banks. The draconian provisions of the Special Powers Act, 1974, enabled the government to detain a person without trial for an unlimited time unless the Supreme Court intervened and offered relief. In his and our case, under the Special Powers Act, the High Court Division intervened, declared the detentions illegal one by one but the Appellate Division, on appeal by the government, stayed operation of the orders of the High Court Division and then sat over them ad infinitum keeping all of us in the jail. Such a monstrosity under the cover of legal procedure at the highest level of adjudication was never observed earlier in our country.

Detention of Salman, Lotus-Kamal and myself was ordered on the allegation that the civil intelligence organ of the government, known as the Special Branch, found three of us meeting at my place on the night of January 27, 2007 to conspire to dislodge the government of Dr. Fakhruddin Ahmed. Lotus-Kamal on that date was out of the country and it was so recorded in his passport. This was mentioned and shown to the two High Court Justices on the day appointed for review of our detentions by the relevant quasi-judicial board that was empowered under law to set us free or detain us further. Obviously the allegations were baseless and tantamount to furnishing of false information to the lawful authority by the government, which ordered such detention. The Justices heard, observed the photocopy of the passport of Lotus-Kamal showing entries in respect of going out and coming back to the country by the Immigration Department, nodded their heads like wizened owls but did not dislodge the detention. The Appellate Division of the Supreme Court had already pigeon-holed the High Court's orders for our release from detention. As it turned out, it became difficult for us to keep our trust in the higher judiciary at this time. We came back to our locked down destination. Salman decided to send his wife out and in two days she left in order that she would not have to suffer such an ignominy of incarceration. We thought about what we should do to save our families.

Lotus-Kamal was a chartered accountant and a gold medalist at that. From a very humble beginning in Comilla, through sheer hard work and merit, he rose up building a number of enterprises.

Quite often he used to lament: "Why I am arrested by this fucking government? I built my enterprises. I paid my taxes. I did not have any transaction with the government or any of its concerns. Why are these ruffians harassing me?" We listened, at times tried to console him, but to no avail.

I had been close with Lotus-Kamal since the late 90s when, at his behest, I as the State Minister for Planning in Sheikh Hasina's government, planned for setting up a public university and an export processing zone in Comilla. Lotus-Kamal was providing employment to more then 7,500 people and serving as a bridge to bring about investment capital from Korea and Saudi Arabia. Incarceration of Lotus-Kamal and harassment of his wife and two daughters have been an anti-enterprise action of the Fakhruddin government. His wife and daughters were very apt entrepreneurs themselves. None in this government seemed to have known in one way or another how the federal and state governments in the U.S. in their early stages helped enterprise of investors and innovators like Carnegie, Morgan, Ford and others.

Quite after sundown, Lotus-Kamal and I sat on two chairs on the grounds in front of our division building and talked about stupidity and cruelty of the government and its cronies. Analyzing the looming import crisis of the government and the impending price spiral, we recalled in appreciation of private enterprise how as early as in September 1915, an entrepreneur like J. P. Morgan by himself had loaned out $1.5 billion to Britain and in the process transformed the U.S. into a capital-exporting country from a capital-importing one. The shrubbery around with gentle breeze blowing along the high walls of the jail could not lessen our anger and anguish at the action of the minions running a government on behalf of those who had nothing but imported arms to suppress their own people. Fortunately for him and us, his wife and two daughters could leave the country at his behest. Lotus-Kamal almost always fondly remembered his only grandson, quite smart and outgoing for his age at 6.

Of others, Mohammad Nasim, Home Minister during the latter part of Sheikh Hasina's government, was calm, quiet and a shade aloof in nature. He used to rise late, miss the morning congregation of prayers, and come late for both lunch and dinner. He was quite concerned about the charge that was being made against his wife as well. Criminal charges for allowing private investment in land telephone, making short payment of income taxes and reporting lesser wealth or assets than what was purported to be his, were all being drummed up against him. Salman told him these were expected as he was a political stalwart who would not budge to support a government hijacked by the armed forces and should, therefore, await a political change for his freedom. In the meanwhile, argued Lotus-Kamal and I, he should send Mrs. Nasim out of the country to avoid her incarceration, designed to make him bow to the powers that be. Arguing for days, he finally agreed, sent message accordingly to his wife and very reluctantly she agreed to leave the country in a clandestine way. We were relieved as was Nasim. Nasim as the Home Minister was the boss of the jail personnel. Most of them were very respectful to him. Only one day Superintendent Matin treated him in a harsh way, sending Nasim to the court in a prison van along with a lifer apprehended and sentenced when Nasim was the Home Minister. Next day I shouted at the Superintendent for this and it was never repeated.

Engineer Mosharraf and Obaidul Kader, as I said earlier, shared a cell. Mosharraf was about my age while Kader was younger, quite healthy in his early 50s but for splinters that were still embedded in his body after he was hit in the grenade attack on Sheikh Hasina and other Awami League leaders in Dhaka on

August 21, 2004. These splinters caused him frequent pain in his thighs and abdomen. I was immediately behind Sheikh Hasina when the grenade attack was made. Fortunately I was more or less unhurt.

Mosharraf had set up a five-star hotel in Chittagong, developed a paunch reflecting good feeding in earlier days, while Kader remained slim. Kader was quiet and dejected most of the time. In their monstrosity, the ACC had filed a criminal case against his wife also. We advised him to send his wife out of the country, to which he agreed; for them separation was somewhat easy as they did not have any child as yet. But young as they were, it was painful seeing Kader lament her absence quite often, losing the dream of living together at a young age. We consoled him; after all, his dear wife would avoid incarceration. Yet his hard eyes shone with desperate grief. As Kader was the ranking Joint Secretary of the Awami League, pressure was more intense on him to change course and toe the line thrown out by those in power. With that end in view, to make him bow, they would certainly have incarcerated his wife.

After some time, Kader reconciled with the reality and came to hammer together a joint life with us as prisoners. He read a lot, wrote his diary regularly and came up with points of discussion one after another. I asked him to get a pair of keds and a track suit for walking in the corridor as well as on the grounds below. This he did and I was satisfied that he was taking care of his health. Engineer Mosharraf was anxious about his wife and grandchildren. His daughter-in-law was Swedish. I pursuaded him to send his wife out of the country along with the other son, the daughter-in-law and the two grandchildren. Following a very circuitous route, Mrs. Mosharraf and her brood could safely get out and reach Sweden. Now, I said, we would all wait with patience to bear the ordeal in our masculine way. Mosharraf accepted, became concerned for the paunch that he had developed, brought in a belly-bending exerciser and started on a strict diet. The diet continued, at least that was what he used to say, but we did not find the exerciser much in use. Mosharraf loved good food and smiled tenderly when caught communing with what he loved.

A. K. M. Mosharraf Hossain was the State Minister for Energy in the government of Khaleda Zia. He was the oldest as well the shortest amongst us. After changing cellmates once or twice, he hitched up with Giasuddin, the erstwhile Member of the Parliament of Narayangonj from the BNP. Mosharraf was divorced from his wife, a socialite of repute since the days of General Ershad.

He took extra care of his hair, applied body lotion quite frequently and brought in a set or two of new bed sheets and covers. These made Kader and Ali Asgar Lobi spread a story that Mosharraf was getting himself ready for wedding with someone famous for her beauty and charm. Silver Selim offered to bring in a horse for him for a bridal ride from the jail gate; offers for sweets as well as wardrobes befitting the occasion came from Lobi. Some amongst us saw Mosharraf blush a little even at this age while all these things were being offered and talked about.

The fairy-bride, however, was not seen to have met him any time during our stay at Kashimpur. His daughter-in-law, a sweet Bangali-American came to see him in the jail from time to time. I found Giasuddin a soft-spoken nice man, taking lot of interest in our food and cooking. The military platooned as the joint force were after him with churning relentlessness. As a result, quite often he was taken to Narayangonj court and placed on remand, tortured, hospitalized and then returned to Kashimpur. He suffered in silence; sought loyal advice from Salman and me and with our support could make Barrister Rafiqul Huq to defend him in a myriad of cases. The pressure of the joint force and their frequent interrogation of him on remand made him suffer a sudden heart attack after about three months. Fortunately he recovered, becoming more intent on silence than on conversation with us.

Silver Selim's full and formal name was A. H. M. Selim. I did not know for sure why he was called Silver; it might have been his nickname; or he acquired the honorific because of his business success after he became a Member of the Parliament from the BNP in Bagerhat area. He was a young man in his 40s, mostly harangued by a series of extortion cases filed against him in the local area, at the behest of the so-called joint force. He had set up a successful spinning mill in Joydebpur area. He saved himself from being taken on remand — torture under legal cover — by feigning heart problems and transferring himself to the Bangabandhu Sheikh Mujib Medical University Hospital. He was a well-mannered person, quite fond of playing cards in which he found willing company in A. K. M. Mosharraf Hossain and Kamal Majumder. For reasons not known to me, he was quite thick with the jail administration. On one occasion, the thickness ruptured for reasons of dissatisfaction of the jail personnel as the ingredients of satisfaction fell short of what was expected as a matter of routine from him and they impounded a built-in VCR from the TV he was earlier allowed to bring into his room and use.

Kamal Majumder in Dhaka's Mirpur area was known as a formidable Awami League leader: moneyed, having organizational capacity and at times given to anger. In size he was small, but in him I found a fighter, almost always fighting to get what were his rights within the jail. He was a meticulous person, used to cleanliness, prompt obedience and immediate satisfaction of demands. An attendant, named Nizam, chosen by the jailors from amongst the well-behaved convicts, having a year or so more to suffer imprisonment, was assigned to him. Kamal used to rebuke him in the morning, sack him in the afternoon, quietly allowed him to do his assigned work in the evening and then packed him off for the night with a handful of fruit and chocolates.

Kamal was not keeping good health; severe diabetes coupled with cardiac problems made him a lonesome person. As he was in the cell next to mine, I had to keep an eye on him and make sure that he had taken his food on time. He was fond of the Korean instant noodles of which he always kept a good supply. His supply of fruit and dry biscuits was adequate and more often than not we were invited down to his makeshift plastic table on the verandah to taste them with herbal tea. He used to be very happy whenever his cook, coming with fish, meat and vegetables of his liking to the jail canteen, located out of the jail walls, cooked them to his taste and could send them in, sharing some with the jail personnel on the way. Of these Kamal ate little but found immense pleasure in distributing them amongst us and hearing how good his cook and cooking were. Kamal embraced me and cried like a child whenever he heard or received bad news or information about me, my wife or sons. Most of the evening, I found him sitting on the verandah in front of his cell and gazing at branches of trees near the jail walls and the sky between them.

Hashem and Naser being late-comers to Kashimpur, were accommodated on the eastern side of the second floor of the division building. Hashem was the Chairman of the Partex Group of industries and a Member of the Parliament from the BNP during Khaleda's government. He was a jovial person, somewhat rolly-polly in appearance and movement, with quite an ostensible weakness for good food. His children were all well-educated and in his absence quite capable of running his enterprises. His nephew was the supplier of food — fruit, dried and cooked — -all in sufficient quantities. We enjoyed delicious food like well-cooked small fishes and especially prepared meat from his kitchen, sent through the jail gate.

He was related to General Moin U. Ahmed, the Chief of the Army, whose government, according to him, it was. When asked despite that why Hashem was arrested, his answer was: the Chief was angry when Hashem suggested a few lines along which the army-backed government should function and advertised them through some national dailies. He said, a substantial subscription to the relief fund of the Army Chief, would buy him freedom. I said, it would not, and then it turned out that, despite Tk. 50 lacs or so contributed from his enterprises to the relief fund of the Army Chief, his freedom could not be secured. That made him somewhat morose and profane saying, after the usual expletives, none in this government or in the previous one kept their word. Naser came from Madaripur; he was an MP for a short while in the interregnum when Khaleda Zia declared herself the winner in the election rigged on February 12, 1996. He was quite loyal to Hashem and took pains to look after him. He kept his medical and court records, medicines and even times Hashem was supposed to take a nap at noon. But at the same time he was an avid walker, walking robustly along with me in the corridor on the top floor and on the grounds every morning and evening.

Asadul Habib Dulu was a deputy minister during the last government of Khaleda Zia. He occupied the cell to the west of Hashem's. He was the youngest amongst us, the political prisoners; he had earned both fame and notoriety as an indiscriminate persecutor of the political opponents in his local area. Once in the winter of 2005, I went to Natore, his locale, and I found our party leaders including Kuddus, who had been a deputy minister himself during Sheikh Hasina's time, quite hesitant to hold a public meeting in Natore where Dulu had his bastion of power. I found Dulu soft-spoken and gentle though somewhat apart from the rest of us. He tried to be chummy with the jail guards so that he could meet his wife for longer time when she came to visit him at the jail gate. Once the jailor complained to us that Dulu did not want to take leave of his wife even when time was up; I asked the jailor what else did he expect of a young couple longing for each other? He looked at me puzzled and then gave me a cryptic smile.

As political or divisional prisoners we were entitled to two newspapers each free of cost except the daily *Janakantha*. We talked amongst ourselves and gave our selections in such a way that combined together we received almost all the dailies except the *Janakantha*. We did not know the reason why the *Janakantha* was banned inside the jail. Its Editor and Publisher Atiqullah

Khan Masud was a nominee of the Awami League for the election slated for January 22 and he was arrested long after that.

We defied the ban by bringing in the *Janakantha,* whenever and whoever went to the court or received food package from outside. The dailies reached us around 10:30 in the morning; we read ours, exchanged with others and then discussed the current happenings. In our assessment, we found the *Daily Star* and the *Prothom Alo* self-serving, at times erratic. Occasionally, editorials in the *Daily Star* were bold and realistic. We voted that the piece that Mahfuz Anam, its editor, wrote under a headline "Milord, We Beg to Differ," differing on the assertion of the then-Chief Justice that the Supreme Court would stay by the nation at the hour of its need as it did in the past, an excellent example of bold and factual assessment.

Some pieces contributed by Abdullah Dewan, a Professor of Michigan State University, U.S., praising the Fakhruddin regime in preference to days earlier than January 11, 2007, were found unprofessional, more so when a few months back we had found the same Professor writing at length in the same paper about people's rights and democratic movements. We found the daily *New Age's* role bold, rational and consistent. In particular its editorials and commentaries contributed by Nurul Kabir and N. M. Harun were assessed as dispassionate and realistic. We were apprehensive the paper would be closed down any day, but luckily it did not happen.

We were surprised to observe that most of the popular columnists of the country except Abdul Gaffar Chowdhury writing from the safety of London, had stopped contributing to our dailies. Salman, being the owner of the daily Independent received occasional information about "pressures" and "self-censorship" imposed on the print media. Barrister Moinul Hossain, one of the owners of the daily *Ittefaq* and holding Information portfolio in addition to that of Law, under his talkative advisorship for the government of the day, said on a number of occasions that the Emergency Powers Rules have laid down "dos and don'ts" for the media and prescribed punishment for violation of the "don'ts," but the government did not want to apply them. We laughed; we wondered how a Barrister such as he was could shamelessly say something which, more than anyone else, he knew to be untrue.

For survival from the severity of imprisonment, we devised and followed an unwritten rule: no one should be left alone. Whenever one was on his bed in an unusual hour or a chair alone, we got the signal. From our respective cells or doings we would go, sit around the loner, sip tea and eat snacks, tell jokes and anecdotes and talk him out of his depression. For everyone sleep was encouraged, as were walking and gossiping, but sitting or staying alone among torn dreams was discouraged and discarded. We took this rule as a collective obligation to follow, and almost always found the victim to gather him up with tender smiles.

The Jail Code amended by the last BNP government, in all probability at the behest of its Law Minister Moudud Ahmed, allowed TV at inmates' cost within the jail on the condition that only the BTV, the government's electronic channel, could be tuned in. In the division building we had TVs in a number of cells. But these were not much used due to drab programs and propagandist nature of news telecast by the BTV. At times, mostly late at night, India's *Durdarshan* could be tuned in showing classic pictures and attractive documentaries. These were popular throughout the jail.

Little did the authorities realize that it was not possible to control telecasts or information that had become technologically borderless even in our part of the world. The interesting part of this tele-control that failed was that at times, given better reception from some of our TVs, the Superintendent and the Jailor used to come by and sit with us to see the officially unseeable telecasts of the *Durdarshan*. Besides, TV as per the Jail Code as amended, all of us had radios that we used to listen to news broadcasts. Almost none tuned in the *Bangladesh Betar*.

The most popular sources of news were the BBC and the VOA followed by *Bangladesh Today*. I used to tune in to the BBC at 6:30 in the morning, then at 7:30 also. Salman after the morning prayer performed in congregation slept till 9:30 and then getting up, came to my cell to find out whether the BBC said something important or relevant for us. The BBC's evening news broadcast was at 7:30 followed by the last one 10:30, which I almost never missed. In between at 10:00 the VOA came on which in its coverage, in our assessment, was not very broad or deep in comparison with that of the BBC. We used to sit for our dinner at around 9:30 just to make sure that we did not miss the VOA at 10:00 and the BBC at 10:30.

Telephone was a taboo in the jail. In the Jail Code use of land telephone or mobile was not mentioned. Given the quick pace of proceedings of cases against us we needed to talk to our lawyers; this we did indirectly through obliging jail personnel using their mobiles to pass on messages and through visitors of common prisoners who came with mobiles to the visitors' room. We used to write our messages on pieces of paper and gave these to friendly prisoners who went to see their visitors; the visitors took our messages outside the visiting room, talked to persons concerned over mobile phones, gave and passed back the messages we needed.

In the Kashimpur Jail, no one except the DIG prison and his guest, usually a journalist or an intelligence officer in disguise, could enter the jail with mobiles. At times, we requested the DIG to pass urgent messages to our dear and near ones, which good-heartedly he did. But since he almost never delegated any responsibility to those below, most of the time he could not pass or take all messages. At times he used to keep his mobile off or muted, so that nothing was taken note of or acted upon, as nothing was heard from our lawyers or family members. This was gamely for him, but quite unkindly for us. For instance, he did not pass the message to me when my elder sister died. Later he apolgized, but it did not matter since I did not expect it of him.

One evening, he came into the division building with a journalist known to me and Salman. After having a chat with them on the verandah in front of Salman's room, I requested the DIG to go to the eastern most cell where Kamal Majumder was lying ill. Kamal's son-in-law was a Major in the army and the DIG's classmate. Sending the DIG off, we took the mobile from the journalist in turn in the semi-darkness of the verandah and talked to our people heartily. When the DIG came back after about 30 minutes and sat with us once again, we had a hearty laugh.

He looked somewhat baffled and asked why we were laughing. I told him that, to make the Jail Code up-to-date, very soon there would be provision for installing telephone facilities for the inmates for use on payment and for limited time. But Asadul Habib Dulu, the youngest amongst us proposed further that duration of such tele-talk should be having inverse relation with the age of the inmate and his wife or girlfriend as the case might be. And then looking at Dulu, his young appearance and having the common knowledge about his propensity to prolong his visiting and talking time with his wife at the jail gate, everybody including the DIG laughed. Later the DIG took us all down to the grounds, stood in our midst in front of a shrub and asked the accompanying journalist to take a number of shots in his digital camera. Use of camera within was not permissible under the Jail Code as far as I knew. But one has to know there were exceptions and such exceptions almost never were made in respect of anything that might favor the prisoners.

(6)

In the jail the attendants that were assigned to us from amongst the convicts were supposed to keep an eye on us and report anything unusual observed about us or found in our cells. But from the way and manner we treated them, all of them without exception became more loyal to us than to the jail administration. At times they used to tell us why and how they were sent to the jail without due process of law and trial and how they were being treated by the jail personnel more or less as slaves and persons without any right to dignity and deserving compassion as human beings. Mizan was Kamal Majumder's attendant. Whimsical as he was, very often Kamal used to rebuke Mizan. At the same time he loved Mizan in his own way; he gave him clothes, made sure he got the same food as he did and even went as far as seeing to the wellbeing of his parents who occasionally came to visit him.

On the other end of the scale, I found Mizan despite the rebukes, very careful and anxious about Kamal's needs. Very often when Kamal got ill, I found Mizan reporting to me about his illness with tears in his eyes. Nizam was Salman's attendant. Looking after Salman's needs with meticulous attention, he did not talk in even a slightly louder voice than others working or moving around him and at the same time remained very alert to respond to any calling from Salman. I saw Nizam giving Salman his myriads of medicines at the appointed time and Salman swallowing them even without looking at them. Salman had placed high trust in him. Salman used to take a glass of freshly squeezed orange juice and nothing else every morning as his breakfast. The supply of oranges was the responsibility of his trusted General Manager Mahbub.

One day it so happened that there was not enough oranges to squeeze to fill a glass. With the glass half-filled and Salman still in bed and sleeping, Nizam came down to me to find out whether I could give him one orange so that he could fill the glass for Salman. Fortunately I found one to spare and I gave it to him without Salman's knowledge. At the same time, I was pleasantly surprised to note how concerned Nizam was to make sure that Salman did not miss his full glass of juice in the morning. This was a small thing but most certainly a response to a call beyond duty, more so for a person incarcerated in the jail.

Saku, a convict of about 18, was assigned to Lotus-Kamal. He had a very funny way of smiling at all times. Perhaps slightly short of hearing, he usually took time to go and finish errands which at times seemed and sounded almost incessant from Lotus-Kamal's end. After about two months, his date for release came and we found the boy shedding tears for Lotus-Kamal and the rest of us.

"Will you not go out of the jail leaving Lotus-Kamal and us behind tomorrow?" I asked him half-jokingly.

"No, I will not," he replied seriously and without any hesitation.

"Then what you will do? They will not allow you to stay in the jail when your term will be over," I reasoned with him.

"I will walk to the jail gate on my way out and there I will hit a jail guard and then they will put me back. I will live with you people," he persisted.

Finally, others joined me in my conversation with him and we persuaded him not to do any such stupid thing and to go out and join his parents, who as he knew were living in Badda area of Dhaka. Salman gave him a note for his General Manager Mahbub so that he could be employed in his mills. Saku went out of the jail at 9:30 the next morning, waited till 4:00 in the afternoon when Salman's General Manager Mahbub came to the jail gate as was usual for him and he gave the note to secure a job for a living and then he came to the southern corner of the jail's periphery, waved at us from outside the wall to bid us good-bye. I was amazed; for securing a decent living as a factory worker, even after he was released, he waited seven hours outside the jail gate. How could a boy of his attitude be incarcerated for three years for alleged criminality and kept out of productive work or education by our administrative-legal system? It seemed our system could not see far and its arm for doing productive work was short and skittering.

A well-built, good-mannered and better-groomed person worked as a cook for us in the kitchen for the division prisoners. In his mid-40s, even with a receding hairline he was quite a handsome man. While taking walks on the grounds below and visiting the kitchen at times, I talked to him about things and wanted to know how and why he landed into the jail. To my utter surprise, I found him to be the younger brother of an incumbent Justice of the High Court Division. He was charged and sentenced for trespassing and hijacking, through the conspiracy of his neighbors. When arrested and being tried, his elder brother, then an almost briefless Advocate, was elevated to the bench. His wife did not have good relations with her mother-in-law. When the mother went to his Justice son for giving legal help and support to his younger brother, she was scowled down and turned out of the

Justice's freshly painted government bungalow. The mother came back never to speak about her eldest son and the accused brother vowed never to visit the Justice incarnate and that was how he landed into the jail for want of legal aid. Life appeared to me once again stranger than fiction even in our so-called close-knit society.

At about the same time, I found out about a small fish-seller of Gazipur incarcerated and rotting in the Kashimpur Jail. A man of small means and with a family consisting of an old mother, a young wife and an infant son, he made his ends meet by selling fish everyday in the local squatter's market. One day, a contingent of three policemen, wanted to see his sale proceeds tucked at his waist in the band of his *lungi*[12] and found a hundred Taka note which they said was a counterfeit one. The poor and illiterate fish-seller could not differentiate between a real and a counterfeit 100 Taka note, nor could he exactly recall who in that morning gave him the note, taking the largest fish from his *thoukri* (basket). To the policeman, the explanation was not satisfactory; the fish-seller must have succumbed to the forbidden deed. He was arrested, charged for counterfeiting and, for want of a lawyer's service, jailed for seven years.

When I found him and came to know how he landed into the jail, three years had gone by. He did not know whether his mother was alive and where and how were his young wife and infant son. Most of the things appeared rotten to me in our State, for and in spite of the police and the magistracy for whom our poor people have been paying. A few days later, the Additional District Magistrate of Gazipur along with a female magistrate, on a visit to the jail, came to my cell and asked me how I was. I told them this misdeed of the police and the Magistracy destroying the life of a poor man. I did not notice that they took note of this as a wrong to be righted in earnest.

Omar was my attendant. He was about 22, meek and soft-spoken. He almost never spoke unless spoken to. I found him a very good hand, a man Friday who catered to my requirements without being asked or prodded. He was very faithful too. I never found him taking any of my loose coins or a thing that might be of some use to him. For about six years he had been in this jail. His home was somewhere near Gazipur, where he had lived with his elder brother, brother's wife and mother. Where his father lived, he never spoke of it. Most probably he was dead.

---

[12] A garment for men and boys loosely resembling a kilt that reaches to mid-calf.

One day his sister-in-law, following a quarrel with his mother, in the absence of her husband had committed suicide. As a result, the police hauled Omar and his mother up and charged them for manslaughter or culpable homicide not amounting to murder. The elder brother was not hauled in as he was at that time not present at home. The family was too poor to meet legal expenses for defense. For four years Omar and his mother were in jail awaiting investigation and facing trial. After about four years, Omar mustered courage to tell the judge:

"Please do not keep both my mother and myself in the jail. Please release my mother so that she can take care of our household, and keep me inside the jail."

"In that case, who had killed your sister-in-law? Will you say that you did it?" asked the judge.

"Yes, I take the responsibility for her death," replied Omar.

So the mother was released, Omar remained in the jail with aching thoughts of love and loss. I asked him to tell me the truth so that I could help him out. He told me with tears in his eyes, he or his mother did not kill the girl. She was somewhat mentally deranged; quite often she ran out of the house and did all sorts of crazy things. All these were known to the neighbors. In fact, she committed suicide after having a fight with his mother.

With a muddy gloom covering his entire face, he said that since they could not satisfy the police, the charge of manslaughter was made against them. I listened in silence and wondered about the nature and system of justice in our country for which we had fought. I promised him, following my release, I would make him file an appeal, pay for his legal counsel and arrange for his release. I did not know at that time that my release would be shrouded in black shadows of domination, stretched long across the pale dirt road of illegitimate ambition of the gun-toters and their henchmen.

(7)

As I found out in course of our stay in Kashimpur, the organizational structure of the jail remained more or less the same as devised by the British Raj. At the time, at the apex of the Kashimpur Jail was Superintendent Matin. He had to put in over 30 years of service to reach that post. A short man with seemingly sad resignation, Matin was an amiable person, as I found. He did not live with his family in the quarters given to him outside the jail walls.

Quite often, on hot days, he was found having a nap in a room adjacent to his office located on the first story of the jail gate. Almost every evening, he used to drop in the division building and chat with us over a cup of tea. He talked mostly about the chances he lost in life, injustice he met on his way up and indifference of his bosses about reforms of the jail administration that he proposed or had in mind. As Superintendent Matin used to say, he wanted to feel secure about the future, as he had lost the present.

In his talks with us, he used to agree to most of the things we suggested to improve his administration, at times called the jailor or the deputy jailors even right in front of us to tell them what needed to be done promptly; and then on the next morning forgot about what he had agreed with us and instructed the officers under him to do. He was on the verge of retirement and quite often wondered about what he would do once he was out of the jail. As he told us, he did not find any time to read the daily newspapers even, so great was, in his assessment, the pressure of his job. But he knew who amongst us were moneyed and could be of help to him in service and when he would be out of it.

Down below was the jailor, Enamul Haq, a man in his early 50s. He was a freedom fighter as he said, but despite that, over years, as he complained, he could not climb up the service ladder as some of his colleagues did. He was portly in appearance, suffered from diabetes, had unshaken faith in herbal medicine, and did not consult or get treatment from the jail's doctor. He almost always greeted me with a wide smile, knowing that from 1996 to 2001 I was the Minister-in-Charge of Kurigram district from where he came and that I helped turn the perennially food-deficit district into a surplus one.

Below him were two deputy jailors, Shahadat Hossain and Jainul Abedin. In his 30s, Shahadat was a handsome young man, not very well-reputed for his treatment of jail guards and prisoners. As the story went, one had to follow a circuitous route to keep him happy and satisfied. Jainul Abedin was in his late 20s, slightly short in his left leg and given to dejected jabberings about almost anything that came to his notice. He was usually helpful but at times moody with his sights spread out beyond the walls of the jail. The deputy jailors supervised the work of six havildars,[13] who in their turn bossed over 46 jail guards known in the jail parlance as *miashaabs*. These havildars and *miashaabs* were the real workhorses of the jail. The jail guards were first called "mi-

[13] A sergeant major in the army.

ashaabs" by Bangabandhu when he was in the Dhaka Central Jail in the 1960s, and from then the title spread throughout all other jails of Bangladesh. As cooking, cleaning, gardening, petty repairing and fixing were all done by convicts, the organizational strength was adequate.

On the top of all was the DIG (Prisons) Major Shamsul Haider Siddiky. For a man from the army, he was quite an amiable and patient person. He tried his best to reduce corruption within the jail administration. In the process, he employed a chosen group of jail guards as his direct informants, who at times could get access to him and could cross over the authority of the Superintendent and even the Jailor. To look after health of all inmates there was a qualified physician Dr. Shamsuddin, assigned from the Directorate General of Health. Sometime later, he was replaced by Dr. Rathindranath Kundu of the same Directorate. He was assisted by a pharmacist named Nuruzzaman.

A number of "writers" worked under the deputy jailors and the pharmacist. They were selected from amongst young educated inmates who could make entries into the relevant registers and keep records. In our time, I could identity eight of them, six working under the deputy jailors and two under the pharmacist. When the Superintendent went on leave, a magistrate assigned from the district magistracy acted on his behalf. In the absence of the jailor, the ranking deputy jailor took over his charge. A lot of vegetables and a reasonable quantity of fruit were grown on the grounds within the four walls of the jail. These were grown by the prisoners; a portion went to their kitchen and a chunk was apportioned amongst the Superintendent, the Jailor and the deputy jailors. Almost nothing (about which the physician complained) went to him or the pharmacist.

There was an infirmary within the jail compound, between the jail gate and the division building. There were 20 beds and separate arrangements for bath and toilet facilities in the infirmary. In addition to genuinely ill inmates, some healthy ones were also found in the infirmary. As the story went, the health personnel of the jail needed to be satisfied, one way or other, to be admitted into the infirmary in good health. Living was better, accommodations uncrowded and food supply separate and somewhat improved over there.

There was a general complaint about the ineffectiveness of the medicines, obtained from the infirmary. Mostly antihistamine, sedatives and anti-diarrheal pills, reportedly ineffective, were available there. When I talked to the physician about this, he told me that the manufacturers of medicines who were selected on the lowest bid did not include all or full ingredients of drugs and medicines into pills and capsules produced for and supplied to the jail in specially printed packets. In order to prevent outside sale of drugs and medicines supplied to the jail, these were labeled on packets as of the Inspectorate General, Prisons, so it was easier for the lowest bidder to cheat on both quantity and quality of drugs packeted for the Prison Inspectorate.

Most of the patients, if they could, preferred to bring medicine prescribed by the jail physician from the open market. In the jail, I found an old crippled person of about 70 years with no leg or hand, requiring compassionate help from other inmates to keep his body clean and non-odorous. I asked Superintendent Matin whether they had recommended his release on the occasion of the last Victory or Independence Day. I was told they did even before that. But he could not obtain his release on the last Independence or Victory Day as there was none to take his brief home through the regulatory labyrinth of the Home Ministry. As it seemed, not many in the jail and the Home Ministry had the wisdom to know what was right and the courage to do it. To them no punishment was too harsh for anyone once inside the four walls of the country's jails.

(8)

Visiting inmates of the jail both those under-trial and convicts was an ordeal interlaced with corrupt practices. For ordinary prisoners, both under-trial and convicts, visitors were allowed once a week. The visitors converged in a one-storied building to the west of the office block at the jail gate and adjacent to its high peripheral walls at around 8:00 in the morning all days of the week. Each visitor deposited at least Tk. 2 to a "writer" to fill in a slip giving particulars of the inmate desired to be seen. The filled-in-slip was then placed before the deputy jailor on duty, who looking at a roster of last visitors of the inmate concerned, or feigning to look at a register looking like that, initialed formal permission. Then the initialed slip was taken inside by a convict wearing an armband, who shouted the name and the *thana* (sub-district) of the prisoner to be visited.

For going to and shouting on the grounds of each building in this manner, there were 24 selected convicts with armbands. Drawn by the shouts, the under-trial person or the convict came down and accompanied the shouter-convict under the surveillance of jail guards, who were standing under nearby trees to the visitors' room. In the visitor's room about 50-75 visitors used to talk at the top of their voices with an equal number of convicts or prisoners still under trial. The usual visiting time was 30 minutes each, extendable up to even six hours on satisfaction of the writer and the deputy jailor concerned. The visitors usually came with dry and cooked food for the inmates to be seen. At times food was freely allowed; at other times refused and dumped aside and then, after a considerable time, allowed on satisfaction of the "writer," the guards or the deputy jailor concerned.

For "division" prisoners, the meeting place was the office room of either the jailor or the deputy jailors or in case of a very well-known person, the conference room adjacent to the Superintendent's office upstairs. The presence of a watcher from the Special Branch of the district police was required. If the Superintendent of the jail was well-disposed and the watcher materially satisfied, the interview could continue far beyond 30 minutes and without the effective or actual presence of the government spook. In that case the spook would loiter outside the visiting room or take tea and snacks elsewhere at the cost of the visitor. In my case, for reasons best known to the Special Branch, very special attention was always given to ensure that the visit did not continue beyond 30 minutes.

On several occasions that my elder brother Dr. Burhanuddin Khan Jahangir and my wife Sitara came to see me, they had to bring in the government spook from Gazipur town, *i.e.*, the district headquarters, in their own vehicle and at their expense. Every time they visited me, I strengthened myself in my mind to be cheerful right from my cell in the division building before walking down to the visiting room with two jail guards guarding me on two sides. I put on a Mujib coat and walked keeping my head high and greeted them warmly and smilingly. Despite loneliness and longing for my family, I did not give them any scope to realize the real state of my mind. I was sure they also did the same. I told them I did not do anything wrong and would never bow down to those illegitimately in power. With tears welling up in her eyes, my wife held my hands and gave support that further strengthened my resolve to stand against the evil with head held high.

On about February 10, I received a notice signed by an Assistant Secretary, Ministry of Home that I along with Salman F. Rahman and Lotus-Kamal had a meeting at my place in Banani on January 27 to hatch a conspiracy to disrupt the government. The notice was based on a grand lie. On the 27th, Lotus-Kamal was out of the country in Malaysia; Salman never visited my place of residence nor did I visit his in a year or so. We in the Awami League did not oppose formation of the government headed by Dr. Fakhruddin on January 11. Along with other members of the Presidium, I was invited to his oath-taking ceremony and I did attend the same. I personally congratulated Dr. Fakhruddin on the assumption of the office of the Chief Advisor and conversed with him right in front of Sheikh Hasina in Bangabhaban. He knew me personally. We were both teachers of Economics in the Dhaka University in 1962-63. We were both members of the erstwhile Civil Service of Pakistan. How could he in his senses bring out a false charge that I had conspired against his government? I could not believe this could come from the government in the Ministry of Home when he was the Advisor-in charge of the Ministry.

When I received the notice I recalled that in 1970, before the Liberation War started, I was Assistant Commissioner, Nowshera, Peshawar district of the North West Frontier Province of Pakistan. Dr. Fakhruddin was then a Deputy Secretary of the Establishment Division of the Government of Pakistan in Islamabad located about 70 miles to the east of Nowshera. In a tribal area on the Khyber Pass adjacent to Peshawar known as Landikotal, a lot of consumer goods smuggled from China and European countries were available without tariff.

On a Sunday Dr. Fakhruddin and his wife Nina drove to Nowshera on their way to Landikotal to buy some Chinese silk and a tape recorder available there free of tariff. We hosted them at a lunch in our place, gave a guide to take them to Landikotal and back. On reaching back to Nowshera with the goodies in the boot of their volkswagon, Nina said they were afraid to cross the Attock Bridge on the eastern border of Nowshera, where a tariff post was in place to prevent smuggling. Sitara gave them tea and then we boarded our Volkswagon and asked them to follow us towards Attock, assisting the Deputy Secretary of the Government of Pakistan and his wife across the tariff post of the same government without payment of due tariff and hassle. We waved goodbye to them for the drive onwards to the governmental citadel. The closeness in service fraternity at that time even covered obvious collaboration in smuggling goodies for the satisfaction of the wife of my colleague visiting from Islamabad.

I wondered how Fakhruddin and his wife could forget all these things. But forget he did, for as I said earlier, he had to prove that blood was always thicker than the watery bond of friendship and fraternity. The notice said that on grounds of conspiracy so hatched, I was arrested under Rule 16(2) of the Emergency Powers Rules, 2007, read with the provision for preventive detention under the Special Powers Act, 1974, and if I so wanted, I could represent to my arrestors about what they should do to me.

With hate unbounded, I decided not to write any representation. And with anguish I recalled that a person arrested under Rule 16(2) could not even apply to be posted on bail. This provision of Rule 16(2) was in obvious and definite violation of the constitutional right that any citizen arrested by the police or any agency of the government would have to be produced before the local magistrate within 24 hours of such arrest. What good it would be to produce an arrested person before the Magistrate if, under no circumstances and irrespective of reasons for such an arrest, he could not be posted on bail?

Needless to say, from this point of view alone, all arrests made by Dr. Fakhruddin's government under Rule 16(2) of the Emergency Powers Rules were in gross violation of the Constitution of the country. As it turned out, the Emergency Powers Rules were drafted by the army long before Dr. Fakhruddin was made the shoeshine Chief Advisor on their behalf. Besides, as he never served as a Deputy Commissioner of a district and Secretary to the government; he had neither the experience nor the courage and integrity of a seasoned bureaucrat to tell the army brass about the constitutional provisions and their implications.

During his university days as a student, Dr. Fakhruddin was a member of the National Student's Federation, the student wing of the Muslim League under the leadership of Monem Khan, Governor of East Pakistan when Ayub Khan was the dictator-President of Pakistan. Just before the Liberation War, he went on a government fellowship to the U.S.A. for higher studies in Economics. Free from the direct tentacles of the Pakistan Government, unlike most of the Bangalis abroad at that time, he did not join or aid the Liberation War.

Liberation attained, he joined the World Bank, being a representative staff symbol in that body from Bangladesh and served that institution till he retired as a Senior Loan Officer in 2001. In 2002 he came back, and was chosen by Khaleda Zia's Finance Minister Saifur Rahman as the Governor of the Bangladesh Bank, *i.e.*, the central bank of the country. Serving some time as a governor he retired and then, to satisfy his almost insatiable propensity to be associated with those in power, he accepted a much lower position as the CEO of the Palli Karmasangsthan Shahayak Foundation, a specialized fund set up earlier by Sheikh Hasina's government to fund creation of rural employment opportunities primarily through the NGOs.

It was learned later that the armed forces, seizing actual government power on January 10, 2007, asked Dr. Mohammed Yunus to be the Chief Advisor and to run the government on their behalf. Earlier failing in his attempt to float a new political party banking on the receipt of the Nobel Peace Prize, Yunus declined, but he suggested that his classmate, Dr. Fakhruddin, be made the Chief Advisor. A dark horse thus appeared from almost nowhere to replace Dr. Iazuddin, another dark horse, who had been made President by Khaleda Zia and then had assumed unique dual charge by appointing himself as the Chief Advisor.

Never in the history of statecraft anywhere had a President of the country appointed himself as his own Chief Advisor like he did. In this context, I discussed the matter at length with my wife when she came to visit me in the jail and decided not to approach Dr. Fakhruddin and his cohorts for anything in connection with my release from incarceration, so ungratefully and indecently imposed on me. In our assessment they were no more than upfront shoeshine boys of demons destroying democracy in the country.

(9)

I knew Dr. Mohammed Yunus. I studied Economics in Dhaka University as he did. He was two years senior to me. We were all proud when he won the Nobel Peace Prize. Along with General Secretary Abdul Jalil and another Presidium Member Motia Chowdhury, I went to his house adjacent to the Grameen Bank building at Mirpur to congratulate him. Motia and I also attended the citizen's reception for him in the Bangabandhu Convention Center at Sher-e-Bangla Nagar. During Sheikh Hasina's time we had built this Center with Chinese help and named it Bangabandhu Convention Center. The BNP government coming into power under Khaleda Zia in 2001 renamed it Bangladesh-China Friendship Convention Center. But for me it was the Bangabandhu Convention Center and would remain so despite the change in name, hammered down distastefully by Khaleda and her cohorts.

On behalf of the Awami League, Motia Chowdhury and I congratulated heartily Yunus once again in the Convention Center. Earlier, following the devastation caused by the country-wide flood in 1998, when the Grameen Bank was in trouble, Sheikh Hasina's government pumped in Tk. 2,000 million as additional capital to the bank. S. M. S. Kibria, the Finance Minister of the time, went out of his way to persuade Prime Minister Sheikh Hasina and her cabinet colleagues to give this support. The Grameen Bank would have collapsed at that time but for this support.

Earlier, when Yunus came up with a proposal for setting up the Grameen Phone (mobile phone company), I, as the State Minister for Planning, gave him unstinted support for getting the license and to use the railway's telelink infrastructure built up earlier with Norwegian aid. Coincidentally, when I was a Joint Secretary in the External Relations Division in the early 1980s, I had negotiated this telelink as aid from Norway. Much before that, when the Grameen Bank was still a concept being experimented by Yunus as a Professor of Chittagong University, Anisuzzaman the then-Managing Director of the Krishi Bank gave him seed money and unqualified support. Anisuzzaman was later made the Agricultural Advisor in Sheikh Hasina's government. Without Anisuzzaman's initial help it was doubtful whether Yunus could have set up his Grameen Bank or exemplified as he did his poverty eradication drive on the basis of micro-credit.

Despite all this assistance, after receipt of the award, in the civic reception arranged to honor Dr. Yunus by the Dhaka City Corporation, he never mentioned these acts of support or his thankfulness for them; he only expressed profusely in favor of the incumbent, *i.e.*, Khaleda's government and the City Corporation led by the BNP's Sadeq Hossain Khoka. He never enquired even in private why, in the civic reception given to him by the City Corporation, no Awami League Leader was invited. He expressed satisfaction when Khaleda Zia formed the government in 2001 following a disputed election. This he did not do when Sheikh Hasina won the election earlier in 1996. He never uttered a word of sympathy when Sheikh Hasina and other Awami League leaders were attacked by grenades on the Bangabandhu Avenue on August 21, 2004 and as many as 24 Awami League leaders and workers were killed.

While we in the Awami League appreciated Yunus's drive to build up the Grameen Bank, informally we suggested that: (1) more voice should be given to the poor (*i.e.*, the borrower-shareholders) in the management of the bank; (2) the propensity to build additional institutions like Grameen Trust, Grameen Mutual Fund, Grameen Food, *etc.* should be reined in both to extend and deepen the operation of the Grameen Bank in the field of micro-credit; (3) the lending rate of the bank averaging over

22% per year should be brought down to reduce the borrower's never-ending dependence on loans, preventing them from crossing the level of subsistence over onto a real path of ever-increasing investment, innovation and wealth creation, like what happened in the post-Civil War America; (4) the Grameen Bank should mop up idle liquidity of the country's commercial banks to supplement its increase in micro-credit operation and (5) the urban poor should be brought under its cover by amending the statute of the bank. But Yunus almost refused to hear about these, let alone consider them.

In view of this backdrop, while sitting in the Kashimpur Jail, we found Yunus waxing eloquent on the need of and support for a non-elected caretaker government led by Dr. Fakhruddin and with the armed forces in the back and we were baffled. To many of us his actions and concerns expressed home and abroad bordered on duplicity, partisanship and opportunism, blemishing the luster of the Nobel Peace Prize. Following victory in major wars — including the First and the Second World Wars — the victors as well as the vanquished demolished their armed forces and invested the peace dividend in wealth and welfare creation in their respective societies. Following the conclusion of the Peace Accord in Chittagong Hill tracts in sequel to the signing of the Treaty on Sharing of the Ganga Water Between Bangladesh and India, we could have taken peace dividends towards wealth and welfare creation at all levels. Yunus, however, did not say a word on these achievements, nor did he lend his support to freeze the nation's ever-increasing expenditure on the military, dissipating avenues for productive investment for societal wealth creation and development.

(10)

On the night of February 2, 2007 I was arrested along with 49 others. From the Awami League we were just 4: Salman F. Rahman, A. H. M. Kamal popularly known as Lotus-Kamal, Mohammad Nasim and I. Following the service of notices of our arrests under R-16(2) of the Emergency Powers Rules, 2007, and the Special Powers Act 1974, on February 20 all the arrested persons received another notice, each under Sections 26 and 27 of the Anti-Corruption Commission Act, 2004, asking them to (i) submit statement of assets (including assets of family members) and (ii) mention sources of the stated assets, in accordance with the procedure determined by the ACC within 72 hours of the notice receipt.

This notice was signed by Mohammad Delwar Hossain, Secretary of the ACC. The ACC was not in place at that time. Earlier the Chairman and two other members, characterized as "jokers" by Major General (Ret.) Matin, an Advisor of Dr. Fakharuddin's government, were forced to resign and nobody was appointed in their place till then. Before giving the notice Mohammed Delwar Hossain went on TV to announce that he had already submitted a statement of his assets. (As reported in the media, besides clothes and utensils, he owned only an air conditioner.) Also, as the country was under the emergency rule, he had issued notices on us accusing us of being corrupt and actionable under the Anti-Corruption Act. He also announced in the media that it was time to cleanse the country of corrupt people. Especially about me, Delwar went out of his way to mention that he had personal knowledge about properties acquired by me in corrupt ways, as he came from the same electoral constituency as I did.

I had occasion to know Delwar for quite a long period. In 1996 when I was the General Secretary of the Civil Service (Administration) Association, Delwar was a sub-district officer in Moulvibazar district. As a sub-district officer he did something terribly wrong, so much so that the Deputy Commissioner, *i.e.*, the district officer, sent a contingent of the police to arrest him. Delwar fled the station and came to me for shelter. I took the Deputy Commissioner to task telling him that under no circumstances could he send the police to arrest a subordinate civil officer under him. I arranged for Delwar's withdrawal from the sub-district and after some time helped him to obtain a fellowship and to go for higher studies abroad. Struggling for two years, he barely passed, came back and sought help to treat his only daughter. I raised subscriptions from our colleagues, arranged for her treatment and he told me he would remain ever grateful to me for what I had done to save him, his job and to treat his daughter. I felt embarrassed; told him I just did what I would have done for any member of my service.

Now I was painfully astonished to find out how grateful he was; his gratitude did not stop here. Some days after the newly-appointed Chairman of the ACC went to Chandpur and met a cross-section of the society over anti-corruption drive, someone asked him what they were going to do with the most corrupt person of the district, meaning the immediate past district minister of Khaleda Zia's government. The Chairman unabashedly replied "the most important" corrupt person of the district (meaning me) had already been arrested and they did not plan to arrest anyone else immediately. The ACC obviously did not know of handcrafted actions taken in all development works in the district by the immediate past district minister. As I came to know later, this was the result of a "brief" on the district's corrupt people given to the Chairman by Delwar Hossain. As it turned out, Delwar Hossain neither knew what was right nor had the courage to do the right thing. In the milieu of perverse self-aggrandizement he thought he could climb up by cutting the throats of even his benefactors and well-wishers.

The Chairman and two other Members were appointed to the ACC sometime in late March. I knew the Chairman, General Hasan Masud Chowdhury, a retired army chief. His elder sister, Sajeda or Saju was my student when I taught Economics in Dhaka University. He chaperoned my wife and me when I went on an official trip to Bangkok sometime in 1999, when he was probably a military attaché there. He was an Advisor for some time in President Iajuddin's first caretaker government. When Iajuddin took upon himself the office of the Chief Advisor, alleging partisan conduct and indecision on part of Iajuddin, Hasan Masud Chowdhury resigned. Before taking up the office, he made Chief Advisor Fakhruddin and President Iajuddin to give him the rank and status of a minister in the government.

At a time when there was no minister in the caretaker government itself in accordance with the constitution and the advisors themselves were not ministers, how the Chairman could be given the status of a minister remained both a puzzle and a mystery of the inner working of the caretaker government. The rumor reached us even in the Kashimpur Jail that while appointing Hasan Masud Chowdhury and two other members of the ACC the procedure prescribed in the law was not followed; they were not recommended by the relevant committee for such appointments as prescribed under the law. On the assumption of office, Chairman Hasan Masud Chowdhury went on a week-long private trip to Pakistan. He started hollering against corruption everywhere, especially of the politicians immediately after his return.

Of the two members, one was Manzur Mannan, once the Collector of Customs in Chittagong, holding perhaps the most important revenue-collecting post of the country. Serving as a Collector and taking pride as a very honest officer he was involved in a car accident at Chowddagram on the Dhaka-Chittagong Highway traveling in a car of a businessman. I was the General Secretary of the Civil Service (Administration) Association and Mannan was an influential Member of the Customs Service at that time. There was an inter-service covert fight in the process of service restructuring of the country at that time. It was likely he was not very kindly disposed towards me as the General Secretary of a rival service of the Republic.

The other member of the ACC, a member of the judicial service of the Republic, had retired as a district judge. We heard that before being appointed as a member of the ACC, he could not make it to the bench of the High Court Division, usually so made by a successful judge at that level. I did not have any occasion to make his acquaintance. The members were given the rank and status of deputy ministers at a time when there was no provision in the constitution for appointment of such ministers. As it turned out, in all subsequent announcements and actions of the ACC, the persons having the status of deputy ministers were imprisoned within the bounds of whims and wishes of the person having the rank of a minister in a minister-less government.

As we came to know subsequently, the private tour of Lieutenant General (Ret.) Hasan Masud Chowdhury to Pakistan after taking over as the Chairman, ACC, was not so private. He collected all information as to how General Pervez Musharraf, after toppling Nawaz Sharif, the popularly elected Prime Minister of Pakistan about nine years back, rode on the bogey of combating corruption, accused the politicians and their supporter businessmen for being corrupt and modified and enacted laws, rules and regulations to maul them down denying them their basic human rights.

In our case, the first action at Chairman Chowdhury's behest was to freeze all bank accounts of the arrested businessmen and politicians and their family members. It was done to make them largely unable to undertake and fight legal battles. This was done first by an oral order to all the banks and financial institutions followed by written instructions by the National Board of Revenue (NBR) under the Income Tax Ordinance. In the income tax law, freezing of bank accounts was about one last measure against a taxpayer after the tax authority fails to collect due taxes through service of notice, hearing, appeal and arbitration. Because of the perceived might of generalship, no civil servant dared to point this out to Chairman Hasan Masud Chowdhury and the incumbent army chief General Moin U. Ahmed, who had installed Fakhruddin's so-called caretaker government.

The second and simultaneous action by Chairman Chowdhury was to form Task Forces, each comprising of security personnel and investigation officers drawn from the ACC and the NBR and led by a Major of the Army and in a few cases, officers of equivalent rank of the Air Force and the Navy. Each Task Force searched, ransacked all records in house and office of every arrested person, terrified their family members and employees and took their political, financial and business records and property documents and denied the arrested one any access to them.

This was a process of deliberate destruction of evidence that could be produced by the arrested persons in courts of law. In my case, as I heard later, all my tax records, cheque books, records of deposits and withdrawals, contracts on consultancy works and manuscripts of reports and books being written were taken away; my personal library was ransacked. All my mobile telephone sets were seized; all documents of sales and purchases of land and share certificates of different companies were bundled off. The objective was very simple and straightforward. Later on whatever they, through formal prosecutors, accused me of, I would find it quite difficult to rebut with sufficient records and documents. This amounted to indisputable denial of due process of law. Incarcerated in jail, I could not even find duplicate copies of these records.

Third, this was followed by threats to prominent and able lawyers. Each of those lawyers initially willing to defend us were told that the Task Force would dig out their income tax records and vilify them as tax-dodgers, dishonest people in the event they dared to stand by our side. Similar threats were given to the judges at the district level and even to the Justices of the Supreme Court. The Chief Justice was called to the President's House, reportedly shown some discrepancies in records pertaining to ownership of land of his family members, and a prima-facie false affidavit sworn earlier by him and a few dubious legal documents. This was done in front of the Army Chief and he was asked to toe the line. In an unprecedented move, the Chairman of the ACC, a party to litigations started and to be followed, called on the Chief Justice officially in the Supreme Court.

All these were done so as to make the courts bend to the wishes of those in power. This became evident subsequently in the soft actions and decisions of the Appellate Division in ignoring constitutional rights and principles of the Rule of Law. This was starkly manifested in putting on hold indefinitely decisions in cases wherein the High Court Division (from which appeal led to the Appellate Division) had declared illegal the incarceration of most of the politicians and businessmen under the Special Power Acts. The Appellate Division kept quiet, in conformity with the long-discarded requirements of the State, as was advanced in Nazi Germany before the Second World War.

Fourth, the Leaders of the Task Force assigned were almost always chosen taking into consideration their political predilections. If the arrested politician was from the Awami League, the Leader of the Task Force assigned to enquire into his assets and deeds was invariably chosen from amongst officers with leaning towards the BNP. In case the arrested person was from the BNP, the leader of the Task Force concerned was similarly chosen from those opposed to the BNP. In the absence of development of professionalism in the armed services, this could be done easily, and of course done without authorization.

And finally, a scheme was drawn up and implemented for setting up special tribunals, selecting pliant subordinate judges aspiring to be promoted, and holding of mock trials under the supervision of the military. The Speaker of the Parliament confirmed his unanimity with the wishes of the army by allowing the setting up of these kangaroo courts or tribunals and prison cells for the incarcerated persons taken there for producing before such courts or tribunals within the Parliament building.

Entry to these courts and tribunals was strictly controlled, making the process nothing other than *in camera* trials. The concerned Leaders of the Task Force, directing the Prosecution and advising the pliant judges were given spaces within the Parliament building to set up their offices. As trials started, personnel of the armed forces and intelligence agencies of the government moving in crisp civil dress could be identified to be almost matching the number of trial lawyers and witnesses. The probable defense witnesses were threatened by the Leader of Task Force concerned and the intelligence agents in general in ways that were never experienced in this country even during the days of united Pakistan. As the story had it, all these actions and steps were advised from Pakistan of the day and carried home by Chairman Hasan Masud Chowdhury through his private trip to the land of his former superiors and trainers.

(11)

As we came to know from various sources while we were incarcerated, a scheme for taking over the government by the armed forces was drawn up long before the Proclamation of Emergency on January 11, 2007. Rumor had it that Bangladesh's Directorate General of the Forces Intelligence was in close touch with the Inter-Service Intelligence of Pakistan and had sent officers in clandestine ways without the knowledge of the government of the day to know and learn ways and means of hauling up politicians and businessmen of independent nature. It was understood that one Syed Ishrat Hossain, once Governor of State Bank of Pakistan under General Parvez Mosharraf had framed policy measures to financially cripple and subdue the politicians over there.

The same set of policy measures were copied from there and under the cover of anti-money laundering measures, the armed forces over here had collected information about deposits over Tk. 50 lacs in any commercial bank of any individual depositor through the central bank of the country. The income tax records, which were not to be disclosed to anyone else unless and until so wanted by competent courts, were collected in the same way. As soon as the Emergency was proclaimed at the behest of the armed forces, both the ACC and the National Board of Revenue started cases against selected individuals.

As the story had it, even the Emergency Powers Rules were copied from Pakistan. General Parvez Mosharraf, to satisfy his ego, wanted Bangladesh to be ruled by the military in the same way he ruled Pakistan and provided the role model for our army brass. They wanted to grab power initially under the cover of a caretaker government, drumbeat the corruptible nature of the politicians of the day, especially of the major two political parties, break them into several groups, form a number of new pliant political parties, bribe and terrorize the media to toe their line, appoint trusted personnel from the armed forces in important organizations and institutions of the State, hold a phony election and then make the army chief President by a consensus vote by the parliamentarians, whitewashed and legitimated through such an election.

This was a classic instance of using all institutions and powers of the State to attain and satisfy the personal ambition of a single person. No other corruption, financial or abusive of political power in local areas, could be worse than such corruption based on the barrel of the gun and its powder. Unfortunately, with the military using such corruption of the gravest nature to drive its roots and extend its sinews, representative ambassadors of some democratic countries gave a helping hand. In their assessment, the economic interests of their respective countries could be better served by a military rule bereft of political support. By terrorizing the people, such a government could provide lease, concessions and rights in favor of these countries; a government based on popular support reflected though free and fair election was assessed as too strong to grant such leases, concessions and rights.

The façade of an interim caretaker government in the front initially and its subsequent replacement by a "popularly" elected military dictator too willing to listen to them and cater to their needs was also in part designed by them. Later, fortunately, reports published in January 2007 by the Human Rights Watch made these roles of usually elected democratic countries quite clear to our people and conscious citizenry in their respective countries. This was a definite betrayal of their democratic tradition and freedom of the common people for the sake of protecting covert economic interests of their transnational companies and investment groups having major influence on foreign policies of their respective governments.

Fortunately, many of the human rights organizations working in their respective countries and internationally could not be blinded to such objectives. Gradually these organizations came to demand withdrawal of the emergency, restoration of human rights, abolition of the kangaroo courts and the reform of the judicial-administrative system in Bangladesh. Of the group of countries, the European Union belatedly came to voice their concern along the lines of these organizations. The U.S. government, from time to time, voiced their concern for violation of human rights by the military-controlled government and for taking all necessary steps for holding free and fair election as expeditiously as possible.

Of the members of the caretaker government, none served the purpose of the military better than Barrister Moinul Hossain, Advisor-in-Charge of Law, Information, Public Works and Land Affairs. Under the garb of democratic reform measures, he criticized the political parties, bashed the prominent amongst them as corrupt, demanded reform of the political parties and manipulated splits among them. I knew Hossain since his University days. While I studied Economics, he went for a degree in Political Science and then, on the strength of his father's financial ability and despite being an unremarkable achiever as a student, for Bar-at-Law in London.

On his return, he enrolled himself as an advocate of the Supreme Court, practiced a little, but ran a daily newspaper, the *Ittefaq,* established in the 1950s by Maulana Bhashani and then taken over by his father Tofazzal Hossain, popularly known as Manik Mia. Hossain supported the national traitor Khandaker Mushtaq Ahmed who was instrumental in killing Bangabandhu, the father of the nation. His association with Khandaker Mushtaq Ahmed put a permanent scar on his political identity; none of the political parties of importance or significance seemed to have any trust in him.

With the advent of the army-controlled caretaker government, Hossain therefore came forward with pent-up venom against the politicians, alleged that all of them were corrupt and tried to create an aura of honesty around himself. He went on proposing all sorts of reforms of the political parties and the election process. From his utterances and actions, it was apparent he was using the military to rise further in power and publicity. And to this end he was instrumental, as the story went, in jailing his own brother Anwar Hossain Manju for keeping a few bottles of liquor in his house. He wanted to throw his brother out of the *Ittefaq*, his power base. All these things he continued till he was thrown out, quite unceremoniously as we had predicted right at the beginning of his jabberings about the reform of political parties, in a later stage of Dr. Fakhruddin's regime.

The Army Chief General Moin U. Ahmed was at the beginning making quite a noise about corruption of politicians and of balance of powers and responsibilities between the President and the Prime Minister being absent in the Constitution. Fed with some support from a group of pseudo-intellectuals led by one Professor Ataur Rahman of Dhaka University, in a conference on Political Science held at Dhaka in the early days of the regime, General Moin presented a paper, reportedly prepared by a pseudo-intellectual aspiring to be an advisor. The paper proposed an institutional sharing of State power by the military through creating a National Security Council with a constitutional mandate to oversee the operation of the entire government.

After a few months, it was publicized that General Moin was invited by the Kennedy School of Government of Harvard University to give a lecture on governance issues of Southeast Asia in general and Bangladesh in particular. While discussing this publicized program of the General with other inmates in the Kashimpur Jail, I said that, as a former student of Boston University and quite acquainted with the neighboring Harvard's tradition of liberal education, I found this unbelievable: Harvard in its history had never invited a military leader or a dictator to visit its institutions, let alone to lecture in them.

As it turned out subsequently, General Moin went to the U.S. almost as a private citizen; he was not received by the U.S. government, or even invited by the Pentagon, nor was he asked by

Harvard to come as a distinguished visitor. Instead, he addressed a makeshift collection of Bangladeshi immigrants in New York, went to Florida to meet his immigrant brother, student son and friends and then came to Harvard's precincts to talk with two academics and about eight students in a side room of the Ash Hall of the Kennedy School. This over, he lugged his own gear onto a plane on a journey bound for Macao. As the story went, in Macao he was not even received by the Chinese government. Why he went to Macao, a fleshpot and a money laundering center of not very good reputation or reliance, remained a mystery if not a secret of Fakhruddin's government.

3 Investigation and Arraignment

(1)

In the meantime, quick steps were taken to investigate my alleged corruption and activities subversive of the State's interest. As I came to know, a Task Force composed of officers of the Police, the Anti-Corruption Commission (ACC) and the National Board of Revenue and led by Major Kamruzzaman of the Army (Second Bengal Regiment) ransacked my house at Banani, threw away my books and manuscripts, personal records, paintings and souvenirs that my wife and I worked on and collected over years, crudely interrogated and wildly threatened my personal staff, gathered records of deposits and withdrawals from our banks and obtained all information in respect of lands and buildings in my ancestral home village. They, through one Jiban Krishna, an officer deputed from the Bangladesh Bank to the ACC, filed a First Information Report (FIR) with the Tejgaon police station, Dhaka, that I had Tk.117 lacs (11.7 million) of time deposits with IFIC Bank Branch at Karwan Bazar, which they alleged was unearned and not shown in my income tax returns filed with the government in 2005-2006 and, therefore, reflective of assets acquired through corruption.

Then on April 7, 2007 they came to see me at the Kashimpur Jail to interrogate me without any previous notice. In this interrogation, the main role was taken by Major Kamruzzaman, a darkish young hungry fellow with carefully disheveled hair, unlike a service person. To my surprise, he started with my education and then dwelt at length with my service career, wife and children, their education and finally quite elaborately on my role in negotiating the Ganga Water Treaty with India and the Chittagong Hill Tracts Peace Accord.

"Why in 1974 were you sent abroad to the U.S.A. for higher studies?" Major Kamruzzaman asked.

"I was sent by the government for higher studies in Economics." I kept my cool and replied.

"Who made the decision?"

"The decision was made by Prime Minister Bangabandhu Sheikh Mujibur Rahman."

"Why did he decide to send you?" He somewhat asked in a raised irreverent tone.

"You would have to ask Bangabandhu if you can bring him alive now," I smiled, and then said "it was a conscious decision that as a newly created State, we needed expertise in financial management in government; I was Deputy Secretary in charge of development in the Ministry of Finance and the selection was made by a committee and then approved by the Prime Minister."

"Who funded your studies in the USA; who funded the study of your wife?"

"The Ford Foundation funded my study in the USA. My wife got a teaching assistantship in the University and funded herself." I explained.

"You were sent to do an MA in Economics. How could you do your Ph.D.?"

"The time set for doing the MA was two years. By taking additional and higher courses, I completed the MA and Ph.D. courses and passed the Ph.D. Comprehensive Examination in one year ten months. Then as instructed by the government I returned, served as the Deputy Commissioner, Jessore, and then I was given a scholarship by the Boston University for writing my Ph.D. thesis. They gave the scholarship as the time taken for the Masters and my completing the Ph.D. course was a record for the University. I wrote my thesis and returned back in six months, which was also a record." I explained with reluctance.

"How did you fund your two son's study in the USA?"

"I paid for their travels; they went and studied on scholarships. They were given scholarships for their results in the TOEFL and SAT examinations held here in the American Center in Dhaka." I was not very sure the Major knew what these examinations were. His look did not betray his ignorance.

"How did your eldest son complete his Ph.D. in such a short time?"

"The Faculty of Brown University, Providence, USA, an Ivy League school from where he obtained his Ph.D., were perhaps at fault for this," I joked.

"How did your youngest son graduate so early from an American University and get a job in Microsoft?"

"The Faculty of the Cornell University were perhaps a bunch of fools to give him the degree in so short a time. The Microsoft people perhaps chose him on a whim," I joked again.

"Are your sons American citizens?" the Major sounded very serious.

"As far as I know, no," I replied reluctantly.

"How much do they earn?"

"I do not know. I don't ask my grown-up boys such questions. And I would not let you know even if I knew. They are independent individuals paying taxes separately here in Bangladesh as they do in the USA," I said in a serious tone.

The Major then changed the subject and asked me who among my relations were in the administration and the defense services. Apprehending harm to them, I said none of my close relations was in administration and defense. Besides, most of my folks were in teaching. Teaching ran in the blood of my family, from my father who retired as a headmaster of a government school and set up a number of private schools in the local area. My eldest brother Misbahuddin Khan started his career as a college teacher and ended as a Member of the Parliament. My elder brother Dr. Burhanuddin Khan Jahangir was a Professor of Dhaka University and retired as the Pro-Vice Chancellor of the National University. His son Dr. Nadim Jahangir was, at that time an Associate Professor in the Independent University of Bangladesh. I started my career as a teacher at Dhaka University. My wife, to start with, taught at the Eden Girl's College in Dhaka. My younger brother, Dr. Arefin was a Professor of Dhaka University. And my eldest son Dr. Jalal Alamgir was an Assistant Professor in the University of Massachusetts, Boston, at that time. My sister's son Dr. Kalimullah was a Professor of Dhaka University as well. I would have continued but stopped, seeing the Major was not interested to hear all these things.

The Major then started talking about matters that could not be thought as his subjects or relating to areas of alleged corruption in my case.

"Why did you negotiate the Ganga Water Treaty with India?" he asked.

"I negotiated the Treaty on authority given by the Prime Minister and in the country's interest." I retorted.

"How can you say it was in the country's interest?" he was audacious enough to ask.

"Young man, I am not accountable to you for the Ganga Treaty that I negotiated with India. The Treaty I negotiated was approved by the cabinet." I became irritated and quite angry.

Then he asked me with a serious tone in his voice, "Why did you write, negotiate and sign the Chittagong Hill Tracts Peace Accord?"

I kept silent. There was hardly anything to explain to this young brute. He paused and then asked, "Did not you recommend slashing the army's budget by over Tk. 3,650 millions a year after negotiating the Peace Accord?"

"I am not accountable to you for the Peace Accord. You know the Accord was approved by the cabinet." I retorted. But at the same time, I finally realized why the army had sent him and let loose the Task Force against me. I did recommend that following the Peace Accord, we should save Tk. 10 millions a day that the army was spending in their attempt to defeat the tribal insurgents and spend the same amount in building up the required infrastructure in the Hill Tracts to integrate them with the rest of Bangladesh. In my consideration, that was the most effective way to solve the insurgency problem once for all. I realized even at the time I was in the government, the army had spooks around us. Placing spooks that way was not only unauthorized but was also illegal. It appeared the democratically elected government of Sheikh Hasina that administered Bangladesh between 1996 and 2001 could not establish full control over the armed forces that ruled the country for the better part of the period since the assassination of Bangabandhu in 1975.

After Major Kamruzzaman's interrogation was over, he asked the representative officer of the National Board of Revenue, Rabiul Hasan Prodhan to question me. Prodhan was an Assistant Income Tax Commissioner who was in charge of my income tax returns. He said politely that they did not have any complaint against me as a taxpayer and that all my taxes due till 2006 were paid. Then Assistant Director, ACC Shermin Ferdousi, a sickly woman in her 40s asked one or two perfunctory questions as regards my Fixed Deposit Receipts (FDRs), which they had located in the IFIC Bank, Karwan, Bazar, Dhaka.

I told her and them that in my statement of assets in Bangla furnished to them, I had mentioned these FDRs. There might have been some discrepancy as to their values as I did not have any access to my financial records (being incarcerated in the jail), but in any event, I had mentioned the value in approximate terms. I also told them that details about these FDRs, as per income tax law, were due to be furnished in the next financial year and as such discrepancy in their values as alleged in the current year was irrelevant. Writing the statement in about 30 minutes sitting in the jailor's office, I could not have given exact values. She said that they did not accept my Bangla version of FDRs as *Amanat Patras*[14] as the formal correct description. In this she was supported by Assistant Director Jiban Krishna who had lodged against me the case or the FIR with the police.

I said the Bangla translation of FDR as I had used in my asset statement was clearly understood and did not leave any room for ambiguity. And if there was any, it should have become clear after they talked with me. To their query, I told them that in my asset statement I did not include my rental income from my house at Banani from 1992 through 2006. I also told them, calculating from 1962 through 2006 my salaried, rental and other incomes yielding on average 8% return per year (compounded) totalled over Tk. 7 crores (Tk. 70 million) which was much more than my assets as stated by me or found by them. I showed them details of annual calculations. It seemed these did not register any meaning in their minds. Concept of annual compounding or annualization seemed to be beyond their comprehension. I told them that in a supplementary statement I would give details of these calculations. They said they would not accept or consider a supplementary statement. The ACC's law did not allow them to consider such a supplementary statement, they explained. They did not record my statement in accordance with Section 161 of the Criminal Procedure Code as was required of them by law.

"He is telling the truth; there is sense in what he explains," whispered Shermin who sat by Major Kamruzzaman.

"But he has to be hooked. That's the order. What else we could do?" whispered back the Major, which did not escape my hearing.

The others kept silent and looked down; none looked at me. As I had looked after their interests as civilian employees of the government against on-and-off onslaught of the military to take their jobs, they were pensive in carrying out their mandate as I overheard. In my capacity as the General Secretary of the Administration Service Association of the country during a long and critical period, they knew my position on service structure of the country and the contribution that I had made to saving them from swirling and arrogant bossing of the military.

At this point, all of a sudden the Major asked me: "Will you sign a paper as we have prepared?"

---

[14] *Amanat Patras* is a kind of security document. As noted, it is equivalent to FDRs or Fixed Deposit Receipts.

"Will you please show me the paper that you have prepared?" I asked.

"Here it is." He held his hand and showed it only to me. I looked at it and said, "Definitely not."

On the paper it was written that Sheikh Hasina had asked and forced me to process approval of a number of specific development projects that were not important and necessary in consideration of the Planning Ministry of which I was the State Minister. I did not know whether others knew about these contents.

"Will you think it over?" the Major asked.

"No," I said firmly. I looked through the window of the jailor's room and saw the stretch of the prison's vegetable patches inside the high walls beyond the carrot he hung for me.

"Is there anything else to discuss?" I asked no one in particular, indicating that I wanted to leave for my cell inside the jail.

"Would you like me to come to you with this paper once again? You may change some words if you want."

"No. You have got my answer, Major." I could not be firmer in my assertion and more obvious in my disgust.

And then in agonized silence they left. I walked back to my cell in the jail convinced that I would face a kangaroo trial. It was the beginning of a warm April and as I returned feeling a gentle swirl of wind, the sun set over the coconut trees lining the rutted routes of fetters inside the Kashimpur Jail.

Leaving aside the carrot shown, the interrogation and conversation that I had with the members of the Task Force led by Major Kamruzzaman was not in accordance with the rules set by the ACC. Rule 8 of the ACC Rules laid down that the accused should be given a hearing before a charge of corruption could be pressed against him. The principle of natural justice also required that an opportunity for such a hearing be given. The hearing was required to be conducted on prior notice on the relevant points of the asset statement that I had furnished to the ACC on February 20, 2007. Obviously, the interrogation and conversations that I had to suffer before the preset and mandated mind of the Task Force was not a hearing within its legal and conventional meaning. The Task Force was tasked to arraign me and in their conduct and treatment of me on that day it became audaciously obvious.

Through some technological improvisation from within the four high walls, I could inform my elder son Jalal in a clear voice about the carrot cloaked behind the allegation to come under the cover of law. He said, too eager to see me free, I should, under the circumstances, consider myself a prisoner of war and get out through any means offered or available. I thought a prisoner of war did not have to leave behind his own country fearing injustice or an act of injustice; if not confronted at the place where injustice was hewed in by the demon, it would encompass everywhere our people and our children would also live with it. I could let him know clearly and in my own voice, betrayal of the truth would be one thing my sons in their solitude and transient sorrow would not hear as imputable to their father. Even when the father would remain in chains for years his sons would have something good to tell to their children in turn. I would fight injustice to inspire them to continue the fight if needed to secure justice for all as our founding father dreamed about for this country. Protection against persecution was our inalienable right and we would hold this as a self-evident truth to preserve, sweat and fight for all time to come. That would be our war of liberation from generation to generation, ceaselessly taking us from one stage of progress to the next.

(2)

On April 29, 2007, I was arraigned, with the charge of concealment of assets not justifiable by income earned by me, before the Senior Special Judge of Dhaka. It was mentioned in the charge-sheet submitted to the Senior Special Judge by the ACC that I had concealed FDs (fixed deposits) of Tk. 117 lacs in my asset statement. The Senior Special Judge, dictated by those in power, did not look into my statement of assets wherein holding of FDs of approximately Tk. 90 lacs was mentioned, disproving the accusation of concealment. He did not look into the notice of the ACC that had not asked me to give particulars of FDs or assets held by me on behalf of others, in this case of my son and of the Sultana Foundation, set up in memory of my mother and which I administered.

I thought the Senior Special Judge was not very well aware of the principle that justice was blind and could not be dictated down or was immune to absurdity imposed from above. He was definitely not aware that the law prescribed cognizance to be taken by the judge in order to ensure proceedings of trial of a *prima facie* guilt and letting off the accused in the event such a *prima facie* guilt was absent. This was a safeguard against harassment of an innocent. Blindly and very quickly, without even hearing what I had to say as a defendant, he took cognizance of the charge so drummed up against me and transferred the case to the Tribunal 3 that had been specially set up in March-April 2007 to try cases of such alleged corruptions.

As many as fifty-tbree days elapsed between filing of the FIR and submission of this charge-sheet on April 29, 2007. During these fifty-three days and thereafter, in accordance with the Emergency Powers Rules under which cognizance of the case was taken, I could not even apply for bail to any court. The Rule denying the right to apply for bail was obviously a blatant violation of the principle of treating all accused as innocent till proved otherwise, and of equal treatment under law guaranteed by the Constitution of the country. The Advisor-in-Charge of the Ministry of Law, Barrister Moinul Hossain, had justified this ordained denial of bail on the grounds that the trial under the Emergency Powers Rules would be very quick and therefore posting of an accused on bail would not be called for. In university days Moinul studied with me. I was painfully amazed to find out how much, despite legal education received, he had degenerated into the cesspool of hypocrisy wrapped in a make-believe moralism. I could see that not everyone in this country possessed values that were worthy of respect.

The Tribunal 3 was set up under the Emergency Powers Rules as a Special Court and was, along with five other such tribunals of the time, located in the *Shangshad Bhaban* or the Parliament Building. These tribunals were hastily furnished by the Public Works Department of the government under the supervision of the military. Before these tribunals became operational to try cases, as reported in the national dailies, Major General Masud Uddin Chowdhury, Principal Staff Officer, Armed Force's Division, which had virtually usurped the Ministry of Defense, organized mock trials of the accused, gave instructions to the court personnel including the Public Prosecutors and the selected witnesses so that every accused could be brought to book and submission to those in power. Under his instructions entry into these tribunals was made very restricted through a number of checkpoints manned by the police and the spooks of the armed forces, derogating openness of trials to be conducted.

Nobody dared to point out that such actions were contrary to the principles of free and independent trial and thus obstructive of justice under the law. Obstruction of justice was codified as a penal offense in the country's penal code. Using the premises of the Parliament by such tribunals was rather unprecedented in our country; it was unconventional in the context of the sovereign nature of the Parliament and the Parliamentary process. The

Speaker of the Parliament, as it seemed, was neither capable of realizing these implications nor courageous enough to stand against the setting up of such tribunals in the Parliament premises where many a member of the Parliament itself were to be framed by mocking and sacrificial trials. Having "iron in the spine" was not strongly apparent in the Speaker's easy and ready consent to setting up these tribunals under his very eyes.

On May 1, I stood up before the Special Judge Shahed Nuruddin, in Tribunal 3, to face the charge for which I was arraigned on April 29. Shahed Nuruddin was in his 40s, looked stocky and well-fed, and had an oval, darkish face. Before the charge could be considered for framing against me on the basis of a full dress hearing, the Prosecution led by the ACC's Prosecutor Mizanur Rahman prayed to the Special Judge for further investigation and time. After the case was transferred for disposal by the Senior Special Judge in sequel to taking it into cognizance, the scope of further investigation on approval of the Special Judge of the Tribunal was obviously not only irregular but also illegal. My lawyer Syed Rezaur Rahman pointed this out. From the cage-like wooden platform on which I was made to stand up as an accused all the while the sessions of the tribunal continued, I also protested. But without batting an eye and with a malignant smile befitting a stifling paternalism adorning his lips, the Special Judge allowed the Prosecution to go ahead with further investigation for about three weeks.

I was saddened by this closed-mindedness of the Special Judge and felt frustrated. For me it was a foretaste of the shoddy trial and the dictated verdict to follow. I was allowed, on humble and repeated requests made by my lawyer, to sit with him and my brother Dr. Jahangir for 30 minutes in the almost empty courtroom after its session for the day was over to discuss the case and the charge to be framed. As soon as 30 minutes were over, the policemen on duty under the supervision of Major Kamruzzaman, Leader of the Task Force let loose against me by the military, took me to the adjacent room turned into a prison hold. They kept me incommunicado and without food and water for four hours before a prison van could be arranged to take me back to the Kashimpur Jail. Neither the court nor the jail administration gave us any meal when we prisoners were taken to and present in the court. If not for food brought by our relations we would have starved during these days. And our relations had to plead with the police guards humbly and pitifully before they allowed in the food packets.

(3)

From conversations with my lawyers and others and then later with other inmates in the jail, I was startled to find out a few things about the Special Judge and the ensuing trial under him. The Special Judge, along with five others of them for the six Special Tribunals, was selected personally by Advisor Barrister Moinul Hossain, in-charge of the Ministry of Law and Justice. He had been asked by the military in the background, so I was told, to select the pliant ones eager to give legal cover to punishment of those selected to be punished by the military. Punishment for corruption would not allow the conscientious and influential politicians to challenge the game plan of the military to occupy power in the garb of common man's interest. The common man's interest would be best served in a landscape of poverty and deprivation, if the corrupt were corralled and punished. So honesty rode into the landscape on the camel of a campaign against corruption.

This was the name of the game in this part of our world since the days of united Pakistan. The pliant judges, in most cases, were themselves corrupt. The carrot hung before them was a promise to elevate them to the bench of the High Court Division of the Supreme Court and to award prize money out of the slush funds of the intelligence agencies following an assessment of the depth and the breadth of their pliant conduct and perpetration of lies and falsehood. The verdict in each case drafted ahead by the Judge-Advocate General of the military would be handed down to them through the leader of the respective Task Force and the Special Judges were expected to marshal their analysis and arguments leading to the handed-down verdicts with legal inputs and cover.

As the daily *New Age* editorialized later (February 25, 2008), 240 persons, out of whom 217 who were involved in politics, were convicted in 61 cases by these tribunals in less than one year, which even the courts with the best prosecution lawyers around the world, could not boast of as a conviction success rate. These were the persons who were arrested by the government and investigated into by the National Coordination Committee to Combat Crime and Corruption led by Major General (Ret.) M. A. Matin Advisor-in-Charge of the Home Ministry. This was done through forming and letting loose as many as thirty Task Forces, each led by a Major from the Army or in a few cases an officer of equivalent rank from the Navy or the Air Force. Major General (Ret.) Matin later on June 24, 2008, admitted that the National Committee led by him till that date and working with these Majors and officers of equivalent rank of the Armed Forces did not have any legal basis for formation or operation.

Earlier Lt. General (Ret.) Hasan Masud Chowdhury, Chairman of the ACC, had stated that in all cases of corruption till then arrests were made by the government and not by the ACC or its investigation officers. All these irregularities obviously left doubt about the entire process, starting from investigations to trials smacking of victimisation by the regime. In this process the single most active and important coordinator was Lt. General Masud Uddin Chowdhury (promoted from Major General since then), Chief Staff Officer of the Armed Forces Division. In this scheme of things, Public Prosecutors were chosen on consideration of willingness to ignore questionable investigation and given remuneration on a scale that far surpassed even the remuneration of the Chief Justice of the Supreme Court. They were to follow, hands-down, instructions to be given by the Leaders of the concerned Task Force, who would not, in any case, be cited or produced as witnesses for the Prosecution. The Prosecution Witnesses would be brought to the offices of the Public Prosecutors before deposition for tutoring right in front of the respective Leaders of the Task Force. Any deviation from the tutored version of the made-up evidence would not be tolerated. Loss of job, business opportunity and even physical assault were threatened in default.

The Leaders of the Task Force set up their offices in rooms adjacent to the offices of the Special Judges in the Parliament building to oversee the functioning of the scheme. The poor cowering Speaker sat helplessly while the Parliament Building was occupied by non-legislative dictatorial forces. The lawyers who would have otherwise represented the defense were threatened with dire consequences. Re-opening of their income tax records and framing up criminal charges with incarceration in prison were two main elements of the threat. Our family lawyers, Barrister Amirul Islam and his daughter Barrister Tania Amir, were threatened and prevented from defending me. Advocate Abdul Matin Khasru, who was the Law Minister in Sheikh Hasina's government and a cordial colleague of mine in those days, shied away from a possible assignment in my defense. Advocate Anisul Huq, who had been appointed by Sheikh Hasina's government as a Special Public Prosecutor in the Bangabandhu murder case and worked quite closely in pursuing the prosecution in that trial, literally absconded. He gave three appointments to my brother Dr. Jahangir on three nights after 11:00 p.m., to discuss my defense but did not keep any.

Only Syed Rezaur Rahman along with his colleague Haider Ali, despite threats from the ACC and the military, stood by me. Advocate Syed Rezaur Rahman was a quite independent and courageous person; he was imprisoned on political grounds during the Pakistan days but could not be made to submit to the then political masters. He was soft-spoken, amiable, deeply and widely experienced and very firm in guarding against confessions and admissions obtained through coercion by the Prosecution. The ACC and the military could not make him budge from his decision to defend me.

Advocate Haider Ali had served as one of the Prosecutors in the Bangabandhu murder case during Sheikh Hasina's government. I knew him as a hard-working trial lawyer prone to go deep into facts and subtle points of law. He started defending me quite well along with Advocate Syed Rezaur Rahman. They had good understanding and working relations between them. Advocate Haider however, after the trial proceeded for some days, was taken off the scene through allurement of an unusual nature. He was appointed a Deputy Attorney General by the government and left my side with regret and reluctant consent from me. Being asked to do things against professional ethics he could not last as a Deputy Attorney General very long. Sometime in June 2008, he resigned and went back to his independent practice.

But by that time my trial in the tribunal was over. The ACC had frozen all bank accounts of myself and my wife and our two sons, denying funds that were required in defending me. But for help and support received from my brother Dr. Jahangir, under the circumstances I would not have been able to pay for even certified copies of court documents that I needed for my defense. Access to records, both government and institutional and to potential defense witnesses and well-wishers were denied. All told, it was a frying pan, if not a fire into which I was thrown. As it appeared, the ACC driven by the military wanted me to plead guilty to the charge that was to be framed against me denying any avenue for rightful and lawful defense. For them, power was honesty, for no one was expected to defy anything said or ordained from the pedestal of raw power.

The ACC was constituted with persons who considered themselves the epitome of honesty. In their opinion, as it seemed from their occasional public jabberings, everyone else other than themselves were part of the worn out and blistered system that was dishonest and thus prosecutable under their stringent law. Little did they realize that their very appointments as chairman and members of the ACC on February 25, 2007 were in violation of the ACC Act and, therefore, illegal *ab initio*. The law provided that the Chairman and the members of the ACC would be appointed by the President from a panel to be selected by a body composed of a judge of the Appellate Division of the Supreme Court, the immediate past Cabinet Secretary of the government and the Comptroller and Auditor-General of the Republic. We were told that this was not followed in the case of appointing retired Lieutenant General Hasan Masud Chowdhury as Chairman, retired Member of the National Board of Revenue Manzur Mannan and Ret. District Judge Habibur Rahman as Members.

I wondered how these persons with their illegal appointments to such posts of profit, power and influence could decide on the legality or otherwise of prosecuting others on grounds of corruption. Honesty could never sprout from a dishonest base and these persons appeared to have been bereft of any association with this dictum. For them power was integrity; lack of power was weakness with abominable inability to protect reputation; and power was knowledge overriding facts and figures and the law of the land. And in their leisurely drift to build their power, they called in officers of the Armed Forces to fill in almost all important positions in the ACC down below.

My brother Dr. Jahangir told me in passing that he had earlier met Faruq Ahmed Chowdhury, his classmate during the university years, a former Foreign Secretary of the government and a brother-in-law of Chief Advisor Dr. Fakhruddin Ahmed and had requested of him to let us know why I had been arrested and so charged. I knew Faruq Chowdhury and his family. Once I along with my wife dined with them at their place with Bina Sikri, the Indian High Commissioner of the time. And once the then-U.S. Ambassador Harry Thomas lunched with me where he was one of the guests. Chowdhurys were well-known for keeping contact with all relevant quarters. Faruq himself served as a foreign policy advisor to Sheikh Hasina when she was the Leader of the Opposition after 2001; his immediate younger brother Enam Ahmed Chowdhury belonged to Khaleda Zia's camp and served her as the Chairman of the Privatization Commission.

Then there was Masum Ahmed Chowdhury, an erstwhile member of the Information and Foreign Services of the government who was appointed Chairman of the Board of Directors of the Oriental Bank by Dr. Fakhruddin Ahmed when he was the Governor of the central bank of the country. The youngest, Iftikhar, an erstwhile member of the Civil and Foreign Services of the government, was Advisor, Foreign Affairs under Dr. Fakhruddin. Faruq had wedded the elder sister of Reaz Rahman who had served as an Advisor, Foreign Affairs, under Khaleda Zia. With links almost everywhere, in position and opposition, opportunism was recognized as a hallmark in Faruq's family. Faruq had told him that he had raised the question with Dr. Fakhruddin but had not received any reply. I did not believe what Faruq had told my brother. But I was moved by his concern for me and willingness to try almost anything to set me at liberty.

I asked him in a choked voice not to approach Faruq or anybody else. There was no need to lower his image before others on this count. I told him, I would wait and fight openly in the court for my freedom, but in the process disgrace was one thing that we as a family would not take. I told the same thing to my wife Sitara when for me she proposed to see Faruq and Fakhruddin both long known to her. I remembered that Martin Luther King in 1963 had written from Birmingham Jail where he was incarcerated that oppressed people could not remain oppressed forever and I told her the same.

(4)

It was a dismal evening, slightly cloudy, with the pleasantness of sunset submerged, when I returned by the archaic and rattling prison van to Kashimpur. On my way to the third floor where my cell was located, I met Tonai Mollah, erstwhile Chairman of Jajira Union Parishad, Shariatpur. He asked me about the Judge of the Special Tribunal. When I said, Shahed Nuruddin was the Judge, he told me as he did earlier, the same Shahed Nuruddin had tried him on charge of a framed-up murder and sentenced him to lifelong imprisonment, despite the fact that there was no evidence to logically and legally do so. He said as he had said earlier, the Judge through an agent had wanted Tk. 5 lacs from him and, on his refusal to meet the demand, the law as well as the evidence was twisted to sentence him the way it was done. Tonai later was honorably acquitted by the High Court Division. He asked me to be especially careful about the Special Judge. What could I do I wondered, as I had wondered earlier. The other inmates, Salman, Nasim, Lotus-Kamal, Kamal Majumder, Giasuddin (of Narayangonj), Engineer Mosharraf (of Chittagong) — all detained on charges of subversion and corruption came out of their cells, embraced me and said they were with me and would remain so throughout the mock-trial slated to be staged by those in power to silence all of us into submission to a process of usurpation of State power.

"You served as a Magistrate, almost as a judge under the rules of the day. Did you behave the way this pack of juris-folks are dispensing their handcrafted remedies these days?" Salman turned himself into a coil of rage and asked, while sitting on the verandah in the suffocating darkness around.

"No, not at all," I replied.

"Why, what was the reason?" asked Nasim.

"Reasons were two; first we were recruited through a stiff competition; bad timbers usually could not find places in our service; second, training; the careful and rigorous training gave us a professional pride that did not open us up to greed and meanness," I explained.

"The meanness and greed of these judges and their practice will not stop to encompass even human sacrifice," commented Engineer Mosharraf. Ali Asgar Lobi and A. K. M. Mosharraf joined at this point and nodded in agreement. I kept silent.

The conversation ended. All of them had poured out their lingering hope for justice and possible success in my case. Justice for all of us, for me, I thought, was a hedge against slights of all who had been educated supposedly with some human values, the ultimate armor against degradation and discrimination thwarting liberty. I would not relent, I resolved. All of us must work so that violence and injustice toward another human being become as abhorrent as eating another's flesh.

I was scheduled to be taken to the Tribunal on May 21, 2007. Foregoing sleep, and without access to records, I started preparing briefs for my lawyers. I borrowed a pen from other inmates, collected pieces of paper from various cells and in my almost illegible handwriting, prepared some notes, gave them to my brother when he came to see me after fifteen days and arranged for their typing by my personal assistant at home. He was well acquainted with my handwriting and I expected that he would be able to give readable preparatory materials to Advocate Syed Rezaur Rahman and his associates.

(5)

While I was passing my days during this period, I could see through the window of my cell, the notorious fundamentalist Shaokh Abdur Rahman, caged in two cells in the infirmary building within the jail premises. The infirmary was located to the north of the "division" building on the third floor on which I was caged in Cell No. 32. In between these two buildings, was the jail pharmacy, a small one-storied building where the jail's doctor and the pharmacist had their offices. Through the window of my cell, I observed Shaokh Rahman rising early in the morning and after prayers, reciting presumably from the holy book and walking to and fro on the verandah in front of his cell. He seemed unruffled, undaunted and carefree. At times, his wife and children came to visit him. Since he was on death row, they were allowed to visit him right in the infirmary building instead of the visiting room at the jail gate.

As the story passed around from the doctor to the pharmacist to the jail guards and the inmates, he was well-behaved and clean-robed, filling aptly the profile of a cold-blooded murderer. After about two months or so, one evening around 7:00 he was taken to the Comilla Central Jail and hanged around 12:00 in the night. His associate Sunny who was on death row in the building located to the west of ours was taken to the adjacent Kashimpur Jail-2 and hanged a little after 12:00 on the same night. In the morning Dr. Shamsuddin, the jail physician at the time, gave us a vivid description of how Sunny was taken out to the gallows, hanged and declared dead. "Does taking away a life that we could not create forfeit the moral language through which we interact in society?" I asked myself in silence.

I recalled, sometime in 2005, during Shaokh's heyday of persecution in Naogaon, Natore and Rajshahi districts, I was asked by Abdul Jalil, General Secretary of my party to hold a public meeting in Bagmara Bazaar, a remote place in between Natore and Rajshahi, to make the local people consciously oppose the fundamentalists and religious bigots. Bagmara was at that time in full control of Bangla Bhai, Siddiqul Islam, Shaokh Rahman and his associates. They had ruled the area like *satraps*[15], enforcing their will and decisions on religious rituals and the conduct of women. They funded their organization through extortion and punished non-conformists by arson, loot, rape and murder. As I gathered from the local people, as many as 27 murders and over 500 rapes had been committed by Bangla Bhai, Shaokh Rahman and his associates in the local area in that year alone.

To reach Bagmara in the afternoon, I had started from Dhaka around 5:00 in the morning, reached Puthia police station past the town of Natore around 8:00. Two top leaders of the party were scheduled to join me at Puthia on my way to Bagmara, but none

---

[15] A *satrap* is a ruler of a dependency, especially a despotic, subordinate official.

appeared on time. At Puthia police station, I was expected to meet Thandu, a former student leader of the Rajshahi University, but he also did not turn up. Realising that none, in fear of his life, would appear and go to Bagmara, I asked the Officer-in-Charge of the police station about the route that I would take to Bagmara. Politely giving me a cup of tea, he along with a female Assistant Superintendent of Police who was visiting the Police Station at the time, advised me to turn back on grounds of personal safety.

The Assistant Superintendent of Police told me in a grateful tone that she was a former student of my elder brother Dr. Jahangir. I told them that since I was expected to address a public meeting there in order to make the local people regain confidence against terror, I could not turn back. If I did, the local people would lose courage to stand against the fundamentalists and terrorists and their yearning for freedom would suffer a setback. Reluctantly, they outlined the route through Tahirpur area and I started towards Bagmara in my old and not so reliable jeep.

As soon as I was on the route, I observed I was followed by three motorbikes with two bearded persons riding each. After about 30 minutes, four motorbikes with eight similarly bearded persons appeared from side paths and were in front of my jeep. My driver looked at me to find out my reaction. I looked straight ahead and asked him to drive steadily. After about two hours, when I reached Bagmara Bazaar, an eerie silence greeted me. There was no visible sign of preparation for holding a public meeting. I got down from the jeep, walked and looked around for the home of the headmaster of the local school. Finding his home, I walked in.

The headmaster was pleasantly surprised to see me. He informed over his mobile phone Khairuzzaman Liton of the Awami League, Fazle Hossain Badsha of the Worker's Party and other local leaders at Rajshahi about my arrival. I ate my lunch there and in about two hours people from all around came. Khairuzzaman Liton, Fazle Hossain Badsha, Thandu and other local leaders joined. I addressed a meeting of about 10 thousand people. Seeing me they seemed to have gotten back their courage to stand up against evil. I told them, we had to fight united the fundamentalists and bigots; if we remained united, the forces of evil would eventually be defeated.

I was shocked to hear about atrocities that the fundamentalists committed in the local area. It was painful to hear about Khajur Ali whose body was cut into 27 pieces when he was killed by the bigots. Tears welled up in my eyes when I met a woman of about

25 who introduced herself as the Chairperson of Tahirpur municipality. Her father was the Chairman before her. He was killed by the bigots and in the consequent election the local people elected her, a student of Rajshahi University at that time, recording their support for the former chairman and opposition to bigotry.

"What do you intend to do in the coming months?" I asked her.

"I will work for the local people and never surrender to the dictates of the bigots. I will do it for my children and for my grandchildren;" she replied with a fire of determination in her eyes. I wondered and admired.

"Can you organize women folks against these bigots?" I asked her.

"Yes, I have already started that. It is not easy but the challenge lies in the difficult, you know." She replied.

In her eyes, I could see the anguish and firm determination of Ferdousi Priyadarshini, a sculptress of repute who had been violated and persecuted by the Pakistani occupation army in 1971. I met Priyadarshini in a meeting of the freedom fighters in Dhaka and to me this young woman Chairperson of Tahipur appeared to have the same honesty of purpose sustaining and cherishing values of self-reliance, self-improvement and risk-taking. She represented a new generation of women in the country's rural areas.

Coming from this determined young woman with the people's support — in an area where the fundamentalists wanted to impose their way of life, putting down women to the background and confining them within the prison of the household — was a definite element of encouragement to me and others who had come to attend the meeting from Rajshahi. I could foresee a social movement in the right direction. With the meeting over a little before sundown, I started for Dhaka via Rajshahi taking a different route on the advice of the local leaders. The fire of determination that I saw in the eyes of the young woman strengthened my resolve to strive with the people to make the country free of bigotry, fundamentalism and terrorism. All the way back I thought of ways to untangle the mess that was to a great extent the making of the government of the time. The execution of Shaokh and his associates appeared to me more as the failure of the government than the scrambling of our identity of secular creed and values with fundamentalist ones.

All these memories streaked in through the gloom of the impending charge that was being framed against me. The further investigation that was allowed illegally by the Special Judge was completed within twenty-two days by Syed Iqbal Hossain, Deputy Director, the ACC. He submitted a supplementary charge-sheet against me to the court of the Special Judge on May 21, 2007. In the supplementary charge-sheet Syed Iqbal Hossain specifically mentioned that he had been mandated and instructed both by the ACC and the Special Judge to produce the charge-sheet against me. It became evident thus that the purpose of this investigation was not to find out the truth but to frame me on a false charge. In the court, I personally pointed this out to the Special Judge. I wanted to know from him whether he had instructed Syed Iqbal Hossain to submit the charge-sheet, *i.e.*, frame up a charge against me or to find out the truth through a dispassionate and objective investigation and put that on record.

That Syed Iqbal Hossain mentioned in the charge-sheet itself that he had been mandated and instructed to submit a supplementary charge-sheet by the court was proof enough that his investigation was not truthful; it was a colorable and mandated exercise of authority, not one meant for undertaking a neutral and objective investigation in search of the truth. The Special Judge, like an owl perched on a lofty citadel of a different world, kept mum and did not even record my objection. To me, he appeared to be an agent illiterate in and innocent of legal knowledge and training but bent upon carrying out the mandate of those in power. His personal ambition and greed calcified into closed-mindedness and cruelty to others. Counting from the date of filing the FIR, the investigation in its two part, took 106 days exceeding by far the 60 days as mandated and laid down in the ACC Rules. He ignored, without any concern or remorse, that the ACC was bound by its own Rules and that the Special Judge had to operate within their bounds.

The court adjourned in the afternoon. In despair and anger, I was made to sit and wait in the cage-like *hajat*[16] in the adjoining room till 6:00 in the evening when I was packed off in a prison van for my journey of about two hours to the Kashimpur Jail. By the time I arrived after 8:00 in the night, the whole jail was blacked out because of loadshedding and appeared like a graveyard in eerie, silent darkness. Despite boastful promises given by the military-controlled Fakhruddin government, nothing could be done to add to the power generating and transmitting capacity of the country. Wondering about the unresponsiveness of the Special Judge and the extent of legal illiteracy from which he suffered, I

---

[16] A holding cell attached to a court of law.

threw myself on the bed, tossed around and tried to sleep over the stifling misery that I had to face in days to come.

4 The Charges

(1)

In two charge-sheets, it was alleged that I:

(1) Concealed Fixed Deposit Receipts (FDRs) of Tk. 117 lacs (Tk. 10.7 million); Tk. 117 lacs of FDRs was beyond my known sources and amounts of income;

(2) Owned land in my village home which I did not mention in my asset statement in terms of quantity and value;

(3) Concealed two buildings owned by me at my village home and their values;

(4) Did not mention a market under construction, named the Biponi Palash, which I owned in Kachua;

(5) Concealed a Petrol Pump named the Sultana Filling Station owned by me at Kachua;

(6) Did not mention a house that I owned in Comilla Housing Estate;

(7) Concealed some bank deposits while giving my balances in the asset statement;

(8) Did not give actual and accurate value of my house in Banani Model Town, Dhaka;

(9) Concealed ownership of three motorcycles; and

(10) Could not reconcile my income as reported in income tax return for the period 1982 to 2006 with the value of my assets as on June 30, 2006.

Seeing the two charge-sheets containing these allegations, my lawyers wanted to see the relevant documents that the Prosecution wanted to submit to the court to prove these. The Special Judge said that these would be shown to them soon and without failure, but went on fixing dates for proceedings without intermission in meticulous pursuance of the Emergency Powers Rules prescribing speedy trial and conviction. Without ensuring that my lawyers had access to the relevant documents and could obtain copies of the statements already made to the ACC's Investigation

Officers under Section 161 of the Criminal Procedure Code by all persons who would be produced as witnesses, the Special Judge fixed May 27 for framing the charge against me. As a matter of law and fact this date would have been for hearing as to whether I could formally be charged for the allegations as made by the ACCs investigators, but in his haste for to try and convict me, the Special Judge had said inadvertently the date would be for framing of charge. I was not surprised. I did not expect anything better from a kangaroo court set up to prove that power was honesty, the law was diktat and justice was a business instead of a mission.

Between May 22 and 26, I along with my lawyers put forward to the court the procedural flaws as well as the apparent mistakes of facts in the allegations against me. We started with the flaws in the notice of the ACC. We pointed out that the notice of the Secretary, ACC sent to me for submission of asset (*i.e.* movable and immovable properties) statement had four built-in misconceived implications and flaws. First, the notice did not define assets. As a matter of fact, nowhere in the ACC Act was "asset" defined in terms of substance, inclusiveness or exclusiveness, difference with the concept of wealth or a stock of wealth or flow of income. Movable and immovable properties construable as wealth were not defined either. Assets yielded by income excluded from total income in accordance with the income tax law (Section 44 read with 6th Schedule), were in variance with what could be construed as an end-product of income that could equal value of assets.

Second, the notice required description of assets and their sources and not their values whereas in the allegation lodged, the notice required me as the recipient to give description of my assets, (undefined as aforesaid) including those held by others on my behalf; it did not require me to describe assets held by me on behalf of others, say a trust or a foundation, a son or a friend.

Third, it was dated (under the signature of the Secretary, ACC) January 18, 2007, *i.e.*, almost a month before I was arrested and put under detention giving it a color of a premeditated measure of harassment and victimization instead of the following of a logical and legal process to bring a really corrupt person to book. We showed the so-dated notice to the Special Judge. He did not blink, nor did he seem to have taken that as a matter of record for the court. The shame of silence in such matters was beyond him. The Buddha-like indifference shown by the Special Judge, as it turned out later, was but a ruse to ignore or not record anything that went to support the defense's position.

While assessing the asset statement, despite these built-in incongruities and flaws, the Prosecution took pains to (i) measure and assess values of items described by me in my asset statement in current market prices through agents of their choice instead of at construction cost index (building), compiled and published by the Bureau of Statistics of the government as should be done in such cases; (ii) include others' assets held by me as mine; (iii) ignore the details of sources of funding for the fixed deposits I had kept in the bank; and (iv) omit and hide the obvious and sinister attempt of a premeditated motive to harass and victimize an innocent, law-abiding, educated citizen even before the time of payment of taxes following a minimum modicum of just and fair process. All these went to prove beyond reasonable doubt that in this case, through serving an incongruous and vague notice and following a dubious and improper procedure, the due process of law was not only ignored but furthermore, sidelined and even obliterated. making the very start of the process of prosecution a colorable and premeditated exercise of witch-hunting on political grounds. We pointed out loudly that this was irregular, unfair, arbitrary and thus untenable in law. This vitiated the very concept of justice as was bestowed on us by the Anglo-Saxon framework and tradition of law. The Special Judge did not take this failure of due process and the vitiation of the concept of justice into consideration. Perched on a citadel of seeming justice and fair play, he looked blank like an owl, at times snoring softly. In fact, he did not deviate from what a pliant arbiter would do.

Furthermore, my lawyer pointed out quite loudly and clearly that Rule 15(d) 5 of the Emergency Powers Rules under which the notice to submit the asset statement was served on me by the Secretary, ACC, was beyond his competence and jurisdiction. Rule 15(d) 5 provided for the service of the notice by a member of the security force or an Investigation Officer specially appointed by the government. The Secretary of the ACC who signed and sent the notice for furnishing the asset statement was neither a member of the security force nor an Investigation Officer within the meaning of Rule 15(d) 5 of the Emergency Powers Rules. By signing and sending the notice under Rule 15(d) 5, the Secretary of the ACC acted with an unreasonable enthusiasm, beyond the limits of his competence and jurisdiction and the bounds of legality. Neither did the provisions of the ACC Act defining the Secretary's duties give him any authority to continue such an onslaught upon the Emergency Powers Rules. Therefore, this notice placed no legal liability or obligation on me and no offense was liable or implicatible to me under the Emergency Powers Rules. Thus, framing of charge or indictment against me under Rule 15 (d) 5 would be *ab initio* illegal and void. This was pointed out to the Special Judge, but with seeming illiteracy in the law and its implication he maintained a lingering owlish silence.

Section 26 of the ACC Act, I pointed out, was not applicable in my case. There were two ingredients of offense as defined under Section 26: (i) satisfaction of the ACC on the basis of information received or inquiry conducted *a priori* that assets of the notice-receiver-to-be were not in conformity with his legitimate sources of income and (ii) submission of the asset statement (and by implication, its sequential assessment) was not in accordance with the procedure set by the Commission. In this instance, before issuing the notice, the Commission was not constituted; therefore the question of satisfaction of the Commission either on the basis of information received or inquiry conducted as to which portion of my assets was not in conformity with my known or legitimate income did not arise. It was also evident that the Commission did not set a procedure or a format for incorporating the asset statement.

As a matter of fact, the Commission was constituted on February 25, *i.e.*, seven days after the notice was served on me and the procedure for furnishing the asset statement under Section 26 of the ACC Act was set by Rule 17 (i) of the ACC Rules on March 29, 2007. This proved that the notice under Section 26 of the ACC Act by the Secretary was vague, incomplete, incongruous and misleading. This was neither tenable nor enforceable under the law. Furthermore, in the notice I was given 72 hours to submit the asset statement when I was incarcerated in the jail without access to my records and lawyer. Given the constraint of writing and communicating in the presence of an intelligence agent (of the police), the time limit of 72 hours turned out to be not more than one. This was done with a prejudice and vindictiveness not warranted by or tenable under the law. All these points were made loud and clear before the Special Judge. He remained unperturbed in his raw-boned, ominous and owlish silence. I could observe a quick exchange of eye-language between him and Major Kamruzzaman, sitting unabashedly by the side of the Public Prosecutor.

My lawyer Syed Rezaur Rahman then in its sequel stated that Section 27 of the ACC Act could not be applied against me. As he said, Section 27 prescribed punishment for having (i) assets acquired through dishonest means and (ii) assets not in conformity with known sources of income. I had given, he pointed out: (i) details of sources of my saving certificates and fixed deposits in my statement of assets mentioning amongst other things that I had opted to take all my pension benefits at one go at the time of retirement from the government service in 1998; (ii) estimate of annualized (at 8%) rental income of Tk. 87.97 lacs (8.797 million) between 1992 and 2006, accepted by the Income Tax Department, in my revised statement of assets submitted to the ACC on April 28, 2007; (iii) sum of savings of my regular salaried income (15% of savings of monthly salary annualized at 8%) between 1963 and 2001 of Tk. 76.46 lacs (7.644 million); (iv) estimated yield from Tk. 65.63 lacs (6.563 million) of investable funds (other than regular salary, *i.e.*, auxiliary and incidental earnings) as shown in the statement of assets with annualized 8% return, totaling Tk. 574 lacs (57.4 million), all in accordance with internationally accepted good accounting practice. These estimates included items that were not mentioned in the first asset statement submitted on February 20 because the ACC failed to specify a format or a procedure in accordance with law for writing the asset statement along with the notice served on me. I along with my lawyer pointed out that these estimates of savings and investable funds proved beyond all reasonable doubt that all my assets were in full conformity with my known and legitimate sources of income.

It was also pointed out that offense under Section 27 of the ACC Act was in sequel to and followed from applicability of Section 26 of the Act. Since Section 26 of the Act could not be applied against me, the Prosecution could not apply Section 27 by any stretch of the imagination. At this point Barrister Tania Amir entered the courtroom. She took a copy of the brief on the charge-sheet and our arguments against it as I had prepared and given to Advocate Syed Rezaur Rahman earlier. It was about three-page brief covering all the points that we made before the Special Judge.

Barrister Tania hurriedly read it and then took the floor. She stated that the charge was fabricated inasmuch as (i) it was made-up on orders after my arrest on political grounds; (ii) the Task Force responsible for this unlawful arrest and unjust and uncalled for investigation was not on the scene before the court; they were not cited as witnesses either; (iii) investigation beyond the scope of the FIR and after the first charge-sheet was submitted was unlawful and untenable; and (iv) there was no specific *prima facie* charge of corruption against the accused.

On these four grounds, Barrister Tania asserted that I could not formally be charged, *i.e.*, arraigned and should therefore be discharged forthwith. Tania, with her usual flair and style, spoke well in my defense. The Special Judge, sitting unmoved and unconcerned, exchanged a few glances with Major Kamruzzaman and the Public Prosecutor; he did not even care to note our presentation. To me he seemed incapable of understanding annualization of income or even savings. He ignored Barrister Tania's assertion totally. I did not see him noting anything on the case papers before him. Tania left, perhaps in disgust. As far as I knew she almost never appeared before a court lower than the High Court. Later, my wife Sitara told me she had come at her special request. She never attended this court after this.

(2)

It was May 27, 2007. Starting from 9:00 in the morning, with a brief break of 30 minutes for lunch, my lawyers presented these arguments and concluded that there was no *prima facie* case against me. The sheen of these arguments and the realities of facts presented did not make any difference at the time of presentation or in their wake. Entry to the courtroom was very restricted. There were hardly twelve persons present besides the lawyers. This restrictiveness said something about the lack of the regime's confidence in open trials. This restriction on entry into the courtroom continued all through.

Around 5:00 in the evening, making the owlish appearance all the more mundane and menacing, the Special Judge, after exchanging meaningful glances with Major Kamruzzaman and the Public Prosecutor but not looking at me even once, read out the charge against me and asked me to say whether I was guilty or not. With more hatred than arrogance, I instantly responded that these allegations were made-up fragments from a world of utter falsehood, and that I was not guilty of these and I demanded a fair trial of the allegations under law. Advocate Rezaur Rahman was mildly bewildered as I had not consulted with him before responding to the Special Judge, but then smiled proudly and came to shake my hand. My brother Dr. Jahangir took time to stand up from his chair. As I stepped down, he embraced me and said the truth would triumph over falsehood and we would fight for the truth; we would defeat the evil that had taken over the country under the guise of fighting corruption.

The charge thus framed against me was under Sections 26(2) and 27(1) of the ACC Act, 2004 and under Rule 15 (d) 5 of the

Emergency Powers Rules. The charge under Section 26(2) was about furnishing false or incorrect statement of assets, implying concealment to the extent of falsity or incorrectness. This was punishable with three years simple imprisonment. The charge under Section 27(1) was about holding of assets disproportionate to known or legitimate income. If proved, this charge was punishable with ten years of rigorous imprisonment and fine. The charge under Rule 15 (d) 5 was of similar nature and punishment. By applying the Emergency Powers Rules, the Special Judge provided for continuous trial of the charge with adjournment of not more than three days if required but all within forty-five working days, extendable up to sixty with information to the High Court Division of the Supreme Court.

By invoking the Emergency Powers Rules, the Special Judge denied me the opportunity to be posted on bail and also to examine at length and depth the statements of the Prosecution witnesses made to the Investigation Officers of the ACC and the exhibits and documents produced by them before the court and to prepare our defense. Earlier by freezing all bank accounts of myself, my wife and sons, the Special Judge denied me funds to pay for the expenses of my defense. All expenses on my lawyers, procurement of certified records and even payment of court fees had to be borne by my brother Dr. Jahangir. My lawyer Syed Rezaur Rahman, along with his associates, was put under threat by Major Kamruzzaman and his associates in civvies for defending me. The associates were the spooks of the Forces Intelligence.

Framing of the charge, phony as it was, came to a close around 5:30 in the afternoon. I was allowed by the Special Judge to sit with my lawyer and brother for about 20 minutes after the charge was framed. They attempted to lift my spirit. I was dismayed, somewhat disoriented, but still courage did not take leave of me. I told them, it should be our attempt to record all testimonies, have all testimonies elaborately cross-examined, obtain certified copies of all testimonies on following days to examine the correctness or otherwise of recording by the Special Judge and select our defense witnesses in the light of depositions of the Prosecution Witnesses in order to rebut their positions.

I told them, as things were going thus far, I did not expect justice from the Special Judge's Court. However, if records of the Prosecution and the trial were presented to the appellate court in detail and without coloring by the Special Judge and the Public Prosecutor, we would be able to give a good fight against the injustice looming large on the horizon. I asked my brother to request all our known journalists to be present in the court as the trial proceeded. Specifically, I requested the presence of my good old friend Forrest Cookson, an American economist working in Bangladesh to be present on one or two occasions to give the trial judge a feeling that his conduct would not go unnoticed beyond the caged court set up under his mandated presidency.

From the courtroom, I was taken to the adjacent prisoner's room or *hajat*. Amongst a dozen policeman and agents of the Directorate General of the Forces Intelligence, I found Iqbal Hasan Tuku (erstwhile State Minister for Energy in Khaleda's government), his wife, son and teenage daughter sitting in a corner. Tuku was an accused before another Special Judge holding court upstairs. Along with Tuku, his wife, son and teenage daughter were accused in the same case. I found his wife and daughter in tears as they told me about the palpable injustice and barbarism they were confronting. With a choked voice, I consoled them and asked them to face the menace with courage and determination to win over the vile violators of freedom. It was but a manifestation of the worst kind of politics by the military to remove the politicians from the scene and occupy the seat of the government. As an avid observer of the Chinese socio-political development since 1945, I recalled Mao Zedong's famous quote of 1938 vintage: "Politics is war without bloodshed while war is politics with bloodshed." In their drive to occupy their own motherland, the military, in our country and at this time as it appeared, took up politics to give it a more sinister embodiment not thought about even by Mao 70 years back.

My brother Dr. Jahangir's optimism sounded over the profane realities of the "police protection" that escorted me into the prison van taking me to the Kashimpur Jail. It was past 9:00 p.m. when the prison van and the police escort delivered me to the entrance of the jail. When I arrived at the jail, I found that other inmates already knew over the radio that the charge had been framed against me. Salman and Kamal Majumder embraced me and consoled me. Lotus-Kamal, Kader and others stood by in silence. Then after a while all of them told me that together we would win over the machinations of those in power. Inaction and silence, they said, would not be ours to match the elements marshaled against us.

Bone-tired I walked to the floor where my cell was located, dragged my body up over the stairs and slumped down on a worn-out plastic chair on the verandah. Two hundred yards to the south, electric lights along the road outside the prison walls and movement of people and vehicles reminded me of liberty. I recalled as early as 1859 John Stuart Mill had warned the citizenry of the dangers of a culture of intellectual repression, in which questioning and criticism of received opinion became taboo. Longing for liberty, I knew through the gaze going beyond the constrictions of the prison to the lights of liberty outside that I was to face that taboo with all my might and determination, fighting a difficult and dishonored existence into which I had been pushed.

One of the junior lawyers assisting Syed Rezaur Rahman had earlier worked as my assistant. He told me that the Special Judge knew him personally. I asked him to find out, if possible, why the court was behaving as that of a kangaroo. In about two days he came back and told me that the court was under the orders of the military at the highest levels and was bent upon inflicting severest punishment on me irrespective of crime committed or not. The court could act otherwise if it received instructions to the contrary. I was also told through the grapevine that, if I could pay the Special Judge Tk. 50 lacs in cash he would try his best, by leaving holes in his judgment to set me free at the stage of appeal. I found these somewhat difficult to believe, a matter of disgrace in lieu of honorable defeat. I was inclined to believe, everything said and done, that both the military brass and the Special Judge had received some lessons giving them the minimum of human values and moral imperatives.

The trial under the Emergency Powers Rules had to be continuous without any break or respite. The Special Judge under this ruled-process of justice could not, excepting weekly and gazetted[17] holidays, adjourn trial for more than three days at a stretch. So on May 29, just two days after the charge was framed, I was made to board the prison van and be present at the court at 9:30 in the morning when the Prosecution started the process with testimonies of their witnesses.

[17] Officially published.

5 Prosecution Witnesses

(1)

The first witness produced by the Prosecution was Jiban Krishna Roy, an Assistant Director of the ACC who had filed the First Information Report against me in Tejgaon Police Station. An overly thin and peptic person with a set of constantly blinking eyes and dirty appearance, he seemed to be a made-to-order crook of the first degree. He stated that on February 20, 2007, I had submitted under my own handwriting and from the jail an 8-page statement of assets through the Superintendent of the jail. On March 1, the Secretary, ACC asked him to scrutinize the statement. Accordingly, after scrutinizing it he submitted a report on March 4, whereupon he was instructed by Nusrat Ara Surat Amin, Deputy Director (Investigation) ACC to investigate my alleged corruption. He said that he had examined my income tax return dated June 30, 2006, submitted to the income tax department along with the statement of assets submitted to the ACC on February 20, 2007. He said he did not find any mention of FDRs that I had held in either of these returns and statements. In cross-examination by Advocate Haider, he stated that he did not know that I was a member of the Presidium of the Awami League but he knew I was a Secretary to the government. He knew I came from a well-known and well-established family of the greater Comilla district but did not enquire as to whether my family was well-to-do or not.

"When did you visit Dr. Alamgir's house first?" asked Advocate Haider.

"I visited before I undertook investigation of the case,"

"Who were with you on this visit to his house?"

"I visited his house along with the Task Force."

"How could you visit Dr. Alamgir's house before you were assigned with investigation against him?" asked Advocate Haider rather loudly.

The witness kept silent. The black cat of premeditated victimization was out of the seemingly white bag of a make-believe story.

He confirmed that in the notice served on me by the Secretary, ACC, I was not asked to describe assets of others held by me. He also confirmed that the Secretary, ACC, signed the notice on January 18, 2007, though on the top of the notice it was dated February 18, 2007.

It became evident from Jiban's testimony that day that (1) no enquiry was conducted in respect of my assets before the investigation was undertaken; this was contrary to the Rules of the ACC; (2) the Investigation Officer did not scrutinize carefully the asset statement submitted by me; holding of FDRs of approximately Tk.90 lacs excluding the amount held by me on behalf of the Sultana Foundation set up by my family members in memory of my mother was deliberately concealed by the Investigation Officer; and (3) the fact or falsity of concealment as in asset statement was relegated to the background in relation to what was stated as wealth in the income tax return for 2006; this was contrary to the requirement of the notice of the ACC served on me under Section 26 of the ACC Act and Rule 15 (d) 5 of the Emergency Powers Rules (EPR) on January 18, 2007; and (4) decision to victimize me on political grounds was taken earlier with preceding action before formal investigation was ordered.

Despite being evident, the Special Judge did not take any notice of these realities. Cross-examination being over for the day, I returned to the Kashimpur Jail in the evening. To recover from the impending dismay with the process of justice, I read through Coelho's "The Fifth Mountain"; I came to believe, as Coelho described so simply and artfully in the face of difference in the best of our wishes and prayers on the one hand and the actual happenings soon thereafter, God has his own ways to mitigate the sufferings and giving help to the just.

On May 30, my lawyer Syed Rezaur Rahman resumed cross-examination of the Prosecution witness Jiban Krishna Roy. It transpired from the cross-examination that I had written my asset statement myself sitting in the jail and submitted the same to the Secretary, ACC, through my brother Dr. Jahangir on 22 February. This contradicted his testimony given on the earlier day that I had submitted my asset statement through the Superintendent of the jail where I was incarcerated. He admitted that I had stated that I was at the time of writing the statement detained illegally in the jail and that I would be ready to give further clarification on getting an opportunity for hearing at the ACC's convenience.

He further admitted that in the asset statement, I had mentioned approximately Tk. 90 lacs of FDRs held by me and had given sources from which these were funded, which he did not mention in the First Information Report (FIR) lodged with the police. He stated that I had mentioned FDRs as *Amanat Patras, i.e.*, term deposit receipts in Bangla. He said my sons were not financially dependent on me. On the contrary, at times of need, they helped me. He admitted that he had not mentioned in the FIR about 20 books including one prize-winning one that I had written and the approximate income that I had received on that account. He said that ten months after I had obtained the FDRs, on April 17 and 18, 2006, he filed the FIR without mentioning the reasons for delay in filing.

"Who wrote the FIR that you lodged against Dr. Alamgir with the police?" asked Advocate Syed Rezaur Rahman.

"I wrote it," replied the witness.

"Here is the photocopy of the FIR. Is it handwritten by you?"

"No; it was printed by a computer."

"Computer does not print, it processes the words as was done in this case. Who processed these words?" asked the Advocate.

"I did not."

"Who did it?"

"I do not remember."

"Did you obtain approval of your supervising officer on the FIR as was composed by a computer or handwritten by you?" asked Advocate Syed Rezaur Rahman.

"No, I did not."

"So the FIR was your handicraft, unapproved by the ACC," observed the Advocate.

The witness kept silent and became grim with a visible worry seen on his face.

He admitted that he did not remember the name of the Manager, IFIC Bank, Karwan Bazar where the fixed deposits were deposited by me; he did not ask the Manager as to whether the Bangla version of FDRs as *Amanat Patras* as I used in my asset statement, correctly reflected the usual English meaning of the same. He admitted that income tax on interest accrued on FDs was deducted at source by the concerned bank and remitted and informed to the tax authority on behalf of the depositor, and holding of FDRs was not or could not be concealed or kept secret as such. He further admitted that in accordance with the relevant rules under the Income Tax Ordinance, annual interest on FDRs obtained on April 17 and 18, 2006, would be accruable at least a year thereafter. Then Syed Rezaur Rahman asked him point blank:

"Did you in course of your investigation know of any year or work when or in respect of which Dr. Alamgir obtained illegal gratification?"

"No, I did not find anything like that in any year in any of his work," replied the Prosecution Witness.

In cross-examination then taken up once again by Advocate Haider, Jiban Krishna admitted that he did not know anything about the Sultana Foundation or its operation by me nor did he investigate it. He said that I had worked in various high posts including chairmanships of a number of public corporations but he did not know or enquire about any corrupt practice ascribable to me while in these positions. He admitted that he did not see or examine the revised asset statement submitted to the ACC by me, nor did he know whether, at the time of arresting me, the arrestors found any incriminating material or document in my house. Responding to cross-examination by Advocate Ayat Ali Patwary thereafter, Jiban Krishna admitted that he did not know of any dishonest action taken by me as a public servant and in that regard he lodged the FIR on mere assumption that I had done such.

While the cross-examination was going on, at times I wanted to ask questions of the Prosecution Witness myself. I told the Special Judge that in accordance with the decision of the High Court the statement made by a witness to the Prosecution before he deposed before the court, was to be made available to the defense for examination and preparation at least seven days before actual deposition to be made before the trial court. This was not done in my case, which was, in my view, obstruction of justice and indicative of partisanship of the court. I also told the Special Judge that since my lawyers served as my agents, I should be allowed to cross-examine the Prosecution Witnesses if I felt like it, more so as I knew more about my conduct and affairs than anyone else and I had served as a District Magistrate, that had given me full acquaintance with the procedure of a trial, specially with the Evidence Act which governed the ways depositions were made and recorded. The Special Judge did not allow me to do so.

"Your lawyers are good enough for you; I do not see why you may speak or ask questions," the Special Judge said.

"If your honor does not permit me to ask questions of the Prosecution Witnesses when I need to do so for my defense, it will be a violation of the legal procedure and also of my right as a defendant," I said firmly.

To this he did not reply.

Then I requested of him that in that case he should give me time to consult with my lawyers immediately after a Prosecution Witness deposed in his *examination-in-chief*, *i.e.*, deposed as led by the Public Prosecutor. He did not respond to this either. Instead, without looking at me, he ruled that I as an accused should not drink water from my bottle standing on the dock as I did. Quenching thirst that way, he said, might be taken as tantamount to contempt of court. I stared at him in anguished silence and wondered about the depth and breadth of the mandate that he had received from up above about disposing my case under the cover of law. When at the end of the day, I got down from the dock, Syed Rezaur Rahman, quite amiable and gentle as he was, said.

"The judge was irritated, perhaps angry with you."

"Did I say something not permitted by law?" I retorted.

"No, but then again — " The rest I did not want to hear as I always believed submissive conduct transgresses, more often than not, rights of persons supposed to be free and brave. Sitara who sat amongst the lawyers and friends passed me two pieces of paper wrapped sandwiches without looking at my eyes. I took them gratefully but did not look at her lest tears well up in our eyes.

These depositions made by Prosecution Witness Jiban Krishna made a number of things evident. First, the investigation conducted by him into allegations against me was mostly unauthorized, incomplete and imposed from above on extra-legal grounds. Second, I as an income taxpayer, did not violate income tax law in any way; I did not conceal anything from the income tax authority in violation of the law. Third, I did mention the holding of FDRs in approximate terms and sources of their funding in my statement of assets furnished to the ACC; it was not reasonable to expect a person incarcerated in the jail to give an exact amount of his financial assets, without having access to his financial records, which in any case in accordance with the procedure pursued by the concerned bank were not or could not be concealed from the tax authority of the government. In going about the cross-examination of the witness, the lawyers tried their best and far beyond the normal course of arguments to point these matters out to the Special Judge. The Special Judge, in his adherence to the dictum seemingly received from above and reiterated through exchange of glances with the Major of the Task Force present in the court, remained unperturbed and unruffled on his way to ignore and truncate the truth.

(2)

It was quite late in the evening when I was dispatched back to the jail in the prison van, a sputtering windowless vehicle of concocted black paint all over. In the darkness all around me in the van I remembered March 7, 1971, the bedrock of our national awakening.

On March 7, 1971, Bangabandhu Sheikh Mujibur Rahman declared in the Race Course (afterwards renamed *Suhrawardy Uddayan*) Dhaka, that the fight of the people thenceforth was for liberation and independence. I along with a dozen colleagues of the then-Civil Service (of Pakistan) was present in the meeting of millions. That evening, in the house of our senior colleague, Al Mamun Sanaul Haq, about fifty of our colleagues sat and decided to support the fight for liberation and independence as was called for by Bangabandhu. The course for all of us was charted out. I was tasked to leave for Comilla, Noakhali and Chittagong and Rangamati to personally tell the respective Deputy Commissioners, Shamsul Haq Khan at Comilla, Manzurul Karim at Noakhali and Mir Mostafizur Rahman at Chittagong and H. T. Imam at Rangamati of this decision, to encourage the Police and the Ansars (the paramilitary) to act accordingly and to open up the district armories for distribution of arms amongst them and the student patriots. The liberation war started, continued for nine months with the support and participation of people from all walks of life and the helping hand of India and was won. And now 36 years thereafter, some goons lusting for political power through the barrel of their guns given to them for protecting our freedom and independence have come to corral us into submission and servitude. In my subconscious, I resolved this could not be allowed; we were not born in 1971 for defeat in 2007.

Between June 1 and 4, the Prosecution examined four witnesses. Of these, Mohammed Idrish Mia, Sub-Inspector of Tejgaon Police Station testified about filing and recording of the First Information Report by the Complainant and Prosecution Witness, Jiban Krishna Roy. He said he did not know of any reason as to the delay in filing the FIR after the alleged occurrence of the offense, *i.e.*, keeping fixed deposits of Tk.117 lacs in the IFIC Bank, Karwan Bazar by me. Then Aminul Islam, First Vice-President of IFIC Bank in charge of its Karwan Bazar branch deposed about six fixed deposits (FDs) deposited in his bank by me on April 17 and 18, 2006. In cross-examination by Syed Rezaur Rahman, he testified that these FDs in accordance with the terms of deposits were maturable so as to yield interest income a year thereafter, *i.e.*, on April 17 and 18, 2007. These were dates much after the date I submitted the asset statement. He said as per the rules of the National Board of Revenue, he had already deducted 10% tax on interest accrued on these deposits and credited the same to the tax authority on my behalf.

"Could any depositor conceal such fixed deposits and tax accrued thereon?" asked Advocate Syed Rezaur Rahman.

"No. It is not possible to conceal fixed deposits. In accordance with the rules set under the Income Tax Ordinance, such deposits along with accrued interest income are required to be reported to the Income Tax Department; tax imposed on interest accrued on such deposits is credited to the Income Tax Department with the particulars of the relevant depositors," replied the witness in clear terms.

He said he could not say whether some of these FDs were held on behalf of the Sultana Foundation or not. Then Gousal Azam Beg, an officer of IFIC Bank working in the same branch deposed that he knew that fixed deposits were literally known as term deposits in Bangla. He could not say whether Bangla equivalent of FDRs was *Amanat Patras* or not. Then A. F. M. Soyeb of the same bank verified the signatures of himself and other officers in reference. In cross-examination by Syed Rezaur Rahman, he admitted that Investigation Officer Jiban Krishna had come to the bank two or three times, but did not record his statement. He said that *Amanat Patras* in Bangla were known as financial instruments in banking parlance.

The significant points that became evident in course of depositions of these four prosecution witnesses were that (i) FDRs in reference were not concealed to tax authority; (ii) as per terms, these deposits were slated to yield interest-income a year after, *i.e.*, not in the financial year ending June 30, 2006, for which the income tax return as mentioned in the FIR was submitted by me and (iii) these financial instruments as far as these were my assets, excluding assets held on behalf of the Sultana Foundation, were mentioned and included in the figure of FDRs or *Amanat Patras* in the asset statement furnished by me to the ACC from the jail. Evidently, as they deposed, I could not be faulted on grounds of giving false statement or concealing facts on this count as alleged by the Prosecution. With silence bordering on being sinister in its eloquence, these facts as I noticed were not noted by the Special Judge.

After the court hours on June 4, with a munificent permission obtained from the Special Judge to consult with my lawyers for just 30 minutes, I sat with my brother Dr. Jahangir, wife Sitara and lawyers Syed Rezaur Rahman and Syed Haider Ali. I told them I did not expect any justice from this court both on grounds of procedural wrongs and misrecording and misplacement of facts. These were serious irregularities that warranted quashment of proceedings in this court. I should therefore file a quashment petition with the High Court Division of the Supreme Court. My brother listened silently and said despite the atmosphere of fear created by the military even within the environs of the Supreme Court, he would discuss the proposition with Barrister Rafiqul Huq. I said I would draft a petition to this end to the High Court the next day for consideration of Barrister Rafiq. Advocate Syed Rezaur Rahman commented that under the circumstances, it seemed unlikely that redress would be available at even that level. Sitara said, even then we should go ahead to save ourselves from this monstrosity looming large under the cover of justice. Major Kamruzzaman, the Leader of the Task Force propelling the Prosecution, observed us from a distance with a grim face. He stared hard both at me and my wife as if we were sitting on a rocky escarpment fearing an immediate fall.

Keeping awake almost throughout the night and despite load-shedding for about three hours, on the back papers of a wall calendar, I drafted a petition for the High Court Division. I outlined the points of inapplicability of the draconian law against me, the flaws in investigation and the deliberate truncation of an expected fair process of trial and gave it to my brother next morning. I had to carefully hide the draft petition while I was taken out of the jail for the court. The jailor would not allow any paper, written or blank, to go out or come into the jail with me. With eyes reddened from lack of sleep and fatigue almost impairing my normal sense, I stood on the dock to see what was in store for me that would be passed as evidence that day.

That day was June 5, 2007. Two witnesses, namely Rezaul Karim, an Inspector of the Income Tax Department and Dipak Kumar Basu, an Upper Division Assistant, Salary Circle 4, Region 4 of Dhaka (Income) Tax Circle were brought in to depose in support of the Prosecution. Rezaul Karim testified about the seizure of my income tax records by the ACC's other Investigation Officer Shermin Ferdousi. In cross-examination by Advocate Syed Rezaur Rahman, he admitted that he did not know of any sign that indicated the seizure of these records and Shermin Ferdousi did not sign or initial every paper that was seized and now presented before the court. He further admitted that his statement had been recorded by Shermin Ferdousi in the office of his superior Assistant Commissioner and he had given his statement as he was asked by his superior officer to do so. Dipak Kumar Basu testified that he had signed the seizure list as a witness.

In cross-examination by Syed Rezaur Rahman, he admitted that what he had seen in the seizure list was not recorded on any paper. Cross-examined by Advocate Haider, Dipak Kumar Basu stated he was not sure whether the income tax register of a VIP like the accused was separately kept or kept in duplicate. Depositions of these two witnesses were more procedural than substantial. Even then it transpired from their testimonies that the seizure and, by implication, the examination of my income tax records by the ACC's Investigation Officers, was neither systematic nor complete for a dispassionate conclusion about the periods, figures and explanatory notes of income tax returns furnished as evidence against me in the court. The Special Judge did not care to take notice of these loopholes and loose ends. At least I did not observe him to note or write anything on the trial file that was in front of him.

Returning to the Kashimpur Jail late in the evening, I started writing down points of cross-examination every night for use by my lawyers for the next day. I was not very satisfied with the cross-examination conducted by them in the past few days. It seemed to me that they did not go deep into the accusations brought against me; various points of law and facts, some quaint but very important in my assessment, were not touched by them. To an extent, it appeared to be an example of shoddy lawyering. Given that the court was that of a kangaroo bent upon imposing punishment on me at the behest of those who had usurped the power of the government through the barrel of the gun, I had expected more seriousness on their part, instead of a perfunctory approach based on instant reaction and supposition arising from the depositions of the prosecution witnesses. This was not reflective of minds capable and prepared to wrap themselves around the enormous construct of falsehood planned and pursued by the Prosecution.

For writing the points rebutting deep into possible deposition, I could procure tidbits of papers, a pen and two pencils and find ways to take them out through the jail gate. The jailor seemed to flinch and I stared hard into his eyes while going out. But I had one difficulty that could not easily be overcome. My handwriting was bad, almost illegible, even for the high-powered glasses worn by Advocate Syed Rezaur Rahman. The Special Judge presiding over the trial seemed to be specially careful and diligent to make sure that I would not consult with my lawyers or pass notes to them when depositions and cross-examinations were going on. But improvisations through eye contacts, pieces of paper and movement of junior lawyers yielded some results.

(3)

On June 6, the Prosecution examined four witnesses. Led by Public Prosecutor Syed Mizanur Rahman, having the look of a well-fed lawyer with his immaculate collar band, they started with Nusrat Ara Surat Amin, Director (Investigation) the ACC. Tall, somewhat plump and straightforward, clad in *salwar kameez*[18] instead of a *sari*[19] as was expected of a Bangali woman of that age, Amin was the supervising officer of both the Investigation Officers Jiban Krishna and Shermin Ferdousi. Amin stated that following the receipt of the asset statement from me, the Secretary ACC, Delwar Hossain ordered for investigation. Accordingly, she instructed Assistant Director Jiban Krishna to lodge the First Information Report with Tejgaon Police Station on March 6, 2007. In the cross-examination by Advocate Haider, she admitted that the notice served on me to furnish the statement of assets under the signature of the Secretary, ACC was dated January 18, 2007, *i.e.*, a fortnight before I was arrested and the notice required me to give description of my assets and not their values.

"Did Dr. Alamgir in the letter forwarding his asset statement ask for an opportunity to be personally heard in respect of anything contained in or omitted from the statement?" asked Advocate Rezaur Rahman.

"Yes, he did," she admitted without hesitation and then added, "but the Commission did not take any step to give him such an opportunity."

She said she did not know that Secretary Delwar's home village was located in the same electoral constituency as mine. The Superintendent of the Kashimpur Jail C. M. Matin was examined then. He deposed about the service of notice of the ACC on me and writing of the asset statement by me on February 20. In cross-examination by Syed Rezaur Rahman, he admitted that I

---

[18] A traditional dress worn by women in South Asia consisting of loose, pajama-like trousers. It is considered the national dress of Pakistan.

[19] The traditional woman's dress, often between 18 to 21 feet long. Women wrap themselves in the sari as their principal item of clothing.

had submitted a second or revised statement of assets to the ACC through the jail authority on April 28, 2007. His deposition was followed by that of Jailor Enamul Haq who simply stated that he was on duty in the Kashimpur Jail on February 20, 2007, when I wrote the asset statement.

Cross-examined by Advocate Syed Rezaur Rahman, he admitted that a second asset statement was forwarded to the ACC through the Deputy Jailor on May 2, 2007. He stated that the personnel of the Special Branch of the police were required to be present when visitors were allowed to see me. He also admitted that the notice of the Secretary, ACC that was served on me was dated January 18, 2007 under his signature (*i.e.* of the Secretary ACC). It came out clear from these depositions that (i) the Secretary, ACC had a personal interest in prosecuting and convicting me of a criminal charge like corruption; once I was convicted, in the electoral constituency that we had in common, he would have an unfettered sail if he wished to contest the national election; (ii) in his unusual enthusiasm to seek and win election, he predated the notice served on me proving that it was an end-product of a premeditated scheme; (iii) the ACC in its haste to prosecute and convict me, did not take into account and consider my second or revised asset statement; if they did, they would not have a ground to allege that I concealed my assets in any way or manner.

Towards the end of 2006, Delwar Hossain was appointed Secretary of the ACC. The appointment swelled him in pride and ego. The Proclamation of Emergency on January 11, 2007, gave a definite boost to his assessment about himself in terms of importance and skillfulness. In sequel to the arrest of 50 politicians and businessmen by the Task Force assigned by the military on the night of February 3, Delwar propelled by his pride and ego, issued notices, reportedly on his own, both under the ACC Act and the Emergency Powers Rules to all of them in detention in jail to furnish statements of their assets within 72 hours. The ACC was not formed and operational at that time. Neither the chairman nor the members were appointed. He was not authorized to issue such notices under the Emergency Powers Rules either. But more like a bull in a china shop, he ran around with notices, appeared in electronic and print media and said that he had to do this in the country's interest at the time of emergency.

So far as I was concerned, Delwar went a step further in the electronic media: he cited me as an example of a corrupt person alleged to having amassed a cold storage facility and a filling station in my electoral constituency. To me all these seemed as small ways of showing how grateful he was to me for saving his job, sending him abroad for higher training and helping him out financially to treat his ailing daughter. I recalled how at his insistence in 1998, during flood, I visited along with him and Fazlul Ahad, another colleague of mine, his home village Lunti within Kachua Police Station on a dark night, just to show my sympathy and fraternal feelings. The poor fellow, wading through knee-deep water in the night along with us two, could not easily get into his home and find his only brother and other relations. When he rapped at the closed doors of a tin-roofed cottage, a bare-chested man with a *lungi* around his waist came out with a lamp, looked intensely at us and then exclaimed at Delwar: "So you found time to see us!" I was convinced, perched on the top of a government job, he did not relish going often to his village home and keeping close touch with his siblings. Now as the Secretary, ACC, he was showing patriotism to his roots and surroundings as if it was about the last refuse of himself as a scoundrel.

(4)

The next witness produced by the Prosecution on that day was Rabiul Hasan Prodhan, Assistant Commissioner of the Income Tax Department. He had the appearance of an experienced and matured officer. He testified about the seizure of three volumes of my income tax records by Investigation Officer Sharmin Ferdousi on April 12, 2007, keeping of my income tax returns since 1981 in these volumes as were filed and mentioning of Tk. 79 lacs 51 thousands 786 as the value of my wealth in 2006 as computed by them. He said that in 1981-82, I had shown Tk. 5.10 lacs as the cost or value of the first two stories of my house at Banani Model town, land valued at Tk. 17.5 thousand in Comilla Housing Estate and 26 decimals of land at Savar. He testified that in 1989-90, I constructed the third and fourth floors of my house at Banani at a cost of Tk.6 lacs of which Tk.5 lacs was reported to have been spent or invested by June 30, 1990.

He affirmed that in accordance with the rules of income tax department, if an asset was acquired by a taxpayer by June 30 in a particular year, it was required of him to mention it in the tax return for the next assessment year. In cross-examination by Syed Rezaur Rahman, he stated that he had not given any statement to the ACC's Investigation Officer Sharmin Ferdousi who seized the accused's income tax records from him. He further stated that the file on income tax return of Dr. Alamgir that he had submitted to the court was a photocopy, not a certified true copy. He admitted that Dr. Alamgir in his income tax return or statement did not hide anything.

While cross-examining him Advocate Haider asked him: "Did the Income Tax Department ever have any objection against Dr. Alamgir as an income taxpayer?"

"No. Dr. Alamgir was a regular income taxpayer. We do not have any objection against his income tax returns earlier or now," Prodhan replied without any hesitation.

He admitted that their records had entries with respect to my rental income from 1982 to 1993 and they had verified construction costs along with sources of funds for my house at Banani from the returns as furnished by me. He stated that Income Tax Department did not have any entry about values of my ancestral property in my home village. He admitted that he did not know anything about Sultana Bhaban and Sitara Bhaban and the Sultana Filling Station alleged to have been my properties. He stated that my commonly owned ancestral house in home village and agricultural land were not demarcated. He admitted that all rental income received by me on account of my house at Banani had been shown in income tax returns since 1981-82. He said he did not bring my income tax files for years prior to 1981-82. He admitted that remuneration and allowances that I had received in U.S. dollars as Director of IDB and UN Consultant in Uganda were tax free. At this point Advocate Haider asked him:

"Did Dr. Alamgir show his earnings in dollars from 1974 to 1976 and in 1990 to 1991 in his tax returns when he was on higher training and service abroad?"

"Yes," Prodhan answered emphatically.

"Were such earnings abroad in dollars tax-free in accordance with the tax law of the country?"

"Certainly," affirmed Rabiul Hasan Prodhan.

"Did Dr. Alamgir show his earnings as author from his publications as creative works in his income tax return?" asked the Advocate.

"Yes, he did," Prodhan replied after looking at his papers.

He said that his department did not have any record of any motorcycle owned by me. He clarified that income tax management or collection was a continuous process; whatever fell short of due payment in a particular year was paid and adjusted in the next year and income tax settled and certified as such in a particular year was not a subject for reopening in the next year. He stated that Dr. Alamgir had and operated a relief fund. He stated that from the files brought by him he could not say whether I had donated lands for a school and an NGO. Had he brought files dating before 1981, he could have verified such donations. He admitted that advance income tax on interest income accrued on FDRs were deducted at source and credited on behalf of the client and that the IT department did not send my income tax files to the court; the ACC did after they had seized them.

It became evident from the testimony of Rabiul Hasan Prodhan that (i) the income tax department did not have any objection or complaint against me as a taxpayer; (ii) values at cost of construction of my house at Banani were reported by me in 1981-82 and 1989-90 as was required by income tax law and were accepted by the Income Tax Department and taxes were paid accordingly; (iii) assets acquired in a particular year, *i.e.*, in 2006 in this case were to be reported in income tax return in 2007 and in this context I did not commit any wrong in respect of my return of income tax in 2006 by not mentioning all those FDRs mentioned in the FIR; (iv) my ancestral home as common property and my rental income from my house in Banani in Dhaka were properly included in my income tax return since 1981-82; (v) my earnings abroad in dollars and from books written by me were properly included in tax returns; (vi) income tax payment was a continuous process in which under or over payment in a particular year was adjusted and rectified in the next year and (vii) interest income accrued on my FDRs in reference were duly credited by the concerned bank to the government on my behalf.

Thus, nothing incriminating against me was testified by Rabiul Hasan Prodhan on behalf of the Income Tax Department. But as it appeared, these facts did not make much of an impression on the Special Judge. Almost all the while he was exchanging meaningful glances with Major Kamruzzaman of the Task Force. The Major was present all the while by the side of the Public Prosecutor. Behind him there sat a crop-cut, well-built young man apparently from the Directorate General of the Forces Intelligence. The process of justice as well as its players seemed to have been well under the unstoppable power of our own armed forces. Evidently for even the Special Judge, power was integrity and facts twisted or fabricated were nothing but fodder for power.

Sitting with my lawyer, brother and wife for 30 minutes munificently allowed by the Special Judge after the testimonies of the prosecution witnesses for the day, I discussed the implication of the day's depositions and preparation for the next day. My brother Dr. Jahangir told me that my detention that was earlier challenged in the High Court Division was declared illegal but immediately thereafter the government took the matter to the Appellate Division which stayed it for a full hearing later. As it turned out, over days and months thereafter, the Appellate Division did not hear these detention cases but put them on hold.

Never in the history of this country had such a submissive attitude and action been shown by our highest court, which had been given the power and responsibility to protect the Constitution and the people's rights guaranteed under it. The rumor had it that the Directorate General of the Forces Intelligence through President Iazuddin let the Chief Justice knew that he had earlier furnished a false affidavit in order to get allotment of a plot of land by RAJUK[20] and if he did not follow the diktat given by the intelligence outfit, the information would be leaked to the press to make him leave his office in disgrace. That was why under the cover of judicial consideration at the highest level he was holding final decisions about the persons whose detentions had been adjudged illegal by the High Court.

It came out in the press, probably as a foretaste of the probable disgrace of the Chief Justice, that the Chairman of the ACC, a party to almost all cases of such illegal detentions, saw the Chief Justice in the Supreme Court and had a meeting with him of an extra-judicial nature. These were all elements of monstrosities created by shoeshine persons elevated to celebrated and responsible positions. I found it hard to believe that as a nation we had gone down to that low a level.

My wife told me in passing it would not be possible for her to come to the court any more for she was being followed by Major Kamruzzaman and his cohorts whenever she went out of the house. I asked her to leave the house, stay somewhere else without letting anybody know except Dr. Jahangir and not to come to the court any more. Late evening, the prison van with the police escort returned me to the jail at Kashimpur. With a severe headache, I hit the bed without taking my meal. Sleep escaped me, as a matter of course.

(5)

The next day June 12 around 8:00 in the morning, I was almost rounded up from my cell by Deputy Jailor Jainul and packed into the prison van to reach the court by 9:30. I was dizzy with a headache and had a bout of diarrhea in the night. But these were

---

[20] Acronym for "Rajdhani Unnayan Kartripakkha," *i.e.*, Capital Development Authority.

not grounds enough to exempt me from the justice being hewed out in the Special Court. The Prosecution brought the Executive Engineer, Chandpur, Public Works Department (PWD) of the government to testify about my allegedly concealed properties in Kachua and my home village. He deposed that he along with his Assistant Engineer made valuation of two buildings "Sitara Bhaban," and "Sultana Bhaban" at Gulbahar, my home village and of an under-construction set of shops by the side of the Gulbahar Cold Store and of the Sultana Filling Station at Kachua. He admitted that he had made the valuation sitting in his office and deducting 18% of the estimated cost on account of overhead and value-added tax. In cross-examination by Advocate Haider, he admitted that the two buildings mentioned by him as Sitara Bhaban and Sultana Bhaban had one single gate and inlet; he did not know who had built these buildings and what was the direction of the frontage of them; he did not use any measurement book or sheet for valuation of these buildings.

"Did you know or record who owned these buildings?" asked Advocate Haider in despaired irritation.

"I do not know. I did not ascertain," replied the witness unabashedly.

"Did you know or record who was the owner of the shops under construction, lumped together as the Biponi Polash by the Prosecution?" asked the somewhat baffled Advocate.

"I did not know. I did not find out," came the unhesitant answer from the witness.

"Did you find out, directly from records or indirectly from persons in charge of construction as to who funded the Biponi Polash?" asked the Advocate breaking across the integrity of the witness and the depth of his findings.

"No."

"Did anybody tell you that Dr. Alamgir was the owner of the Biponi Polash and he funded its construction?" Advocate Haider's push for the truth came to a shove.

"Nobody told me so. I have no knowledge of ownership and funding of the Biponi Polash," the witness responded with seeming abandonment of the strain that lay in cross-examination.

He said he did not ascertain what types of materials were used in constructing these buildings; he could not say plot and *khatian*[21] numbers of lands on which these buildings were located. Then he admitted that various departments of the govern-

[21] Account book or ledger of revenue records.

ment had varying schedules of rates for construction and that he did not know whether an under-construction set of shops such as the Biponi Polash not yet constructed constituted an asset or not.

The deposition of the Executive Engineer, PWD, Chandpur, was followed by that of Sufi[22] Abul Hasnat, Subdivisional Engineer of the same department of the same location. He deposed that along with an Assistant Engineer, he had verified construction of the Sitara Bhaban and the Sultana Bhaban at Gulbahar village, the Sultana Filling Station and the Biponi Polash at Kachua. At the time of measurement of Sultana and Sitara *Bhabans*, an employee of the Sultana Filling Station was present. He stated that cost of the under-construction Biponi Polash was verified on the basis of its drawings. He said that, based on questioning local people, he assumed 1987 as the period of construction and accordingly used schedule of rates/cost of that year in estimating the cost of Sultana and Sitara Bhabans. In cross-examination by Advocate Syed Rezaur Rahman, the Executive Engineer admitted that while estimating cost of buildings at Gulbahar he did not consult with the Chairman or local members of the Union Parishad and did not observe that the Al Asheq was the name of the home. He said he had taken about 30 minutes to complete the estimation, had not seen the blueprint or drawing in the process and could not enter into the house as the keys were not available.

"Did you verify and find out *khatian* and plot numbers of the holdings on which these buildings, the Sultana–Sitara Bhaban, the Sultana Filling Station and the Biponi Polash were located?" asked Advocate Syed Rezaur Rahman.

"No, I did not," the words strutted out of the witness.

He stated that he could not say whether the Sultana Filling station was owned by the accused's son Dr. Jalal Alamgir nor did he report it. He said, he did not in fact know whether Dr. Alamgir was the owner of the filling station. In the same way, he admitted that he could not say anything about the ownership of the under-construction shops lumped under the name the Biponi Polash. In cross-examination by Advocate Haider, the witness could not say how many rooms were there in the twin building in the accused's village home, what type of bathroom fittings were there, whether the rooms were plastered or not. He could not say how much of the Biponi Polash was constructed. He said, he did not dig or bore down any portion of the building and did not know about the

---

[22] A Muslim holy man, who typically travels from place to place in order to preach; in this case a family title.

thickness of the plaster. In response to a query made by Advocate Ayat Ali Patwary, he admitted that in rural areas usually the Local Government Engineering Department and the Facilities Department of the Education Ministry undertook and completed construction of buildings; the Public Works Department usually concentrated on construction in the urban areas. In this context he could not explain as to why only the current schedule of construction costs of the PWD (Public Works Department) was used in measuring costs of these buildings to the exclusion of schedules of other government departments bestowed with more construction work in the rural areas.

"Do you know the difference between current and constant costs?" asked Advocate Patwary. His eyes had an alert, humorless glare.

The witness remained silent for some time and then said "no."

Then the Assistant Engineer, PWD, Chandpur, was examined. He deposed that he had estimated values/costs of three establishments, namely, the Sultana Filling Station and the Biponi Polash, Kachua, and the Sultana-Sitara Bhaban, Gulbahar village. He said while he was making rough measurement of the Sultana Filling Station, its manager was present; the work on this over, he went to Gulbahar village along with a person given to him by the Manager of the Filling Station and then he came back to Kachua and verified the under-construction Biponi Polash along with the Manager of the Cold Store on the premises of which the shops under-construction were located. Put under cross-examination by Advocate Haider, he admitted that his report on measurement did not bear any official reference number, though all such works were required to be entered into official measurement books. He admitted that in the measurement done in respect of these three buildings, he did not maintain any measurement book for them in their office; he did not know in which file were kept the office papers relating to these works or measurements. As he said, there were some piecemeal writings on some papers about these. He said that measurement and estimate of costs (in respect of a building) were different from each other.

"While undertaking measurement and estimating costs of these buildings did you see or follow the relevant site plans, architectural and structural designs and plumbing and electrical drawings? Asked Advocate Haider.

"No."

"Why not?"

"I did not feel any need for these plans, designs and drawings." His answer made the hairs on my head stand on end.

"Can one or an engineer measure or estimate construction cost without reference to these plans, designs and drawings?" asked the Advocate in anguish.

"No, perhaps no," came a delayed and strutted reply. He seemed to have no further contribution to make on the subject.

When this cross-examination by Advocate Haider was going on, at about 4:00 in the afternoon the Special Judge abruptly stood up, adjourned the proceedings and left for his office room. The Public Prosecutor along with Major Kamruzzaman followed him in response to his glance. Through the grapevine, we came to know that the Law Secretary with an important message from the Law Advisor Barrister Moinul Hossain had come to meet them.

I knew for certain the message was for manipulation: irrespective of evidence I was to be convicted; irrespective of the way the evidence was presented, ways and means had to be found out for bending them to give the sinister process a make-believe judicial cover. I had known Barrister Moinul Hossain for a long time. In the early 1980s, he and his wife invited me and my wife once or twice to his beautiful new house at Baridhara. Sitting in a split level marble-floored living room and looking at a mid-roof sky-light, over delicious meals and soft conversations, I wondered how he could bend RAJUK's rules to get the spacious plot for his house despite his father's ownership of a few in various locations in Dhaka.

Obviously he had signed an inaccurate affidavit and made the RAJUK authority accept it as true by pulling a string here and two there. I was not, therefore, very surprised when Moinul Hossain became a vociferous Law Advisor of the military-controlled government of this time and tried to ride over his vices and misdeeds under the cover of speedy and extensive trial of corrupt businessmen and politicians. I was not very surprised when he had stated in an answer to a question raised by a journalist that to him and his government completion of trial of the killers of Bangabandhu was not a priority item of business.

I also recalled that in 1971 after the military crackdown of the Pakistanis against the innocent, freedom-demanding Bangalis, Hossain and his cohorts did not hesitate to accept a sizable amount from Governor Tikka Khan to restart the daily paper *Ittefaq* that he had inherited from his father Tofazzal Hossain, Manik Mia. Tikka Khan earned infamy as the butcher of the then-East Pakistan for the genocide that was committed by him and his cohorts during the liberation war. Moinul's brother was Anwar Hossain, who as the co-owner, edited the daily. The two brothers were at daggers drawn over the management, especially about the distasteful but tax-free distribution of daily cash income from classified advertisements paid for in cash and as reports had it, even gruesome murders were committed in the paper's office between the two groups supporting each of the feuding brothers. Recalling all these things, I fell into a deeper despair, almost unable to breath the sad dormant air around.

The Special Judge did not return from the meeting with the Law Secretary that afternoon. After waiting in the dock for more than an hour I, yawning and exhausted, was led to the adjacent cage-like room earmarked for the accused. I found Pankaj Debnath, Secretary, the Awami Sechhasevak League and Amanullah Aman, a former State Minister in Khaleda Zia's government and his wife there. Pankaj Debnath was a leader since his student days. He was now under detention and prosecution for an alleged violation of income tax law along with his wife. His wife worked in a bank and, with borrowing from there they had bought an apartment. Both of them were accused of not reporting the purchase in full detail to the income tax authority. Amanullah Aman along with his wife was prosecuted under the Anti-Corruption Commission Act. The charge against him was primarily under the Income Tax Ordinance, which allowed for rectification of under- and over-payments over time following a process of noticing, reviewing, appealing and arbitration. As I could understand from its reading, the ACC Act was not relevant and applicable in his case. I wondered how in a civilized society wives could be brought under incarceration as a matter of course on alleged charge of corruption or misdeeds of their husbands. Pankaj was in his 30s, well-built, handsome and confident. I told him never to lose courage and not to allow his wife to surrender before the kangaroo court and be incarcerated into the vile jail on a flimsy charge. The regime, we agreed, wanted to keep going a campaign of combating corruption in order to perpetuate their holding onto power and clinging to the reins of the government. I felt like flinging cow dung in their faces.

I boarded the prison van around 8:00 in the evening and reached the jail after 10:00 in the night. Still, Salman and Lotus-Kamal were waiting for me with anxiety. A squall was rippling and swirling against the high walls of the jail. "How did it go?" they cried in unison. "Splendid," I replied painfully smiling back at them. They understood. While we ate our meager meal, somewhat cold and almost impossible to swallow, we did not speak.

For us silence was a cover for our continuous suffering in the country for the independence of which we all contributed our might. Despite the cover, the smell of *Rajanigandha* grown on the borders of vegetable patches in front of the division building with the soft rustle of its twigs and leaves wafted over as if it was yearning to open small windows in our almost locked hearts. In the late night, unable to sleep, I paged through Alan Farst's *Voyage*, a story about indomitable courage and determination of a captain of a ship taking him and his sailors on a voyage through the enemy line in the Mediterranean and the Baltic during the Second World War. I could reaffirm my belief: a determined man never wavered from his mission. He would remain undefeated despite brutal odds and grinding distress, unlocking his heart to the limitless bounties of possibilities.

Next day on June 13, Advocate Haider continued cross-examination of the Assistant Engineer. He admitted that he had estimated the costs/values of the installations in reference in accordance with the PWD's (Public Works Department) schedule of rates sitting in his office. He said that he did not have any quantity surveyor with him nor did he have any training in surveying quantity. He admitted that my ancestral home and buildings thereon were commonly owned by four brothers and four sisters and their inheritors. He clearly stated that the Sultana Filling Station was owned by my son Dr. Jalal Alamgir, and the Biponi Polash by the Gulbahar Himagar[23] Ltd., a private limited company.

"Are you sure? How can you say so?" Advocate Haider wanted to be dauntingly clear.

"I am sure. I scrutinized the land records and gathered information locally," the witness answered candidly. Smiling with satisfaction, Advocate Haider said he had no more questions to ask of the Prosecution Witness.

Testimonies of these three Prosecution Witnesses in essence made a number of facts clear. First, their scrutiny and verification of various installations in reference were perfunctory and not rigorous and therefore, their reported findings on their costs or values were way off the limits of credibility. Second, except one, none of them verified the ownership of these buildings; on the

[23] A commercial cold storage facility, usually for potatoes, filling the purpose of the "root cellar" once common in more temperate climates.

contrary, their combined testimony revealed that buildings at my village home were common and un-demarcated ancestral properties; the Sultana Filling Station was owned by my son Dr. Jalal Alamgir and the under-construction set of shops lumped as the Biponi Polash was owned by the Gulbahar Himagar Ltd., a private limited company. In essence, there was nothing incriminating against me in their testimonies. Unfortunately, the Special Judge was not disposed towards taking these testimonies at their face value and arriving at a dispassionate conclusion. His attitude was not only naive; it was totally injudicious and blatantly biased.

On the same day around 11:30 in the morning, Public Prosecutor Mizanur Rahman produced the Executive Engineer, PWD, Comilla to depose about a house in Comilla Housing Estate alleged to be under my ownership. The witness deposed that at the request of the ACC's Investigation Officer Jiban Krishna, on May 3, 2007, he had assessed the value/cost of a one-storied house on Plot 8, block – N of Comilla Housing Estate at Tk. 20 lac 2 thousand and 9 hundred in accordance with the PWD's (Public Works Department) schedule of rates as were prevalent in 1992.

"Did you ascertain the ownership of the plot or of the house?" Advocate Haider asked the witness in cross-examination.

"No, I did not."

"Do you know that a branch of the Agrani Bank is located in that house?"

"Yes, I know," pat came the reply.

"Did you ascertain whether the Agrani Bank funded its construction by loan and payment of rent in advance?"

"No, I did not," the witness answered after a considerable pause.

"Did you ask anyone working in that branch of the Agrani Bank as to how the construction of the house was funded?"

"No."

"Did you examine the lease deed of the house given on rent to the Agrani Bank?"

"No, I did not."

He admitted that he did not examine the site plan, architectural and structural designs and electrical and plumbing blueprints at the time of assessment of the value/cost of the house and he could not say what type of iron rods, etc. were used in its construction. Then in cross-examination by Advocate Syed Rezaur Rahman, he said that he did not know that Joy Alamgir, the accused's second son was the owner of the house.

"Do you know then who owned the house or the plot?" asked the Advocate with a sardonic smile.

"No, I don't."

"Was the house owned by Dr. Alamgir, Joy Alamgir's father?"

"I do not know," answered the witness.

"Do you know or can you tell us the plot number on which the house was located?"

"No, I cannot. I did not enquire and find that out," the witness answered quite candidly.

He admitted that the house was built in 1986-87 while he assessed its cost in prices of 1992. He also admitted that schedules of rates of construction of various government departments like the LGED, the Facilities Department and the Water Development Board were different and he had not taken these differences with the rates of the PWD (Public Works Department) into consideration while assessing the cost of the building. He said that he knew that the government published cost indexes of construction in its Statistical Year Book, but these indexes were not used by him in arriving at the cost estimate of the house in reference. Nothing substantial or different was deposed by the next Prosecution Witness Helal Ahmed, an Assistant Engineer who worked under the Executive Engineer in the same division.

Factually, three points became evident in these depositions about the house at Comilla allegedly owned by me. First, the measurement of cost was perfunctory and overly approximated and irrelevant and inapplicable for the time of construction of the house. In accordance with the relevant law, valuation of a house was always done at cost at the time of its construction. Second, none of the witnesses verified the ownership of the house, which was actually of the accused's son who was a separate income taxpayer working and living in the U.S.A. and on whom the ACC did not serve any notice to give a statement of assets. And third, none of the witnesses knew or cared to find out how the house was funded or to what extent the Agrani Bank funded its construction to locate its branch there.

Obviously before funding, the Agrani Bank assessed its total estimated cost on the basis of prevalent market rates of materials and labor and took the land and the building under its mortgage. And nobody cared to reconcile the cost of construction in accordance with the official Construction Cost Indexes published annually by the government and the estimate based on the PWD's schedule of construction rates for a recent year, which were indicative rather than actual, and that the actual cost of contracts for construction given by the PWD was, more often than not, either less or more than the rates shown in the schedule. As a summing up, no incriminating evidence against me as the accused could be posited by these witnesses. The Special Judge, however, in silence and unruffled appearance, did not seem to have been affected by these testimonies in his thought or consideration. To me, he appeared to have not changed at all from the course charted for him by those in power. The concept of ethical nicety in recording facts, let alone acting on them as a judge, was unknown to him.

(6)

During the break for lunch, though not formally allowed to talk or consult with my brother, wife and lawyers, I pushed the barrier nearer to them. My brother told me he had a long discussion with Barrister Rafiqul Huq about taking the case to the High Court for a stay on procedural grounds and misjoinder of charges. Barrister Rafiq agreed that it was a very good case for placing before the High Court, especially in the division bench presided over by Justice Shah Abu Naim Mominur Rahman, but he was afraid the moment it would be taken up for hearing, the Chief Justice, acting at the beck and call of those in power, would withdraw the bench's writ jurisdiction or even if he did not do so, would stall the decision in the Appellate Division thereafter. He suggested that until significant public opinion arose against the submissive conduct of the judges and the persecution of innocent people under the popular cover of combating corruption, we should wait.

My wife Sitara told me she was being followed and interrogated quite frequently over mobile phone by Major Kamruzzaman of the Task Force. I asked her to get ready to leave the country. I told her that despite staying behind the bars, I would be able to make the arrangements for her leaving through my friends and contacts and that she should keep it to herself. In the meanwhile, she should remain in touch with our good old friend Forrest Cookson to make sure her visa status was alright. Amidst the people surrounding us, tears welled up in Sitara's eyes, the emotion behind which only I could realize. Almost driven to the adjoining cage (where the accused like us were consigned when the Special Judge was out), I ate a bite of lunch given by Pankaj Debnath and supplemented by two sandwiches packed by Sitara. Pankaj's sister had brought his lunch as his wife with her newborn baby had by that time left the country for which Pankaj fought three decades back. "Are his captors the guileless beneficiaries of superior breeding and inheritors of commendable virtues?" I wondered.

Around 3:00 in the afternoon, the Prosecution brought in the Executive Engineer, PWD, Sher-e-Bangla Nagar and one of his associates of the same division, to depose on the cost of my house at Banani Model Town, Dhaka. Curiously enough, Banani Model Town was within the jurisdiction of Executive Engineer, PWD, Gulshan who was not brought in probably because he was not considered as pliable as the former. This pliable one deposed that he estimated the cost/value of my house as directed; he was assisted by a team consisting of Sub-divisional Engineer Mohammed Nasim, Sub-assistant Engineers Mohammed Mostafa and Mafizul Islam and Work Assistants Makbul Hossain and Mohammed Abdul Khaleq. He measured the house on site on April 8 and submitted his report on April 25. His report consisted of two parts, civil and electrical, the sum total of which figured at Tk. 86 lacs 28 thousand and 562 as the cost of my house in accordance with the PWD's schedule of rates. He said he was informed of the time of construction of the house by my brother Dr. Jahangir.

Advocate Haider started with the cross-examination of the Executive Engineer, Sher-e-Bangla Nagar.

"Do you as the Executive Engineer, PWD Sher-e-Bangla Nagar, have jurisdiction over Banani area where Dr. Alamgir's house is located," asked Advocate Haider.

"No."

"Then how come you went to measure and value his house in Banani?"

"I was selected to do so. I was asked by the Leader of the Task Force to measure and value the building," the Executive Engineer gave out the reason without an outraged sense of right and wrong.

He said he did not know per square foot cost of construction of the Sangshad Bhaban or Suhrawardy Hospital located in his area of jurisdiction. He admitted that various government departments had various schedules of costs of construction; he did not know whether the government statistically compiled differing costs of construction of buildings, nor did he ever see the Statistical Year Book containing Cost of Construction (Building) Indexes published by the government. He stated somewhat shamelessly that he and his associates did not apply the official cost of construction indexes compiled and published by the government through the Bureau of Statistics. He knew that the House Building Finance Corporation, financing construction of buildings carefully, scrutinized cost estimates thereof. He admitted with a slight ragged quickness of breath that he did not sign every page of his report; the report did not mention of any measurement book, while the grand total of cost was mentioned in the report only in figures and not in words, leaving space and scope for manipulation.

"For how long were you present at the site for measuring and assessing the cost of the building?" Advocate Haider asked him.

"For about 30 to 40 minutes," answered the witness.

"Can one measure and value a 4-storied building with each story of about 1,450 sq. ft. in area and built in two stages, ten years apart in 30 to 40 minutes?" Advocate Haider wanted to know.

"Actual measurement and valuation in such a short time is difficult to make," the witness replied with tongue smacking somewhat sour.

He admitted that he did not mention in his statement given to the investigation officer that he had been present at the site and that he gave his statement to the investigation officer some days after he had submitted the report. He admitted that he did not examine the earthwork and wind tolerance of the building and that he could not say who composed the report on cost or valuation in the computer.

The Sub-divisional Engineer in his deposition stated that he had prepared the report on cost/value of my house in Banani on instructions from his Executive Engineer. He admitted that the actual year of construction was not available to him; at the same time, he punctuated his statement by saying that Dr. Jahangir, the accused's brother by a letter written on April 19, 2007, informed him that the house was constructed in two stages, in 1981-82 and 1991-92. He said that they had estimated costs according to their own schedule of rates of construction. In cross-examination by Advocate Haider, he admitted with a visible queasiness that he could not obtain the plan of the house as approved by RAJUK (*i.e.* Capital Development Authority) nor could he obtain the time of its construction from them, *i.e.*, RAJUK.

"Did you, in your estimation of cost, take into account the difference in labor cost 1981-82 when the first two floors of the house were built and the current labor cost on which your estimate is based?" asked Advocate Haider.

"No, I did not."

"Did you ascertain specifications of iron rods and other building materials used in constructing this building?"

"No," came the hesitant answer.

"Did you, in your report on cost or value of the building as you estimated, take into account increase in cost of sand, cement and other building materials over years since the time of actual construction?"

"No, I did not," answered the witness, flickering his eyes.

Then the witness admitted that in the schedule of rates (of the PWD that he used) costs of overhead, project preparation, income tax and vat were not included.

In the cross-examination emphasis should have been given on assessment of the cost of the building in 1981-82 and 1991-92 by the Income Tax Department in accordance with the PWD's schedule of rates. If costs at that time were accepted, as indeed these were by the Income Tax Department, and taxes were paid accordingly, these could not now be reopened to perfunctory and mandated assessment by the personnel of a division of the PWD having no jurisdiction over the area in which my house was located. In this context, I wanted to cross-examine the Prosecution Witnesses myself and sought permission of the Special Judge to do so. Despite no bar to do so in law, he, for reasons best known to him, said no. But before saying no, he exchanged meaningful glances unabashedly with Major Kamruzzaman sitting by the side of the Public Prosecutor. I realized how effective the remote control of the Leader of the Task Force was over the Special Judge. The Special Judge evidently was going through the motions of a trial, which in my case was actually conducted by the Major from behind.

The next day on June 18, the Prosecution produced Mohammed Mostafa, Sub-Assistant Engineer, PWD, Sher-e-Bangla Nagar, as their witness. He deposed that as per information given by my brother Dr. Jahangir, the first two floors of my house were constructed in 1981-82 and the second two floors in 1990-91. He stated that from the schedule of the PWD's current rates for construction cost, they deducted 1% for every year till they reached back years of actual construction to arrive at the cost of the house. This meant the rate of inflation between 1981 and 1992 and then between 1992 and 2006 was just 1% a year which was unrealistically far below the rates of inflation as computed by the government itself. As per the procedure they followed, the cost of the house as a whole figured at Tk. 86 lacs, 28 thousand 562. Under cross-examination by Advocate Haider, he admitted that Banani area where my house was located was within the jurisdiction of Gulshan division of the PWD, not Sher-e-Bangla Nagar where the witness worked.

"Why, despite your work area being different from the work area where Dr. Alamgir's house was located, you were assigned to measure and value his house?" asked Advocate Haider.

"I do not know . . . I was selected by higher ups." the witness attempted at an answer.

He said he did not have a quantity surveyor with him when he assessed the cost of the house. He admitted that a contractor might construct an establishment or house at a cost less than the cost given in the schedule of rates approved or used by the PWD. He stated that his report on cost of my house did not take into account the rate of inflation between 1981 and 2006. He admitted that it took seventeen days for him and his associates to prepare the report on my house.

After Mohammed Mostafa, Sub-divisional Engineer (Sher-e-Bangla Nagar) Mahbubul Haq Chowdhury was produced by the Prosecution as a witness. He deposed that he had measured my house at the request of the Deputy Director, ACC. He said that he prepared the report on the cost/value of electrical installations of the house. Under cross-examination of Advocate Haider, he stated that the house was 5-storied, the 5th story being built in part. Here he differed with his superiors and associates who had described the house as having four stories. He admitted that he did not know what was stored on the 5th story of the house, could not remember the types of electrical installations on the other stories, could not state or specify how many electrical outlets there were in the house or in each story of the house.

"Can you describe the type of electrical materials, jigs and fixtures used in the house?" asked Advocate Haider.

"No."

"At what prices, current or at prices of 1981-82 and 1991-92 did you value the electrical installations of the house."

"I used current prices; I did not know anything about prices of the times when the house was built," replied the witness, shocking the Prosecution.

He could not state how many kilowatt loads were needed for the house or how many circuit breakers were installed there. After him Nurul Alam Sarker, Sub-assistant Engineer, PWD, Sher-e-Bangla Nagar, deposed that he was a member of the measurement team. My lawyers declined to cross-examine him.

From the deposition of these witnesses drawn from the PWD, Sher-e-Bangla Nagar, it became evident that:

(1) They were selected from outside the PWD's work division in which my house was located, as they were considered pliable in making depositions against me in so far as valuation of my house in Banani was concerned;

(2) They measured the house perfunctorily, differing in terms of number of stories of the house even and mostly at current prices without any reference to measurement and valuation done by the income tax authority at the time the house was constructed; they did not take into account change in Construction Cost Index compiled and published by the government either;

(3) They did not examine the structural, electrical and plumbing blueprints of the house, nor did they verify the type and quantities of materials used in its construction making their exercise in valuation unrealistic and irrelevant; and

(4) There were substantial inconsistencies and material contradictions in their process of measurement and valuation as deposed by them.

All these made their evidence bereft of credibility and did not leave room for incrimination of me in respect to either concealment of assets or their disproportionateness to my known or legitimate income. In the notice asking me to furnish statement of my assets, I was asked to describe and not to give their value or cost (of assets). And in my asset statement furnished on February 20, 2006, I had given description of the house amongst other assets as wanted, mentioning costs as far as I remembered, as recorded in my income tax returns for the relevant years. The Special Judge, mandated as he seemed to have been, ignored all these loopholes and inconsistencies in their testimonies. As a matter of fact, as I observed from the dock, he did not bother to note these depositions and mark their built-in inconsistencies and contradictions. It was, to me, not only a case of judicial neglect, arrogance and dishonesty but also an illiteracy of the form and intent of the appropriate judicial procedure.

(7)

After Sub-divisional Engineer Nurul Alam Sarker, the Prosecution produced Abdul Majid, Zila Registrar, Chandpur, as their witness. He deposed that at the request of Investigation Officer Jiban Krishna, he had furnished a three-page report on properties belonging to me, my wife Sitara Alamgir and sons Jalal Alamgir and Joy Alamgir for the last 12 years. He said that particulars of these (landed) properties were obtained from Kachua Subregistry and he did not have any information in respect of property held by us in any other subregistry. Under cross-examination by Advocate Haider, he stated that his report did not give classification of these lands and properties, nor did it mention about lands obtained on exchange and given as donations to various schools and the Institute of Integrated Rural Development, a non-government organization.

After him Sheikh Mohammed Anwarul Haq, Sub-Registrar, Kachua subdistrict was brought in to depose for the Prosecution. He stated that he collected particulars of our landed properties in Kachua and sent them to the District Registrar for preparing his report. He stated that in his report, he had mentioned about ten or twelve documents pertaining to these properties. In cross-examination by Advocate Haider, he admitted that the report sent to the District Registrar by him was not written by him and the report did not contain particulars of our lands that were donated to various educational and other institutions. Nothing incriminating against me or my family or contradicting commonality of these properties as stated in my asset statement came out in the evidence of these two Prosecution Witnesses.

The court's working hour on June 18 ended with the Subregistrar's deposition. The Special Judge while leaving his high chair-borne judicial position reluctantly allowed me to sit and consult with my brother Dr. Jahangir, other relations and the lawyers. Sitara was not coming to the court since the day I forbade her from doing so, on grounds of possible harassment by Major Kamruzamman. My brother told me that on the previous day, the Major followed his car after the court hours down to a hospital where he had gone to see a patient-friend. When he left the car, the Major pounced upon his innocent driver and found out from him the new address where Sitara was staying without letting others know. As reported by the driver, Major Kamruzamman muttered to himself in vengeance that he would find her out and make her depose against me or make me sign some papers against Sheikh Hasina. I became concerned and asked my brother to make her go elsewhere and keep her under his close supervision. As the Prosecution did not give us the names of witnesses they would produce the next day, there was hardly anything to consult with the lawyers. Giving time to consult with lawyers after depositions of the witnesses was nothing but a mockery of a judicial process even beyond applying narrow rules and arcane procedures pursued by the Special Judge. Thirty minutes over, I was led into the adjacent lockup for prisoners. There I found Mahmud Hasan cent lockup for prisoners. There I found Mahmud Hasan Tuku, State Minister for Power in Khaleda Zia's government, his wife and young daughter sitting with gloomy faces. I asked them how they were being treated by their Special Judge and how was the process of trial they were facing. To my dismay, I found their brush with the made-up law and the process of remote-controlled justice no better than what I was facing.

Hours later, the prison van, along with other unfortunate prisoners facing trials in the Special Courts set up in the Sangshad Bhaban, took us back to the Kashimpur Jail. Climbing up the stairs, I found a dilapidated plastic chair on the verandah in front of my cell. With raw emotion and mental tiredness, I slumped on the chair, looked at the flower plants on the sill of the iron grills heaving in the gentle and soothing air and trying to pop up defeating all sorts of adversities from the half-broken water bottles and used earthen jars for yogurt on which I had planted them. Looking out through the iron grills, I recalled Robert Frost: "But I have promises to keep,/And miles to go before I sleep." That reinforced my will to fight the evil and the injustice with dignity.

Evening meal over, I sat over some predated newspapers that I brought with me unseen by the jail guards. It was quite difficult to get newspapers of our choice within the jail. As "division" prisoners, we were entitled to receive two dailies each, but their choice was not ours. The jail officers cleared the worst type of dailies on the pretext that those were within the list approved by the government. That was why whenever I could find an avenue or an opportunity, I used to bring dailies, specially the *Janakantha* and the *Daily Star* from outside, evoking images of free thinking and opinion. That night I winced at two items of statements and comments. As the report had it, Dr. Kamal Hossain, known as an eminent jurist of the country, supported the steps taken by the government to punish, in his words, corrupt politicians who had already been arrested. I wondered how a person trained in law could knowingly ascribe people arrested as corrupt persons before they were proved to be so through a fair and impartial process of trial. To me it appeared as a tenuous backdoor attempt to climb up the ladder of leadership, like what the world witnessed in Vichy France during the Second World War.

Similar condemnation was found in comments of one Professor Abdullah Dewan of Eastern Michigan University, USA, congratulating the military-led government of Bangladesh for arresting corrupt politicians. He tried to capture the days by saying that all politicians of Bangladesh, past and present, were corrupt; none of them contributed anything for the development of the country. During the days of political government about nine months back in the very same newspaper, I had found the Professor proclaiming support for freedom and people's rights with an overtone of support for the Awami League. It was painful for me to observe a Professor prone to raw opportunism unbecoming of his profession. It was all the more painful to see the Professor deviating from the principle of dispassionate analysis before writing something; a Professor by training could not twist confusion to serve his selfish purpose or support his own predilection.

I recalled how eager Dr. Kamal Hossain had been to sit by the side of the Awami League President Sheikh Hasina in public meetings and crying hoarse for free and fair election and democracy before the military-led government took over. I was not surprised at his comments. Dispassionate adherence to principles was never a strong point with him. I recalled how unabashedly, by using friendship of his brother-in-law Amanullah, then Manager of the Commerce Bank in Dhaka, with General Mitha of Pakistan Occupation Army, in late March 1971, he eased into a convenient and cozy surrender and restful detention in West Pakistan far away from the armed struggle for independence of Bangladesh. At the time Bangabandhu was murdered in 1975, Dr. Kamal as his Foreign Minister was in London but could not be persuaded to come up with a simple statement condemning the killing. It was more than a morsel of proof of the low level of integrity as was expected of a person, who aspired to be the Prime Minister of the country through military machination and by promising to serve as their celebrated shoeshine person.

(8)

On June 19, a steno-typist of the ACC was examined by the Prosecution. He testified about the preparation of the seizure list of papers consisting of three pages. Under cross-examination by Advocate Syed Rezaur Rahman, he admitted that the seizure list attested by him then and now produced before the court seemed to be a carbon copy. Every day the Special Judge usually wanted to hasten the proceedings on the plea that he had to complete the trial within days fixed by the law. But on this day he did not. In whispered consultation with the Public Prosecutor; he did not allow examination of any other witness after the steno-typist. He left the court, as we learnt through the grapevine of his office, for a meeting convened by the Law Advisor Barrister Moinul Hossain in the Ministry of Law.

As the rumor had it, the meeting was attended by the Chairman, ACC, other Special Judges and also the Law Secretary. It was painfully surprising to all of us, an affliction of still quietness. Only a few days ago, the Law Advisor had announced and boasted of complete separation of the judiciary from the executive and its independence to ensure unfettered justice in this country. As it turned out to us, under his partisanship and scheme, the judiciary became separate but not really independent of those in power. The judiciary still had a long way to go to walk on a firm stretch of dispassionateness outside the diktat of raw power.

In the courtroom left by the Special Judge, Mafiz, Manager of our family business, told me that in the morning Major Kamruzzaman had come to our house in Banani and demanded that Sitara should be present before him in 30 minutes. In the face of his irksome shouting laced with obscenities, Mafiz told him that he did not know her whereabouts and could not bring her to his presence then but would try to reach her the message. The Major threatened that if Sitara did not see him immediately he would make the ACC issue a notice on her demanding statement of her assets in accordance with Section 26 of the ACC Act and then prosecute her under Section 27 of the same Act for having assets disproportionate to her income. In their accounting, the law could be bent any way depending on who was involved and who was required to be sized down. I asked Mafiz to tell Sitara not to see Major Kamruzzaman anywhere anytime. I asked him instead to send her a message to see me at the jail gate at Kashimpur late that afternoon without letting others know. I wanted her to take an unknown or hired transport to dodge the Major and his cohorts on her way to Kashimpur and back and asked Mafiz to make arrangements that way.

Accordingly she managed to see me at the Kashimpur Jail around 5:00 in the afternoon, almost at the time of lockup of all inmates and closure of the main gate. She told me, true to his words, Major Kamruzzaman made the ACC issue a notice on her to furnish a statement of her assets in seven days from that day. She was in tears and I was sorry that my dash into politics landed her into this difficulty and disgrace. My head spun with the thought of all things that should have been different. Hurriedly, I told her that she should prepare her asset statement as per a format that I would write in the night and reach her next day. While filling in the form, she should give as much detail as possible about her movable and immovable assets. For this, she should obtain her income tax records from our income tax advisor.

I told her, since there was no possibility of getting justice under this regime and Major Kamruzzaman and his cohorts would arrest her and she would not be posted on bail as per the law of emergency period, she should leave the country immediately after furnishing her asset statement. I told her to make three reservations by air from three different travel agents for three different destinations, one for Bangkok, one for Singapore and another for Calcutta on and after the day of her submission of asset statement. Included in the passenger manifest of the relevant airline, it was likely her name would be known to the immigration personnel at the Dhaka Airport. Following the service of the ACC's notice on her, the regime would likely enter her name in the restriction list of the computer of the immigration department, if they had not already done so after I had been arrested. She should not make the first and the second flight as per reservations made. When they would see that despite reservations she did not make the slated flights, they would lower their vigil and then she would make her choice of the actual flight.

I told her in addition, I would make reservation for and get her a ticket through a diplomat friend of mine from his embassy's travel agent to Boston where our children stayed on the day following submission of her asset statement to the ACC. She should carry only a handbag and be attired in ordinary dress and wait in a restaurant in Pallabi that we knew, about 1 hour before the scheduled departure of the flight. My friend, after getting her passport through the immigration using his diplomatic clout, would give her a ring over a mobile phone so that she could arrive at a given point at the entrance of the airport to be escorted in a rush to the plane through the rather loosely guarded VIP channel ten or so minutes before the take-off.

Sitara hesitated, then on my insistence agreed to act and leave according to the plan that was drawn up. She was in tears; I was on the verge. I told her, reason should take precedence over emotion and there was no sense in getting both of us locked up in jail on drummed-up charges over here. That way we would be helping the very enemy we wanted to defeat. I stood up and whispered "I love you with all my heart, every drop of my blood." I told her *Inshallah*[24] we would meet soon and embraced her in the little corner of the jail gate. "I love you and I will be loving you," she said in a lingering embrace. With tears in eyes that had shone like solace and tranquility of the bird's nest to me in course of 38

[24] "God willing."

years of our married life, she took leave of me a minute before the main gate of the jail was locked up and I was taken back to my cell. That night I prayed to Allah for a long time for the safety of my wife and our two sons.

On June 20, the prison van, rattling and emitting choking smoke as usual, took me to the Special Court around 9:30 in the morning. On the way I vomited and felt feverish, but more than anything else, I was worried about Sitara and the plan that I drew up for her escape into freedom. Despite enough gripes to contend with, I had sent a message the night before to my diplomat friend to see me in the court next day. Salman helped me to send the message and to make the plan foolproof, as far as we could from our end. Earlier he had sent his wife out on the same consideration and more or less in the same way. The friend met me in the court, confirmed the arrangements I made with Sitara and I gave him the contact number and the code to be used for identification while calling her to come to the airport.

That morning, the Prosecution first produced Tofazzal Hossain, Assistant Inspector, ACC as their witness. He deposed that on May 12, 2007, he had seized from the Sultana Filling Station two papers: first, a *challan* (purchase memo or invoice) for three motorcycles and second, a receipt for compensation paid to me for land acquired by the government (for Kachua Bypass Road). Under cross-examination by Advocate Syed Rezaur Rahman, the witness admitted in broad details that three motorcycles were not registered in anybody's name and one could not be sure as to who bought these cycles just by seeing the purchase memo. He stated candidly that seeing just the purchase memo one could not say who were owners of these cycles. He stated that receipt for compensation for land seized by him was a photocopy without anybody's signature. The land for which compensation was received was located to the east of the land on which the Sultana Filling Station was built up by my son on the basis of gift of the same to him by me. Much before the accusation was brought up against me, the portion of the land for which compensation was received had become a part of the Kachua Bypass Road, *i.e.*, land acquired by the government. The receipt of compensation for this did not in any way incriminate me with the ownership of the Sultana Filling Station. Its evidentiary value was zero.

"Whose land is it now for which compensation has been paid by the government?" asked Advocate Syed Rezaur Rahman.

"The government's," answered the witness.

"If the ownership of the land is of the government at this time, can you, or one in authority, ascribe ownership of the same to Dr. Alamgir?"

"No."

"Then what do you prove or assert by producing this receipt for compensation for land acquired for road?"

"I, no, we do not or cannot prove anything incriminating Dr. Alamgir in this regard." The witness was quite candid in his admission avoiding bare-faced falsity expected from him by the Prosecution.

From his testimony, it was not proved that three motorcycles in question were mine; the photocopy of receipt for compensation of land by the roadside acquired and adjacent to the Filling Station by the government, as candidly admitted by the witness, did not prove in any way that the land on which the filling station was located was under my ownership at that time. I had earlier gifted the land on which the filling station was located to my son following the Islamic principle of *heba*.[25]

The next Prosecution Witness produced was Khurshid Anwar, District Intelligence Officer (Police), Comilla. He deposed that on May 12, 2007, he witnessed that Syed Iqbal Hossain, Deputy Director, ACC, Dhaka seized 1 *challan*[26] showing purchase of one motorcycle in my name and another challan showing two motorcycles purchased in the name of Dr. Jalal Alamgir and one paper of Land Acquisition Branch of the Office of the Deputy Commissioner, Chandpur, relating to acquisition of land adjacent to the Sultana Filling Station for building the Kachua Bypass Road. Under cross-examination by Advocate Rezaur Rahman, he admitted that he did not remember when he had signed the seizure list as a witness; Syed Iqbal Hossain did not sign the same in his presence either.

"Does a *challan* or invoice of one or two motorcycles by itself prove that payment of prices was made for the purchase?" asked Advocate Syed Rezaur Rahman.

"No," answered the witness.

"Did you observe on the *challan* seized by the Deputy Director, ACC, any seal or signature of the seller stamping or stating or in any other way acknowledging receipt of payment of prices of the motorcycles?" queried the Advocate, seeking clarification.

---

[25] Deed conveying a gift according to Islamic custom.

[26] Invoice.

"No, I did not see or observe any such stamp or sign of acknowledgement of receipt of prices," the witness clarified candidly.

The deposition as a whole, as it thus turned out, was imprecise and did not prove the procedure of seizure of papers as correct and legally noticeable and, more important, did not prove anything in terms of actual ownership of land on which the Sultana Filling Station was located and of three motorcycles alleged by the Prosecution as my assets.

Then Masudur Rahman, Manager, the Sultana Filling Station, was produced as a witness by the Prosecution. He testified that Dr. Jalal Alamgir (my son aged 35) was the owner of the Sultana Filling Station. He said that all transactions of the filling station were on cash basis. In cross-examination by Advocate Haider later, he said that all sanction and approval letters pertaining to the filling station from the relevant authorities were in the name of Dr. Jalal Alamgir. He also said that Dr. Jalal Alamgir had asked him to borrow from his father in case he faced some difficulty or had to meet unforeseen needs in operating the filling station and at times he did borrow accordingly. After Masudur Rahman, Morshedul Islam, an Upper-division Assistant of the Special Branch (Police), Chandpur, was brought in to identify some items in the seizure list. My lawyers declined to cross-examine him. Summed up, these two witnesses did not say anything incriminating against me for concealing and holding assets disproportionate to my known and legitimate income in any way.

(9)

Then the Prosecution brought in Haren Mitra, Manager, Bangladesh Krishi Bank, Gulbahar. He stated that in two accounts, one savings and the other current, I had on May 13, 2007, Tk. 62,169/ and Tk. 26,409/ respectively as balances. Under cross-examination by Advocate Haider, he stated that I was the first one to open an account in his bank (when it set up its branch in my village Gulbahar). He admitted that there were over-writings and corrections in bank statements that he had submitted to the Investigation Officer and that he did not sign every page of the statement. Importantly, in reference to the Prosecution's expectation that I would be able to state the exact amount of balance in my bank accounts on the day I furnished my asset statement, Advocate Haider asked him.

"What is the balance in your personal account in the Krishi Bank, Gulbahar today?"

"I cannot say exactly," the witness answered.

"Did Dr. Alamgir used to go to your branch for transactions, for depositing and withdrawing money?"

"No. His deposits and withdrawals were usually done by his caretaker of the village home." Haren Mitra answered immediately.

"Did you send him statement of his accounts quarterly or half-yearly, and did he reconcile these statements frequently and regularly?" asked Syed Rezaur Rahman.

"No. I never sent him statement of his accounts and he never raised any question of reconcilement either," answered the witness.

After the cross-examination, the Special Judge made him wait for about two hours for signing the depositions made by him and recorded by the former. While leaving, Haren Mitra raised his right hand in a silent *salaam*[27] to me. Seemingly he was perturbed finding me on the dock and in a distress of conspiracy whose depths he would never know.

The last Prosecution Witness of the day was Kamal, Manager, the Gulbahar Himagar Ltd., a private limited company operating a cold store owned by our family members with some shares apportioned to me also. He deposed that the under-construction shops lumped as the Biponi Polash were located on lands of the Himagar. He stated that on the blueprint for these shops submitted to the Kachua Pourashava (*i.e.* municipality) for obtaining the local body's approval, under the horizontal column titled owner's name, "Dr. Muhiuddin Khan Alamgir *for* Gulbahar Himagar" was mentioned. On cross-examination by Advocate Haider, he stated that he had been serving as the Manager of the Himagar for about last ten years; it was owned by four brothers and other family members; it had a memorandum and articles of association as a private limited company set up and registered under law. He admitted categorically that the Biponi Polash was the property of the Himagar and he had all papers and vouchers relating to its construction as such.

"Did the Investigation Officer see and examine these papers and vouchers kept with you?" asked Advocate Syed Rezaur Rahman.

"No," the Manager answered.

"Did the Investigation Officer examine the records of land on which these shops were located?"

"No," the Manager answered again.

---

[27] "Peace be with you."

The deposition made by Manager Kamal made it clear beyond all reasonable doubt that the Biponi Polash, as falsely alleged by the Prosecution, was not my personal property or asset. The Special Judge, as I looked at him when the deposition was being made, remained unmoved by the truth that was revealed to him. I doubted whether he made a note of Kamal's deposition or its implications. I noticed Major Kamruzzaman, the Leader of the Task Force formed to punish me, right or wrong, sitting stubborn and tired by the side by the Public Prosecutor Mizanur Rahman as usual. He looked somewhat grim and perturbed by the deposition made by the witness.

It was 5:30 in the afternoon when the Special Judge left for the day. Before he left, in his owlish style, at the request of my lawyer Syed Rezaur Rahman, he allowed me 20 minutes to talk to my lawyers and relations. Sitara, as arranged, had not come that day. She, however, did not forget to send me sandwiches that I liked. I downed those delicious sandwiches with a stale cup of tea brought from the makeshift canteen set up outside in the north-eastern corner of the hall by the side of the courtroom. The owner of the tea bar would not accept money for the tea given to me. I could not recollect whether we were known to each other. I looked at both Advocates Rahman and Haider.

"How did it go?" I asked them.

"We could establish the truth," said Rahman.

"Truth has been established but I doubt whether the Judge will be truthful," observed Advocate Haider rather dryly. My brother, almost always soft-spoken, did not say anything. I passed some notes for Sitara to him asking her not to falter on preparation for leaving. At that moment, Nilufar, my sister, passed her mobile phone to me telling that Sitara was on the line. Hardly had I said hello when at the instigation of Major Kamruzzaman standing outside the courtroom and keenly observing us, a police sentry shouted and took off the phone. He said a prisoner could not speak on the mobile. I could not recall any such prohibitory provision in the Jail Code and the Criminal Procedure Code. I realized a prisoner was supposed to suffer and be punished before conviction at the altar of personal ambition of a few armed men, raising heads over other faces multiplied across the landscape in desperation and hunger and yet yearning for freedom; if I burned, my tears would never put it out.

"Keep your cool," I said smilingly to the police sentry. And then I added, "Your worries may soon be over; the whole country is fast becoming a prison and you may end up as my jail mate."

He looked bewildered at me and then led me to the adjoining prison cell away from my lawyers and relations. I found Mir Nasir, a former State Minister in Khaleda Zia's government and his young Barrister son Helal sitting on two half-broken chairs in the prison cell. Both of them were prisoners and facing trial on similar charges like me. Nasir was over 50 and wore a sullen and despaired look. He embraced me and wept. I tried to console him, encouraged his son Helal not to lose courage and surrender to the forces of evil, bent upon choking merit and the youthful resources of the land. A few evil men could not erase decades of evolution of an independent society, I assured him. Helal was just married before he was arrested along with his father. About what his father did, I almost never cared to know. But I was certain Helal was innocent. He had an altercation with a man in power, which was the cause for his incarceration. At sundown, we all prayed. Prayer I found was a wonderful solace against suffering and a cornucopia of never-dying hope to overcome brute injustice that we faced in a country almost conquered by its own armed forces and their cronies in proxy in front.

With loadshedding of power all around, it was quite dark by the time I journeyed back to the prison in the rattling and smoke-emitting prison van. At the enclosure of the "division" prison building, I was greeted by Mufti Shahidul Islam, a member of the previous Parliament and an overly religious man who, as it seemed, had been waiting for me. Mufti Shahidul Islam had voluntarily taken charge of our kitchen overseeing marketing, cleaning, cooking and serving food for all political prisoners incarcerated in the Kashimpur Jail. In addition, he led us in prayer five times a day whenever he was present in the division building, *i.e.*, whenever he had not gone to the court. A pious, humble man with dedication to the poor, he faced similar drummed-up charges of concealment of assets and holding them in quantities disproportionate to his known income. He was gentle, amiable, always eager and willing to help others. I felt sorry that such an amiable and religious gentleman should face such an ignominious charge. His fault was the same as mine. We did not like usurpation of State power by non-representative forces under any circumstances. We opposed sacrifice of conscience to expediency and greed.

Everybody around the improvised dining table asked me how did it go in the court that day. I narrated the depositions and said if there was an iota of justice in the process they would not be able to punish me. Lotus-Kamal did not agree.

"Justice is manufacturable now in this country," he said.

"It will soon be a purchasable good saleable to the highest bidder," he added after a moment.

With experience gained in these months, it seemed others around did not find much of a ground to contradict him.

Sleep being elusive, I lay down with a novel on Churchill titled *Never Surrender*. The author was Michael Dobbs. It was sent by Sitara to keep up my spirits to win over the odds, to overcome the impediments and obstacles on the way, and to strengthen our common belief that confidence was the secret to people's success. The novel pictured Churchill in his fight for freedom in years before and during the Second World War, his determination mingled with his emotion to fight even on the beaches and never to surrender to the enemy. I might have felt confidence, for in the morning when I awoke, I found Churchill halfway through and still open on my chest. I slept a precious late sleep, despite its earlier elusiveness in the evil-emblazoned darkness.

(10)

A worrisome surprise awaited me on the next morning, June 24. The Public Prosecutor Mizanur Rahman recalled their star witness Rabiul Hasan Prodhan, Assistant Commissioner, Income Tax, who had earlier deposed for three days on June 6, 7 and 11. This was irregular and an attempt at filling in loose holes in his depositions already made and recorded. My lawyer Syed Rezaur Rahman pointed this out, but the Special Judge took no notice. Prodhan was made to depose that on April 15, 2007 while being examined by Investigation Officer Jiban Krishna, he had submitted a six-page statement summing up my income tax returns submitted since 1981-82. He totaled my income on one side and total assets in the other from 1982 to 2006 without realizing and mentioning that sum-total of assets in 2006 was the end-product of income from 1965 when I started my earning through 2006 when I was arrested by this government and they mistakenly showed that my assets exceeded my income.

In addition, little did he understand or state that (i) total income as stated as per income tax law was exclusive of exemptions made in terms of religious application of income, investment in government security and post office savings banks, pension and gratuity received, receipt from provident fund, interest received from government saving certificates, earnings from literary work, etc. as spelled out in the 6th schedule of the Income Tax Ordinance; (ii) assets were reflective of creation out of these exemptions, also outside the total income defined under income tax law as well as of income earned earlier than 1982, in my case since 1963 when I had started my life's work and (iii) assets shown in income tax records were at cost-value while assets as assessed by the ACC's Investigation Officers were shown mostly in current prices (valuation of house property made by them, for example); (iv) assets as assessed by the Investigation Officers of ACC were inclusive of assets owned commonly, and by my two adult sons and wife who were separate income taxpayers; (v) assets were inclusive of inheritance before my earning began. Therefore, value of assets in a period as assessed by the ACC would reasonably be more than income that I earned in the same period.

My lawyer Syed Rezaur Rahman, with a prodding from me through passing of a note, pointed this out and wanted the entire statement given by the Prosecution Witness for examination in depth by us, but the Special Judge would not listen. Dumbfounded, I whispered to him to formally announce no confidence against the Special Judge, postpone the cross-examination and ask for a change of the trial court. But he advised me against it. The other court would also be under the direction of the Leader of the Task Force and no better in accounting income and asset. In view of the Special Court's moronic and inept treatment of our pleadings, at the stage of appeal in the High Court Division later, we would be able to score favorable procedural and factual points, he whispered back. I let the issue go, with a wounded feeling about justice that one would expect in good accounting as a part of a civilized process of trial.

Another painful surprise awaited me that morning. When I was on the dock, my brother Dr. Jahangir sent me a note that my other advocate Haider Ali who had been cross-examining the Prosecution Witnesses quite well had been appointed Deputy Attorney General of the government yesterday. First, he had been threatened by the ACC and the intelligence agents of the government for representing me in this case. Failing that, the government at the prodding of the ACC had kicked him up into the Attorney General's Office in the Supreme Court so that he could not defend me any longer. My brother said Haider had expressed sorrow leaving me, but becoming Deputy Attorney General was an opportunity of a lifetime for him. I kept mum and maintained my cool. My brother assured me the other Advocate Syed Rezaur Rahman would not leave my side despite bizarre threats he had been receiving from the Leader of the Task Force and his cohorts.

I was not very sure. Though he said so, I could feel elements of delicate pessimism wound down his chest.

Advocate Syed Rezaur Rahman, despite hostile and partisan attitude of the Special Judge and opportunity and time not given to examine in depth the papers produced by the recalled Prosecution Witness Prodhan, took up his cross-examination. Prodhan admitted that on three earlier days when he had deposed as a Prosecution Witness, he had not mentioned anything about what he said and produced today; he had not mentioned about these papers earlier to Investigation Officer Sharmin Ferdousi either. His today's statement contained in these papers had not been included in three volumes of income tax returns that he had earlier submitted to the court. He said that this statement was to the exclusion of information contained in those tax returns and documents submitted earlier. He admitted that today's statement was a carbon copy, with corrections, erasures and over-writings on various pages without his initials and with just figures put in at least 17 places without written corroborative words.

"At whose prodding or orders did you come to produce these papers and the statement today?" an irritated Advocate Syed Rezaur Rahman asked the witness.

"I came as desired by the Public Prosecutor. The Public Prosecutor told me my earlier depositions will be difficult to understand and as a result controversy will arise once too often unless I produce the statement based on these papers," the witness answered, leaving telltale indications of a tutored deposition.

Evidently thus, (i) income and asset shown in the statement purported to be mine were incomparable and not incriminating in terms of either concealment or disproportionateness of assets with known income and (ii) the statement along with the papers on which it was based itself left sufficient room for credibility and authenticity. As I could observe with disdain, the valueless nature of the evidence did not make a noticeable impact on the Special Judge. He was more intent on exchanging glances with his mentor Major Kamruzzaman and the Public Prosecutor than on attempting to separate the grain of truth from the mound of chaff thrown around by the Prosecution.

During the brief lunch break at 2:00 in the afternoon, I was taken to the prison cell on orders of the Special Judge. Despite his arduous efforts at keeping me incommunicado, through a sympathetic police sentry, I received a note from Sitara. She said she was being shadowed by cohorts of Major Kamruzzaman and not receiving cooperation from some people we knew as trustworthy in preparing her asset statement. I sent a note back: come what may, she should get herself ready to leave the country as arranged. I also passed a message to my diplomat friend that she would leave as arranged earlier.

During the break, I met Barrister Nazmul Huda and his wife Barrister Sigma Huda in the prison cell. They were both incarcerated and accused of concealment and holding of assets beyond their known incomes as in the case of others and also for extortion. Being Barristers, I found both of them somewhat confident that the legal framework that still existed in the country would save them from punishment designed for them by the regime. I told them about my experience with the Special Judge and his disdain for simple accounting and subservient conduct. My conversation with the Barrister couple made me apprehensive: justice would not be done under the circumstances at these levels of courts of which kangaroo had became the call-sign; for reaching justice in an appropriate institutional framework, our people would have to take the issues to the streets. For us death was designed by gravediggers who have taken over the guns. And for us death was designed to kill life through creating fear.

In the afternoon, the Prosecution examined Anwar, Manager, the Grameen Bank, Gulbahar. He was the spectacle of a nervous and shoddy person. He deposed that in a saving account in his bank, I had a balance of Tk. 11 thousand as on December 5, 2006. Though irrelevant to the fact-in-issue, he stated that my wife Sitara had Tk. 56 thousand 1 hundred and 38 in a saving account in the same bank. Despite its irrelevancy to the fact-in-issue and consequent inadmissibility as an element of evidence against me in accordance with the Law of Evidence, I observed the Special Judge had noted this. Under cross-examination by Advocate Syed Rezaur Rahman, the witness stated that he knew Sitara was operating an orphanage in the village; that anyone, including the caretaker of the house, could deposit money in Dr. Alamgir's Account; that the witness did not inform me about my balance in the account in writing ever, as I never wanted it that way, and that he did not survey out whether my family was popular or not in the area. Then as an after-thought, he admitted, however, that my family had a good name in the local area.

"Did Dr. Alamgir ever go to your bank personally to deposit or withdraw any amount?" Advocate Syed Rezaur Rahman asked him.

"No," the witness answered.

"Then who used to deposit into and withdraw money from his account?"

"The caretaker of his village home used to do that," confirmed the witness.

He admitted that he did not remember whether he had given any statement to the ACC's Investigation Officer Syed Iqbal Hossain about my account in his bank or my conduct as an account-holder or client. Summed up, he did not testify anything incriminating against me. He raised his hand hesitatingly in *salaam* to me while leaving the courtroom and then was scolded down by the Public Prosecutor to sit down and wait, till blindly signing of the deposition recorded by the Special Judge.

Prosecution Witness Anwar was followed by Mohammed Abdul Jabber, Second Officer, Janata Bank, Kachua. Led by the Public Prosecutor, he deposed that I had a current account in his bank with a balance of Tk. 145,322/ on February 5, 2007 and had submitted a 10-page statement of transactions in this account to the Investigation Officer. Under cross-examination, he admitted that in his statement there were over-writings and corrections not backed by initials and entries of double payments on separate days against a single cheque bearing the same number in the statement of account produced before the court.

Advocate Syed Rezaur Rahman showed him the two entries of double payment and asked.

"How was it done in a bank?"

The witness kept mum. The Public Prosecutor followed by the Special Judge prodded him to reply.

"It was a mistake," the witness finally said.

"How come a mistaken payment of over Tk. 1 lac was not noticed by you and how could you carry this mistake in the statement of accounts produced before the Investigation Officer and the court?" Anger was quite discernible in the voice of the otherwise soft-spoken Advocate.

"Can we or any authority in such a backdrop of either cheating or utter negligence, consider the statement of accounts as prepared and submitted by you as correct?" asked the Advocate in a similar tone.

"It was a mistake," the witness attempted at an explanation once again.

"Your entire statement of account was a mistake," retorted the Advocate in ingratiating anguish and, to the relief of the witness, sat down.

In essence, therefore, his statement left sufficient room for doubt as evidence and he did not say anything that incriminated me in any way. In the process, his ineptitude and incompetence, if not a comprehensible scheming of the Prosecution came under sharp focus before all those present in the court excepting the Special Judge, the Public Prosecutor and the Major in attendance.

(11)

I got a respite from continuous attendance of the court the next day. The Public Prosecutor on personal grounds regretted his inability to come that day and without blinking an eye, the Special Judge agreed. Earlier he had refused to give me a day's respite on medical grounds even. Evidently he was always eager and ready to accede to any wish or request of the Prosecution.

Keeping awake in the night before morning, I decided to list the witnesses in my defense and the points that I would make in my statement under Sections 342 and 265 of the Criminal Procedure Code rebutting the charges framed against me. Of the probable defense witnesses, I wanted testimonies in respect of my reputation, lifestyle and correctness of estimation of my income and saving for 38 years starting in 1965. I thought my friend Forrest Cookson, an American economist working for a long time in Bangladesh, would be an acceptable witness to testify about correctness of estimates of my income, savings and investment. My friend Lotus-Kamal recommended his former associate S. A. Ahmed, a Chartered Accountant, to testify in this respect also. But as I came to know later, he hesitated to testify in such a case in fear of losing hearty relations that he maintained with a few top men of the time. I thought M. A. Muhit, a former Secretary and Minister of Finance under whom I worked, would be a good choice to testify about my work, integrity and reputation. He was, in my assessment, a man of integrity with courage and straightforward approach. I also thought that Dr. Akbar Ali Khan, a former Finance Secretary, Chairman of the National Board of Revenue and Advisor in the earlier caretaker government, being acquainted with my work and attainments would be an appropriate choice. I decided that in addition, Dr. Abul Barkat, Professor of Economics of the Dhaka University and General Secretary of the Bangladesh Economic Association would be an expert witness to prove that what I mentioned as the Bangla equivalent of fixed deposits in my asset statement was correct and should, therefore, be acceptable. I thought that Iqbal Sobhan Chowdhury, Editor, the *Bangladesh Observer*, being known to me since university days, would be a credible witness about my general reputation, as would be my colleagues in service, Dr. S. A. Samad, Principal Secretary to the former Prime Minister Sheikh Hasina, and Dr. Mashiur Rahman, a former Secretary of Economic Relations Division and Chairman, National Board of Revenue. I hoped that Abdul Hamid Chowdhury, who worked under me as Secretary, Ministry of Planning and A. S. M. Shahjahan, a former Inspector General of the Police and Advisor to the caretaker government under Justice Latifur Rahman in 2001, my age-mate and classmate in university days, would testify about my works and conduct. And I thought Engineer Shahid of Messers Shahid Associates (who had prepared the blueprint for my house at Banani and who was about the best-known structural engineer of the country) would be the most appropriate expert to testify about the cost of its construction, which was greatly inflated by the Prosecution. I have known Engineer Shahid as a man of principle, integrity, courage and social consciousness since long. And finally, I decided that architect Alamin of Union Construction Ltd. (who drew up the plan for the Biponi Polash) would be the most credible witness to testify about the ownership and estimated cost of the set of shops that I was alleged to have owned and constructed. Architect Alamin was a freedom fighter. He had drawn up the blueprint for the Gulbahar Himagar of which the Biponi Polash was an additional investment. I also thought of Lt. General (Ret.) Nuruddin Khan who knew me since I was the Deputy Commissioner, Jesore, and who was a colleague of mine in Sheikh Hasina's government, as one who would be a very good witness to testify about my work and conduct. I decided that I would ask my brother Dr. Jahangir and nephew Dr. Muntassir Mamun to approach these persons, make them talk to my lawyer, if possible, and prepare them to be witnesses in my defense. I noted all these on two pieces of papers to hand them over the next court day.

Throughout the next day, sitting in my cell in the Kashimpur Jail, I wrote my statement of defense under Sections 342 and 265 of the Criminal Procedure Code. I analyzed the testimonies of the Prosecution Witnesses given thus far, the legal loopholes and irregularities that were revealed in the process and decided on the documents that I would append to the statement. I thought it would be a good idea to collect these documents right from the next day and give a copy of the statement to my lawyers sufficiently ahead of time for their comments. I decided to give a few advance copies to my friends in the diplomatic circle so that they would know the kind of kangaroo court by which I was being tried. It was quite an exercise to procure paper and pen and find a solitary corner in the jail to write the statement. I labored throughout the day and till around 11:00 in the night; though I could not complete it, I became satisfied with the actual progress in writing and jotting down of points to continue the same the day and the night thereafter. I completed calculation of annualized yields of my estimated investment and saving and of rental income with the help of a calculator given to me by a deputy jailor. I thought it would be a good idea to give the base figures to Sitara to fax them up to my son Jalal Alamgir for final calculation by a computer and add explanatory comments and clarifications where needed.

Thus prepared, I arrived in the court on June 26 around 10:00 in the morning and found the Special Judge waiting for me. In a not very benign voice he asked,

"Why are you so late?"

"Your honor, I am your prisoner. I can't move at my will. Please ask the police escort and the driver of the prison van why they took so long," I replied, feeling amused.

"Don't repeat it in the future," he responded perplexedly without looking at me.

I did not feel any need to respond to such a ridiculous accusation for which most certainly I was not accountable. As it seemed, it was a foretaste of being held liable for punishment despite others in his court being responsible and accountable.

(12)

On this day, the Prosecution brought in Investigation Officer Jiban Krishna once again to present in detail his purported findings. He deposed that he had been appointed Investigation Officer formally by the ACC; he found Fixed Deposit Receipts valued Tk. 117 lacs in my name in the IFIC Bank, Karwan Bazar, and seized them. He kept the original FDRs in the custody of the Manager, IFIC Bank and took their photocopies with him. On March 22, 2007, he requested the District Registrars, Dhaka and Chandpur to send him all information as regards ownership and transaction of properties of Dr. Alamgir, his wife Sitara and sons Jalal and Joy Alamgir; he requested the Executive Engineer of the PWD, Sher-e-Bangla Nagar, to let him know of measurements and values of Dr. Alamgir's buildings and establishments. On March 27, he went to the IFIC Bank, Motijheel to obtain particulars of Dr. Alamgir's bank account. On March 29, he went to the Central Enquiry Cell of the National Board of Revenue and examined the income tax files of Dr. Alamgir, his wife Sitara Alamgir and his two sons, Jalal Alamgir and Joy Alamgir. On orders of the ACC, on April 4, 2007 he handed over Dr. Alamgir's case file to the next appointed Investigation Officer Shermin Ferdousi. He stated that the reports on Dr. Alamgir that he had received were addressed in his name even after he had handed over the case file to Shermin Ferdousi. Shermin Ferdousi handed over the file on May 7, 2007, to Syed Iqbal Hossain, who was appointed the Investigation Officer after her. He also stated that he had handed over reports received on income tax payments and bank accounts of Dr. Alamgir to Syed Iqbal Hossain in the same way.

Under cross-examination on the same day, Jiban Krishna stated that while serving as an Investigation Officer, he was on deputation, not absorbed in the service of the ACC. He admitted that he was assigned with investigation on February 22; he submitted a partial report on March 4, lodged the First Information Report with the police two days thereafter on March 6. He admitted that during these days he met with the members of the Task Force on this investigation led my Major Khandaker Kamruzzaman of the Second Bengal Regiment, Jalal Uddin Ahmed, Assistant Commissioner (Income Tax) and Atiar Rahman of the police.

"Why the Prosecution did not produce Major Kamruzzaman and other members of the Task Force as you mentioned as witnesses?" asked my lawyer Syed Rezaur Rahman.

"I do not know the reason; it was not my decision," replied the Investigation Officer and Prosecution Witness Jiban Krishna.

"As an Investigation Officer, don't you feel, you, we and the court would have known more, the whole truth if these persons tasked with unearthing the allegations in this case, were brought in before the court for deposition and cross-examination? Did not you recommend that they should be so produced as witnesses?" Advocate Rezaur Rahman wanted to know.

Investigation Officer Jiban Krishna did not reply. He strutted a few inaudible words and then stopped.

"Your task force acted as a secret force tasked to torture, pressurize and force selected persons to serve personal, illegitimate and even audacious ambitions of a few," the Advocate commented very slowly. I could see the Special Judge ignored the comment and did not record it.

"Does the Army Act authorize and empower a Major of the army to serve as the Leader of a Task Force such as this one?" asked the Advocate after a pause.

"I do not know," the witness replied.

He then admitted that he had investigated into this case for just five days and that his assignment as an Investigation Officer was not notified in the government's Gazette in accordance with the relevant ACC Rules. He stated that he discussed this case with the next Investigation Officer, Shermin Ferdousi but could not recall the number of occasions of such discussions. He admitted that during investigation no opportunity was given to Dr. Alamgir for a hearing. He stated that during investigation he came to know that Delwar Hossain, Secretary, ACC came from village Lunti, within Kachua Police Station, *i.e.*, the same electoral constituency as that of Dr. Alamgir. He admitted that he had received the first of the two asset statements submitted by Dr. Alamgir; he had seen in the first asset statement that Dr. Alamgir had mentioned Tk. 90 lacs approximately as the value of fixed deposits held by him and he had not visited Dr. Alamgir's home village and the house at Comilla Housing Estate allegedly belonging to him in course of his investigation.

Advocate Syed Rezaur Rahman's cross-examination ended for the day at this point. The day after was fixed for continuation of the cross-examination as the Public Prosecutor said he would be busy with personal work the next day. The Special Judge as usual was only too willing to oblige him. I did not mind; I got a day's respite without a request from my end. After talking to my lawyers, brothers and few relations, I walked to the rattling prison van that took me to the Kashimpur prison. My companion prisoners, received me, heard an account of what went on in the Special Court and consoled me that the investigator had revealed weaknesses and irregularities in the investigation process sufficient to prove elements of partiality and incredibility in his work. Reaching the jail, over a meal that I could not eat, I listened to the news broadcast of the Radio Today between 9:45 to 10:00 and then of the BBC between 10:30 to 11:00 in the night and slumped down on my bed. The *Radio Today* reported that I had been in the Special Court and the Investigation Officer's depositions were recorded by the court.

The next day, I took time to go through newspapers that I could not read with attention earlier in the last few days. I was painfully surprised to know that the Awami League, the political party that I belonged to, did not make any protest against the arrest of myself, Salman, Lotus-Kamal, Engineer Mosharraf, Kamal Majumder and others. On the contrary, General Secretary of the Party, Abdul Jalil, on more than one occasion, both at home and abroad, stated that the Awami League would not tolerate corrupt members within its fold. To us, it appeared as a ridiculous sycophancy on their part to avoid being arrested or otherwise harassed by the military-backed government led by Dr. Fakhruddin. To me it appeared that the leadership at that level had degenerated into protection of self-interest and cowardice far from the ideals once spearheaded by Bangabandhu. It was a blind misery and grit into which the leadership had been drowned.

It reminded me of the people's indifference to persecution and injustice in Nazi Germany in the 1930s. When a friend or a neighbor was taken off from home by the Nazi cadres on a drummed-up accusation of treachery, no one protested, reasoning that the persecution had not touched them. And then when came the turn of the non-protestor, he found no one left to turn to and no one having the courage to stand by his side. The tragedy of indifference was written in white letters with black in the background on the side of a memorial path remembering the victims of holocaust laid near the JFK Federal Building in Boston. I along with Sitara walked this path with agony and tears a number of times while we were studying in Boston. Recalling the tragedy that followed from indifference, I said aloud, these sycophants would be used by the regime, as far as they would degenerate into lackeys, and then be thrown off as squeezed out sugarcanes.

From the newspapers, I also noticed that the members of the Supreme Court Bar Association, excepting Barristers Rafiqul Huq and Shafiq Ahmed, Advocates Mahbubey Alam, Yusuf Humayun and a few others, were silent fellow travelers of the illegitimate regime trying to rule the country by intimidation and thriving on persecution. The voice in support of rule of law, justice, and the citizen's inalienable rights, which had always helped the nation to stand against misrule and persecution, seemed to have been drowned, at least in the short run, in the quagmire of fear and self-preservation. In their verdicts and pronouncements, most of the judges of the Supreme Court appeared similarly to be eloquently silent with respect to the unabated violation of the due process of law. To me it seemed to show the vulnerability of justice and of just and life-pulsating society at the hands of weaklings. As the first black Justice of the U.S. Supreme Court, Marshall told the second black Justice, Clarence Thomas on assumption of the office by the latter: "I did in my time what I had to do; you now have to do in your time what you have to do." Could these people, perceived as the most educated, conscious and responsible of this generation, say the same to their progeny? I asked this with a sudden punch of dread and pondered, but did not find an answer.

I noticed that there was countrywide shortage of power, fertilizer and spiraling price of food and essentials of life and living and Nero-like playing of flutes by the regime in the face of the gathering crisis. I was bemused by the boasts of the Chairman ACC that he and his associates had become almost successful in combating corruption throughout the country. Giving press notes on illegally amassed wealth of so-called corrupt arrestees, especially of businessmen, in my assessment, they had done away with the fiduciary trust reposed in banks and financial institutions and led to frenzied trials and punishments through the media. Certainly, this was not a way to tread along towards prosperity through private enterprise.

I observed that almost all the columnists of repute had stopped writing; a few traitors to the class, along with some drawn from the academia, were trumpeting the corralling of the so-called corrupt, without following the due process of law and keeping kangaroos in the special courts set up hurriedly and selectively for make-believe trials. These people seemed to be painfully unconcerned about the question of and difference between right and wrong, good and bad, virtue and vice and loyalty and treachery in the society. They were oblivious of a fundamental process of reasoning and progress; they were ignorant of history's lesson that no morality could ever be found and justified in raw authority over society, based an unbridled and uncivilized intimidation.

Till late in the night, I read John Grisham's *The Innocent*. This was a true story of an innocent black man who became a victim of misapplication and misinterpretation of law even in a country like the U.S.. The book was sent to me by Sitara knowing that Grisham was one of my favorite storytellers. She had an unerring ability to identify and encourage my best impulses. I did not consider myself a person who could easily be bruised and blistered or was prone to growing disappointment and fear generated by crude brutality. Despite that, as told by Grisham, at the helplessness of an innocent man facing almost a slaughter under the cover of law, tears welled up in my eyes. My mind turned to hundreds of prisoners holed down here in Kashimpur, who even in the assessment of their jailors were innocent. I found and heard that all of 67 jails of the country were bursting with glowering youth, an entire generation thrown into moral darkness without any material prospect. I could not finish reading the book. I decided to return it to Sitara if I could, before she left the country.

Next day June 28 dawned drab. The sky was like a spread out gray slate of despair and hopelessness. In sweating humidity, the windowless rattling and smoke-emitting prison van took me to the Special Court around 10:00 in the morning. Before I could consult my lawyers and brief them about what needed to be focused in the cross-examination, the Special Judge started the proceedings. As cross-examined by Syed Rezaur Rahman, Prosecution witness Jiban Krishna stated contrary to his statement made the day before yesterday, that the investigation of my case after him was taken over in two sequences by Shermin Ferdousi and Syed Iqbal Hossain. He stated that Bangla version of fixed deposit receipts or FDRs was permanent *amanats* and not *amanat patras* as had been used in Dr. Alamgir's asset statement.

"In that event, why did not you get a clarification from him, give him an opportunity to be heard in person?" asked my lawyer.

"It was not to be my decision," answered the witness.

"Did you ask for such a decision from your supervising officer, or the Leader of the Task Force if he was the leader over your supervisors?" the lawyer wanted to know.

Jiban Krishna mumbled something inaudible.

"Permanent *amanat* or *amanat patras*, these were assets of approximately Tk. 90 lacs as mentioned by Dr. Alamgir. Why did not you take this into account while alleging concealment of assets by him?" asked the Advocate.

The witness kept silent. The Special Judge did not press him to come out with a reply. Then he said that he did not in course of his investigation interrogate anyone in the Janata Bank, Kachua; he said he did not examine double payment against a single cheque made by the Janata Bank, Kachua out of Dr. Alamgir's account with them. He admitted that witness Rabiul Hasan Prodhan, Assistant Commissioner (Income Tax), did not give him a six-page comparative statement of my income and assets during the time he investigated into the case nor did he mention about this in his case diary. He said that on May 7, when he was not in charge of the investigation, he handed over the comparative statement in a list of inventory of papers and documents to the third Investigation Officer Syed Iqbal, though he was not asked to do so by the Secretary, ACC. He stated that he did not tell Rabiul Hasan Prodhan either on April 14 or later that he was no longer in-charge of investigation and that the new Investigation Officer was Shermin Ferdousi. He admitted that Dr. Alamgir had mentioned that he held Tk. 90 lacs approximately as FDRs/saving certificates and 25 sources from which they were funded in his statement of assets, but while lodging the First Information Report with the police, he did not mention about these.

"Don't you think by not mentioning or better concealing these, you concealed the very core of the allegation mentioned against Dr. Alamgir in your FIR?" asked Advocate Rezaur Rahman very quietly but firmly.

The witness strutted to say something but could not.

"Was it not a blatant and willful misrepresentation of facts leading to denial of freedom and causing financial damage to the accused?" the Advocate demanded.

Silence became eloquent in the non-response of the witness. Truth was not told by him, though he was under oath to tell it in full excluding all falsities. He said he did not mention in the First Information Report about Tk.19 lacs or so received by Dr. Alamgir as his one-time pension and the cumulative yield of Tk. 20 lacs or so out of saving certificates held by him since 1972. In the same vein, he stated that he did not mention in the First Information Report that Dr. Alamgir had received Tk. 2 lacs 60 thousand from his books, authored by him at an average rate of Tk. 20 thousand per book. He further admitted that in course of his investigation for fourteen days, he found in part that Dr. Alamgir was an educated, democratically minded political leader. He said that it was not true that he had lodged the First Information Report against Dr. Alamgir with a view to be rewarded through absorption into the regular service of the ACC.

We came to know at this time that Jiban Krishna was originally an employee of the Bangladesh Bank, *i.e.*, the Central Bank of the country, who had been assigned to find out politicians who held more than Tk. 100 lacs (10 million) as FDRs or saving certificates in various banks, more than eight months before I was arrested. His activities were hewn into a scheme drawn up by the army, borrowing from Pervez Musharraf's Pakistan, about a year before the army-backed caretaker government with Dr. Fakhruddin on the front took over. The provisions of the Emergency Powers Act about allegation, investigation and trial relating to income tax were also similarly borrowed and the potential leaders of the Task Force were trained more than six months before the Dr. Fakhruddin government took over.

An analysis of the deposition of Jiban Krishna made it clear that (i) he was not authorized under the Rules of the ACC to investigate into the case; (ii) his investigation was perfunctory and also incomplete inasmuch as he had examined only the first asset statement, and not the second one, submitted by me; (iii) the procedure followed by him denied me my right to natural justice in so far as I was not given an opportunity for hearing; (iv) he omitted in his First Information Report lodged with the Police that I had indeed mentioned about FDRs and Saving Certificates held by me and given sources of their funding and (v) he did not find any instance of illegal earnings by me. The depositions made by Jiban Krishna alone were sufficient to prove that charges against me were drummed-up on grounds other than what was warranted by law and ways of justice. But as I observed the Special Judge from the dock, it would have been kind for anyone to perceive that he was endowed with an analytical capability to realize all these things. Transforming judicial power into justice and fair play was unknown to him either as a value to be cherished or a duty to be performed.

A witness under cross-examination remains under the control of the defense lawyer till the latter completes his examination. Despite this, without even looking at Advocate Syed Rezaur Rahman, the Special Judge closed the proceedings.

"That would be enough for the witness," he said, before rising from his chair.

"Yes, your honor," the Public Prosecutor almost instantly crowed back. Everyone else sat in silence. Jiban Krishna as a Prosecution Witness was released before signing the depositions as recorded.

(13)

In the afternoon, Shermin Ferdousi, the second Investigation Officer was brought in as the prosecution witness. Led by the Public Prosecutor, she stated that on April 3, 2007, she started to investigate into my case on orders from the ACC. She stated that I had kept Tk.117 lacs as fixed deposits in the IFIC bank, Karwan Bazar, which I did not mention in my income tax return for 2006. She did not say that the year for mentioning particulars of these fixed deposits in accordance with the filing procedure of income tax returns was 2007 and not 2006. She said that she could not find any source of funding for these fixed deposits, despite the fact that in my first asset statement furnished to the ACC, I had mentioned that I held fixed deposits of approximately Tk. 90 lacs and had elaborately given as many as 25 sources of their funding. According to her, I had concealed assets worth Tk.117 lacs to the ACC. She stated that she had submitted a charge-sheet to this effect on April 29, 2007 though the ACC approved of such submission on April 30, *i.e.*, a day later. The charge-sheet against me, as she said, was submitted under sections 26 and 27 of the ACC Act and Rules 15 (d) 5 of the Emergency Powers Rules.

She was cross-examined by Advocate Syed Rezaur Rahman. I myself wanted to cross-examine her on some points. The Special Judge did not allow me to do it. Under cross-examination by Syed Rezaur Rahman, she admitted that the notice to submit the asset statement served on me in the jail by the Secretary ACC was dated January 18, 2007, *i.e.*, a fortnight before I was arrested; the notice gave me 72 hours to furnish the statement:

"Was not such a predated notice indicative of premeditated prejudiced action against the accused?" asked Advocate Syed Rezaur Rahman.

"I can't say," answered Prosecution Witness Shermin Ferdousi.

"As an Investigation Officer, could you act in accordance with law on a notice signed on January 18, 2007, and actually served on the accused on February 20, 2007, giving the accused 72 hours from the date of the notice to send in his asset statement?" the Advocate wanted to know.

Shermin Ferdousi did not answer.

"Does Section 26 of the ACC Act prescribe any time limit for submission of asset statement?" asked the Advocate.

"No," said the Prosecution Witness.

"Under Section 26 of the ACC Act as notified by the ACC, Dr. Alamgir was asked to submit asset statement. Was he asked to submit asset or wealth statement under the Income Tax Ordinance, 1984?" asked the Advocate.

"No."

"Then how could you say his omission on June 30, 2006, to mention six FDRs, scheduled to yield him interest income in fiscal year 2007, was a concealment of assets within the meaning of S-26 of the ACC Act? Did not Dr. Alamgir mention about holding of these FDRs in approximate value in his asset statement?" asked the Advocate seeking clarifications.

The witness kept silent. I observed the Special Judge did not note this question and response from the witness on the case papers in front of him.

"Even if we assume that Dr. Alamgir had not mentioned about these FDRs in his income tax return in 2006, but in reality mentioned about the same in his asset statement submitted to the ACC, can you prosecute him under Section 26 of the ACC Act for not mentioning them in his income tax return?"

"No, I am not sure," mumbled the Prosecution witness.

"Does concealment of assets, as mentioned in Section 26 of the ACC Act, mean or include concealment elsewhere than in the asset statement submitted in accordance with Section 26 of the said Act?"

The witness did not answer. The Special Judge did not ask her to answer either. Nor did the Special Judge, as I observed, note anything on the case file in front of him.

Seventy-two hours was fixed as the time limit for submission of the asset statement at a time when the ACC Rules on such submission were not framed by them, she admitted. Under the ACC Rules drawn up later, instead of 72 hours at least seven working days were fixed for submission of asset statement. She stated that under the ACC Act, the Secretary did not have power or authority to serve notice on anyone to submit an asset statement. She further admitted that the notice in question was served under both the ACC Act and the Emergency Powers Rules and she was not aware of any inconsistency as between the Act and the Rules. She said that during investigation she came to know that Delwar Hossain, Secretary ACC had his village home at Lunti within Kachua Police Station, *i.e.*, the same electoral constituency that I came from.

She admitted that despite that the Secretary ACC (1) issued notice on me to submit an asset statement; (2) instructed her to investigate into the case (3) received the investigation report; and (4) he was not cited as a witness nor was examined by the Investigation Officer. She admitted that in the notice served on me to submit an asset statement, asset was not defined and values of assets were not asked for. She stated that she did not know who were the members of the Task Force assigned to the case even though she along with Major Kamruzzaman and other members of the Task Force met me in the Kashimpur Jail on April 7, 2007. Advocate Rezaur Rahman said at this point that she was lying under oath and committing a criminal offense. The Special Judge did not take any notice of it. She stated that she could not say whether the Task Force pressured me in the jail to write the asset statement in 2 or 3 hours. She also stated that she did not know whether I submitted a supplementary or second asset statement on April 28, 2007. At this point Advocate Syed Rezaur Rahman showed her the receipt of the second asset statement by the ACC.

"Did anyone in the ACC tell you about or give you the second asset statement, as was received?" the Advocate asked.

"No," she said after a considerable pause.

She admitted that she considered only the first asset statement, which I had forwarded with a note to discuss with me anything contained in the same statement for clarification, if so needed; she also admitted that while meeting me in jail on April 7, she did not record my statement in accordance with Section 161 of the Criminal Procedure Code, despite that I had stated to her and other members of the Task Force my salaries and other incomes and annualized return on my savings and investment. In fact she did not record anything except that the Task Force met me and interrogated me, she admitted. During investigation by her, as she stated, she had recorded the statement of seven persons, including Assistant Commissioner (Income Tax) Rabiul Hasan Prodhan. She admitted that Rabiul Hasan Prodhan in his statement recorded by her under Section 161 of the Criminal Procedure Code had not mentioned of any discrepancy in my income tax records. She also admitted that she was not notified as an Investigation Officer for this case in the official Gazette of the government though it was so required by the ACC Rules.

"Was not acting as the Investigation Officer, without being notified so in the official Gazette in accordance with the ACC's Rules, illegal; making your entire investigation unlawful?" asked the Advocate.

"No . . . I do not know," came the hesitant answer.

Then she stated that she took fifteen days, April 3 to 19, to investigate into the case before the third Investigation Officer Syed Iqbal took over the assignment from her. She could not say how many days were taken by three investigation officers assigned in sequence to the case to complete the investigation nor could she say whether they could complete the investigation within the time limit set by the law. She admitted that during investigation, she did not visit my village home in Kachua Police Station and the Comilla housing estate where a house allegedly of mine was located. She admitted that my wife and two sons were established persons in their respective fields in the U.S. and they financially helped me whenever needed. She stated that in my asset statement I had mentioned that I held Fixed Deposits of approximately Tk. 140 lacs and 25 sources of their funding. She said that in the asset statement, my investment in the Investment Corporation of Bangladesh (mutual fund), and the Bay Pacific Limited, pension deposits in the Bangladesh Shilpa Bank, receipt of Tk. 8 lacs as sale proceeds of a jeep and repayment of bank loan of the Gulbahar Himagar Ltd. (of which I was a shareholder) have been mentioned. She admitted that in my asset statement under a heading of "relevant facts," earnings of my wife Sitara, sons Dr. Jalal Alamgir (over Tk. 120 Lacs annually) and Joy Alamgir (over Tk. 91 lacs annually) and their financial independence and status as separate income taxpayers were mentioned. She said that in the asset statement I had mentioned about 13 publications from which I had received on average Tk. 20,000/ each and approximately Tk. 19 lacs that I had received as a one-time pension. She admitted that in the charge-sheet, despite all these, she had not mentioned that my incomes were legitimate and proper.

"Was not such deliberate omission a concealment of facts reflecting prejudice and material damage to the accused?" asked Advocate Syed Rezaur Rahman at this point.

"No, but I should have avoided these omissions," she replied.

"If you would have mentioned these as required of you to find and tell the whole truth and nothing but the truth, there would not have been any case against the accused," the Advocate commented, slowly in his typical way. And then he asked, "Was not your submission of charge-sheet a day before it was approved for such submission, unauthorized and, therefore, illegal?"

She looked uncomfortable, wanted to say something, but was stopped by the Public Prosecutor, directing her to be silent by putting his forefinger on his lips. Major Kamruzzaman, as usual was sitting by his side like a crude intrusion. I observed that he looked at Shermin Ferdousi at this point with reddened eyes inspiring fear in her. Then she stated that her supervising officer was Tanjil Haque who was not cited as a witness in this case. She could not give any reason why Tanjil Haque was kept out of the scene. She denied that she had not prepared the charge against me as instructed by the Secretary ACC, outside the ambit of supervision of her supervising officer Tanjil Haque.

From the deposition of Shermin Ferdousi, a number of facts came out in the open. In the first place, her assignment as an Investigation Officer, not being notified in the official Gazette of the government as required by law, was unlawful, which made the entire investigation unauthorized and therefore untenable in law. Secondly, the allegation of concealment of assets by me as made by her was not substantiated by facts: the alleged concealment did not even pertain to the ACC Act (Section 26); on the contrary, violating norms of neutral investigation, she concealed that I had mentioned holding of fixed deposits and sources of their funding in my asset statement. Thirdly, the law did not permit the Secretary, ACC to issue notice on me to submit asset statement and the notice was a premeditated action of prejudice as it was dated prior to my arrest and gave me officially just 72 hours, as a matter of fact functionally not more than 1 hour, to submit the same. Fourthly, her investigation was incomplete and perfunctory in so far as she did not take into account all my income and earnings, examine my second asset statement, record my statement under S-161 of Criminal Procedure Code, visit my home village and Comilla Housing Estate, where I was alleged to be owning a house, and submitted the charge-sheet against me without authorization of the ACC. These facts, as it turned out, were not noted by the Special Judge bent upon ignoring or bypassing any deposition that was in my favor or that rebutted allegations made in the charge-sheet.

(14)

Immediately after Shermin Ferdousi's deposition was over, the third and final Investigation Officer Syed Iqbal Hossain was called in by the Prosecution. Led by the Public Prosecutor he deposed that he had received approval for undertaking further investigation into allegations mentioned in the FIR on May 12, 2007. He stated that he had submitted photocopies of reports of the Executive Engineer, Public Works Department, Sher-e-Bangla Nagar and the District Registrar, Chandpur and of statement of my account from the Janata Bank, Kachua, invoices or *challans* of three motorcycles and certificate of Land Acquisition Branch of the Deputy Commissioner's Office, Chandpur. He said on May 12, he recorded statements of other Prosecution Witnesses in accordance with Section 161 of the Criminal Procedure Code. Then, he said, he went to Comilla and fixed up the Executive Engineer of the Public Works Department as a witness. He said then he took statements of my accounts with the Krishi Bank, Kachua and the Grameen Bank, Gulbahar. All told he found me owning assets valued at a figure much higher than I had mentioned in my statement of assets submitted to the ACC. On this basis, he submitted the supplementary charge-sheet against me under Sections 26 and 27 of the ACC Act and Rule 15(d) 5 of the Emergency Powers Rules after obtaining approval of the ACC. The approval of the ACC was signed by its Commissioner Manzur Mannan and none other, *i.e.*, not by the Commission, as provided in the law.

Standing in the dock, I recorded all these depositions as I did on other days. By the time the Prosecution was through with witness Syed Iqbal Hossain, it was 7:30 in the evening. It was all deep dark around me, not so much from low-powered bulbs fixed on walls, as from acculturation of a systemic institutional mechanism, where truth was kept miles off from real and relevant facts. Bowing a *salaam* to me while going out, more in shame of himself than out of respect for me as a former civil servant protecting the civil administration from the onslaught of militarization for at least two decades, Syed Iqbal Hossain left to be whisked out in a microbus escorted by plainclothesmen. I was surprised, painfully, to see how the educated people in the prosecution and judgeship came into an easy collaboration with a process of predetermined injustice, exiling from their moral compass the responsibility of doing right. I found essential values lacking in the environment, which made it difficult to see the desired destination to hope for, or to translate into reality the self-evident truths of inalienable rights of people in an independent society.

Unable to sleep in my cell in the jail, I read Clarence Thomas' *My Grandparents' Son* till the small hours of the morning. This was an autobiography of a black American who, through persistence, values, integrity and support of his white wife Virginia and friends and associates, rose to the judgeship of the Supreme Court of the U.S. despite betrayal of a woman, Anita Hill, of his own black community. At the end of his story, with resolve as a Justice, he prayed silently: "Lord grant me wisdom to know what is right and the courage to do it." I did not know when and how people in garbs of Special Judges of our country mandated to truncate and ignore the truth in the area of their assigned responsibility would realize the value and the profundity of such a prayer and wish.

The next date was July 3 slated for cross-examination of the Prosecution Witness Syed Iqbal Hossain. Before the cross-examination could start, I thought I would try to solve a vexing and at the end a very frustrating problem: squabbles among my lawyers. Advocate Syed Rezaur Rahman was soft-spoken, but with strong likes and dislikes. Advocate Haider, till he was lured away as a Deputy Attorney General, had good working relations with Rahman. But Rahman did not like or even tolerate Advocate Ayat Ali Patwary. Advocate Patwary came from my area, was acculturated in literary fields and came to defend me on his own and at no cost of mine. I wanted him to take the role of Haider but in a good working relationship with Rahman. But Rahman would not allow it; he would not even give opportunity or time to Patwary to cross-examine the Prosecution Witnesses.

I requested both Rahman and Patwary to cooperate with each other for my sake. Rahman smiled, but as it turned out remained adamant. I could not be very firm with Rahman, as he was the senior lawyer and came to defend me despite threats from the ACC as well as the Task Force Leader. Instead, Rahman came with another advocate, Tipu Sultan, whom I knew since my days at Jessore as the Deputy Commissioner. Tipu was a good political organizer but lacked in depth and diligence expected of a good trial lawyer. As it turned out, after a perfunctory cross-examination of Prosecution Witness Syed Iqbal Hossain for about 15 minutes, Tipu was taken off the scene by Rahman. I also found Sultan's cross-examination lacking in depth and acumen. The day after this, Tipu did not come to the court; he sent in a message that he was threatened by the Task Force Leader as well as the personnel of the Forces Intelligence. It was a good riddance, but non-cooperation between Rahman and Patwary continued. I could not do anything to put an end to this squabble. Rahman continued his pivotal but almost unassisted role; Patwary stayed with me but could not contribute his best. It seemed, I was in a cesspool of smallness, almost helpless in the face of stifling constraints in the heart of darkness, created mostly of made-up evidences for a compliant court, helped in the open field by professional jealousies of the defense lawyers themselves.

In the cross-examination led by Advocate Rezaur Rahman on July 3, Investigation Officer Syed Iqbal Hossain admitted that, in the notice served on me to submit asset statement, asset was not defined, valuation of asset was not asked for and particulars of other person's assets kept with the recipient of the notice was not called for. At this point Advocate Syed Rezaur Rahman asked him, "Can you, in that case, fault Dr. Alamgir for not mentioning assets that he held on behalf of others, for example, the Sultana Foundation and his son Dr. Jalal Alamgir?"

"No, we could not do that," conceded the witness.

"Did you ask Dr. Alamgir at any stage of investigation about the assets that he might have held on behalf of others?"

"No, we did not," admitted the witness quite candidly.

"Did you interrogate Dr. Alamgir or give an opportunity of hearing to him?"

"No," answered the witness with seeming guilt.

He stated that the Prosecution had submitted the charge-sheet in fifty-five days instead of forty-five days as directed under law and that he had not applied to his Director to extend the time for investigation as required under the ACC's Rules. He said that Shermin Ferdousi, who had submitted the original or the first charge-sheet, had not mentioned that the allegations against Dr.

Alamgir had been proved or borne out by facts. She had not mentioned anything to this effect in her memorandum of evidence either. He admitted that despite being mandated in the law, none of the investigations of the Investigation Officers, of he himself, Shermin Ferdousi's and Jiban Krishna's were supervised. He admitted that his statement in the supplementary charge-sheet submitted by him that the Court had instructed him to submit the same was not correct and proper; rather the court had ordered for further investigation and report based on such an investigation.

"Then why did you mention in the charge-sheet itself that the court had ordered you to submit it irrespective of your findings as regards guilt or innocence?" asked the Advocate.

"It was a mistake," responded witness Syed Iqbal.

"I wish you were the victim of such a mistake rather than Dr. Alamgir," dryly commented Advocate Syed Rezaur Rahman.

Then the witness stated that he had not seen the second or the supplementary asset statement submitted by me, that his investigation was based on only the first asset statement. He admitted that he had not said anything about Dr. Alamgir's Fixed Deposits with the IFIC Bank, Karwan Bazar, as had been mentioned in the First Information Report, nor about the place of occurrence of the alleged crime centering around these deposits. He further admitted that he had not given me an opportunity to be heard on the allegations made against me: he had discussed with the Task Force as to how he could submit a supplementary charge-sheet as he did. He stated that he had taken papers and documents on this case from Jiban Krishna Roy before he (*i.e.* Syed Iqbal) was assigned as an Investigation Officer; he had not taken any paper and document from Shermin Ferdousi.

"Then how come Shermin Ferdousi came in between two of you as an Investigation Officer and what did she do in that role?" asked a perplexed Syed Rezaur Rahman.

"I . . . I . . . can't . . ."

The witness did not say anything more in reply on a signal given by the Public Prosecutor.

At this point the cross-examination was over for the day. It was 7:30 in the evening and I felt tired and frustrated. Words jumbled up in my head. I had been passing notes to Advocate Rezaur Rahman all the while the cross-examination went on. My handwriting was bad, almost to the point of illegibility and Rahman's eyesight was very poor. I found him missing points that seemed important to me. A number of times, I had tried to cross-examine the witness myself, but the Special Judge would not allow it. Thus I was gripped with anger also. My brother Dr. Jahangir held my hand firmly and said not to give up and not to panic at the prospect of a botched up trial. Truth would prevail despite the intermittent march of falsehood, he said. The prison van, rattled back with me to Kashimpur carrying a heavy and putrid odor of despair and bizarre prospect.

Once in the jail, I found other inmates, Salman, Lotus-Kamal, Engineer Mosharraf and Nasim discussing about the price spiral, power shortage and the pervasive failure of the Fakhruddin government. I joined them without strength to hold back a swirling blackness. We found that the country was reeling under the pressure of unbridled self-interest and personal ambition of a few; the entire State machinery was pressed in to serve this purpose and to speed up the process of the decay of a democratic and pluralistic society concerned with the wellbeing of the common man. In this twisting vulnerability of the society, a few like Lt. General Masud Uddin Chowdhury, who was reportedly spearheading the onslaught on the politicians and businessmen, were reveling in their anticipated victory.

"Using the entire State machinery to serve personal interests and ambitions of a few at the expense of all others is the worst form of corruption," I said in desperation.

"Yes, you are right. But this definition of corruption does not find a place in our ACC Act," Lotus-Kamal pointed out.

"Definition of corruption in the ACC Act was imported from Pakistan. This is a gift of Pervez Musharraf and company to spur their counterparts in our country," interjected Tuku, who joined us in the meantime.

"Then how about Moudud and Nazmul Huda who had crafted this law in our land?" asked Engineer Mosharraf of Chittagong.

"They were, have always been lackeys of dictatorship and self-interest, now unfortunately caught in the net woven by themselves," said Ali Asgar Lobi, who came with a bowl of nuts, distributed handfuls among all and sat with us. He was a member of the defunct Parliament from the BNP and reportedly quite close to the ruling BNP-Jamaat coalition government.

"Have patience; wait a few more days, maybe till December. The situation is untenable, extremely untenable. People's anger and anguish will burst out soon, any day I would say," Salman wanted to pontificate and console and admonish down the crippling despair.

The blackness swirling around me did not leave. Lotus-Kamal understood, took my hand and led me to my cell of twisting pain and moronic despair. Despite the pain cutting through my guts, I sat with a pen and a piece of paper and noted down the points of cross-examination that should be pursued next day.

Next morning cross-examination by Advocate Rezaur Rahman started at 10:00. Before the start, I handed him over the piece of paper wherein I had noted the points of emphasis in the ensuing cross-examination. I had written the notes till the small hours of the morning. I was hoping that I would not find a lackluster response, which would be a more ominous strain on me. In the cross-examination, Syed Iqbal Hossain admitted that in the course of investigation, he had not examined my wife Sitara and my brother Dr. Jahangir and had not found it necessary to know how much my two sons living and working in the U.S. earned and how many brothers and sisters I had. He admitted that he did not know where in Gulbahar village, my ancestral home was located. He said that he did not examine the Chairman of the relevant Union Parishad and the concerned Member of the ward of the Union Parishad to find out whether my eldest brother had been a member of the Parliament or not.

"Then how could you say that all of the twin houses and lands in Dr. Alamgir's ancestral home were his alone?" Advocate Syed Rezaur Rahman asked in shimmering anger.

"I could say, for I was told to say so," Syed Iqbal Hossain responded without shame. It did not sound like an improvised response.

The Prosecution had alleged in the charge-sheet that in the asset statement I did not exactly give the balance that I had in various bank accounts. In view of the fact that I was given virtually an hour or two to write my asset statement, I made Advocate Rahman ask the witness how much the witness had in his account on May 8, 2007. As expected, he said he could not say with exactitude. In terms of reasonableness, could one expect a person to give exactly his balance in bank accounts on a certain day without seeing records? Would not they expect such reasonableness when assessing an answer to such a question given by the accused? These questions were asked both of the Prosecution and the Special Judge. They looked up and kept silent. Syed Iqbal Hossain admitted that the "synopsized" statement of my income tax records, *i.e.*, figures of my income since 1982 and assessed value of my assets in 2006 as given by Prosecution Witness Prodhan, had not been mentioned in his deposition given earlier;

this "synopsized" statement was given by him when he was recalled later. The witness stated that the "synopsized" statement had been sent earlier to Jiban Krishna on April 15 when he (*i.e.* Jiban Krishna) was no longer in charge of the investigation.

"In that case the investigation input provided by Jiban Krishna alleging disproportionateness of earnings and assets of Dr. Alamgir was unauthorized, unlawful and cannot be judicially noticed," pointed out Advocate Syed Rezaur Rahman.

The witness kept quiet. The Special Judge squinted but did not say a word. The Public Prosecutor jumped up from his chair.

"It is my turn to cross-examine, you have no right to interrupt or disrupt," Advocate Syed Rezaur Rahman told him sharply.

So he scampered back to his chair much to the dismay of his mentor Major. All the while the Special Judge looked unruffled and unconcerned almost to the point of lifelessness.

At this point, I wanted to cross-examine the witness myself to find out how in a reasonable mind they could compare income between 1982 and 2006, that is income of 24 years, with the value of assets in 2006 which were acquired in course of 38 years of my work-life and even from before through inheritance and whether income as reported by the Income Tax Department was net of exemptions for investments and savings in selected fields as given under the income tax law and such exemptions were embodied in assets of the taxpayer. But I was not allowed to do so by the Special Judge. A sudden awakening into motion out of masterly inaction was observed in his conduct.

I passed a note to Syed Rezaur Rahman to ask these of Syed Iqbal Hossain. Syed Rezaur Rahman, not much acquainted with the intricacies of the income tax law missed the points. Responding to pointed questions of Syed Rezaur Rahman, Investigation Officer Syed Iqbal Hossain clearly and unhesitatingly admitted that he had not ascertained the ownership of our ancestral home at Gulbahar, examined its revenue records or *porcha*,[28] enquired into the ownership of the Gulbahar Himagar, the Biponi Polash, the Sultana Filling Station and of the house in the Comilla Housing Estate, all alleged to have been mine and concealed by me in my asset statement. As a matter of fact, I had given particulars of ownership of all these in my asset statement. The ancestral home was the common and un-demarcated property of all my brothers and sisters; the Gulbahar Himagar was a private limited company and the Biponi Polash was an under-construction set of

[28] A document relating to land, most closely resembling a settlement record.

shops under its ownership and located on its lands; the Sultana Filling Station was owned by my eldest son, Dr. Jalal Alamgir aged 36, and the house in the Comilla Housing Estate was owned at that time by my youngest son Joy Alamgir aged 28, both living and working abroad and separate income taxpayers. I was not very sure whether the Special Judge in his enthusiasm to be very compliant of the wishes of those in power noted these points of truths and falsehoods. At this time he appeared to be in somewhat grinding distress having seen something produced and stated before him that he did not want to see and hear or record.

Syed Iqbal Hossain further admitted that in estimating the value of my house at Banani they did not take into account the Cost of Construction Index (Building) as compiled by the Bureau of Statistics of the government and applicable in cases of both public and private sectors and urban and rural areas. He stated that he had not ascertained when my house at Banani was constructed as he had not ascertained costs of bricks, rods and cement in the years of construction. In respect of three motorcycles alleged to have been mine and unreported by me in my asset statement, he admitted that ownership of vehicles were to be proved on the basis of registration with the relevant department of the government and he did find that these were not registered in my name.

"Did you see any or all of these motorcycles?" asked Advocate Syed Rezaur Rahman at my prodding.

"No, I did not," answered the witness.

"Did you or anyone from the ACC seize these motorcycles from the possession of Dr. Alamgir or anyone of his employees or relations?" asked the Advocate for clarification.

"No. These motorcycles were not found or seized," replied Syed Iqbal Hossain.

"You found just two *challans* or invoices without any proof of payment made against them, right?" proffered the Advocate.

"Yes. That is right," admitted the witness.

"So these cycles came as manna from heaven to fabricate your case against Dr. Alamgir; you could not come out with a proof of their existence in the world we live in," observed the Advocate, not with exaggeration. The Prosecution did not respond.

In the same cross-examination by Advocate Syed Rezaur Rahman, Investigation Officer Syed Iqbal admitted that, in my first asset statement written from the jail, I had stated that I had approximately Tk. 90 lacs worth of fixed deposit receipts or *amanat patras*. This they did not mention in the charge-sheet submitted to the court by them. To a pointed question asked by Advocate Rezaur Rahman, the Investigation Officer admitted that I had sent a second or supplementary asset statement from the jail to the ACC and it was received by them but they did not take it into consideration while crafting the first and the supplementary charge-sheets against me. He admitted, more or less as the normal stuff of negligence, that in course of his investigation he did not come to know anything about the Sultana Foundation and its capital fund that was in custody of Dr. Alamgir. The Sultana Foundation was a trust designed to be set up in memory of the mother of Dr. Alamgir, his brothers and sisters and to encourage others of the family to help the needy students and the poor people of the local area with contributions from all of the family kept in custody of Dr. Alamgir. In this backdrop, Advocate Rezaur Rahman asked:

"You say you completed your investigation with due care and diligence, looked into all aspects of assets under ownership and management of Dr. Alamgir and took into account and consideration help and support that was organized for the students in need and the poor people of the locality by his family?"

Witness Syed Iqbal strutted to say something in reply. But the Special Judge intervened and ruled that the witness was not required to respond to this question. Knowing the provisions of the Evidence Act as I did, I was startled at this ruling that was evidently and ridiculously partial to the Prosecution. The witness then admitted that the notice that had been served on Dr. Alamgir to describe his assets did not require him to give particulars of assets of others, like of this foundation and perhaps that was why in the first asset statement he had not mentioned about this. The Investigation Officer, in a crestfallen way, admitted that he had not, in course of his investigation, visited Kachua where most of Dr. Alamgir's alleged assets were located. He stated that he had visited Chandpur town, where none of his alleged assets was located.

"Do you think, in the context of what you have stated, that your investigation into assets of Dr. Alamgir was complete and adequate enough to accuse him for concealment and disproportionateness with his earnings?" asked Advocate Rezaur Rahman, at this point.

"No . . . Yes, it was complete and adequate in consideration of my superior officers," answered the witness indicating his difficult and perhaps frightened existence in the Commission.

Then he admitted that the house in the Comilla Housing Estate alleged to have been owned by Dr. Alamgir was on lease to the Agrani Bank and the Agrani Bank had earlier funded its construction. He admitted that he was not certain that the ownership of this house was of Dr. Alamgir at the time he submitted his asset statement. He stated that three Investigation Officers of the case including him were not supervised by a superior officer guarding against any arbitrary action and proceedings. He admitted that he did not record any statement of Dr. Alamgir in accordance with Section 161 of the Criminal Procedure Code, nor did he give him an opportunity for hearing.

After Advocate Syed Rezaur Rahman, Advocate Tipu Sultan who came in to replace the lifted off Advocate Haider for a while asked a number of pointed questions to Investigation Officer Syed Iqbal. In response to these questions he admitted, without a seeming lack of guile, that he had not ascertained when and for how many years Dr. Alamgir worked in various posts and positions and at what salaries and scale of remuneration and how much Dr. Alamgir had earned in dollars while working abroad. He admitted that he had ascertained how much Dr. Alamgir had received as salaries and allowances as the State Minister of the government. Quite candidly he admitted that he had not found any discrepancy in Dr. Alamgir's income tax returns; he stated that he had found all of Dr. Alamgir's income tax returns were correct.

"If tax returns were accepted as correct by the Income Tax department, can the same department or the ACC reopen the assessment and prosecute him for any omission or mistake without giving him opportunities for explanation, review, appeal and rectification under the income tax law?" asked Advocate Syed Rezaur Rahman at this point.

"I don't know," answered the witness.

He did not respond when he was asked to say whether in his careful assessment one being in jail could correctly and comprehensively write his asset statement in 72 hours and whether he knew correct English translation of the Bangla term *"amanat."*

As the day wore on, Advocate Ayat Ali Patwary took over the cross-examination of Investigation Officer Syed Iqbal. Tearing through a bedrock of make-believe depositions made earlier, in the cross-examination Syed Iqbal had to admit that his supplementary charge-sheet was not based on the supplementary or the second asset statement of Dr. Alamgir, that Dr. Alamgir did not conceal any asset in his statements, that his FDRs as mentioned in his statement were to be mentioned in the income tax return next year and that these were in the know of the National Board of Revenue or the tax authority and that this along with deduction of tax on interest income accrued on these Fixed Deposits at source on behalf of the depositor had been so acknowledged by the relevant personnel of the IFIC Bank.

Breaking the barricades of made-up depositions presented by Investigation Officer Syed Iqbal till sundown, I along with my lawyers felt tired. Despite being tired, I felt relieved, as the Prosecution Witness Syed Iqbal could not even in the tedium of his jabberings substantially prove anything incriminating against me. On the contrary, amongst others, he made evident (1) the incompleteness and perfunctory nature of their investigation, (2) lack of understanding of the accounting procedure and income tax laws, (3) ignorance about ownership of properties alleged to have been mine, (4) non-examination of two asset statements furnished by me, (5) unauthorized nature and process of investigation pursued and the admission that the filing of the charge-sheet was not authorized by the Commission in accordance with law of the ACC itself, and finally (6) his biased and unlawful intent to file the charge-sheet on the basis of further investigation instead of reporting the whole truth and nothing but the truth through dispassionate investigation.

Obviously the Prosecution had been pushed far beyond their rational comprehension. The Special Judge, without any seeming sign of understanding these matters, or change in heart or mind, or move to let me go, rose from his high chair-borne position and declared that depositions of all Prosecution Witnesses had come to a close and the next date of session would be July 9. I said on that day I would present the relevant documents in my defense in terms of a statement under Sections 342 and 265 of the Criminal Procedure Code. I hoped to break through the barrages of false accusations made against me and to cut through the sordid accounting of income and assets as had been done by the Prosecution in that statement. The Prosecution left the court as if they carried a creel of withered roots of guilt and falsehood.

(15)

Through a humid and faltering rainfall, at once inchoate and oppressive, the prison van rattled and took me back towards the Kashimpur Jail. Once over the flyover at Mohakhali, I noticed Dr. Sarwar Ali, an executive of Renata Ltd. with whom I was well-acquainted, and a known left-bent social speaker coming along in a car. He saw me as I saw him. I waved at him but he turned his face away in awkward contortions. The barrage of propaganda against us as corrupt persons even before we were adjudged so through the due process of law must have eaten through his rationality, molded his view of our past and changed his attitude towards me. It seemed that for only the fickle-minded impression of a moment, all that was created or gone on thus far was carried away. My thought also turned backward towards propaganda machinery of the Nazis in the pre-war Germany that tried the political opposition more in media than in open courts, in the process of the most hated State persecution in history. The present regime, which was bent upon taking over and sustaining power through the barrel of the gun, seemed to have been succeeding with its brand of verbal legerdemain designed along the lines etched by Goebbels.

Meal over, I tried to sleep in my cell in the Kashimpur Jail. But sleep seemed elusive; raindrops against the ceiling with occasional bursts of wind made an eerie expunging of the world as I knew. Against a brute group bent upon consolidating power to themselves, I did not know how the nation at large could hew out a new life of freedom, survive the ongoing storm of armed arrogance to reach a solid bank of rationality and pursuit of happiness befitting a land of the really free and brave. I thought of desperate measures, for, to me, these were desperate times threatening our very existence as an independent and democratic society. I also thought of the need for raising collective conscience of the society recognising what Dr. Martin Luther King recognized as early as 1963 in the U.S.: that injustice anywhere was a threat to justice everywhere.

6 My Statement

(1)

July 9 was fixed for presentation of my statement under Sections 342 and 265 of the Criminal Procedure Code. This gave me some time to write down the statement and collect the relevant documents that would be appended to it. I concentrated on this and by July 7, came up with a fairly well-written statement, along with supporting documents that my brother Dr. Jahangir collected and gave to me from time to time. From the jail, I could manage to send an advance copy of the statement to my lawyer Syed Rezaur Rahman for comments. He did not send any, except one cryptic line stating that "I would adduce my witnesses in support of my statement." Ahad, my assistant and nephew, helped me with typing out the statement.

Along with this preparation, I had to make arrangements for Sitara to leave the country immediately after submitting her asset statement. Through some friends, I could procure the relevant documents and papers for writing her statement of assets. In addition to my diplomat friend, Salman and his able assistant Mahbub helped me to make preparations for her departure through the net of prohibitions set by the regime covering all airports and land routes. Reservation in as many as five flights on three routes were made in her name; none other than my brother Dr. Jahangir, myself and our diplomat friend knew about her departure; none except two were in the know of her actual flight and Mahbub and the diplomat friend were assigned to check her in 10 minutes before the flight and to take her quietly and quickly through a rather loose immigration control set up on the western part of the airport for the VIPs of the regime, as we had planned earlier.

On July 6 Sitara came to see me alone at the Kashimpur Jail. She said, despite the arrangements made, she would not go; she said, if she went out we would not be able to meet in years. I reasoned with her, controlling tears in my eyes. I said there was no reason why she should, in addition to me, be detained in the jail or be put up before a kangaroo court. I said her presence here would not be much of a help; rather her presence abroad in freedom would help us to remain in touch with friends and well-wishers who would help. Since justice did not reign in our land and power was synonymous with honesty at the time, I said it would be prudent to inform others of the reigning injustice to make a collective and determined dent into it. Finding a few moments of absence of the jail personnel, we embraced and bade farewell to each other. With tears and courage she left me; with determination to stand against the evil forces and a sense of common stake in freedom and honor, I passed through the huge iron gate to be inside the jail, the citadel of injustice built up and filled in almost to the brim to satisfy the lust for unjust power of one or a few. John Francis Shade, (1898-1959) that reclusive American poet came to my mind: "One opal cloudlet in an oval form reflects the rainbow of a thunderstorm, which in a distant valley has been staged, for we are most artistically caged." Were we? I asked myself somewhat apprehensive of a limpid depth.

Distributed through limitless space and unbounded time, I passed the night in the dark. In the morning Salman came up with the news. Sitara had left last night. It was the Emirates with stopovers at Dubai and London. At Dhaka, it was a touch and go between brute forces of a king-aspirant and conscious good fortune bestowed by two good souls towering over the moronic persecution. She had walked out on through the tight rope. Our sons had been informed by Mahbub over the phone about the arrival of their mother. I sank into a momentary swoon of thankfulness to God. Then I blacked out in a swirling fatigue. After months of agony and anxiety, the black around me was a relief and sublime existence. Hatred and despair were nowhere to stop the beating of my heart, which I pressed with both my hands.

Between July 6 and 8 I read intermittently *A Thousand Splendid Suns* by the famous Afghan author Khaledi. Earlier I had read his first novel, *The Kite Runner*. I was impressed more by his theme than his style. In *The Kite Runner*; he showed how values sustained and cherished by a poor and neglected Afghan boy, gave him qualities of a noble human being in a hostile world. In *A Thousand Splendid Suns*, the author depicted the triumph of love through the ordeals and pains of the Afghan turmoil, fomented by the Taliban and their cohorts. Both these novels were glimmers of hope in the distress and despondency in which I was incarcerated.

I was not quite finished with *A Thousand Splendid Suns* when July 9 dawned. With a prepared text and in a somber mood, I boarded the rattling and smoke-emitting prison van and arrived at the Special Court at about 10:00 in the morning. The police escort made me sit alone in the cell adjacent to the courtroom; that gave me time and opportunity to put the appended documents in order. At 12 noon I was taken to the courtroom, placed on the dock of the accused to wait for the arrival of the Special Judge. When the Judge perched himself on his high chair, Musharraf Hossain Kajal, an advocate appointed by the ACC in another case, in the absence of Public Prosecutor Mizanur Rahman, stood up and stated like an usher in the court of a Sultan of bygone days:

"You, Dr. Muhiuddin Khan Alamgir, on the basis of evidence adduced by the Prosecution thus far, are accused of offense under Sections 26 and 27 of the ACC Act and Rule 15 (d) 5 of the Emergency Powers Rules. Do you have anything to say?"

"I will state my defense to the court and not to you nor at your behest or direction," I retorted.

I knew Advocate Kajal since 1997, when he was appointed by us in the government as a junior prosecuting lawyer in the Bangabandhu murder case. I had some contribution to make in hauling up the murderers of the father of the nation and preparing their prosecution 23 years after the ghastly crime was committed. I was surprised to see him now representing the ACC, and that too against me, hired from another case. I knew him as an intelligent, hardworking and honest person. In those days, once he requested me to make a *tadbir*[29] for admitting his son into a well-known English medium school in Dhaka. I told him smilingly that I did not make *tadbir* of such nature. When he pressed me further, I told him somewhat curtly that I would not make *tadbir* for admission for my own son even and I had not done so, ever. Since admission of one implied denial to another, any deviation from following the principle of merit-based admission was implicative of injustice and I would not be a conduit for it. That made him crestfallen and silent. But he worked diligently as a prosecuting lawyer in the Bangabandhu murder case. I was told he was once incarcerated in jail as a political activist. Observing my mood, Kajal became silent and slowly sat down by the side of the ever-present Major Kamruzzaman. The Major sat with his hands clamped behind, in obvious fury, as if he wanted more visibility in a clearer field of fire.

---

[29] Using one's influence to obtain a favor for another, not necessarily based on merit.

(2)

I started my statement under Sections 342 and 265 of the Criminal Procedure Code loudly and clearly, keeping my eyes on the Special Judge. At the outset, I stated I was innocent and I denied totally the charge framed against me. I pleaded not guilty. And said, I would adduce witnesses in my defense and in support of my statement.

I started with my career. I stated I was a member of the Presidium of the Bangladesh Awami League. In the late 1990s till 2001, I was the State Minister of the Ministry of Planning. In addition, in various parts of the same period, I was the State Minister-in-Charge of the Ministry of Civil Aviation & Tourism and of the Ministry of Science & Technology. With a Masters in Economics from the Dhaka University, I entered the erstwhile CSP (Civil Service of Pakistan) in 1965. In many phases of my career, I served with distinction as a teacher of the Dhaka University, Deputy Secretary, Ministry of Finance, Deputy Commissioner, Jessore, Joint Secretary, External Relations Division, Additional Secretary, Ministry of Finance, Executive Director, Islamic Development Bank, Jeddah, Managing Director, Bangladesh Shilpa Bank, Chairman, Boards of Directors of Bangladesh Krishi Bank, Investment Corporation of Bangladesh, Bangladesh Shilpa Rin Sangstha, Member, Directing Staff, Public Administration Training Center, Chairman, Tariff Commission, Secretary, Ministry of Science & Technology, Member, Planning Commission, and Secretary to the Prime Minister (1996-98) when I retired voluntarily from the Civil Service. I was the member-secretary of the Civil Administration Restoration Committee (1972-74) and contributed to setting up the structure of the Bangladesh government after Independence. I was member-secretary of the Land Reform Committee (1984), on the basis of the report of which ceiling on ownership of agricultural land was lowered down to 60 bighas[30] and the owner's share of the produce of agricultural land given to sharecropping was limited to one third of the produce by law. During my tenure as Executive Director, Islamic Development Bank (IDB), I also served in Boards of Directors of a number of international companies located in Indonesia and Turkey in which IDB was a shareholder. I contributed to open up the oil-rich middle-eastern countries as an important source of develop-

---

[30] A bigha is a unit of land measure that varies from region to region, but is usually approximately a third of an acre.

ment aid for Bangladesh. I opened up similar productive economic relations with the socialist countries, especially USSR and China.

While in service, I obtained an M.A. in Political Economy, an M.A. in Economics and a Ph.D. in Economics from Boston University, U.S.A. in the shortest possible time. I served as the lead consultant of UNCDF (UN Capital Development Fund), preparing reconstruction program for Uganda, Africa, (1980) and as a Distinguished Visitor to the U.S.-sponsored Asia Foundation and affiliated to Penn State University, State College, Pennsylvania, (1989). I authored quite a number of books and articles on Economics, published nationally and internationally; I was President of the Bangladesh Economic Association and General Secretary of the Civil Service (Administration) Association. I was a life-member of the Bangla Academy. I contributed to the setting up of the Bangla Department in the University of Sindh (1970). I set up quite a number of educational institutions and social welfare organizations. I was a life-member of the American Alumni Association, Bangladesh. I was the founder and chief patron of the Bangladesh Non-Government Primary Teachers Association. I also set up the Jessore Shikkha Trust and the Kachua Shikkha Trust for giving financial help and support to the poor and meritorious students.

After retiring from the service of the Republic, I served as the State Minister, Ministries of Planning, Civil Aviation & Tourism, and of Science & Technology. While serving as Secretary to the Prime Minister, I negotiated the historic Ganga Water Sharing Treaty with India, and the Peace Accord of Chittagong Hill Tracts. I was the main author of the Fifth Five-Year Plan (1997-2001) under the aegis of which the country attained a growth rate of 6.7% per year, literacy rate of 65% and average life expectancy of 62 years, all highest since 1974.

After the Coalition Government of Khaleda and Nizami came to power in 2001, while returning from the U.S. after medical treatment, on February 15, 2002, I was arrested under the Special Powers Act on prejudicial political grounds and framed falsely in a number of criminal cases. My detention under the Special Powers Act, protested against by national and international professional associations and human rights bodies, was subsequently declared illegal and proceedings under all other aforesaid cases stayed by the Supreme Court (High Court Division).

I stated that I took part in normal, legal and peaceful political activities after my release from the jail in September 2002. As a member of the Presidium, the Awami League, I was quite conscious of my duties and obligations as a citizen of an independent and democratic country administered under the Constitution. As a member of the Presidium, between 2003 and 2005, I visited, on invitation, the USA, Australia, France, Germany, Austria, Spain, Switzerland and the U.K. I was nominated by the Awami League as a candidate to the Parliament in the national election slated for January 22, 2007. Following cancellation of the election and declaration of the emergency in the country on January 11, 2007, I supported the emergency measures along with my party and attended, on invitation, the oath-taking ceremony of the Caretaker Government led by Dr. Fakhruddin Ahmed. Then on February 3, 2007, at about midnight, I was arrested without warrant from my residence at Banani, Dhaka by a team of the RAB (the Rapid Action Battalion of the Police), kept confined in their headquarters for more than two days (*i.e.* more than 24 hours, violating my constitutional right) and then produced before a metropolitan magistrate, who detained me under the Special Powers Act for prevention of activities purported to be subversive of the State. My detention was subsequently declared illegal by the High Court Division.

While in detention in the Kashimpur Jail 1, on February 20, 2007, I was notified by the Secretary, ACC by a letter signed premeditatively on January 18, 2007 (the letter was on record with the court) to submit within 72 hours of receipt, a statement of my assets. At the time the notice was served on me, with its first Chairman and Members having left in resignation the ACC was not in existence; it was yet to be formed with a new Chairman and Members. The notice given under Sections 26 and 27 of the ACC Act and Rule 15 (d) 5 of the Emergency Powers Rules by the Secretary, ACC required me to give description of my assets and sources of their funding, including assets held in other's name on my behalf but excluding assets that might have been held by me on behalf of others. No format was given or procedure laid down in accordance with Section 26 of the ACC Act in the notice to write in the statement of assets. Nor was "asset" defined in the notice to make it meaningful in terms of inclusiveness or exclusiveness.

I said that being in jail without access to my records and papers and being denied consultation with my income tax advisor and lawyers and with a medical condition of early streaks of Alzheimer's at an age of 66 and within constrained time limit, I wrote my statement of assets in presence of the personnel of the

Special Branch (the Police) and the jailor in less than an hour and handed it over to my brother Dr. Burhanuddin Khan Jahangir on February 20, 2007 for reaching the same to the ACC within the time limit set by its Secretary. As a political detainee, I could not have taken even one hour, not to speak of a day more to write my asset statement, as nobody would have been allowed to see me before the expiry of fifteen days after February 20, 2007 (when my brother and wife were allowed by authorities to see me in detention in jail) and take my asset statement to the ACC as my authorized representative in time so set. In the circumstances I in good faith gave the required statement without concealing anything. And I had no intention to conceal anything.

In my statement of assets, constrained as I was by lack of time, access to relevant papers and consultation with my income tax advisor and lawyer, and a medical condition originating in aging, as required by the notice, I described from memory my immovable and movable assets earned over a life-time, with sources/incomes. I stated, amongst other facts, that (1) costs/values mentioned against each item of the statement were estimates or approximations; (2) my wife Sitara Alamgir, a Masters in Economics from Boston University, U.S.A., (the first woman from Bangladesh to get such a degree from the U.S.A.) aged 60, my elder son, Dr. Jalal Alamgir, an Assistant Professor in the University of Massachusetts, Boston, U.S.A. aged 36, and my younger son, Joy Alamgir, Chief Executive Officer of Consilience Inc., a software firm also in the U.S.A., aged 28, were, insofar as their incomes originating in Bangladesh, separate income taxpayers without their being in any way economically dependent on me. In the letter covering my statement, I stated that in the event the ACC required any explanation in respect of any information given in the statement, it would be appropriate for them and conducive of their purpose to see me there in the jail where I was detained or at their option, in the ACC's office. The statement was on record with the court, I added.

Without seeing and obtaining any clarification on any item of the statement from me, the ACC froze the bank accounts of mine, my wife and sons, filed an FIR (first information report) under the Emergency Powers Ordinance 2007 {rule 15 of sro 15; 15(a) (b) and (c) } and the Anti-Corruption Commission Act, 2004 (sections 26 & 27) and the Prevention of Corruption Act, 1947 {section 5(2)} with Tejgaon Police Station, Dhaka on March 6, 2007 alleging that I didn't mention in my statement of assets about (a) 6 FDRs (fixed deposit receipts) valued at Tk. 117 lacs (Tk. 11.7 million) and (b) sources/incomes from which these were obtained and thus purported to have concealed them.

In the FIR so filed, it was not mentioned that in my asset statement in reference, I had in fact stated that I had *Sanchay Patras* and *Amanat Patras, i.e.*, FDRs valued approximately at Tk. 90 lacs with their proximate sources of funding. Instead it was mentioned in the FIR by way of obfuscating the truth that these FDRs were not mentioned in the wealth statement pertaining to my income tax return for FY 2006 earlier furnished to the Income Tax Department. The FIR was on record with the court for its perusal and examination at length, I pointed out.

(3)

I stated that filing of the FIR was followed by investigation by Jiban Krishna Roy and Shermin Ferdousi of the ACC for fifty-three days and submission of a charge-sheet (that is arraignment) on April 29, 2007. In the operational part of the charge-sheet, it was alleged that I had concealed holding of 6 FDRs valued at Tk. 117 lacs, which was beyond my known sources of income. Before the charge could be considered for framing on the basis of this, the Prosecution at the time prayed for further investigation and, after obtaining permission for the purpose, got the FIR investigated further beyond the scope of allegation mentioned therein by Syed Iqbal Hossain, Deputy Director, ACC, and then submitted a Supplementary Charge-sheet on May 21, 2007.

Counting from the date of filing the FIR, the investigation in its two parts thus took 106 days, exceeding by far the 60 days mandated and prescribed under the ACC Rules. In the Supplementary Charge-sheet, on assessment of ancestral and family assets purported to be mine alone, it was alleged that I had concealed assets worth Tk. 2,10,88,465 (Tk. 2 crore 10 lac, 88 thousand and 465) in addition to FDRs of Tk. 117 lacs as mentioned in the original charge-sheet. Thus, it was alleged, I committed offenses under Sections 26 (2), and 27 (1) of the ACC Act and R-15 (d) 5 of the Emergency Powers Rules, 2007. These charge-sheets were on record with the court and I requested the court to examine them in depth.

Earlier on April 7, 2007, a Task Force led by Major Khandaker Kamruzzaman met me in the office of the jailor, Kashimpur Jail, and conversed with me about my work, assets and whereabouts of my family members in the presence of the deputy jailor. This was recorded in the testimony of Jailor Enamul Haq dated June 6, 2007. On the basis of this conversation, rather than a hearing on notice on specific items of my asset statement dated February 20, 2007, on April 28, 2007, through the jailor I submitted a revision/addition to my asset statement dated February 20, 2007. As it turned out, though they received it (as testified by the Superintendent of the Kashimpur Jail on June 6, 2007) the IOs (Investigation Officers) did not take into account these revisions and additions and clarifications while they prepared the aforesaid charge-sheet. Obviously, I stressed, they obviated from the dictum of telling the whole truth to the court.

Here I paused, observed that the Special Judge was listening with a grim face while Major Kamruzzaman was sitting in the courtroom by the side of Musharraf Hossain Kazal, giving proxy for the Public Prosecutor on that day. I drank a glass of water and stated that filing of these two charge-sheets and framing of charges against me on their basis were not the end-product of a due process of law and diligent investigation. First, the central ingredient of offense under Rule 15 (d) 5 was the notice or order given by a member of the law enforcement force or an Investigation Officer (IO) as per Rule 15 (c) of the Emergency Powers Rules. The Secretary, ACC who signed and sent the notice to me for furnishing of the asset statement was neither a member of the law enforcement force nor an IO within the meaning of Rule 15 (c) of the Emergency Powers Rules. By signing and sending the notice under Rule 15 (d) 5, the Secretary, ACC acted with unreasonable enthusiasm, beyond his limits of jurisdiction and the bounds of legality. Section 16 of the ACC Act defining the Secretary's duties does not give any authority to him to go on with such an onslaught of the Rule 15 (d) 5 of the Emergency Powers Rules either. Therefore, with all the emphasis in my command, I said, no legal liability or obligation was placed on me by this notice, and no offense was liable or could be implicated to me under Rule 15 (d) 5 of the Emergency Powers Rules. Thus framing of charge against me under R 15 (d) 5 was *ab initio* illegal and void.

Second, I went on, the two ingredients of ascribing offense under Section 26 of the ACC Act were: (i) satisfaction of the Commission on the basis of information received or inquiry conducted that assets of the notice-receiver-to-be were not in conformity with his legitimate sources of income and (ii) submission of asset statement (and by implication, its sequential assessment) not in accordance with the procedure set by the Commission. It transpired from the testimonies of IOs that in this instance, before issuing the notice, the Commission, neither on the basis of information received nor inquiry conducted, knew or was satisfied as to which portion of my assets was not in conformity with my known and legitimate income. It was also evident that the Commission did not set a procedure or format for incorporating the asset statement by me.

As a matter of fact, I emphasized, the procedure for incorporating the asset statement that could be submitted under Section 26 of the ACC Act was set by Rule 17 (1) of the ACC Rules and form 5 pertaining to this Rule on March 29, 2007, which was more than a month after the notice was served on me. Therefore, the notice under Section 26 of the ACC Act issued by the Secretary on me was vague, incomplete, incongruous and misleading and thus not tenable to the discomfiture of the notice-recipient (me). Further, Section 26 of the ACC Act did not set 72 hours as the time limit for submission of asset statement. This was done by the Secretary, ACC in case of me with a prejudice and vindictiveness not warranted by or tenable under the law, I pointed out. Subsequently when examining the asset statement as was submitted by me, the ACC evidently assessed its format, contents, inclusiveness and exclusiveness by the standard of procedure set forth by Rule 17 (1) of the ACC Rules and form 5 pertaining to this Rule. Any purported deviation from this standard set forth subsequently was not a liability and responsibility of incomplete discharge of a lawful requirement for which an offense could reasonably be imputed to me. Summed up as such, Section 26 of the ACC Act in terms of these aforesaid two ingredients did not apply to my discomfiture in ways it was applied by the IOs.

Third, I said, Section 27 of the ACC Act has two ingredients of offense: (i) assets acquired through dishonest ways and (ii) assets not in conformity with known sources of income. I had given (i) details of sources of my *Sanchay Patras and Amanat Patras* (FDRs) on p. 3 item 4 of my statement of assets of February 20, 2007 mentioning, amongst other things, that (i) I had opted to take all my pension benefits all at once (1998); (ii) I had annualized (at 8%) rental income from my house at Banani of Tk. 87.97 lacs between 1992 and 2006 in my revised statement of assets submitted on April 28, 2007; (iii) estimate of savings of my regular salaried income (@15% savings of monthly salary annualized at 8%) between 1963 and 2001 of Tk. 76.46 lacs; (v) estimated yield from Tk. 65.63 lacs of investable funds (total of sub-item from (ka) through (ha) of item 4 of statement of assets of February 20, 2007 with annualized 8% return totaling a minimum of Tk. 305 lacs and a maximum of Tk. 574 lacs, all in accordance with internationally accepted good accounting practices. These estimates included items that were not mentioned in the asset statement of February 20, 2007, because the ACC failed to specify a format or procedure in accordance with Section 26 of the ACC Act for writing the asset statement along with the notice served on me. These did not in any way negate the principle on the basis of which the aforesaid first statement of assets was written.

These estimates of my savings and investable funds proved that all my assets were in full conformity with my known or legitimate sources of income. This, coupled with the Prosecution's failure or inability to point out that I had acquired any asset in a dishonest way, proved beyond all reasonable doubt that Section 27 of the ACC Act could not be applied in my case. Even IO Jiban Krishna who had filed the FIR admitted in his testimony of May 30, 2007, that he had not known of any specific instance of acquisition of assets in a dishonest way by me. Similarly, Prosecution Witness Rabiul Hasan Prodhan, Assistant Commissioner, Income Tax, admitted in his testimony on June 6, 2007 that IT (Income Tax) department did not ever have any objection against me as an IT assessee and payer. I categorically stated that all throughout my life I maintained strict frugality and hence my savings.

Then I turned my attention to flaws in investigation. As per Rule 15 (c) of the Emergency Powers Rules, FIR or complaint against the accused was to be investigated and completed by an IO (Investigation Officer) appointed by the government for the purpose. This was not done so. Instead, in this case investigation was undertaken and completed by three IOs in succession as appointed by the ACC. The investigation was, therefore, unauthorized and without any legal applicability as per Rule 15 (c) 5 of the EPR. For investigation under the ACC Act, in this case under Sections 26 and 27, IOs were to be appointed as per Rule 24 of the ACC Rules. Such an appointment was required to be notified in the government's Gazette under Section 20 (2) of the ACC Act. This was never done. For scrutinizing the asset statements furnished by me, the procedure prescribed by Rule 17 (5) of the ACC Rules was not followed; filing of FIR was not in accordance with Rule 17 (6) of the ACC Rules (as the ACC Rules came into force on March 29, 2007, the FIR supposed to have been preceded by a scrutiny was filed on March 6, 2007); no instance of complaint of corruption against me could be cited by the IOs or by following the set procedure of scrutiny of complaints by a committee comprising, amongst others, a non-official honest and acclaimed member of the society as per Rule 5 of the ACC Rules; this was posited on record. IO Jiban Krishna in his testimony of May 29,

2007 admitted that he did not even obtain approval of his supervisor Nusrat Ara Surat Amin for filing the FIR against me.

I was not given an opportunity to be heard on my asset statement or alleged offense in accordance with Section 22 of the ACC Act and Rule 8 of the ACC Rules and the principle of natural justice. In conducting investigation, the concerned IO under the tutelage of the leader of the relevant task force could not follow the principle and modicum laid down by the Criminal Procedure Code, especially Section 4 (1) (1) for an unimpeded, independent and impartial investigation. As testified by Investigation Officer Syed Iqbal, the charge-sheet for prosecution in the court was approved by only one member, namely, Manzur Mannan.

The law prescribed that all decisions of the Commission would have to be taken in meetings of the Commission, *i.e.*, jointly by the Chairman and two members of the Commission. In my case this was not so done. Surely Manzur Mannan by himself alone did not constitute and represent the ACC. For all these procedural omissions, irregularities and violations, vitiation of justice was the resultant predicament against the unbreakable principles of rule of law, justice and fair play. This, I emphasized, was a classic example of truncation of the dictum of telling of the whole truth to the end of dispensing justice under the principle of rule of law in a just society constitutionally obligated to give every citizen equal protection under law. This forfeited legal as well as moral authority of the ACC for prosecuting me, I added.

Then I drew attention of the Special Court to the flaws of the notice. The notice of the Secretary, ACC sent to me for submission of asset (*i.e.* movable and immovable properties) statement had four built-in definite flaws and misconceived implications. First, the notice did not define assets: As a matter of fact, nowhere in the ACC Act "assets" was defined in terms of substance, inclusiveness or exclusiveness, difference with the concept of wealth, or a stock of wealth or a flow of income. Movable and immovable properties were not defined either. Second, the notice required description of assets and their sources, not their values. I added that this was also admitted by Prosecution Witness Nusrat Ara Surat Amin in her testimony of June 6, 2007. Third, the notice wanted me to give description of my assets (undefined as aforesaid) including those held by others on my behalf; it did not require me to describe assets held by me on behalf of others, say a trust or a foundation, a son or a friend. Fourth, it was dated (under the signature of the Secretary, ACC) January 18, 2007, *i.e.*, almost a month before I was arrested and put under detention giving it a smack of premeditated measure of harassment and victimization instead of a follow-up of logical and legal measures to take a really corrupt person to book. The notice so dated constituted a part of the court's record and I requested the court to examine it in depth.

While assessing the asset statement, despite these built-in-incongruities and flaws, the IOs and the Prosecution took pains to (i) measure and assess values of every item described by me in my asset statement in current market prices through agents of their choice instead of at cost at the time of acquisition and on the basis of Construction Cost Indexes (Building) compiled and published by the government as was or should have been done usually in such a case; (ii) include other's assets held by me as mine own and (iii) omit and hide the obvious and evidently sinister attempt at premeditated motive to harass and victimize an innocent law-abiding, educated citizen even before the time or occasion so demanded following a minimum modicum of just and fair process. All these go to prove beyond reasonable doubt that in my case, through serving an incongruous and vague notice and following a dubious and improper procedure, the due process of law based on diligent and impartial investigation was not only ignored but way beyond, sidelined and even obliterated turning the entire process of prosecution into a colorable and partial exercise of witch-hunting untenable in law.

(4)

Then I drew attention to FDRs and the allegation about their concealment. The allegation in the first charge-sheet that I didn't mention FDRs in my statement of assets was not at all correct and I totally denied the same. I pointed out that on p. 3 item 4 of my statement of assets furnished to the ACC in Bangla, I had mentioned the value of my *Sanchaya Patras* and *Amanat Patras* at approximately Tk. 90 lacs. *Amanat Patra* is the Bangla translation of FDR. Evidently the Bangla translation of FDR was ignored by those who examined the statement and filed the FIR and the charge-sheet. In the statement furnished from jail without access to papers and documents and income tax advisor and lawyer, such an approximation was reflective of bona fide reporting. A minor variation in exactitude, under the circumstances was not indicative of, nor did it connote, concealment of financial instruments kept in a public institution like a scheduled bank, bearing names and other relevant particulars of depositors or of a mala fide intention to do so.

In my second statement of April 28, 2007, written out once again from memory and under constrained circumstances of being in jail without access to records, I stated that I had *Sanchaya Patras and Amanat Patras* of approximately Tk.120 lacs. In this figure, I included *Amanat Patras* or FDRs of approximately Tk. 25 lacs that I held on behalf of the Sultana Foundation. Subsequently I found the accumulated fund of the Sultana Foundation was marginally more. The Sultana Foundation, with an initial capital contribution of Tk. 31 lacs or so was agreed to be set up in 1988 by our family as a trust in memory of our mother for providing educational support to deserving students and financial assistance to the poor. As per this Agreement signed by almost all family members, pending raising its paid-up capital to at least Tk. 50 lacs and its formal registration under the Trust Act, its capital money was to be in my custody and its work and operation in the interim in furtherance of its objectives within the ambit of my responsibility on behalf of other family members. In 2006 the Foundation's assets or capital amounted to approximately Tk. 34 lacs, which I held along with my savings in FDR's. I placed a copy of the notarized Agreement on Foundation to the court for record and in-depth examination. I stated, the IOs never investigated into the creation and operation of this Foundation. As per the requirement of the notice of the Secretary, ACC, I was not required to mention assets held by me on behalf of others and that was why I did not mention the Foundation's capital fund with me in the first asset statement. I asserted that added to Tk.90 lacs (more or less) mentioned in the first asset statement, these together in approximations figured more than Tk.117 lacs and removed any scope for understatement or concealment.

Further, in this figure of Tk. 117 lacs was included Tk. 47 lacs of my son Dr. Jalal Alamgir. Dr. Jalal Alamgir aged, 36, was an Assistant Professor in the University of Massachusetts, Boston, U.S.A. earning over US$ 100,000, or Tk. 70 lacs a year. This was evidenced in his tax return to the U.S. Federal Government. I presented a copy of his tax return to the U.S. Federal Government for the court's perusal. Dr. Jalal Alamgir was allotted a NAM flat by RAJUK in 2001 at a price of Tk. 47 lacs 16 thousand 8 hundred & 50. For paying the price he kept with me Tk. 50 lacs. After paying three installments totaling only Tk. 33 lacs 1 thousand 7 hundred and 95, RAJUK unilaterally cancelled the allotment and returned Tk. 33 lacs 1 thousand seven hundred and 94 on January 5, 2006, *i.e.*, after five years and without any interest. I produced the relevant documents on these to the court as evidence for its examination. Since Dr. Jalal Alamgir was abroad at that time, at his request, I kept this amount along with the rest of Tk. 47 lacs in FDRs in my name on April 17, 2007 and April 18, 2007 together with my savings in IFIC Bank, Karwan Bazar, so that I could return the money on time and he could buy a flat of his choice when he would get back and settle down in his homeland in the summer of 2007. This left for Tk. 36 lacs stated in my wealth statement furnished to income tax (IT) authority in FY 2006, which conformed to my IT records for FY 2006. Thus, in essence, there was no mis-statement and concealment of facts to income tax authorities by me as alleged by the ACC. The income tax authority never complained about a mis-statement or concealment either.

Then I indicated the sources of my FDRs, savings and investment capacity. I stated that leaving aside Dr. Jalal Alamgir's Tk. 50 lacs or so kept with me, the proximate sources of such *Sanchaya Patras and Amanat Patras* or FDRs had been mentioned in item 4, from sub-items (ka) through (khiya) on pages 4 and 5 in the statement of assets dated February 20, 2007 furnished by me. The statement was on record with the court as an evidentiary exhibit. The total of these figured at Tk. 95.73 lacs, more or less, justifying holding of these Sanchaya Patras and FDRs (excluding those of the Sultana Foundation) by me. Over this amount, in sub-item (ha) it was mentioned that I had not opted for monthly pension on my retirement in 1998; instead I had opted to draw my entire gratuity, provident fund accumulations and pension capital totaling approximately Tk. 19 lacs at one go. Reasonably capitalizing this amount (*i.e.* Tk. 19 lacs) at 8% annual return as obtainable from *Sanchaya Patras*/FDRs as informal or formal investment would, through addition of yield, double this amount by 2006, *i.e.*, make the total investable fund on this count figure at Tk. 145.73 lacs, (95.73 + 19 + 31 lacs, the latter being approximation of capital fund of the Sultana Foundation held by me). This amount of investment capability, however did not exactly mean that it was fully utilized in investment. It indicated the reasonably known, legal and bona fide financial capability to invest or legitimate resource envelope that could be used for such investment by me.

Then I drew the attention of the Special Judge to the yield from savings of my non-salary income. The return from investment of savings/income as mentioned in sub-items from (ka) through (ha) of item 4 amounting to Tk. 65.73 lacs as mentioned in the first asset statement on the basis of base figures given by me was subsequently calculated through computer assuming 8% annual return, reasonably assuming that a half of total receipts from subitems (ka) through (ha) amounting to Tk. 65.73 lacs for 38 years from 1965 to 2006 (time span of such receipts) was invested in one form or other, formally or informally, and thus yielded a total return of Tk. 5 crores, 74 lacs, 40 thousand and 337.

A more conservative and sophisticated procedure based on arithmetic progression in capacity to invest more in later years than in earlier ones, yielded a total return of Tk. 3 crores 5 lacs 66 thousand and 926. Following internationally accepted accounting procedures in such a case, these figures indicated reasonable extent of receipts or yields from *Sanchaya Patras, Amanat Patras* and other financial instruments or formal or informal investments prior to 2007 justifying my bona fide capacity to hold financial instruments or FDRs valued much more than Tk. 117 lacs, alleged to have been beyond my means in the charge-sheet. Yearly calculation of such yields, following both these procedures, were given on computer print-outs. These I produced before the court for its inspection and record. The Public Prosecutor came over his table to see these. By way of clarification, I said, I had mentioned these figures in my second statement of assets as addition and revision, which were conveniently ignored by the IOs.

Then I stated, the ACC while giving me the notice did not prescribe any procedure, *i.e.*, form or format in which the statement of assets as per Section 26 of the ACC Act was to be furnished. That was why in my statement of assets furnished to the ACC, I did not describe or mention my rental income from letting out 1st and 2nd stories of my residential house (at Banani) following completion of its 3rd and 4th stories in 1992. I received an average monthly rent of approximately Tk. 30,000/, *i.e.*, 3,60,000 a year, from which deducting two month's rental (a year) for maintenance and (city) corporation's tax, from 1992 to 2006, my total receipt amounted to approximately Tk. 42 lacs.

As admitted by Prosecution Witness Assistant Income Tax Commissioner, Prodhan, this income in approximate terms was accounted for in my income tax returns for the relevant period. Added to my investable fund of Tk. 148.73 lacs as spelled out earlier, this totaled my investable surplus alone at Tk. 190.73 lacs at the minimum (excluding annualized return as shown earlier). Assuming that this rental amount (Tk. 42 lacs) was invested in one form or other, in monetized financial instruments or non-monetized embodiments yielding an annual return of 8%, the extent of income from this source amounted to Tk. 87 lacs 97 thousand and 285. Added together these justified more than adequately my capacity to hold FDRs and *Sanchaya Patras* and other assets much over Tk. 117 lacs. The details of these calculations made by computer on the basis of base figures given by me were presented before the Special Judge. This amount was mentioned in my second asset statement dated April 28, 2007 and despite that conveniently ignored by the IOs.

Then I concentrated on my savings from salary income. Since despite the legal requirement, no form or format was given or prescribed at the time the notice was served, in my first asset statement to the ACC, I said, I did not indicate the extent of my savings from regular salary income. In item 4 from sub-item (ka) through (khiya), of my asset statement of February 20, 2007 corrected or annualized at 8%, my receipt from non-regular extra or adjunct salary income only was accounted for. In addition, if it was reasonably assumed that starting from 1963 (when I entered Dhaka University as a teacher) till 2000 (when I ceased to receive salary) I saved at a rate of 15% of my salary income every month/year, and such savings gave me an annual return of 8% in one form or other (to save erosion of value of savings given an assumed conservative annual inflation rate of 6%), yield on this count worked out at Tk. 48 lacs 18 thousand and 310 Taka.

This on the basis of base figures given by me was spelled out in the computer print-out that I produced before the court. This I had stated in my second asset statement of April 28, 2007, which was likewise ignored by the IOs. Added to other receipts as given above and read with my entire statement of assets (dated February 20, 2007 and April 28, 2007) furnished to the ACC, this amount of savings, I asserted, adequately justified holding of all my present immovable and movable assets. And these, beyond all reasonable doubt, proved that I was never ever involved in corruption or with ways unbecoming of a responsible public servant and citizen.

(5)

After this I took up explanation of payment of income tax. I stated that I had been paying income taxes since 1962, as was required of me under the income tax laws as were amended and enforced from time to time. Given that income as used in income tax laws was a concept of flow and statement of wealth and that the prescribed format relevant to this concept and required to be submitted along with income tax return was of comparatively recent vintage and was more of a flow instead of a stock, there was a difference as to inclusions in such a statement and a general asset statement outside a given format and bereft of a definition of an asset, as was furnished to the ACC by me under constrained circumstances such as being in jail and without access to relevant records and lawyers. Besides, income tax was paid in installments, *i.e.*, at sources of income and in advance of assessment, and at most of the time, in case of me (being a servant of the Republic) deemed to have been paid by the government at various stages of assessment and tax and financial years.

In this process, spread over time, underpayment for a particular year was made up, overpayment adjusted through a process of advance filing and due-dated filing, preliminary assessment, final assessment and also through reviews and appeals, arbitration and rectification. The Law of Limitation did not apply in case of income tax payment, making the process continuous and open-ended. In view of this situation, in the event it was found that there had been a case of omission, underpayment or overpayment for any year, this could be made up and adjusted according to the law and prescribed procedure. I pointed out that all these matters were admitted in the testimony given by the Assistant Commissioner (Income Tax) on June 10, 2007. Anything left to be done, from the side of the payee or the payer in this process being adjustable, rectifiable and open-ended and unencumbered by the Law of Limitation as such and could not be construed to have an element of corruption or corrupt practice as was given to be understood or purported in the charge-sheet against me.

Then I drew the attention of the Special Court to the payment of income tax on FDRs. The six Fixed Deposits (FDs), mentioned to have been kept by me in the relevant bank on April 17, 2006 and April 18, 2006 and maturable on April 17, 2007 and April 18, 2007 as mentioned in the charge-sheet, remained to yield interest or income to me on April 17, 2007 and April 18, 2007 when I was in jail, past and beyond the date of submission of statement of assets. Besides, income tax payable on yields from them remained to be paid in advance by June 30, 2007 and finally by September/October 2007, which was eight months after I had submitted the same statement when final assessment on income and tax payable on such income would have been made. Therefore, the time for including these FDs in the statement of assets relevant for income for the financial year 2006-07 could not be said to have expired to my discomfiture and disadvantage, attracting the mischief of the law. As a matter of fact, it was not required of me to mention these FDs in my income tax return for the fiscal year ending June 30, 2006. Besides, as per the income tax law and rules as were in force, tax payable on these FDs remained to be deducted at source by the relevant bank. For FY 2007, as testified by the AVP, IFIC bank, Karwan Bazar, (on May 30, 2007) 10% tax on interest accrued on these FDs had already been credited to the Deputy Commissioner (Income Tax) concerned on April 18, 2007 on my behalf and in my name.

This means there was no scope for me as a depositor to conceal these FDs or to go without paying tax on them. Information on such deduction, including particulars of the taxpayer on whose behalf such deduction was or would have been made, was sent to the NBR or the income tax department following a set procedure. This was also admitted by the Assistant Commissioner (IT) in course of his testimony before the court on June 11, 2007. This meant the NBR or the income tax authority was always in the legal and dutiful know of such FDRs or financial instruments making the question of concealment an impossible and irrelevant issue and not ascribable in any incriminating way to me. The only sequential requirement in this case for me remained to mention these in my statement of assets to be given finally with my income tax return in September/October next or even in later years when I would have encashed[31] these FDRs. Thus the allegation of concealment of these FDRs under Section 26 and 27 of ACC Act and 15 (d) 5 of the Emergency Powers Rules and their being beyond lawful income or bounds of reasonable knowledge of the IT authority as made in the charge-sheet was a mistake of law as well as of fact and consequently did not stand in terms of incrimination against me.

(6)

Allegations against me made in the first charge-sheet having thus been proved inapplicable and untenable under law, I turned my attention to the untenable nature of the charges made in the supplementary charge-sheet dated May 21, 2007 under the relevant heads.

Land: In the supplementary charge-sheet, it was mentioned that (i) Kachua Subregistry reported that I had in my own and joint names 3.79 acres of land valued at Tk. 7,93,712 (Tk. 7 lacs, ninety-three thousand and seven hundred twelve) acquired over last 12 years; (ii) Kachua Police reported that in Kachua area I and my family have 15.83 acres of land of an approximate value

[31] Liquidated, turned into cash.

of Tk. 79 lacs; and (iii) I did not give an estimate of value of my lands as reported in my statement of assets. In my statement of assets (p. 1, item 2) written under constrained circumstances of being in jail without access to records, I had stated that I had 15 to 16 acres of land in and around village Gulbahar of which approximately 10 to 12 acres were purchased by me. There was no substantial or material difference in quantity of land as reported by the Sub-Registry and the Police on the one hand and myself on the other. Village Gulbahar was within Kachua P.S. and separated from Kachua Pourashava by two villages in between and, therefore, lands in and around Gulbahar were inclusive of lands in Kachua as reported by the Sub-Registry and the police. Land reported by the Sub-Registry (3.79 acres) as the end-product of purchases and sales in the last 12 years by me and my family was evidently included in lands reported by the Police (15.83 acres).

Value of land was not stated by me in my statement of assets, as the notice from the ACC's Secretary did not require me to do so. I was asked to describe such assets, which I did in my statement of assets. Besides, constrained by detention in jail, such valuation either at cost (verifying deeds of sale) or market price (verifying current sale deeds from the Sub-Registry) was not possible and could not, therefore, be said to be reasonably expected of me. Besides, value of land as reported by the police was obviously approximate present market value, not purchase cost. Cost of purchase of land was evidently within the bounds of my saving/investment capacity as spelled out earlier by me.

Building at Home: The IO reported that I had two buildings at our village home, one named "Sitara Bhaban" and the other named "Sultana Bhaban," built by me at my cost, estimated by them at Tk. 57 lacs 46 thousand and 6 hundred and 21. This was not correct. We have a jointly owned twin house at our village home. Nowhere in this twin house was the word "Bhaban" inscribed. We were four brothers and four sisters. In our ancestral home we had a twin-building owned by all brothers and sisters jointly and built at stages from 1980 to 1999 with contribution made by all from time to time. The ancestral home was named Al-Asheq and it was inscribed on the wall of the front gate. Construction of the twin house was supervised by my eldest brother Misbahuddin Khan (a former Member of the Parliament, who retired as Vice-Chairman, Dock Labor Management Board, Chittagong Port Trust), now deceased.

The twin building, with still unpainted walls and unfinished work and having one common kitchen, cost approximately Tk. 12

lacs (Tk. 5 lacs in the first stage and Tk. 7 lacs in the second stage approximately). Contribution of myself to this cost was approximately Tk. 2 lacs given over 18 years. Sale produce of land, ponds and receipts from sharecroppers also went into its construction. The cost estimate of this twin house as made by the Executive Engineer, the PWD (Public Works Department), Chandpur, was obviously at later or current prices and purported to represent cost at the time of actual construction and thus was way off the mark of a realistic valuation of the actual cost.

It needs to be mentioned that following Construction Cost Index (Building), compiled and published by the Bureau of Statistics (BBS) of the government every year, which was applicable to all sectors, public and private and all areas, rural and urban, cost estimate of this twin house in 2006 prices would be much different from the cost estimate made by the PWD (*vide*, *Statistical Year Book of Bangladesh 2004*, p. 468) purportedly for the actual years of construction.

But such difference between actual cost incurred at the time of construction and cost calculated on the basis of or because of change in schedule of a particular department of the IO's choosing, did not bear any implication whatsoever in terms of concealment or *mala fide* intention on my part. Following the BBS's official Construction Cost Index, cost calculated in 2006 prices, if worked backwards shedding off increases in cost indexes for the relevant year would approximately equal or conform to the cost incurred in years of actual construction imputing no liability of concealment on me. Here by way of explanation, I stated that details of calculation of cost of construction following Construction Cost Index compiled by the BBS in case of my residential house, as I would spell out later, might be cited as an instance.

Positing the aforesaid, I asserted that peripheral in terms of examination of site and ignoring the architectural, structural, sanitation and electrical plans, cost estimate as made by the PWD's personnel, sitting in their offices in accordance with the PWD's schedule of specifications and rates, as admitted by them (in their testimony on 12/06/2007), did not reflect realistic reconciliation of rate of inflation or increase in building cost as between dates of construction and current estimation and difference in schedule of rates of the PWD on the one hand and of the LGED (Local Government Engineering Department) and the Facilities Department of the Ministry of Education on the other. The estimate did not take into account depreciation of the building over 18 years or so.

The PWD's (Public Works Department) personnel did not enquire about and find out ownership and land records of the building also. On one wall of the house "Sultana," being our mother's name, was inscribed as a token of remembrance of her sacrifices to rear the family and on another wall "Sitara" (name of my wife), was inscribed to recognize her social work in the local area including establishing and operating an orphanage and in appreciation of her responsibility in maintaining the house in the absence of other wives, deceased and ill. Wife of my youngest brother Dr. Arefin was long dead. Wife of my elder brother Dr. Jahangir was also dead. Wife of the eldest, Misbahuddin Khan, was ill and did not visit the village home.

Inside the eastern part of the twin house, there were portraits of all brothers and sisters and our father, Asheq Ali Khan, the founder of the family. This was not mentioned by the IO. The founder of the family, our father, was the first Muslim graduate of Chandpur District. The family had taken a decision in early 2006 to inscribe names of all members on walls of the hallroom of the house for remembrance by posterity. Most importantly, in terms of fact-in-issue, the twin house was situated on our ancestral homestead and jointly owned (four brothers and four sisters and their heirs) and undemarcated, and so mentioned by me in the statement of assets of February 20, 2007. The *porcha* (land record) of this homestead had the house specifically mentioned with all brothers and sisters and their heirs as owners.

I produced the *porcha* before the Special Court for perusal, scrutiny and record. The Special Judge squinted but did not say anything. He, however, exchanged meaningful glances with Major Kamruzzaman and the Public Prosecutor. I stated that no partition of the property at our home ever took place. Therefore, the accusation that I had two buildings in my home village that I concealed, as alleged by the Prosecution, did not stand ground. No value of the homestead and the house was stated in the asset statement as the notice of the ACC's Secretary did not require it to be mentioned as such. As the ACC's notice did not call for valuation of the house, attempt at its valuation now, even on perfunctory basis as was made by the Prosecution, smacked of an overly enthusiastic and made-to-order exercise by the PWD not warranted by the requirements of law. This valuation did not conform with the cost data officially compiled by the BBS. The notice required descriptions of assets, and I mentioned the homestead and the house, jointly owned and undemarcated accordingly.

Therefore I said loudly and clearly to the court, no liability on this count could be imputed to me.

Biponi Polash: The IO reported in the supplementary charge-sheet that these under-construction shops were owned by me and that these shops, incomplete as they were, were valued at Tk. 2,992,181/. As testified by Prosecution Witness A. S. A. Kamal, the blueprint for the shops showed that (i) in the slot for owner's name mine was mentioned as "for," *i.e.*, on behalf of Gulbahar Himagar; without my signature above or underneath (meaning non-ownership by me) and (ii) it was situated on plot no. 50 Mouza Charal Kheal, *upazila* Kachua, exactly corresponding to Plot No. 50 owned by the Gulbahar Himagar Ltd. as shown in land records or the *porcha*.

I produced both the blueprint and the *porcha* of the land and showed them to the Special Judge. He saw and smiled sardonically and once again exchanged glances with his mentor. As evidenced in testimonies of the Executive Engineer, PWD, Chandpur, and his colleagues and the Manager of the *Himagar*, as Prosecution Witnesses, the shops were incomplete, not rentable at their present state and did not, therefore, constitute an asset. The PWD personnel themselves admitted that they did not estimate the cost with due diligence and care, reconcile or check their figures with on-the-spot measurements posted in departmental measurement books, adjust figures with scheduled specifications and rates of government departments other than the PWD (*e.g.*, the LGED, the Facilities Department, and the Water Development Board), correct prices/costs for inflation. They did not even check on ownership of land on which these under-construction shops were located. With an investment of Tk. 19 lacs or so (quite a shade different from the PWD's peripheral and indiligent estimate) from the Gulbahar's Himagar fund, as of then, that was a liability rather than an asset. This amount of investment was borne out of depreciation allowances shown in the *Himagar's* tax returns for 2005-06.

I produced before the Special Judge these tax returns as evidence. He saw, did not comment and returned them to me before I resumed. I had mentioned about these shops under construction adjacent to the *Himagar* in my asset statement of 20/02/2007 (p. 5, item 6, bottom line). In terms of asset or valuation, this could not, therefore, be imputed incriminatingly to me. Here the difference in estimate of cost and actual cost incurred by the *Himagar* was not the fact-in-issue. The fact-in-issue was the ownership, which was undeniably that of the Gulbahar Himagar, a private limited company of which I was just a shareholder. Thus established as an investment of the Gulbahar Himagar Ltd., beyond the realm of my personal and sole ownership, the cost estimated obviously at current prices and following the PWD's schedule did not lend it, I asserted emphatically, to be of factual and incriminating relevance against me.

Sultana Filling Station: The IO in the supplementary charge-sheet reported that this Petrol Pump or filling station was owned by me. This was not based on fact. This was owned and funded by my son Dr. Jalal Alamgir, aged 36, and earning over US $100,000 per year. His tax return filed with U.S. Government, along with copies of letters from Bangladesh Petroleum Corporation, Meghna Petroleum Company, Department of Explosives, Deputy Commissioner's Office, Chandpur and Kachua Pourashava all showing Jalal Alamgir as the owner, bore testimonies to this.

I produced copies of all these documents before the Special Judge. He looked at them, asked me whether I needed a drink of water and returned them to me. I then stated that the land on which the pump was situated was given to my son as a gift from me by a notarized deed of gift according to the Islamic principle of *heba* for use as a filling station. This piece of land was included in the total of approximately 15 to 16 acres of land of mine as stated in the statement of assets of February 20, 2007. I said that I desired my son to settle back in Bangladesh. The filling station with its cost of Tk. 24 lacs 39 thousand 694 as estimated by the PWD could not, therefore, be ascribed as my asset nor could I be alleged to have concealed this. I stated that at the end of my asset statement dated February 20, 2007, I had mentioned specifically that Dr. Jalal Alamgir was a separate income tax returnee and payer and at his age and position was not dependent on me in any way. I was neither able nor liable to describe his assets either in Bangladesh or in the U.S. where he lived and worked. I could and have produced before the court documentary proof of his income adequate enough for constructing this filling station by him.

(7)

House at Comilla Housing Estate: The IO in the supplementary charge-sheet stated that this house valued by the PWD (obviously at prices much later than the year of its construction) at Tk. 20 lacs, 2 thousand and 965 was not reported in terms of value by me (p. 18 of the supplementary charge-sheet). I stated that as testified by the PWD's engineers of Comilla, their estimate of cost was peripheral, largely inconsistent, utterly out-of-date and completely incoherent with comparable schedules of specifications and rates of the LGED, the Facilities Department and the WDB (Water Development Board). More important, their estimate of cost was not based on official Construction Cost Index (Building), compiled by the BBS on behalf of the Government.

I stated that I funded construction of this house out of advance rent and loan given by the Agrani Bank and then gifted it off to my younger son Joy Alamgir (by notarized *heba, i.e.*, the Islamic way of giving gift). I showed the notarized *heba* or deed of gift to the Special Judge. He gave it a cursory glance and let out a loud belch. The Agrani Bank had set up its branch there. It was reported, and described in my statement of assets of February 20, 2007 as required of me by the ACC's notice. As admitted by the IO, its construction cost of Tk. 10 lacs 86 thousand 200, was reported by Joy Alamgir in his income tax return for the relevant year and accordingly accepted by the income tax authority. So this could not be ascribed as my asset on February 20, 2007, *i.e.*, the date of the asset statement.

The fact-in-issue in this case was the ownership on the date of asset statement and not the cost, and the ownership was not of mine on that date and I did not conceal it. In terms of relevancy of fact, I informed the court that Joy Alamgir earned over US$144,000 (Tk.100 lacs) in the U.S. per year and was fully independent of me as his father. His tax return to U.S tax authorities of 2006 testified to his financial ability and independence. I presented a copy of his tax return to U.S tax authority to the court. All advances taken from the Agrani Bank had long since been adjusted as rent. The Agrani Bank still operated its branch in this house and paid rent by crossed cheque/pay order to Joy Alamgir in accordance with the relevant lease agreement.

There had been no objection or complaint centering on ownership, taxes, rents or services about this property from anyone having any *locus standi*. The question of somebody filing a case centered on this, therefore, could not arise and was evidently irrelevant for the allegation in reference, I asserted in full voice. The IO's reporting in this matter was not only dubious but also indiligent and misleading; it reflected a colorable exercise of authority and responsibility outside the ambit of the due process of law, I said aloud. Whether this made any impression on the Special Judge, I did not notice or know. All others present in the court, however, listened in somber silence. The Major sitting by the side of the Public Prosecutor slightly flinched.

Bank Balance: Under constrained circumstances of being in detention and without any access to my records, I, in my asset statement of February 20, 2007, stated from memory that I had in my bank accounts in various banks approximately Tk. 90 thousand. The IO had reported that total of balance in my bank accounts on various dates around February 20, 2007 — *i.e.*, the date of asset statement, worked out at Tk. 244,900/ — I stated that being in detention I had no way to reconcile this discrepancy from memory. In my careful assessment, this discrepancy was the result of any or all of the following: (i) approximation from memory without access to bank records and in less than an hour of time; (ii) variation of dates of balances as between the date of asset statement and dates of balances as reported by banks to the IOs on the basis of last transactions; (iii) deposits made by our family caretaker at our home of annual rental of or sale of produce from land, usually received in February and March, without my instant knowledge; (iv) repayment of temporary loan into the current account in the Janata Bank, Kachua taken earlier from me for supplementing the working capital of my son's filling station (he was working abroad), owing to increase of oil prices by the Bangladesh Petroleum Corporation and the Meghna Petroleum, Ltd. without instant intimation to me; (v) usual practice of reconciling bank accounts by me once a year; (vi) mistakes made by the concerned banks in statements furnished to the IOs; and (vii) treating balance in current account, yielding no interest income besides a statement of transaction, as asset by the Prosecution. Prosecution Witness Masudur Rahman in his testimony before the court had stated that on instructions from the owner of the filling station he used to take temporary loans from me, coming to me personally to operate business and then return it into my account evidently without my instant knowledge.

Through cross-examination of Prosecution Witness Abdul Jabbar, second officer, the Janata Bank, Kachua, on June 24, 2007, it was found that in their account statement furnished to the IO in addition to over-writings and corrections, backed without initials of any concerned officer, against one and the same cheque (being No. 5066701) they made two payments, on two days, of which one alone amounted to Tk.125,000. This was indicative of made-up nature and incredibility of bank statements or figures for balance as posited by the Prosecution. Summed up as evidence, I asserted, figures, corrected, overwritten balance yielding no interest income and reflective of false or cheated transactions are bereft of value imputing reasonable liability to me on this account. Had I been given fourteen days to state my assets or balance in banks with access to records, such discrepancy would not have been there. The responsibility for this discrepancy rested squarely on the shoulders of those who did not give me adequate time and access to records of any kind. I said that some Prosecution Witnesses, even drawn from the bank management and living in freedom unlike me, could not give their exact balances in the bank on particular dates.

Interestingly, when the procedure was subsequently laid down, as per Section 26 of the ACC Act or Form 5 in three parts (one each for immovable, movable assets and liability and loans), the bank balance was not even asked for as a component of asset statement under R 17 (1) of the ACC Rules. Further, the discrepancy was not reflective of any criminal motive or *mens rea* on my part. Furthermore, the allegation of concealment or understatement in these, as alleged by the IO, was blatantly unreasonable and tantamount to harassment of an honest citizen in order to serve an evil purpose set forth by the interested parties.

(8)

House at Banani: The IO in the supplementary charge-sheet alleged that I had understated the value of my house at Banani and thereby concealed my asset (p. 26 of the supplementary CS). I stated that this allegation could not stand on four grounds. First, the notice of the Secretary, ACC of January 18, 2007, asking for a statement of assets purported to be as per Sections 26 and 27 of the ACC Act and Rule 15 (d) 5 of the EPR, required me to give description of assets and sources of funding, not their values. This notice did not prescribe a procedure as mentioned in Section 26 of the ACC Act for writing and submitting such a statement. The procedure was subsequently (on April 29, 2007) prescribed by Rule 17 (5) of the ACC Rules and thus was not applicable to me when I was required to write and submit my asset statement under constrained circumstances of being in jail without access to the relevant records of the house and its construction. As required of me, I gave description of this house and of sources of its funding as faithfully as I could (p. 3 of the asset statement dated February 20, 2007). I could not, therefore, be faulted or held liable for not furnishing something in my asset statement that I was not asked and required to do by the notice. Second, the cost of its construction at two stages (1981-82 for the ground and the first floors and 1991-92 for the second and the third floors) and sources of their funding were furnished along with my IT returns to the income tax (IT) authority in the relevant years. The IT authority scrutinized the costs on the basis of thorough inspections as per their procedure and accepted them (with marginal modifications in some items) as correct and assessed and collected due taxes accordingly.

Their assessed cost of the first and second floors constructed in 1981-82 figured, as testified by the Assistant Commissioner (Income Tax) as a Prosecution Witness on June 6, 2007 was Tk. 4.10 lacs excluding Tk. 1 lac or so as the cost of land; the cost of the second and third floors was assessed at Tk. 6 lacs which was marginally higher than the cost given by me in the asset statement from memory. In costs so assessed by the IT authority, supervision and auxiliary costs were imputed; in my costing, I excluded that, as I personally supervised construction and purchased rod, cement, etc. from TCB, BCIC and timber from the Forest Department on permit. Be that as it may, their procedure of scrutiny and acceptance at that time included among other things, consideration of market prices of building materials, blueprint and specifications of the building, cost appraisal made by the HBFC (House Building Finance Corporation) before sanction of the house building loan, with which the house was constructed, specifications and schedules of RAJUK (Capital Development Authority), the PWD, the LGED and other relevant government departments and bodies. The fact of such scrutiny of costs and their acceptance had already been testified by the Assistant Commissioner, IT, before this court. Once so accepted by the IT authority, costs or valuation could not be modified or changed subsequently as was attempted by the IO in this case, I asserted. Besides, the principle of estoppel of the Evidence Act did not permit such a subsequent modification of cost/value. Besides being barred by law, this amounted, as I stated, to swimming backstream toward the site of one's own conception, despite change in the size of the swimmer and his circumstances.

Assistant Commissioner (IT) had testified that in their procedure, income tax settled in one year did not remain a subject matter for valuation or assessment in subsequent years (his testimony of June 12, 2007). He had also testified that IT department did not have, either through their intelligence outfit or regular establishment, any objection or reservation about me as an IT assessee any time till date. Therefore, mounting objection against cost/value of my house already scrutinized and accepted by the IT Department in 1981-82 and 1991-92, now in 2007 by the IO and trying to place liability of a made-up under-valuation and cooked-up concealment of value by implication did not stand ground.

Third, and by the way, (as it was not the fact-in-issue here) valuation made by the PWD of my house in 2007, was subjective, wide-off-the-mark of realism, inapplicable and untenable. From the testimonies of the Executive Engineer and his subordinate engineers, Sher-e-Bangla-Nagar, it became evident that: (i) their valuation was based on the PWD's schedule of specifications and rates without any adjustment with specifications and rates of the RAJUK (Capital Development Authority), the LGED, the City Corporation and the private builders; (ii) they did not make valuation in reference to or in the light of the blueprint of the building, as approved by RAJUK, following which the house was built; (iii) they did not adjust their scheduled rates for building materials and labor for increase in general price index, specially index of increase in prices of construction materials compiled by the government and published annually in the Statistical Year Book by the Bureau of Statistics; (iv) they did not find out whether specifications of building materials, as in their schedule, conformed with specifications of rod, cement, brick, sand, plumbing, sanitary and other materials used in this building; (v) they discounted annual cost by 1% from their scheduled rates of the current year or the year in which the scheduled rates were prepared to figure out cost or value down to the actual year of construction which, given the experienced rate of inflation, was unrealistic; (vi) they did their measurement and estimation perfunctorily — without reference to the house's architectural, structural, electrical and plumbing drawings; without the survey by a qualified quantity surveyor, without examination of wind and earthquake tolerance of the construction, and, with the Executive Engineer leading the team, spending not more than 30 to 40 minutes on site; (vii) they wrote the report sitting in office bereft of reference to properly maintainable measurement books; (viii) they did not take into account renovations and modifications made by me or tenants in the period between 1982 and 1996; and (ix) they ignored depreciation of the building since its construction.

All these went to prove that the valuation of the building in reference, uncalled for and untenable after its scrutinized valuation at cost in 1981-82 and 1991-92 by the IT authority, was mandated by the IO for reasons beyond legality, and the way it was done, left sufficient room for serious, realistic, impartial and correct costing/valuation. Inapplicable in the context of the principle of estoppel, as already mentioned and untenable in law in view of its completion and acceptance earlier in 1981-82 and 1991-92 by the IT authority, the IO with the PWD engineers drawn from outside the usual area of their work at his (the IO's) behest, in this exercise tried to malign the character and bring disrepute to a citizen whose honor and reputation, besides life and property, were protectable by the State in accordance with article 31 of the Constitution, I pointed out.

Estimate in Accordance with Cost Index of the BBS: The Bangladesh Bureau of Statistics (BBS) of the Ministry of Planning, Government of Bangladesh, compiles and publishes Construction Cost Index (Building) every year. These cost data are reflective of costs of construction for all sectors, public and private and all areas, urban and rural, and as such are appropriately applicable to this case. According to the BBS, Construction Cost Index increased from 100 in 1969-70 to 2,235.62 in 2003-04, *i.e.*, at a rate of 67.72% per year in 33 years (This may be seen in, BBS, the Statistical Year Book of Bangladesh 2004, Table 10.20, p. 468).

I presented the relevant page of the Statistical Year Book, 2004, before the Special Judge. He looked at it with a seeming disinterest and pushed it back to me. I said, it could reasonably be assumed that even after 2003-04, this rate of annual increase in cost continued till 2006 although the actual rate of increase in this period was much higher. In my asset statement of February 20, 2006, I had mentioned cost of construction of the ground and the first floors of my house in 1981-82 at approximately Tk. 3 lacs (excluding cost of land of approximately Tk. 1 lac.) In 24 years between 1982 and 2006 at a simple average rate of 67.72% per year, as shown in the government's Cost of Construction Index cost in 2006 can reasonably be said to have increased by 1625% (67.72 x 24) or 16.25 times. This makes cost of Tk. 3 lacs in prices of 1981-82, Tk. 48.75 lacs in prices of 2006. In my asset statement of February 20, 2006 (p. 1 item 3) I had mentioned the cost of the 2nd and the 3rd floors at approximately Tk. 4.25 lacs in prices of 1991-92. In 14 years in between 1992 and 2006, at a rate of 67.72% increase per year, in prices of 2006 cost of construction can reasonably be taken to have increased by 948% (67.72 x 14) or 9.48 times, *i.e.*, to Tk. 40.29 lacs (Tk. 4.25 x 9.48). The total construction cost of these four floors of the house in 2006 prices thus figured at Tk. 89.04 lacs nearer to the figure imputed by the PWD as the cost of construction of the house in two stages in 1981-82 and 1991-92.

This also meant working backward in time from 2006, the cost of the house as I mentioned in the asset statement in prices of

1981-82 and 1991-92 as correct, imputing no liability or responsibility of concealment. To arrive at a value of the house on the basis of this cost in 2006 prices, depreciation has to be deducted and housing scarcity and location value have to be inducted. Assessed as such the cost/value following the BBS data applicable to all sectors and areas would be different from the cost/value presumably based on their schedule of recent years (the PWD personnel in their testimonies could not give the year of their schedule then in use or used in estimation of the cost of the house in reference) and imputable for the years of actual construction estimated perfunctorily, as was made by the PWD at the behest or threat of the IOs of the ACC. By any stretch of the imagination, given the difference between approximate cost of construction in 1981-82 and 1991-92 as in the asset statement on the one hand and the current cost on the other, I could not be held liable for the difference or imputed concealment.

I had given this cost estimate based on the BBS data just to prove that the PWD's cost estimate purportedly imputable for the time of construction was incorrect and could not be used as an indication of the fact or extent of concealment of cost or value by me. I said that I wanted to emphasize as a trained economist that without taking into consideration the context and basis of calculation in reference to a base year and without using the officially compiled data, an untrained and evidently prodded exercise, as was this case, could lead one to jump to false conclusions, detrimental to the objective of finding and telling the whole truth and nothing but the whole truth, which was avowedly pursued by the IOs and the Prosecution Witnesses. Evidently thus, the Prosecution's calculation of the cost of construction of my house in Banani was incorrect, and the liability imputed therefrom on me misplaced, misleading, incongruous, inapplicable and thus not tenable in law and legal process.

Motorcycles: Three motorcycles stated by the IO in the charge-sheet as owned by me was not correct. These motorcycles were not owned by me and were not registered in my name. Dr. Jalal Alamgir, my son contributed some money (Tk. 30,000 or so) to buy these for local party workers. Mr. Iqbal, Vice-President of the local Awami League, contributed Tk. 60,000. The rest approximately Tk. 50,000 was taken out of savings of our party workers contributing to the expenses of the election in 2001. These were neither my assets nor intended for my personal use. The workers were of similar age as of my son, which perhaps led him to contribute. In the *challan* (invoice) of these cycles my name and my son's name might have been inscribed (at the behest of party workers who bought them) either by mistake, or through over-enthusiasm of workers or possibly to avoid extortion by the police on their transportation from Dhaka to Kachua. The IO, as he testified before the court, could not show in whose name these cycles were registered or from whose possession these were recovered and did not explain the long difference in time between purported purchase and expected registration or actual recovery as the case may be. The IO could not differentiate between a *challan* and a cash memo. Registration in my name would have implied my ownership, which the Prosecution could not prove in this case, I asserted. Assistant Inspector, the ACC, Hossain in his testimony of June 20, 2007 admitted that these motorcycles were in fact not registered in anybody's name. The *challan* shown by the Prosecution did not bear my or my son's signature either, nor did these *challans* show that prices as quoted therein were paid or not. This came out in the testimony of Prosecution Witness Khurshid Anwar on June 20, 2007. The IO did not realize, for instance that VAT paid by one's assistant while buying a toaster or a music center and inserting his name in the cash memo or the *challan,* consciously or unconsciously, did not necessarily make the assistant the owner of the toaster or the music center. Similarly, customs duty paid on a generator imported from abroad by our cold store manager did not make the manager owner of such a generator that needed registration of ownership. I stated these points by way of examples. Therefore, this allegation that those three motorcycles were my assets was based on a mistake of fact and did not stand ground. The allegation was not only frivolous but also misconceived and false and not tenable in law.

Investigative Officer's Mistake in Asset Valuation in Comparison with Income Received: The IO in his supplementary charge-sheet stated that (p. 27 of the supplementary CS) he had compared my income as reported by income tax authority between 1983-84 and 2006 (p. 26, bottom of the supplementary CS) and the purported value of my assets earned during my lifetime of work (1963-2006) and even before, as in case of inherited ancestral properties or assets, and found the value of assets in excess of my earnings. He admitted that he had not considered that in computing income of an income tax assessee as per the 6th Schedule of the Income Tax Ordinance, 1984, quite a number of exemptions and rebates were excluded while these were naturally embodied as assets.

In support of the allegation, the Prosecution on June 26, 2007, recalled Prosecution Witness Prodhan, Assistant Commissioner (IT) to place a 5-page statement of income and expenditure purported to be mine for the period 1983-84 to 2006-07. He did not in course of his testimony given on three days earlier (on June 6, 7 and 11, 2007) mention about this statement nor had he mentioned about this at any time to the IO either. In course of cross-examination, the statement turned out to be a carbon copy, full of overwritings and corrections without initials and figures in numbers bereft of corroborating words. Be that as it may, the comparison between income and expenditure from 1983 to 2006 (23 years), net of exemptions and rebates under the law with cost/value of assets acquired from 1962 to 2006 (44 years) with embodiment of such exemptions and rebates into assets, was evidently incorrect, deceitful and thus not legally tenable. Besides, assets as valued by this Prosecution Witness were in total variance with assets valued by the Prosecution in the charge-sheet — the very basis of the allegation against me. This was a premeditated, wrongful way to misrepresent facts and figures.

I emphasized once again that I had already shown in accordance with internationally accepted good accounting practice reasonable estimates of my investable surplus/savings or resource envelope earned throughout my lifetime till today, which more than justified holding of all my movable and immovable assets. The deceitful and confusing accounting of my income and assets placed by the Prosecution before the court was nothing but a sinister attempt to proffer that in the continuing control over the affairs of the State; power had become the fount as well as the regulator of even accounting knowledge. I stated with emphasis for realization by the court that the dictum of telling nothing but the whole truth in adjudication followed in countries ruled by law was not only sidelined, but totally ignored deliberately by the Prosecution in this case.

Allegation in Respect of Shares: It was alleged by the IO that I had bought shares worth Tk. 6 lacs out of sale proceeds of my vehicle in the Gulbahar Himager Ltd. and the Bay Pacific Carriers Ltd., both private companies owned since long by our family members, but did not reflect these in my wealth statement furnished to IT department for FY 2006 showing total of my wealth amounting to Tk. 91,94,853 (*vide* p. 14 of the Supplementary CS.). I was not given access to my own records of income tax returns. The Task Force led by Major Kamruzzaman, while ransacking my house, either threw out or took away these. The IO did not with certitude press this charge against me nor adduce any witness or evidence in its support, but seemed to have included this amount of Tk. 6 lacs as a concealed asset.

This was not factually correct, I pointed out. On p. 5, item 6 under the heading "Others" of the asset statement furnished by me on February 20, 2007, purchase of these shares from my eldest brother, now deceased and the source of funding (sale price of the vehicle) were mentioned. Transformation of one kind of asset, a vehicle, into shares of a private limited company as in this case, did not increase in net terms wealth to be elaborately reflected in a wealth statement furnishable to the IT authority. The form of wealth statement was less than ¼ in size of a foolscap page having no scope of containing all such details. I showed this form to the Special Judge. The purchase of these shares was reported and approved by the Registrar of Joint Stock Companies as required by law. Therefore, no wrong was done by me in this case; in IT return of the private limited company its shareholdings and taxes payable and paid were reported. The Special Judge failed to realize these facts despite my production of relevant papers in support of my statement. A glance from Major Kamruzzaman to the Special Judge seemed to have given a death blow to the sense of justice and fair play expected from him on this count. As it appeared, the Special Judge remained oblivious of even the narrow rules and arcane procedure that he should have followed while considering such an allegation.

Conclusion: I asserted that considering the facts-in-issue and the relevant facts as I had stated, the summed up allegations of the IO made in the supplementary charge-sheet that I had acquired assets valued at Tk. 3,27,88,465 (inclusive of FDRs of Tk.117 lacs mentioned in the original CS) beyond my known income and concealed them (p. 27 of the supplementary CS) was false, fabricated, deceitful and untenable in law. I also pointed out that the summation of allegedly concealed assets as was made by the IO was arithmetically wrong. While making valuation he followed mostly current prices of assets instead of valuation at cost following the basic principle of accounting. In the process of his arbitrary, fabricated, inflated, deceitful, arithmetically wrong and incorrect testimony, from the viewpoint of accepted accounting practice of valuation of assets at cost and thus legally untenable estimate of assets and partial accounting of my legitimate income and savings (*i.e.* from 1983 to 2006), he wanted to impute a liability of under-statement or concealment by me which was not maintainable out of the requirements as spelled out in the notice of the of the Secretary, ACC. In its deceitful arithmetic and incorrect accounting the Prosecution presented even my pension, savings from salary, tax paid rental income, earnings in dollars accepted by the Income Tax Department as tax free elements of concealment. The Prosecution, in the process concealed my income and savings for 38 long years holding in the process that serving in the highest service of the Republic and rising to the highest post that a service of the Republic could provide to its member, leaving aside the post of a State Minister for about four years, I earned almost nothing and lived in their wisdom and sense of justness on mere air or doles. "Is this the way we transform State power into justice and fair play?" I asked loudly, deviating from my written text of the statement.

Then I said, I had spelled out the failing of IOs in pursuing due process of law and diligence in sufficient detail in my statement. I had pointed out the inapplicability of Sections 26 and 27 of the ACC Act and R 15 (d) 5 of the Emergency Powers Rules. I had elaborately explained incorrect and fabricated nature of the alleged concealment of FDRs. From the testimonies of the Prosecution Witnesses themselves and the relevant documents, I had proved beyond reasonable doubt the falsehood and the untenability of allegations made in the supplementary charge-sheet against me. I had pointed out that the process pursued by the IO in this case violated my inalienable right to be treated in accordance with law. In this case, I asserted, the Prosecution Witnesses produced and examined by the Prosecution did not corroborate in material particulars the charge framed against me. The process pursued by the Prosecution was tantamount to an action detrimental to my liberty, honor and reputation as a citizen, violating all norms of due process of law. This amounted to stretching one's lucidly wicked imagination beyond the point of breaking, sufficient to prove the guilt of the investigator rather than of the investigated and to warrant an immediate discharge of me as an accused. Obviously in the annals of dispensation of justice in this country, in matters dealing with a citizen's conduct, integrity, honesty, reputation and honor, I said loudly, this would be recorded and remembered as a case of (a) avowedly not telling the truth, (b) deliberately truncating and obliterating the whole truth and (c) arbitrarily and deceitfully not only sidelining, but also utterly ignoring, the responsibility of telling nothing but the truth by the Prosecution.

I said that my electoral constituency was Kachua Upazila within the district of Chandpur; there my popularity was at its peak. A conspiracy was hatched up not to allow me to contest in the ensuing Parliamentary election by framing these charges against me. This case was utterly false, concocted and based on an ulterior motive; this was the outcome of a conspiracy of military-led usurpers of State power and authority not to allow me to seek public office and serve my people to the end of democracy and freedom. I said the case would not have been lodged and I would not have been thrown into this fry pan of misery had I agreed to lend my support to those in power and allowed my conscience to be sold for profit, greed and expediency.

I was 66 years old at the time I made this statement. As a teacher and a civil servant, I had put in over 36 years of service. I stated that I served my country and people to the best of my ability and intention. In my service and work I received international as well as national recognition. Never ever any allegation of corruption and misdemeanor was lodged or raised against me in these years. Now after about nine years from my retirement as a public servant, this frivolous, deceitful, vexatious, and totally false allegation was brought against me. The allegation against me was wrongfully given the cover of Emergency Powers Rules (R 15 (d) 5), keeping me behind the bar without even the right to be posted on bail. As spelled out in terms of law and facts, none of the allegations against me under Sections 26 and 27 of the ACC Act were or could be proved in any way or manner. The entire exercise of the Prosecution in this regard was of harassment and persecution. In conclusion, in this context, in consideration of the inability and failure of the Prosecution to prove in any way my liability for concealment of assets and acquisition thereof beyond my known and legitimate sources of income, I demanded discharge of myself as an accused forthwith. And then I said, I would adduce witnesses in my defense, in support of my contention and in justifying my demanded discharge.

While stepping down from the dock, I handed over a copy of my statement along with relevant documents to the court not having very strong points or reputation in noting the arguments and records of the defense. When I finished, surprisingly the Special Judge did not examine me on the statement that I had made under Section 342 of the Criminal Procedure Code. In accordance with Section 265 of the Code, it was obligatory on his part to examine me to find out the truth, to remove any doubt about what I stated and to obtain clarification as regards facts and figures mentioned by me. The demeanor of the Special Judge in this respect was of stifling indifference, calling for relinquishing whatever was still left as responsibility of the Special Courts operating under law. It seemed adjudication under the regime was a business and not a mission for justice and due process of law for a judgeship, which quite easily thwarted trust and respect and acted as a paid agency for vendetta against perceived political opposition.

7 Defense Witnesses

(1)

Next day, July 10 was fixed for production of the Defense Witnesses. The Special Judge while stating this made it clear that as he was short of time, as prescribed in law all defense witnesses should be produced without break. This did not give me and my lawyers reasonable time to select the defense witnesses and arrange for their production, suiting their convenience. A. M. A. Muhith, one of my potentially star witnesses was out of the country at the time and would not return till the 14th. Before he left he had written a testimonial on my work and conduct for production before the court in case he could not return in time to depose, affirming that I had all through been an efficient, honest and patriotic civil servant. Editor Iqbal Sobhan Chowdhury of the *Bangladesh Observer*, because of pressure of his work could not be contacted in the constrained circumstances. Dr. S. A. Samad, my erstwhile colleague and former Principal Secretary to the Prime Minister, I was told, was threatened by the Forces Intelligence of dire consequence, if he would come to depose as a defense witness. The same was the situation with former Secretaries Abdul Hamid Chowdhury and Dr. Mashiur Rahman. They excused themselves in somewhat cowardly defense of themselves. A. S. M. Shahjahan, a former Advisor of the 2001 caretaker government, could not be contacted within such a short time; my nephew Dr. Muntassir Mamun told me that he being a former chief of the National Security Intelligence and of the police, simply avoided being contacted.

My brother Dr. Jahangir had contacted Lt. General Nuruddin Khan, but he refused to be a witness on the advice, as he said, of the Directorate General of the Forces Intelligence. I knew Lt. General (Ret.) Nuruddin as an amiable gentleman with the courage befitting a soldier. I was disappointed to see that he cowered down before the intelligence officers who had been under his command earlier. What tamed him to be behind his juniors irrespective of what was right or wrong I did not know. But I recalled in 1991 when he was the army chief he had not given support to the then self-styled President Ershad and as a consequence Ershad had to resign. I realized even a seemingly glorious role, unless based on a bedrock of values, could not remain a road sign for guiding others. But since failure was more expensive than shortcoming, we decided we would do our best. I clamped by hands behind myself and asked my brother Dr. Jahangir to contact and request the willing and courageous ones to come to my defense.

We adduced six Defense Witnesses. The first one was Dr. Akbar Ali Khan, Finance Advisor of the former caretaker government, having extensive experience with the working of the government in positions inclusive of Finance Secretary, Chairman, National Board of Revenue and finally Cabinet Secretary. He testified that the accused, Dr. Alamgir, was well known as an able and efficient civil servant; efficiency connoted, amongst other attributes, a built-in ability to avoid waste, *i.e.*, an adherence to integrity in conduct of public affairs and discharge of responsibilities as a servant of the Republic. He had known Dr. Alamgir since 1961 and never saw him leading a luxurious life. He stated he had seen a testimonial written by A. M. A. Muhith, a former Secretary and Finance Minister under whom Dr. Alamgir worked. Muhith put on record Dr. Alamgir's ability, efficiency, hard work and integrity and Dr. Akbar Ali Khan agreed with him about these abilities and attributes of Dr. Alamgir. Dr. Akbar testified about Dr. Alamgir's work as the Executive Director, I. D. B. (Islamic Development Bank) and as a consultant home and abroad and of higher remuneration that he used to receive compared to that of his peers. According to him, Dr. Alamgir, as a State Minister of Planning completed development projects very expeditiously and efficiently, the like of which was not observed earlier.

Muhith's letter appreciating Dr. Alamgir's efficiency, integrity and work was placed before the trial court. In cross-examination by Public Prosecutor Mizanur Rahman, Dr. Akbar admitted that he did not know in exact terms what were the accusations against Dr. Alamgir and he did not work together with him in the same department any time except on various inter-ministerial committees. He also admitted that he did not know how much daily allowances I drew as the Executive Director of the Islamic Development Bank, but he knew the rate of daily allowance of the IDB was quite high. The Special Judge, as it turned out, did not take Dr. Akbar Ali Khan's testimony in effective and positive consideration despite his wide recognition and unquestioned reputation. He, however, bowed a *salaam* to him at the close of the cross-examination, when he left.

The second Defense Witness was Dr. Forrest Cookson, an American national, economist of repute and a financial analyst of international recognition, who had received his education in Princeton and Georgetown Universities, U.S.A. He worked in Bangladesh as a consultant of the Bangladesh Bank, the Ministry of Planning, the World Bank and the Asian Development Bank. He was the President of the American Bangladesh Chamber of Commerce (AMCHAM). He testified that he had known Dr. Alamgir since 1989. In his assessment, Dr. Alamgir was a man of honesty, patriotism, devotion and determination for eradication of poverty. He mentioned how Dr. Alamgir when he was Secretary to the Prime Minister in 1997 protected Bangladesh's interest while negotiating with the American Ambassador David Merrill who called on him, with prompting from the then-Vice-President Dick Cheney. He testified that calculations of savings/investment capabilities of Dr. Alamgir on the basis of his known, legitimate, rental, salary, and auxiliary and incidental income, as stated in his statement under Section 342 of the Criminal Procedure Code and shown to the court in computer printouts appended to his statement, were in accordance with internationally recognized good accounting practices and correct. This implied that all movable and immovable assets of Dr. Alamgir were well within the bounds of his known income.

Without commenting or deliberating on the correctness of my savings/investment capacity as stated by Dr. Cookson and shown in these annexures, the Special Judge did not accept them as serious evidences. These annexures were earlier given in the statement I made under Section 342 of the Criminal Procedure Code and in reference to figures of savings/investment mentioned in the second asset statement submitted to the ACC. The Special Judge could not disregard these as unacceptable or trivial under the provisions of the Evidence Act. Intervening in an unashamed support of the Special Judge, the Public Prosecutor could not cite any section of the Evidence Act under which these could not be accepted. My lawyer pointed out that as integral parts of the statement made under section 342 of the Criminal Procedure Code, a refusal to consider these estimates of savings and investment capacity as reflected in the relevant annexures was an arbitrariness contrary to the provision of law and principles of justice and fair play. Dr. Cookson also testified that as per Household Expenditure Survey conducted by the Bureau of Statistics of the government, average household savings in Bangladesh was about 25% of income and in comparison with that Dr. Alamgir's calculation of savings at 15% of his salary income was conservative and thus acceptable as a very reasonable estimate. He also testified about the correctness of tax returns submitted by Dr. Alamgir's two sons, Jalal and Joy working in the USA. The Public Prosecutor seemed to have no capacity to cross-examine Dr. Cookson effectively or in depth.

"Did Dr. Alamgir sign the estimate of savings and investment as given in annexures annexed to his statement?" he asked.

"These estimates are generated by computers on the basis of realistic base figures and parameters given by Dr. Alamgir. Computer-generated figures or estimates need not be signed. They are taken as authenticated by the computer as a matter of course," Dr. Cookson tried to make the computer-illiterate Public Prosecutor understand.

"How these figures could be generated by the computer when Dr. Alamgir was in jail?" asked the Public Prosecutor.

"He has already explained in his statement that these figures were generated on the basis of base figures and parameters given by him. Base figures and parameters can be and were given for such generation even from laptop computers outside the jail. This was possible and this is how a computer generates data," explained Dr. Cookson.

The Public Prosecutor sat down. Along with my brother and his few teaching colleagues from the University present in the court, I was astonished at the ignorance of the Prosecution of the technology so widely used in calculation in our country. Despite these explanations and the unquestioned reputation and credibility of Dr. Forrest Cookson, the Special Judge seemed to have not given adequate credence and importance to his testimony by openly taking the side of the Prosecution. I wondered, "Can ignorance be regarded as bliss for the judges as well as for the lawyers?"

(2)

After Dr. Cookson, Dr. Abul Barkat, Professor of Economics of Dhaka University and General Secretary of the Bangladesh Economic Association, testified as a Defense Witness. He said that Dr. Alamgir, once President of the same Economic Association, was, in his assessment, the most enlightened amongst the country's bureaucrats. Dr. Alamgir was well-known, he said, as an early user of Bangla in teaching of and research in Economics; some of Dr. Alamgir's books were used as references in teaching of Economics in Dhaka University even in present days. The Fifth Five-Year Plan (1997-2001), authored by Dr. Alamgir, was a distinguished work. Dr. Alamgir used *"Amanat Patra"* as the Bangla version of FDR, which was correct. According to Dr. Barkat, in calculation of construction cost of building, Construction Cost Index exemplified on p. 468 of Bangladesh Statistical Year Book, 2004, should be used in preference to other estimates or procedures, in reference to calculation of present or past cost of buildings as in the cost of Dr. Alamgir's house at Banani. He stated that Construction Cost Index (building) was the official index of the government and could not, therefore, be substituted by other estimates as was done by the Prosecution in the case of Dr. Alamgir's house at Banani. Dr. Barkat affirmed that cost estimation was the field of expertise of applied economists and accountants and not of engineers who were employed in calculating the cost of Dr. Alamgir's house. The Public Prosecutor taking up cross-examination at this stage dryly commented that when he was a student himself, he regarded statistics and statistical calculations as unrealistic:

"When I was a student, for correctness we had to count how many crows crowed over a tree; the statistician used to estimate instead of counting. How can an estimate be more correct than counting?" the Public Prosecutor asked with a grin.

"The state of knowledge in all subjects including Statistics had progressed far since the days you were a student and to assume otherwise would be tantamount to ignoring knowledge and its blessings. Statistics as a subject or discipline of knowledge has not been innovated and extended thus far for the benefit of crows," Dr. Abul Barkat laughed and responded.

The Public Prosecutor did not pursue his comments any further. I could tell from his appearance, he did not understand from Dr. Barkat's response the underlying wrath and derision for the ignorant. Contorting his face and voice, he sat down, despite finger-pointing to the contrary by the remote-controller Major Kamruzzaman. Regrettably, the Special Judge did not seem to take into account Dr. Barkat's testimony, which interpreted *Amanat Patra* as the Bangla version of FDR and raised the inauthenticity and unacceptability of the PWD's cost calculation of my house at Banani or our ancestral common and undemarcated twin house at village Gulbahar. Nor did the Special Judge cite any cogent ground for not doing so. As I would see later, this lame-brained attitude made his conclusions in these respects arbitrary and unreasonable and subservient to the diktat he had received.

Cross-examination of Dr. Barkat over, the Special Judge announced that he would hear the other defense witnesses the next day. He stroked his forehead in time with the rotating fan overhead for a minute or two, looked for something, probably a handkerchief in the right hand pocket of his pant and finding none shouted something to his attendant and left. I came out of the dock, sat with my brother Dr. Jahangir, sister Nilufar, nephew Dr. Mamun and the lawyers for about 30 minutes and discussed about the impact of the depositions made.

My brother Dr. Jahangir appreciated Dr. Akbar Ali Khan's straightforwardness; his deposition as a defense witness must have made the regime queasy if not uncomfortable, he said. Dr. Mamun was skeptical. He said, Dr. Akbar should have been more elaborate and to the point. He did work with you in various committees and could have said more about his experience of working together. Advocate Rezaur Rahman and Dr. Jahangir agreed that Dr. Cookson's deposition was to the point and the best. I said, the Special Judge did not look like he gave credence and importance to Dr. Cookson's deposition. Dr. Mamun opined that Dr. Abul Barkat's performance was the best. The Public Prosecutor could not make him bend in any way. Advocate Rezaur Rahman, with his experience with the conduct of the Special Judge, sounded skeptical. "Let us see what the Judge makes out of these depositions," he said to himself. Then I walked back to the prison-van that rattled its way down to the Kashimpur Jail.

In the night, till late hours, to lessen the despair in me I tried to read Tapan Chowdhury's *Bangal Nama*. Tapan Chowdhury was the Professor of Indian History and Civilization in Oxford University. He was born in Barisal, in Bangladesh during the Raj and had seen the social and political upheavals in both the united and divided India. He struggled hard to establish himself and on the way never took leave of human values. I could not finish the whole book — a sort of autobiography written in very simple but appealing Bangla. But before I fell asleep with the book left unconsciously on my chest, I could share his feelings about the soil on which he was born and the societal framework in which he was brought up. The societal framework in many ways resembled the one in which my father was brought up, as I learned from reading his diary after his death in 1974. I got up late in the next morning and skipping breakfast, hurriedly boarded the prison van that took me to the court.

Sheikh Md. Shahid, Managing Director of M/S Shahid Associates (set up in 1970), one of the most recognized structural engineers of the country, aged about 75, was produced as our witness next day July 11. Led by my lawyer Syed Rezaur Rahman, he testified that he had prepared the design and the blueprint of my house at Banani. He stated that he had made an economic or low-cost design for the house. As stated by him, the first two stories of the house were built in 1981-82 and the second two stories, *i.e.*, second and third floors in 1991-92. According to him, following the PWD's rough guidelines, approximate cost of the ground floor and the first floor along with plinth in 1981-82 for 1,400 sq. ft. with 20% deduction on account of self-supervision and purchase of materials was about Tk. 5.6 lacs (Tk. 250 per sq ft x 1,400 sq. ft. of floor space = Tk.3.56 lacs of which 80% = 2.80 lacs) For the first floor his estimate of cost figured at Tk.2.43 lacs (Tk.190 per sq. ft. x 1,450 sq. ft. floor space = 2.66 lacs of which 80% = Tk. 2.12 lacs) totaling construction cost of the first two floors at no more than Tk. 4.92 lacs. He said the actual cost would be lower because the staircase and verandahs were not that well finished and covered by walls. This figure approximately corresponded to the cost figure as assessed and accepted by the Income Tax department as the cost of the house in the same year.

Defense Witness Shahid did not give his estimate of cost of second and third floors in 1991-92 prices as he did not bring with him the rates prevalent or applicable at that time. He stated that there was a large discrepancy as between the PWD's rates and actual cost of private builders. According to him the PWD's rates, though widely used, were not authentic, implying thereby that the PWD's rates inclusive of cost of supervision, contractor's profit and tax were comparatively higher than the actual incurred by private builders. Cost figures mentioned by Defense Witness Shahid were thus similar or very close to the cost figures given by me and accepted by the IT authority. Defense Witness Shahid further testified that he knew the accused since the latter was Deputy Commissioner, Jessore, and he was of help to the witness in pursuing some of his social and charitable works and programs there and also in Dhaka.

"So you are deposing in support of Dr. Alamgir as a friend and benefactor?" the Public Prosecutor taking up cross-examination at this stage asked.

"I am deposing as the Engineer who had prepared the blueprint of his house and in support of an honest civil servant," retorted the Defense Witness.

"Did Dr. Alamgir as Executive Director, Islamic Development Bank or Minister of Planning help you in any way, say, getting contracts for architectural and structural job for you?"

"No, never in any way. Contracts were won by me on merit and not on *tadbir* by anyone," responded Sheikh Shahid.

At this point the Public Prosecutor lurched up and went up to him standing on the witness box and tried to snatch off a piece of paper on which the Defense Witness presumably had his notes on estimates of cost.

"These are my notes for helping me in remembering the calculations and the salient points of the blueprint of the house that I had prepared. You cannot have them; you have no lawful claim on them. I refuse to show them to you even," with a gentle swirl of hand, pocketing the paper, Sheikh Shahid firmly told him.

Flexing his toes, with visible irritation, the Public Prosecutor retreated and sat down; he seemed to be a rutted shadow of the Major, flinching from the obvious insult, yielded by their own audacious conduct. Regrettably, as I observed, the Special Judge did not note down the full deposition of the renowned structural engineer Shahid and the figures of costs as evidenced by him and similar to costs as assessed by the IT department in 1981-82. Specially, I saw him not noting the details and explanations given by the Defense Witness. His conduct, as it seemed was immune to absurdity.

The next Defense Witness was Alamin, an architect-engineer. He was a valiant freedom fighter in 1971. He said he had prepared the blueprint for the Biponi Polash, a number of shops under construction within the premises of the Gulbahar Himagar, a private limited company at Kachua. He testified that the ownership of these shops under-construction was that of the Gulbahar Himagar, Ltd. and not of Dr. Alamgir. He stated that the name of Dr. Alamgir was mentioned under the relevant space for owner as "for," *i.e.*, on behalf of Gulbahar Himagar Ltd. of which he was just a shareholder. As testified by him, he had inscribed Dr. Alamgir's name "for," *i.e.*, on behalf of the Gulbahar Himagar, Ltd.; Dr. Alamgir did not sign under his name so inscribed. In the cross-examination of the witness, the Public Prosecutor wanted to know about the witness's acquaintance with Dr. Alamgir and his eldest brother, a former Member of the Parliament from the area, at that time deceased. It seemed he cautiously ignored the deposition of this witness. Grabbing on the lack of focus on him by the Prosecution, the Special Judge seemed to have ignored the truth revealed through the deposition of this independent and expert witness, having hands down experience of the shops under construction in reference.

Architect Alamin had deposed as a defense witness ignoring the threat of the Forces Intelligence. The very day he deposed, his wife serving as the deputy chief architect of the RAJUK was laid off on orders of the intelligence people. This exemplified how the truth was being hammered down into a prefabricated mould by the regime, bent upon solidifying its hold by crude intimidation and cruel treatment.

Reaching the Kashimpur Jail, I hit the bed without a meal. I did not want a conversation with anyone. When my anguish softened somewhat, I took once again Tapan Chowdhury's *Bangal Nama.* While reading the latter part, I realized how the favorable environment of Oxford University helped blossom the intellectual depth and fervor of Professor Chowdhury. I realized that an environment for letting a thousand flowers bloom had to be created, sustained and cherished for the refinement of values and quality of life of a society. Sometime in 2003, I and Sitara visited Oxford University, breathed the air of free expression and creativity and understood the fount of its flourishing over centuries. I thought, despite the wrong done, havoc created, organized throttling of thought and expression, of destruction wrought down, this nation, owing a debt to the blood sacrificed by 3 million martyrs for its independence, would be able to recreate what was being destroyed at the time. *Bangal Nama* was given to me by Munir of Chandpur — an erstwhile ardent activist and leader of the Students' League, the student wing of the Awami League. I thanked this representative of the young generation and hoped that what we could not do for the country, they would be able to do. With an unseen smile for him and his associates in the dark, I feared that they would face more difficult days to overcome the enemy. It was over for us. We were lucky. Our generation would soon be dead, leaving the future ones to the more difficult days.

(3)

On July 12 the next day came Mir Mohammad Iqbal, Managing Director of the Monowara Hospital, Dhaka, and the General Sales Agent of Japan Airlines and Air Shahara in Bangladesh, Vice-President of the Kachua Thana Awami League, as the Defense Witness. In his testimony to the Special Court, he stated that he had purchased three motorcycles from Nobel House, Tejgaon, Dhaka sometime in June 2006. The cost in total was about Tk.1,50,000 that was funded by the accused's son Dr. Jalal Alamgir (Tk. 30,000), and out of savings of the election budget for 2001 (Tk. 60,000) and by Mir Iqbal (Tk. 60,000) himself. These motorcycles were intended for use by the party workers for the election slated for January 22, 2007. He corroborated Prosecution Witness Assistant Inspector Hossain that these cycles were not registered till then, *i.e.*, after more than nine months, in anybody's or the accused's name. He affirmed that the accused did not have any connection with either ownership or use of these motorcycles. As stated by him, these motorcycles could not be registered till then in names of party workers – Presidents of the Thana Jubo League, Students League and Sechhasevak League as time was not opportune in those turbulent days. In cross-examination, the Public Prosecutor stated with a patronizing tone:

"I knew Mr. Iqbal's late father very intimately. I am surprised to see his able son in the witness box. Haven't I noticed you in the courtroom earlier on a number of days?"

"Yes, you did. I have been present in the court some days. I wanted to observe how the Prosecution presents a case of absurdities against an honorable person," said Iqbal.

Seeing this way he would not be able to make the witness slide down to his side, the Public Prosecutor asked "What were the colors of these three motorcycles?"

"Each of these, as I remember, was bi-colored; I don't exactly remember the color combination each had," replied the Defense Witness.

Finding nothing else to ask, the Public Prosecutor sat down. The Special Judge, despite this deposition of the VP of the Thana Awami League and position elaborately clarified, seemed to be continuing with the wrong imputation of ownership of these motorcycles on me.

Then Dr. Burhanuddin Khan Jahangir, my elder brother, a former Professor of the Dhaka University and Pro-Vice Chancellor of the National University, testified as the last Defense Witness. He stated that the twin house at village Gulbahar, alleged to be mine alone, was actually the jointly owned undemarcated property of our four brothers and four sisters. He deposed that the twin house was constructed between 1981 and 1999 by our eldest brother, Misbahuddin Khan, a former Member of the Parliament now deceased, at an approximate cost of Tk.12 lacs contributed by all brothers and sisters from time to time. He also stated that the Sultana Foundation, was a trust created to commemorate the memory of our mother and to help the poor and the meritorious students of the area with an initial capital of Tk. 27 lacs or so with contributions by all members of the family, in accordance with an agreement among themselves.

The Agreement was placed before the Special Judge earlier while I made a statement under Section 342 of the Criminal Procedure Code. As per this Agreement, Dr. Jahangir deposed, the Foundation's fund was to be in the custody of Dr. Alamgir. As a proof of joint and undemarcated ownership of the homestead and the twin house situated on it, Dr. Jahangir placed before the court a copy of the land record or *porcha* that mentioned all brothers and sisters and their heirs as owners of the homestead and by implication the house in question. Prosecution Witnesses, who purportedly valued this property, had admitted earlier that they had not enquired about and found out the ownership of this house or property in reference. The Public Prosecutor could not make Dr. Jahangir budge from his position.

"You were most of the time in your life outside the country?" The Public Prosecutor wanted to know.

"Not most of the time; but quite often I was out in foreign universities, teaching and researching," replied Dr. Jahangir.

"Why, your eldest brother Misbahuddin Khan gifted all his shares of the Gulbahar Himagar to your one brother Dr. Alamgir and not others?" asked the Public Prosecutor.

"He did not gift off the shares; these were bought by Dr. Alamgir from him before he died."

"Why did not you buy?"

"I was never interested in business enterprise. I have been an academic throughout my life," responded Dr. Jahangir.

The Public Prosecutor slowly slumped down on his chair. Sitting there with eyes downwards, he said,

"Please do not mind. I had to ask you these questions doing my duty."

"It seems you have been doing your duty and serving your employers well," dryly commented my brother and left the witness box.

At this point Dr. Jahangir produced proofs of his associations and accreditations with various universities and institutions of international repute and showed them to the Special Judge. He did not care to look at them. He returned them to Dr. Jahangir as if he had seen such things once too often. Civility and humility were not his well-groomed hallmarks.

All the while Major Kamruzzaman remained tightly clamped on his seat with audible signs of discomfort. Despite the deposition made and proof produced, the Special Judge as it seemed, did not care to consider the house in village Gulbahar as jointly owned, undemarcated property, instead of solely mine as alleged but not proved by the Prosecution. Further, the Special Judge did not seem like taking into account the current capital fund of Tk. 31 lacs (inclusive of interest earned net of charities made annually) of the Sultana Foundation as fund not owned by but in custody of me. To me he appeared to be a man bent upon erasing evidence instead of evaluating it to grasp the truth. The environs around him were smudged with the ragged aim of lies and servitude.

July 12 was Thursday. July 13 and 14 were weekly holidays. Muhith was expected back in the country on July 14. Advocate Syed Rezaur Rahman requested the Special Judge to allow us to produce Muhith as our last witness on July 15. But the Special Judge did not agree on the grounds that the law required him to complete the trial within a given time. Regarding the time set by law for investigation, his interpretation was that it was directive rather than mandatory. Regarding the time set for trial without intermission of more than three days at a stretch, by the same law, it was mandatory instead of directive to him. So he fixed July 16 as the day for arguments of the Prosecution. Little did he take into consideration that he had given six times more time to the Prosecution to produce their witnesses and present their depositions. Keeping July 16 for the Prosecution arguments, he could have easily fixed July 15 for Muhith's deposition. Obviously he did not have any intention to introduce even a semblance of equality between the Prosecution and the Defense. Here zealotry became the other name for impartiality, blurring the vision between the just and the wrong.

In the end, with a rational sense of having been aggrieved in the process of trial and being a witness to shedding of responsibility for ensuring due process of law by the administrator of law himself, I boarded the prison van on my way to the Kashimpur Jail with which I had become quite familiar.

As I walked to the division building, the sun was setting, breaking its golden rays through the afternoon clouds. I found Lotus-Kamal sitting on a plastic chair with a clutch of weeds that had grown against the south-eastern corner of the jail's walls. Lotus-Kamal got up, walked me to the grove of trees to the south of the walkway and showed me two *shalik* birds perched side by side on a branch and teetering and stealing looks at each other with profound love and affection. For his love of birds, we the inmates of the jail named him Abu Taiyara, *i.e.*, father of birds following the Prophet's companion Abu Horaira, the father of cats. He was named so by the Prophet for his love of cats in those days.

"In the bird's world, there is no jail; look how happy and content they are." Lotus-Kamal told me.

"Yes. They are happy but then again, in a thousand years they have been so teetering and looking at each other with no progress in their living — they live in the same kind of nests and on the same kind of insects and worms," I said.

"Then with progress attained in the living of your, our people, we have invented jail to punish the innocent so that the voracious could get everything they don't deserve," replied Lotus-Kamal.

Seized with despair and anger, Lotus-Kamal pulled up the weeds that sprouted colored flowers from their knotted roots. I took his hands and walked him along the bended walkway up the stairs to the cells of our incarceration provided by the seemingly unremediable raw power.

8 Arguments: Prosecution

(1)

On July 16, as arranged, I was taken to the court early in the morning. Public Prosecutor Mizanur Rahman in his flamboyant and mischievous manner, started summing up the Prosecution's case against me. It seemed, he did not analyze the depositions in depth. It also seemed, he did not have to. For him it was a stubborn attempt to capture and convict innocence. He was a paid agent to devastate the truth, not to find it out towards the end of justice. The Leader of the Task Force Major Kamruzzaman sat by his side to stifle any element of truth that might come out of his sayings. Shamelessly, but with considerable confidence, he said that the Special Judge understood the Prosecution's case in full, which therefore needed not much elucidation and elaboration from his side. For him, as it became evident, victory came not from the pursuit of truth but a sinister plan and a set of tools given to implement the scheme to thwart it and drown it into cesspools of falsities.

Standing in the dock, I looked at my brothers Drs. Jahangir and Arefin, who appeared crestfallen, losing the grasp of the present. My lawyer Syed Rezaur Rahman gave me a look of despair, somewhat angry at the pomposity of the Public Prosecutor. Other friends sat in silence, almost dumbfounded by the hypocritical swirling of moronic mistakes and falsities that spewed out of the Public Prosecutor at public cost. In accordance with the recent dispensation of public resources by the "independent" ACC, the Public Prosecutor assigned to anti-corruption cases received higher remuneration even than the Chief Justice of the Supreme Court of the country.

Beefed up with the unbridled evil strength by his side and encouraging demeanor of the Special Judge, Public Prosecutor Mizanur Rahman stated rather briefly that they had found all elements of blackness behind the white *kurta* and *pajama* that I had always worn. His eyes were glassy, set in a gleeful raw-boned face of a heavyweight boxer sure of his victory in the case. He gave an impression that his impending success in playing with justice would always leave all those who would come to seek justice in front of a judicial demon, feigning capability of evaluating harsh evidences of good and bad, right and wrong, and even life and death. The demeanor was too ridiculous to inspire anger in us; we were dumbfounded, witnessing a horrible drama being unfolded before our eyes sludged with the morass of unashamed lies and hypocrisies.

(2)

Shamelessly, without even referring to specific depositions, in about 30 minutes flat, the Public Prosecutor recanted that I had concealed Tk. 117 lacs of fixed deposits, two houses in my ancestral home valued at Tk. 57 lacs, Tk. 134 lacs of bank deposits, a filling station at Kachua valued at Tk. 26 lacs, a house at Comilla Housing Estate valued at Tk. 20 lacs, agricultural lands of about 15 acres valued at Tk. 79 lacs, a house at Banani costing Tk. 87 lacs and a set of shops named the Biponi Polash costing Tk. 29 lacs. While giving these costs and values, he did not care to realize that their total did not tally with the figure mentioned formally in the charge-sheet. It was also beyond him to understand that his figures were not net of figures that I had mentioned as cost/values in my asset statements. He did not care to mention that they had not considered my second asset statement along with the first wherein I gave details of fixed deposits and income tax payments. Without flinching, he brushed aside the fact that the ancestral houses were commonly owned, undemarcated property. Also, the filling station was owned by my elder son, aged 36 and earning about Tk. 100 lacs a year in the U.S. The house at Comilla was funded by the Agrani Bank for setting up a branch over there, and was under the ownership of my younger son, aged 28 and earning over Tk. 120 lacs a year in the U.S. Additionally the Biponi Polash was owned and funded by the Gulbahar Himagar Limited, a private limited company of which I was just a shareholder. Most important, I had mentioned all these and the agricultural lands around our ancestral home in my first asset statement. He did not refer to any of the documents that we had presented in support of my position. As it appeared from what he posited, an omission in the tax return (even if there was one), was not an omission or concealment within the meaning of Section 26 of the ACC Act as long as no such omission was found in the statement required to be furnished under the Act.

With an owlish face, directed more towards Major Kamruzzaman of the Task Force (sitting by the side of the Public Prosecutor) than to papers and evidential documents at hand, the Special Judge seemed to be under a degenerated kind of power over him and the court's proceedings. The Special Judge occasionally nodded with bizarre disdain, as if to satisfy the power that mandated him to sit on the judge's row along with some ten others in other courts on chairs placed high above the common citizenry, trumpeting the triumph of power flowing from the barrel of the gun.

The Public Prosecutor, with visible encouragement from both Major Kamruzzaman and the Special Judge, made some ludicrous comments in the process. These indicated the Prosecution's poverty in identification and analysis of facts-in-issue. Shameful presentation of this was made as if poverty in understanding was a good proof of simplicity, straightforwardness and perhaps truthfulness. He said in respect of my second asset statement that they could not evaluate it as it was turned in late. A correction or an addition late, but while evidence was being produced and sifted, in his assessment was a reason enough to ignore the truth contained therein and press for conviction based on incomplete evidence or half-truths. He stated that the Prosecution did not take into account Tk. 25 lacs or so of the Sultana Foundation kept with Dr. Alamgir, as he had not mentioned it in his first asset statement in addition to approximately Tk. 90 lacs of fixed deposits.

Little did it occur to him that the notice served on Dr. Alamgir to describe his assets did not require him to mention assets held by him on behalf of others, in this case, of the Sultana Foundation. The Prosecution did not even consider the approximate figure of Tk. 90 lacs as my fixed deposits as stated in the first asset statement. Apprehending misconception, I corrected the figure by mentioning the asset of the Sultana Foundation held by me in my second asset statement, which they would not take into consideration either. Very simplistically, he stated that Dr. Alamgir's two sons stayed and worked abroad and earned high incomes but they could not give him any idea about their "savings."

In making this assertion, the Public Prosecutor forgot that copies of their income tax returns to U.S. treasury were submitted along with my statement made under Section 342 of the Criminal Procedure Code and that their incomes and savings as submitted were never put into question by the Prosecution at that time or through cross-examination of the testimonies of financial analysts or experts. The Public Prosecutor made an overtly false statement that my eldest brother gifted all his shares of the Gulbahar Himagar Limited to me and not to Dr. Jahangir and the other brother. As a matter of fact Dr. Jahangir was a shareholder of the company right from the start while I was not and that the eldest brother had sold his shares to me before he died, which the Public Prosecutor did not find out or state while trumpeting the mandated falsehood.

Prompted by Major Kamruzzaman, he stated falsely that I employed three drivers, two maids and eight *ansars* in my house. As a matter of fact, two drivers were in the employ of business concerns that rented the ground floor of my house in Banani; and one messenger working in my office located on the first floor knew how to drive. These three could not be taken to be my drivers reflecting my allegedly posh life-style. Of the two maids alleged to have been in my employ, one was an old lady, a victim of river erosion who had worked in our house and raised our two sons for a long time and was now retired. She occasionally visited and took meals with us. My sons, because of service rendered and out of deep affection for her, gave her a monthly allowance which they termed retirement benefits. Her daughter-in-law now worked in the house as a maid and a cook. These facts eluded the Investigation Officers as well as Major Kamruzzaman, prodding them to snuff out the truth. These were never ascertained by the Public Prosecutor, who in the public interest was pressing the charge for the highest punishment on me.

Little did he know, unknown perhaps in the circumstances around him, that none of our employees ever left us; we looked after them well and they lived with and worked for us almost as members of the same family. The ansars were employed by the two business concerns that had offices downstairs for protection against the onslaught of goons and thugs of the political opponents who since October 2001, when the BNP was made to win the national election, came to ransack the house on more than one occasion. The Prosecution, if desirous of being truthful and conscious of public interest, could have ascertained this from the office of the District Adjutant of Ansars, which was a law-and-order outfit of the government itself.

One funny assertion of the Public Prosecutor regarded the ownership and registration of three motorcycles that I was alleged to have owned and concealed. He said that I could not give any satisfactory explanation as to why these were not registered in my name and that was why these should be taken as owned by me. He said this despite the Prosecution Witnesses' deposition that registration was the proof of ownership of such vehicles and these were neither registered in my name nor recovered from my possession, and without being so registered and being under my possession, one could not say these were mine.

(3)

About depositions made by the defense witnesses, the Public Prosecutor's evaluation indicated his lack of legal education and professional ethics. As regards the deposition made by Dr. Akbar Ali Khan, a former Advisor of the caretaker government and a Cabinet Secretary (*i.e.*, the top bureaucrat of the country), the Public Prosecutor said that the evidentiary value of his deposition was zero as he could not exactly say what were the charges against me and how much I drew for traveling and daily allowances as an Executive Director of the Islamic Development Bank.

Regarding the assertion of Defense Witness Dr. Cookson (an internationally acknowledged financial analyst) that my computation with a computer of my savings and investment capacity out of my salaried, rental and incidental incomes was correct and in accordance with internationally accepted good accounting practice, the Public Prosecutor stated that these could not be accepted as I had not signed them on every page. The Public Prosecutor could not say how in the Evidence Act of 1867, authenticity or otherwise of computation through computer invented about 150 years thereafter could have been ruled in or out merely on the grounds of its being signed or unsigned by me. Obviously it was beyond his knowledge that computer-generated data did not require the signature of persons who used computer programs to make the relevant calculations.

The Public Prosecutor's abhorrence of current technology and knowledge became all the more evident when he stated rather loudly that the Construction Cost Indexes compiled by the government and published through its Bureau of Statistics were not authentic as deposed by Dr. Abul Barkat, Professor of Economics, the Dhaka University and General Secretary of the Bangladesh Economic Association. As he stated, depositions of Dr. Barkat were not reliable and acceptable as expert's evidence. In the Public Prosecutor's opinion, stated without blinking his eyes, depositions made by Defense Witness Sheikh Shahid, a renowned architect and structural engineer of the country as well as that of Alamin, the architect of the Biponi Polash, were unreliable. Sheikh Shahid, as the architect and structural engineer of my house in Banani, deposed that the costs of construction of the house in two stages, in 1981-82 and 1991-92 were more or less the same as I had stated in my asset statement or recorded in my income tax returns for the relevant years and accepted by the Income Tax authority.

Mr. Alamin deposed that the land on which the under-construction Biponi Polash was located was not mine and that the Biponi Polash was a project of the Gulbahar Himager Ltd. and not mine. With a prodding from the Major sitting by his side and an encouraging, mischievous smile from the Special Judge, he even dismissed my brother Dr. Jahangir's deposition that our ancestral house and lands were common and undemarcated properties of all members, all of whom contributed to the capital fund of the Sultana Foundation. In this he and the Special Judge ignored the land records of the ownership of the ancestral lands and the documentary proof of the formation of and capital contribution to the Sultana Foundation. Words jumbled up in my head as, unauthorized and unable to speak standing in the dock of the accused, I was for a moment gripped with panic in this swirling of lies and misinterpreted or ignored documents. Then the panic gave way to anger as I realized that, under the circumstances, government in our land had been innovated and pressed forward to persecute the innocent for the benefit of the illegitimate ambitions of a few. Optimism was snuffed out almost to the last point, but I did not resign myself altogether to disappointment.

Dashing through the demands of respectability expected of a Public Prosecutor, Mizanur Rahman spoke with feigned confidence a number of other lies. These could not hide a heavy putrid odor of certain decay in values expected of an educated man. He said that according to Prosecution Witness 3, Assistant Vice President, the IFIC Bank, Karwan Bazar, I had concealed six Fixed Deposit Receipts. The Prosecution Witness had clearly stated that fixed deposits were not matters that could be concealed, as these were reported to the National Board of Revenue or the tax authority as a matter of procedure under law. Public Prosecutor Rahman stated that the alleged fact of concealment was not denied by the defense, which was not true.

In addition to the deposition of the Prosecution Witness concerned, I explained in great detail in my statement under Section 342 of the Criminal Procedure Code that these fixed deposits were in part mine, and accordingly, to that extent, reported in the wealth statement accompanying the income tax return for the relevant year. I also explained that all of these together were slated to be stated in the next financial year's returns, as and when interest income from them would have been yielded. Clinging to a knot to bind his accusation, the Public Prosecutor said that Prosecution Witness 12, Executive Engineer, Chandpur, gave valuation of the house at Gulbahar village and the Biponi Polash at Kachua, but then he quite dishonestly omitted to mention that the Executive Engineer himself had admitted his ignorance about the ownership of these properties. The Public Prosecutor could not understand that the fact-at-issue here was the ownership and not valuation and the ownership was never ascribed to me by the Prosecution Witnesses or proved by documents produced by the Prosecution.

At this point of swirling falsehood and half-truths, the Public Prosecutor stopped for the day. With the permission of the Special Judge, I sat with my brother Dr. Jahangir, my sisters Kohinoor and Nilufar and my lawyers Syed Rezaur Rahman and Ayat Ali Patwary for about 30 minutes. We talked about the Prosecution's production of truncated evidence and arguments. I asked my lawyer to be ready with apt rebuttal the next day when the Public Prosecutor would finish his jabberings. Then by the rattling and smoke emitting prison van, I returned to the Kashimpur Jail.

Sitting very late in the night, dark and grim, I discussed the pros and cons of the Prosecution's arguments with Salman, Lotus-Kamal and Engineer Mosharraf. We all agreed: the courtroom was nothing but a front, showing the verdict that had already been decided upon and transmitted to the Special Judge by the armor of power represented by Major Kamruzzaman. The Advisor for Law, as the rumor went, had already given his instructions. Around 2:00 in the night I hit the bed, but both sleep and rest alluded me despite the darkness, thick and heavy. I clamped my eyes shut but shivered in anxiety, stared at distant shadows of a chained life and prayed for the daylight.

(4)

On the morning of July 17, once again in the Special Court, Public Prosecutor Mizanur Rahman along with his cohorts was at the site of his perceived platform. There were not, as it seemed, more details to the construct of his own falsehood. He started with the flaws in the notice that was served on me to submit the asset statement, as we had pointed out. Earlier, while cross-examining Prosecution Witnesses Jiban Krishna and Syed Iqbal, my lawyer had pointed out that the notice had been signed by the Secretary ACC on January 18, 2007, *i.e.*, on a date earlier than when I was arrested. This to us reflected a premeditated and prejudiced action of harassment, not warranted by the findings of an enquiry against me after I was arrested. In this context, Public

Prosecutor Mizanur Rahman said, it had been a "natural mistake" indicating that the Secretary had not been unusually and overly attentive to my case. Had he been so attentive, he would not have committed such a mistake, he stated.

He admitted that in the notice, values of assets had not been specifically asked for. But despite that I had given values of assets in the case of some items, and since I had given so, it was to be assumed, he argued, that "values" were really asked for. I almost laughed aloud along with most others present in the courtroom at the naiveté of the argument that could wrap one's mind in such an improvisation. He stated that I had in my asset statement given explanation of sources of my income but the Prosecution could not find "definitiveness" about them. This was obviously a lie shared with his prompter Major Kamruzzaman. This was not so stated by any of the Prosecution Witnesses. He stated that he had seen many a book authored by me in the market but could not ascertain income that was earned against them.

This was a dismal distortion inasmuch as in the first asset statement in an appended appendix, I had given book-wise estimates of my earnings. About the second asset statement that I had submitted, he posited with a pampering relaxation that it was submitted at a very late stage. Little did he comprehend that the time between April 28 when it was submitted and July 17 when he made his argument on this line was time enough for any reasonable Public Prosecutor to consider this supplementation and that the second statement was produced before the court only when we had pressed for its production time and again and after submitting proof of its receipt by the Secretary, ACC. He alleged that the computer printouts detailing estimates of my salaried, rental and incidental income over decades (from 1963 to 2006) were made out of the jail and, therefore, not authentic.

This was at best an argument or excuse of a person illiterate in ways of modern computation or use of computers. The court in this context was obligated to assess and conclude on the reasonableness of estimates or figures generated by the computer. The court could not throw out the computer-generated data on the grounds that the computer was not in the jail where I was incarcerated. He admitted that the supplementary charge-sheet submitted by Investigation Officer Syed Iqbal was not given in the prescribed form. Little did he understand that the form was prescribed by the High Court and none below that court could ignore or violate it without sparing vitiation of proceedings.

According to him, Public Witness Prodhan, Assistant Income Tax Commissioner, by inadvertent mistake did not present the summary of my income tax records spelled out in terms of income on one side and assets on the other while he had deposed for three consecutive working days at the first instance. He stated that to cover up this mistake, it was presented to the court by recalling him and making him depose once again. While giving this explanation, he did not mention how illogical it was to compare income of 24 years earned between 1982 and 2006 with assets built up over a period of 38 years since 1962 and even before, as in case of inherited properties. In effect, it was tantamount to attempting to compare the chair on which he sat with the table in front of the Special Judge. He did not mention that in the total income mentionable in income tax returns, exemptions as given in the 6th,7th and 8th schedules of the Income Tax Ordinance, 1984, were not to be included, though these constituted elements of or contributed to the build-up of the total assets or wealth of an income tax payee. He could not comprehend that income tax of government officers deemed to have been paid by the government was shown substracted from total income, though in actuality it should not have been. Such substraction reduced income but contributed to the build-up of assets.

By his arguments, the Public Prosecutor made it abundantly clear that in his world of prosecution in the public interest there were no surrounding safeguards of ethics. For him, success lay in perfecting the art for a malicious cause, in relinquishing one's best self for the sake of centering on nothing else but self-interest. By his actions and utterings he had jettisoned the very concept of public interest from public prosecution.

This was the result out of the total absence of checks and balances in the ACC's prosecution procedure. In the U.S., prosecution for criminal offense originates in the Sheriff's office and is authorized by the district attorney, who acts as the check on probable maliciousness. Over there in the ACC, the public prosecutor merely obeys the order or malicious wishes of the ACC without having any authority to serve as a check. This makes the procedure rife with unchecked error and bias, questionable investigation tactics and ultimately shoddy lawyering from the side of a Commission announced to have been set up as an independent body to uphold public interest. Here group or private expediency overrides public interest and cherished human values that stand against transformation of the State into an instrument of persecution and tyranny. And the instrument remains unbridled, unbecoming of a democratic society in the absence of a conduit for appointing public defendants by the judge from amongst diligent and experienced lawyers.

The role played by the Prosecution in my case was an eloquent testimony to this. It was beyond the realization of the judge in particular and the administration of criminal justice of the regime in general that prevention of injustice meant and included sustenance of a society of amity, coherence, tolerance and a built-in process of development with the stake of all. Such a society, furthermore, could not be founded and cherished despite mere political independence. No one, irrespective of promise given or background touted, should be given the absolute role of the czar of honesty in a pluralistic society aspiring to encourage and develop enterprise and creativity.

9 Arguments: Defense

(1)

The Public Prosecutor spewed out from a heart of darkness. The darkness centered around a cesspool of make-believe, spitting out the falsehood otherwise inspired by the Special Court itself. His jabbering was over by lunchtime. At 1:30 p.m. the Special Judge, disgracefully belching out satisfaction of servitude, rose and gave us an hour to prepare for our defense and start arguments. It was a difficult task. For obviously the Public Prosecutor's tales were mostly words to hide behind, not words that could carry a message of protecting public interest guarding against public persecution.

At 2:30 in the afternoon, as soon as the black-robed Special Judge gravely perched himself in an owlish manner on his elevated chair, my lawyer Advocate Syed Rezaur Rahman started his arguments and rebuttal of the Prosecution's charges. He said, it was difficult for us to be sure whether this case was filed against Dr. Alamgir by the State or the ACC or whether this case should be titled Jiban Krishna Roy vs. Dr. Alamgir. Jiban Krishna Roy was the complainant in this case. He had filed the First Information Report (FIR) in this case to the police, without completing the required enquiry in accordance with the Rules of the ACC. He could have taken adequate time to complete the enquiry in full but he did not, for he wanted to secure an award from the ACC for filing the FIR in the shortest possible time.

Jiban Krishna Roy asserted that for proceeding against Dr. Alamgir expeditiously and beyond the call of normal duty, he along with his supervising officer Surat Amin were awarded cash prizes on June 28, 2007 as reported in the national dailies. It was obvious they were let loose, or rather lured, to go after Dr. Alamgir to serve an evil motive of themselves and their superiors. Investigation Officer Jiban Krishna Roy had admitted, said Advocate Syed Rezaur Rahman, he had not received any complaint against Dr. Alamgir before lodging the FIR; he had lodged the FIR against Dr. Alamgir on instructions of the Secretary, ACC. Jiban Krishna admitted that the ACC had not given any format for furnishing the asset statement by Dr. Alamgir as required by law. This they did, Advocate Syed Rezaur Rahman asserted, to frame Dr. Alamgir for inadvertently omitting certain parts of his assets required to be given in the prescribed format.

The notice, pointed out Syed Rezaur Rahman, did not require Dr. Alamgir to give particulars of assets held by him on behalf of others, in his case that of the Sultana Foundation. It was evident, he stated, the Secretary, ACC had decided long before he asked for Dr. Alamgir's assets, that he would frame Dr. Alamgir, an enlightened person by any standard. The Secretary, who came from the same electoral constituency as that of Dr. Alamgir, wanted to clear his way by eliminating potentially the most powerful and popular contestor. As a matter of fact, the Secretary, ACC, did not have any authority under the law to serve notice on Dr. Alamgir to furnish a statement of assets. As it became evident, he was too eager to serve such a notice on him and by doing so, he misused his power and authority. He had signed the notice ahead of Dr. Alamgir's arrest.

The Prosecution could not hide this. In order to obviate his discomfiture and prejudiced attitude, the Prosecution did not cite and produce the Secretary to be examined and cross-examined as a witness under oath. Dr. Alamgir, being incarcerated in the jail, was given notice to give his statement of assets within 72 hours. He should have been given at least fourteen days as in the case of others who were arrested along with him or were similarly given notice. While writing the statement, he was not given time and opportunity to consult his lawyer or tax advisor or access to his financial records. Asking Dr. Alamgir in detention to give the statement of his assets in 72 hours was tantamount to persecution under the seeming cover of law. The law was misused in his case to create circumstances adverse to his rights as a citizen.

In his letter forwarding the statement of assets, Dr. Alamgir stated that he should be given an opportunity to explain his statement or to be heard in person in respect of any matter contained therein, the Advocate pointed out. He was not given such an opportunity, which was in violation of the law as well as the universally recognized principle of natural justice and fair play. On page 4 of his statement of assets, Dr. Alamgir had stated that he had approximately Tk. 90 lacs of fixed deposits. This was not mentioned by Investigation Officer Jiban Krishna in the First Information Report. Its omission in the charge-sheet was conspicuous. This was a deliberate and motivated concealment of a vital fact to the lawful authority to frame Dr. Alamgir.

The Prosecution went ahead with the supposition that *"amanat patras"* was not the Bangla version of fixed deposit receipts; this was ludicrous, disgraceful and wrapped in an ulterior motive. No less a person than Defense Witness Dr. Barkat, Professor of Economics, Dhaka University and General Secretary of the Bangladesh Economic Association testified before the court that *"amanat patras"* was the Bangla version of fixed deposit receipts. Even then the Prosecution went ahead with a phony accusation that Dr. Alamgir did not mention his fixed deposits in his asset statement. This was nothing but a perverse attempt to frame an innocent person, Advocate Syed Rezaur Rahman asserted. In his statement of assets, Dr. Alamgir had mentioned that his wife and two sons were not financially dependent on him; rather in times of need, they provided financial assistance to him. Investigation Officer Jiban Krishna did not bother to inquire into this. His report was not only incomplete, but perversely motivated and lathered with partiality unbecoming of a public servant.

Advocate Syed Rezaur Rahman stated that as was required by law, Investigation Officer Jiban Krishna did not mention in Exhibit 4 on whose order or authorization he had filed the First Information Report against Dr. Alamgir. He had not mentioned the date and the place of the alleged occurrences, events and offenses. He stated that there was a startling discrepancy about the place of alleged occurrences and events as mentioned in the first and second charge-sheets. He pointed out that the FIR was lodged about ten months after the alleged occurrence of depositing fixed deposits. This delay itself had cast serious doubt about the entire case based on the alleged occurrence. He stated that the Investigation Officer did not by himself process and print the FIR, which was done through a computer by somebody else.

None could say who processed the words of the FIR in the computer; nobody signed the so-processed-out FIR. When the FIR was lodged, as was admitted by Investigation Officer Jiban Krishna, there were as many as 33 officers in the ACC who could have done this. Despite this, Advocate Syed Rezaur Rahman pointed out, Jiban Krishna alone acted as the lodger of the FIR and Investigation Officer, violating the ACC's own rules. Jiban Krishna's appointment as the Investigation Officer was never gazetted, officially violating the law. This was an unauthorized, colorable and perverted exercise of authority by the ACC and Jiban Krishna to frame an innocent person on political grounds, he asserted. Advocate Syed Rezaur Rahman said that the Investigation Officer did not investigate into the ancestral properties of Dr. Alamgir; and without completing a thorough investigation of these properties and assets (on the grounds of purported shortage of time), submitted the charge-sheet, seemingly meeting the time limit set by the law. This was an exercise in obviating the substance for the sake of meeting a deadline — amounting to a formality and disgraceful injustice.

Advocate Syed Rezaur Rahman made it clear that Investigation Officer Jiban Krishna did not investigate to find out or actually find out whether Dr. Alamgir ever earned income or assets in dishonest ways nor did he mention in the FIR or the investigation report anything about such a finding. As a public servant, it was his duty to mention this and by deliberately not mentioning this, he failed in his duty to protect public interest in terms of telling the whole truth and nothing but the truth. This was not only an inept and incompetent performance, but way beyond, a dishonest and perverse act unlawful for a public servant given such a responsibility. Therefore, it was evident, assets as reported by Dr. Alamgir were not earned through dishonest ways in any way. And by omitting to make this clear, Advocate Syed Rezaur Rahman asserted, Investigation Officer Jiban Krishna in addition, thwarted the independent functioning of the ACC as provided for in the law.

Then Advocate Syed Rezaur Rahman turned his attention to item 4(a) of the asset statement of Dr. Alamgir wherein he had mentioned sources of his incidental income that went into funding his fixed deposits. As admitted by Investigation Officer Jiban Krishna himself, he had not investigated into these sources. If he had, he would have found out the truthfulness of these sources. His investigation, therefore, was bereft of truthfulness and consequently could not be accepted for drawing any conclusion as regards dishonest earnings by the accused. Investigation Officer Jiban Krishna had further admitted that the accused had told him about the Sultana Foundation, its formation, funding and functioning but did not show him any supporting paper.

This, Advocate Rezaur Rahman emphatically pointed out, was not true. A notarized copy of the agreement setting up the Foundation was shown to the court and elaborated upon in the accused's statement made under Section 342 of the Criminal Procedure Code and also corroborated in the deposition of Defense Witness Dr. Jahangir. Investigation Officer Jiban Krishna had stated in his deposition that he had not found any evidence of dishonest earning and living by the accused and that he did not scrutinize the second asset statement furnished by the accused.

In view of these things, no reasonable conclusion could be reached that the accused's income or earnings, in whole or part, were dishonest or beyond his known and legitimate sources of income, Advocate Syed Rezaur Rahman pointed out. The deposition of Investigation Officer Jiban Krishna was thus an amalgam of lies, distortion, negligence, ill-motive, prejudice and confusion which taken together in terms of implications warranted discharge of the accused, the Advocate asserted.

(2)

Then Advocate Syed Rezaur Rahman focused on other weaknesses, inadequacies and inapplicability of depositions of the Prosecution Witnesses. He stated that (1) payment of income taxes was a continuous process with lawful avenues for making up short payments and evening-out over-payments over years without any criminal implication adverse to the payee; (2) the notice to submit the asset statement was dated January 18, 2007, *i.e.*, before the accused was detained, indicating premeditated, biased and prejudiced, and therefore legally untenable, action by the ACC; (3) the notice to submit the asset statement was served on the accused in the Kashimpur Jail without permission of the Ministry of Home as was required under law in the case of a person in detention under the Special Powers Act as was the accused at that time; (4) the second or the supplementary asset statement though submitted later to the ACC was duly received in time for its scrutiny and consideration and produced before the court and accepted as a part of its records, ruling out its unacceptability and inconsideration to the detriment of truth and justice; neither the Prosecution, nor the Court took the second asset statement into consideration; (5) providing 72 hours notice to write and submit the statement of assets in jail, a judicial custody (where the police could not enter, per the law) in presence of the personnel of the Special Branch of the Police instead of seven days as was given in case of similar detainees was discriminatory and unlawful; (6) the only place of occurrence of the alleged crime was mentioned to be the IFIC Bank, Karwan Bazar, whereas other relevant events and occurrences were not specified with places and times making the elements of the allegation unspecified and incongruous in terms of essentiality and definitiveness of the ingredients of offense and, therefore, untenable in law; (7) the fixed deposits mentioned as concealed in the FIR were not, in fact concealed insofar as these were mentioned in approximate terms excluding the portion belonging to the Sultana Foundation in the asset statement and as under law these were to be reported to the tax authority and taxes on their interest income deductible at source by the bank on maturity in 2007-08 and not in 2006-07, *i.e.*, when the statement was written and submitted, as was posited by the Prosecution and (8) the fixed deposits were not bank accounts as was given to understand in the FIR and the charge-sheet making the question of concealment of bank accounts in this case an irrelevant issue, untenable and not actionable in law.

Then Advocate Syed Rezaur Rahman analyzed the depositions of Prosecution Witnesses Gausal Azam Beg and A. F. M. Soyeb, Senior Assistant Vice-President and Assistant Vice-President respectively of the IFIC Bank, Karwan Bazar, Dhaka. Prosecution Witness Beg deposed that he did not know or study the Banking Companies Books of Evidence Act, which *inter alia* provided for presumption of truth in favor of all entries in the books of a bank. This meant all authorities were bound to presume information on fixed deposits given and payment of taxes on their interest incomes made to the tax authority by the IFIC Bank on behalf of the holder, in this case the accused, as true unless proved otherwise with the onus of proof lying on the contestor. Prosecution Witness Soyeb's deposition that fixed deposits of a bank were also known as financial instruments did not imply any incrimination on the accused in respect of connotation of *"amanat patras,"* as used by him in his statement of assets to mean and include fixed deposits.

Prosecution Witness Rezaul Karim's deposition, as pointed out by Advocate Syed Rezaur Rahman, made it clear that ACC's investigation officer Shermin Ferdousi, seized the income tax file of the accused from him but did not put any mark of identification, serial numbers on parts and pages and sign the pages selected as *"alamats."*[32] These inadequacies and negligence in work stood against the unquestioned acceptance of the accused's income tax file and its contents as produced by the Prosecution to the court. The depositions of Prosecution Witness Rezaul Karim and Kumar Basu, both personnel of the Income Tax Department, did not have any incriminating element or implication on the accused.

Advocate Syed Rezaur Rahman pointed out that Prosecution Witness Prodhan, Assistant Income Tax Commissioner, had deposed that the Income Tax Department did not have any objection against the income tax payment of the accused any time earlier and till the date of filing the case against the accused. He admit-

---

[32] Means signs and proofs of relevant event or transaction.

ted that the twin house Sultana-Sitara in the accused's home village was not included in his file as sole properties of the accused. He stated candidly that he did not know whether non-resident Bangladeshis pay income tax in Bangladesh or not and that he did not know who was the owner of the house in the Comilla Housing Estate, the Sultana Filling Station and the under-construction shops lumped as the Biponi Polash all alleged to have been owned by the accused.

This Prosecution Witness affirmed that fixed deposits were not taxable but their interest incomes were as and when these were accrued or encashed by the depositor after a year or at the end of the term following the year when such amounts were deposited on clearly defined fixed terms and conditions. He also affirmed, as pointed out by Advocate Syed Rezaur Rahman that, in accordance with law, tax on interest income accruing to fixed deposits were deducted at source on term or year-end and credited to the tax authority on behalf of the depositor.

He asserted that the "synopsized" statement of income and assets produced before the court on April 15, in addition to 3-part income tax files of the accused produced earlier, was not acceptable as evidence inasmuch as in that statement (i) income shown was for the period 1981-82 to 2006 as against assets earned in between 1962 and 2006, *i.e.*, since 1962 when the accused had started earning income and even before as in case of inherited properties; (ii) income as shown in income tax files was net of exemptions given in the 6th,7th and 8th schedules of the Income Tax Ordinance, 1984, while the amount of money retained as exemptions was or could be embodied as assets and (iii) taxes deemed to have been paid by the government on behalf of the accused as a government servant since 1972, actually did not diminish his total income except in records of the Income Tax Department, making Prodhan's statement unrealistic. Advocate Rezaur Rahman pointed out that the specter of this additional statement from Prosecution Witness Prodhan was pushed in through the cracks, shoved by the Prosecution to convict and consequently debar Dr. Alamgir from participating in the forthcoming national election.

Advocate Syed Rezaur Rahman then sifted through the depositions of the District Registrar, Chandpur, and the Sub-registrar, Kachua and made it evident that they did not say anything incriminating against Dr. Alamgir or supporting the fragments of half-truths flapped out in the sweating fabrication by an ill-motivated Prosecution. Their depositions distinguished these two as prosecution witnesses basing their depositions from permanent records of the government and separated them from sharing a conspiratorial current to abuse, abhor and discard the rule of law designed to the end of knowing the whole truth and nothing but the truth.

(3)

It was late in the evening when Advocate Syed Rezaur Rahman rested his argument for the day. The Special Judge Shahed Nuruddin left his chair with an agonized and glimmerless face. I was freed from the accused's dock, which was kept under lock and key till the court rose. Coming down from the dock, I sat with my brothers Drs. Jahangir and Arefin and sisters Kohinoor and Nilufar. Kohinoor Apa was about 80, quite weak and fragile but still ardent in her affection for me. At that time I heard from an American friend, who dropped in with a smiling face, that Sitara had reached Boston and was united with our sons. Amongst stilting constraints lumped together by the ongoing hypocrisy and the bullshit going under the cover of law, the information was a very welcome relief.

Sitara and I were married in 1968 and never ever in 39 years of our marriage was I more worried about her safety. The information blurred the edges of my memory but gave me a confidence that I along with others could change the blind and mindless course that had been charted for us, our society and the country by a horde of usurpers and traitors. I became all the more determined to choose dignity in place of the disgrace and servitude that was handcrafted by illegitimate ambitions flowing through the barrels of guns and by a morality preached far and wide on the strength of gunpowder.

Reaching the Kashimpur Jail very late in the night I sat and talked with Salman, Nasim, Lotus-Kamal, Engineer Mosharraf and Kader about what went on in the court that day. They were all happy and relieved to hear of Sitara's reaching the destination of safety. I thanked heartily and sincerely Salman for his help in organizing the journey. The events of the day and the hypocrisy and betrayal looming large on the horizon kept me burdened with anxiety and hate that could not be thrown off easily. Swept over by fatigue and on-and-off sleep, in the small hours of the morning, I dreamed like Hemingway's Santiago, the old man living on the bounty of, and facing the cruelty of, the sea. I dreamed of the sunlit shores of prosperity, of destruction before defeat and of victory beyond anger or despair, in sync with the rhythm of the breath of life. As an author Hemingway showed, in almost all his writings, how determined resolve could distinguish a person in terms of values of the intrepid and the virtuous, the rhythm of life itself.

I also recalled John Steinbeck — his *Grapes of Wrath* — showing how sacrifices in terms of hard work and determination could transform an unyielding dust bowl into a productive palette of green and gold, a cornucopia of life with quality. "Had these usurpers ever heard of Hemingway and Steinbeck?" I wondered. Ghengiz Khan, brutality and suppression, beastly behaviour and destruction must have been their trappings of life and its mission. A *tiktiki* (lizard) cackled from the ceiling perhaps to say I was not wrong in my thinking. Am I becoming superstitious? I rebuked myself and then echoing Poet Nazrul Islam resolved that I would not rest till the knives and swords of persecution of these subhumans were stopped in shame and defeat.

Early next day on July 18, the prison van and the armed escorts took me to that seeming citadel of justice presided over by the Special Judge Shahed Nuruddin. My lawyer Syed Rezaur Rahman started with an analysis of depositions of other Prosecution Witnesses. First, it was pointed out that the Manager, the Bangladesh Krishi Bank, Kachua, had admitted that the statement of my balance in the account in his bank, as furnished by the Prosecution, did not bear his signatures on all pages; he could not tell how many accounts his bank branch had and what was their total; he could not say with certainty what was the balance in his own account in his bank branch on that particular day.

These, asserted Advocate Syed Rezaur Rahman, cast serious doubt on the correctness of the Manager's statement about the accused's balance in the bank account kept in his bank, and exemplified the unreasonableness to expect a person to state in exact figure the balance in his own account in his own bank on a particular day. This made it evident that it was not reasonably expected that I as an accused confined in the jail would be able to exactly state the balance in my bank accounts in front of the jailor and the spook of the police, without access to relevant records and papers. In this context, to ascribe the guilt of concealment on someone for not being able to give the exact balance in his bank account on a particular day would be unreasonable and the principle of law did not warrant punishment of a person on nonfulfillment of an unreasonable expectation or obligation. The argument was coherent and unassailable.

But looking at the Special Judge, I did not feel that the coherence of the argument made any impact on him. In the second place, Advocate Syed Rezaur Rahman had a low-down on the deposition of the Second Officer of the Janata Bank, Kachua. From his deposition, as Syed Rezaur Rahman spelled out in clear terms, the bank statement of the accused, as prepared and submitted to the Prosecution and then to the court by the bank, as against one and the same cheque number on two different dates for Tk. 10,000 and Tk. 125,000 respectively, were paid. These mistaken entries and payments could not be reconciled with records kept with the depositor and the bank's own relevant ledgers. There were numerous examples of writing of entries in the statement unbacked by signatures or initials of concerned officers, which made this witness's statement highly unreliable. Calling for any incrimination in terms of concealment by the accused was unthinkable. Besides, the account in the Janata Bank, Kachua was a current one, yielding no interest income and thus was not an asset but a record of financial transactions only.

As I noticed, Special Judge Nuruddin did not bother to check the bank statement in question placed in front of him and remained unmoved by the clarity contained in the argument; I was unsure whether the Special Judge understood asset-yielding characterstics of a bank balance. Seeing Major Kamruzzaman sitting with brash profanity by the side of the Public Prosecutor and exchanging glances with the Special Judge in fleeting moments, I felt the rabble in my head free to run riot. A precious silent look from my brother Dr. Jahangir restrained me from taking leave of my senses. I found bodies of the few friends and relations allowed to sit in the courtroom frozen in awkward but conspicuous contortions.

Then Advocate Syed Rezaur Rahman turned his attention to the deposition made by Prosecution Witness Lokman Hakim Mallick, Superintendent Engineer, Public Works Department, Chandpur (then posted at Jessore). He pointed out that the Prosecution Witness sending reports on the accused's ancestral house in village Gulbahar and under-construction shops named as the Biponi Polash at Kachua, allegedly owned by the accused, had not inquired into the ownership of these properties, records and measures of lands on which these were located and periods of their construction and based his findings on measurement books having details of materials used; he had not even visited these properties. All these inadequacies, asserted Advocate Syed Rezaur Rahman, made his deposition and reports unreliable and unacceptable in arriving at any conclusion about the values and ownership of these properties.

In the same vein, Advocate Syed Rezaur Rahman analyzed the deposition of Prosecution Witness Abul Hasnat, Sub-divisional Engineer, Public Works Department, Chandpur. The witness had admitted, as pointed out by the Advocate, that he had submitted a report on the accused's ancestral home, the Sultana Filling Station and under-construction shops lumped as the Biponi Polash on mere assumptions. He had not verified the relevant land records and ownership of the accused's ancestral home, had not taken any quantity surveyor with him, had not verified as to how many rooms the ancestral house consisted, and had not scrutinized ownership of the Sultana Filling Station and of the Biponi Polash. He could not name any person who had claimed that the properties were actually owned by Dr. Alamgir, nor testify how much of the Biponi Polash was actually constructed.

Thus, the deposition made by Prosecution Witness Abul Hasnat was perfunctory and casual and the end-product of negligent observation and wispy verification and thus did not merit any consideration in terms of incriminating Dr. Alamgir on any point as alleged by the Prosecution. Similarly, scrutinizing depositions made by Prosecution Witness Abdur Rab, another Sub-divisional Engineer, Chandpur, Advocate Syed Rezaur Rahman pointed out that the witness had not ascertained ownership of the twin house in the accused's village home, age of the septic tank and times of construction of various stories of the house for the purpose of valuation, nor verified the foundation of the house even. He admitted that he had not taken any quantity surveyor with him and he did not know what a quantity surveyor could say about quantity of materials used in construction. Thus, as it turned out, his deposition could not reasonably be relied upon for concluding anything about the extent of ownership and value of Dr. Alamgir's ancestral home.

After this, Advocate Syed Rezaur Rahman presented his analysis of the deposition made by Prosecution Witness Tripurari, Executive Engineer, Public Works Department, Comilla in respect of ownership and valuation of the house in the Comilla Housing Estate, alleged to have been owned and concealed by the accused. As pointed out by the Advocate, the Prosecution Witness, in this case, did neither scrutinize and report about the ownership of the house in question, nor apply the Construction Cost Indexes (Building) compiled by the government's Bureau of Statistics in its valuation in reference to the year of actual construction. Advocate Syed Rezaur Rahman, scrutinizing the depositions of Tripurari's associate, Sub-divisional Engineer Helal, pointed out that he had measured the house in reference on April 5, 2007, while his supervising officer Tripurari had stated that he had taken two weeks to prepare the report on the construction and valuation of the house. It was further pointed out by the Advocate that the report was not signed on its every page by either Tripurari or Helal, leaving ample scope for alterations and insertions by the Prosecution to throw the accused into a slick mire of make-believe guilt.

In respect of valuation of the accused's house at Banani, the Prosecution had produced four witnesses. In my first asset statement, I had mentioned that I had constructed the house at two stages, the ground and the first floors in 1981 and 1982 and the second and the third floors in 1991 and 1992 at approximate cost of Tk. 4 and Tk. 6 lacs respectively. These costs were accepted by the income tax authority in the relevant years while scrutinizing my income tax returns and payments. Against these accepted costs, the Prosecution with the made-up reports from these four witnesses put up a cost of Tk. 87 lacs for the entire house without stating whether the valuation was made in constant or current prices.

In the backdrop of this position, a scrutiny of depositions of these four prosecution witnesses drawn from the Public Works Department, revealed *inter alia* that (i) Banani area where my house was located was not Prosecution Witness Executive Engineer's area of assignment, *i.e.*, he was chosen by the Prosecution selectively to estimate the value of my house in preference to the Executive Engineer of the area who would have done this work in association with his associates in the normal course of events; (ii) the valuation of the house was made by them in accordance with their departmental schedule of rates, the applicability of which in terms of years was not definite to them; (iii) in their measurement the Construction Cost Indexes (Building) of the government, compiled by its Bureau of Statistics, were not applied; that proved their method of costing as inappropriate, arbitrary and unauthorized; (iv) their measurement of quantity and quality of construction was casual and perfunctory and without reference to the relevant blueprint or plan as approved by the Capital Development Authority (RAJUK), *i.e.*, the government's agency that authorized, approved and supervised such construction in Banani. These evidently made their valuation of my house unreliable and unacceptable as evidence.

While Advocate Syed Rezaur Rahman made these points, I noticed a mischievous smile adorning the otherwise tight lips of the

Special Judge Shahed Nuruddin and his sight more often than not directed at Major Khandaker Kamruzzaman, sitting as a profane watchdog by the side of the Public Prosecutor Mizanur Rahman. To me, he appeared to be giving an impression that being honest was a military thing in our country and morality had the color and odor of brute force that could silence the rest into an eloquent silence and submission.

Advocate Syed Rezaur Rahman then took up the scrutiny of the depositions made by Prosecution Witness Idris, who had recorded the case in Tejgoan Police Station. It was pointed out that as the recording officer of the case, Idris noted in the official book that the First Information Report in format prescribed by the High Court as was received by him was a handwritten one. But in the record of the court, the same was found to have been processed by a computer. It was thus evident that the complainant at first lodged a handwritten First Information Report and then replaced it by one processed by a computer, but unsigned by the lodger. This had made the First Information Report as was put by the Prosecution in the record of the court dubious and, therefore, not actionable under law. He mentioned that the aforesaid First Information Report was lodged about ten months after the alleged occurrence of offense took place and no reason was given for such a delay. Obviously delay in lodging the First Information Report affected its authenticity and legal actionability.

Then Advocate Syed Rezaur Rahman dwelt on the anomalies in the deposition of Prosecution Witeness Surat Ara Amin, Deputy Director, ACC. It was pointed out that in her testimony Surat Ara Amin had admitted that (i) the notice served on the accused to furnish statement of his assets asked for description of assets, not their values; (ii) no procedure or format was given along with the notice to fill in the asset statement in accordance with Section 26 of the ACC Act; (iii) he was not given any opportunity to be heard on the allegations, First Information Report lodged and the charge-sheet framed against him; (iv) the complaint against him was not scrutinized by a committee of the ACC comprising amongst others, a non-official neutral person, in accordance with the Rules of the ACC; and (v) permission of appropriate authority was not obtained for serving notice on him.

The Advocate asserted that (i) giving Dr. Alamgir 72 hours, which under the circumstances of being in secluded detention amounted to not more than an hour, to write and turn in the statement of assets in the jail instead of the usual minimum of seven workdays, was undoubtedly illogical, grimly discriminatory and starkly contrary to the principle of law; (ii) not allowing him to consult his lawyers and have access to his records before writing in the asset statement was unfair and violative of the principle of natural justice; (iii) ignoring his second or supplementary asset statement was tantamount to perverse persecution instead of a dispassionate investigation and prosecution in public interest and (iv) writing the notice by the Secretary, ACC to furnish an asset statement on January 18, 2007, *i.e.*, about a fortnight before Dr. Alamgir's arrest indicated premeditated, prejudiced and perversely biased action targetted against him, not tenable in law.

These were points warranting serious consideration in any process of dispensing justice under the Anglo-Saxon framework and tradition of law. But as I could see, the owlish silence of the Special Judge Shahed Nuruddin and his occasional exchanges of meaningful glances with the Leader of the Task Force, wearing civvies and sitting by the Public Prosecutor, provided eloquent testimony on the poverty of values needed for integrity in action and dispensation of justice. To me, it appeared beyond all reasonable doubt that the Special Judge was blindly proceeding toward the site of a construct containing nothing but falsehood, covered conveniently by the traditional black robe. This was yet another dark obstacle on our way to capture the dream of a democratic homeland dreamt of by the founding fathers.

Ms. Sharmin Ferdousi, Assistant Director, ACC, was the next Prosecution Witness to come under scrutiny. As analyzed by Advocate Syed Rezaur Rahman, her deposition revealed that (i) she took the charge of investigation from Assistant Director Jiban Krishna on April 3, 2007 as Jiban Krishna's appointment as an investigation officer was not gazetted in accordance with the relevant law and rule of the ACC; (ii) as Jiban Krishna's appointment was not lawful, the first charge-sheet submitted by him to the court of the senior judge taking cognizance of the case was unlawful; (iii) Delwar Hossain, Secretary, the ACC, who signed the notice on Dr. Alamgir to furnish the asset statement premeditatively, prejudicially and perversely before his actual arrest, was not made a prosecution witness, nor was the Leader of the Task Force Major Kamruzzaman who had led the investigation against him; (iv) no statement of the accused was recorded in accordance with Section 161 of the Criminal Procedure Code; (v) the second or supplementary charge-sheet was submitted without considering the second or supplementary asset statement furnished by the accused; (vi) the Assistant Income Tax Commissioner did not state that there had been any discrepancy in income tax records of Dr. Alamgir at any time; (vii) the income tax department had, in accordance with law, completed valuation of Dr. Alamgir's house at Banani as it was constructed in two stages, in 1981-82 and 1991-92, and accepted the costs of construction and sources of funding as accounted by him and (viii) as an investigation officer, Sharmin Ferdousi never visited Chandpur, Gulbahar and Comilla. Sifting through her depositions, I determined that these facts made her accusation against me not only phony but also an exercise in deliberate and perverse truncation of truth, unexpected and unbecoming of a public servant bestowed with the duty to protect public interest and to obey the Constitution and the law of the land.

Then Advocate Syed Rezaur Rahman took the depositions of Prosecution Witnesses Masudur Rahman, Manager, the Sultana Filling Station and Kamal Hossain, Manager of the Gulbahar Himagar Limited. Masudur Rahman, pointed out Advocate Syed Rezaur Rahman, testified clearly that the Sultana Filling Station was owned by Dr. Jalal Alamgir; elder son of Dr. Muhiuddin Khan Alamgir. Dr. Jalal Alamgir lived and worked in the U.S. All papers and documents in respect of operation of the Filling Station from the Meghna Petroleum Ltd., the Bangladesh Petroleum Corporation, the Department of Explosives, the Roads and Highways Department, the Deputy Commissioner, Chandpur and the Kachua Pourashava wherein it was located, were in the name of Dr. Jalal Alamgir. The land on which the Filling Station was located was gifted by Dr. Alamgir to his son Dr. Jalal following the Muslim procedure of *heba*. So, Dr. Alamgir could not be regarded as the owner of the Filling Station at or after the time the asset statement was given.

Prosecution Witness Kamal Hossain testified that the Gulbahar Himagar operating a cold storage facility was a private limited company in which Dr. Alamgir was a minority shareholder. He stated that the Biponi Polash was a set of under-construction shops owned and funded by the Gulbahar Himagar Limited. His testimony along with the land records and the income tax returns of the company proved beyond reasonable doubt that these were not properties owned by Dr. Alamgir as a person and he did not conceal them in his statement of assets either. Despite these proofs, as I could notice, the Special Judge's look at me remained alien, apart and at times grim and menacing.

After this, Advocate Syed Rezaur Rahman focused on the deposition of Syed Iqbal, the last investigator. He pointed out that Syed Iqbal deviated from the principle of dispassionate investigation by stating in his charge-sheet that he had been instructed by the Special Judge to file the supplementary charge-sheet, not to investigate the truth. Syed Iqbal admitted that he did not visit the accused's ancestral home, his properties in Kachua, verify the ownership of the house in the Comilla Housing Estate alleged to have been owned by him, or scrutinize whether three motorcycles alleged to be Dr. Alamgir's were actually registered in his name. Without verification and scrutiny of these, Syed Iqbal added up current values of properties not owned by Dr. Alamgir and imputed falsely their ownership, and by implication concealment of them in his incrimination. As a matter of fact, Syed Iqbal furnished false information to the lawful authority of the ACC, for which he was liable for punishment as a public servant.

Syed Iqbal did not examine the first asset statement of the accused carefully and could not identify a single source of income beyond his known means or legitimacy. He totally ignored the second asset statement of assets, making his report and consequent charge-sheet incomplete and a truncation of truth. He was a student of philosophy and innocent of any association with good accounting practice. Annualization of income, difference between current and constant price, cost of construction index compiled by the government and its implications in calculating cost of buildings were unknown to him; he could not differentiate between income taxes due in an assessment year and income tax not yet accrued and due. He was not aware of rebates, etc. given under the 6th and the 7th schedules of the income tax laws. He did not know that pension amount was not taxable. His entire testimony was not only superfluous, but also irrelevant and incorrect. Even his arithmetic was wrong insofar as he did not deduct the value of assets shown in the asset statement from the assets impugned to have been found by him. His only ability was to follow the diktat of the leader of the Task Force irrespective of his findings in terms of truth or falsehood.

(4)

Following summing up of the depositions of all Prosecution Witnesses, Advocate Syed Rezaur Rahman took up the legal irregularities that characterized the entire proceedings pursued by the Prosecution. He pointed out that the notice to submit the asset statement was issued by the Secretary, ACC, on a day on which the ACC was vacant following resignation of its chairman and all members; Section 16 (c) of the ACC Act defining the duties and responsibilities of the Secretary did not empower him to act as if he was the Commission. In this case, the Secretary acted beyond his competence and jurisdiction with prejudiced motives, which was not tenable under law.

Advocate Syed Rezaur Rahman stated that in accordance with Section 26 of the ACC Act, only the ACC could issue such notice on the basis of a complaint received and upon its satisfaction preceded by an investigation. The notice issued by the Secretary when the Commission was not installed in office was evidently not issued by the Commission for such an investigation and for its satisfaction. This notice issued by the Secretary was thus without any lawful authority and as such totally void *ab initio* or right from the start. This made all subsequent actions following the illegal notice illegal and bearing no legal effect or implication except transgression of legal authority and limits, violating a citizen's lawful rights.

In a seeming effort to cover up the illegality of the notice, the government by an Ordinance inserted sub-section (2) in section 18 of the ACC Act purporting to give retroactive approval of all actions by the officers of the Commission prior to the assuming office by its Chairman and Members. Such retroactive approval was applicable only to actions that could be delegated by the Commission to its officers. Satisfaction of the Commission was a subjective matter on the basis of which a notice to submit asset statement could be issued in accordance with law. This could not be delegated. This made the retroactive effect of the notice on behalf of the Commission null and void.

Advocate Syed Rezaur Rahman stated that the notice issued by the Secretary on the accused was incomplete and insufficient, as it required the accused to give description of his assets that were held in his and other's names; it did not require description of assets of others held by him. Therefore, if the accused had not given description of assets of others, say of his adult and non-resident sons (separate income taxpayers themselves) or of a family foundation held by him in his first asset statement, he could not be faulted on that count. Further, the notice did not require the accused to give values of his assets nor did it provide him with the procedure, *i.e.*, the format prescribed by law (Section 26 of the ACC Act) to write in the asset statement. This notice was thus vague, incoherent, incongruous and consequently not legally tenable. The basic ingredient of offense under Section 26 of the ACC Act was non-submission of asset statement as per prescribed procedure or format. As the notice did not provide any such procedure or format, for any possible omission, the statement submitted by the accused could not be used as an element of mischief conceivable under law against him. Advocate Syed Rezaur Rahman made it clear that the notice issued on the accused did not require him to state as to what was his valid source of income, nor did it identify or quantify which of his assets was disproportionate to his legal or valid income.

It was stated by Advocate Syed Rezaur Rahman that the accused was not given a copy of the investigation report nor was he apprised of the exact allegation against him that emanated out of the report. The accused was not given an opportunity to be heard despite provision in the law to give him such an opportunity. The Prosecution, Advocate Syed Rezaur Rahman pointed out, did not take into account the second or revised asset statement submitted by the accused and did not thoroughly examine even the first asset statement.

Advocate Syed Rezaur Rahman, at this point, stated that at the time (1965-2001) the offense was allegedly committed by Dr. Alamgir he was a public servant as defined in S-21 of the Penal Code. Following the provision in the Criminal Procedure Code, for prosecuting a public servant a formal sanction of the government in the Cabinet Division was required. Such sanction was never obtained by the Prosecution. Therefore, the Prosecution in its entirety was unauthorized and *ab initio* illegal demonstrating highhandedness, arbitrariness and selectivity in application of penal laws of the country on prejudiced political grounds (*vide*, Sheikh Mujibur Rahman vs. State, 15 DLR, 549).

Advocate Syed Rezaur Rahman then pointed out that trial of two offenses defined by Sections 26 and 27 of the ACC Act together was illegal in view of Section 233 of the Criminal Procedure Code. Section 233 of the Criminal Procedure Code provided for separate trial of every distinct offense except those mentioned in Sections 234, 235, 236 and 239 of the same. The charges under Sections 26 and 27 of the ACC Act were not covered by these exceptions. As a result of such a misjoinder of charges, the charge-sheet submitted (*i.e.*, arraignment pressed against the accused) was illegal and the entire trial was vitiated with illegality.

The advocate stated that allowing further investigation of charges beyond the scope of the first charge-sheet and the First Information Report, as was done by the trial court in this case, was illegal. It made it evident that the trial court derailed itself from its lawful neutrality and acted as if it was the prosecution itself. It was a definite abuse of the process of the court. Besides, Advocate Syed Rezaur Rahman pointed out, the investigation so allowed exceeded the time limit for its completion set by the ACC's Rules (Rule 10). The ACC was bound by its own Rules and did not have any authority or power to violate the Rules that bounded its operation lawfully. It made the supplementary charge-sheet as was submitted by the Prosecution and considered by the court, illegal.

Advocate Syed Rezaur Rahman then pointed out the inapplicability of Rule 15 (d) 5 of the Emergency Powers Rules against the accused. The central ingredient of offense under this Rule was the notice or order given by a member of the law enforcement force or an investigation officer in accordance with Rule 15(c) of the Emergency Powers Rules. The Secretary, ACC, who signed and sent the notice for furnishing the asset statement to the accused was neither a member of the law enforcement force nor an investigation officer within the meaning of the Emergency Powers Rules. Further, the alleged occurrence of the offense having taken place long before these Rules came into force, the accused could not be charged under this Rule. Therefore, no legal liability or obligation was placed on the accused by this notice and no offense was liable or implicatible to him under the Emergency Powers Rules.

Pinning down Section 26 of the ACC Act, he stated that the two ingredients which could compose offense under it were (i) satisfaction of the Commission on the basis of information received and investigation conducted that the assets of the notice receiver-to-be were not in conformity with his legitimate source of income and (ii) non-submission of asset statement and its sequential assessment not in accordance with the procedure set by the Commission. Evidently these two ingredients were not present in the case drummed-up against the accused.

And finally, treading the tapestry of legal jargon, Advocate Syed Rezaur Rahman posited that Section 27 has two ingredients of offense: (i) assets acquired through dishonest ways and (ii) non-conformity of such assets with known sources of income. The accused had given: (i) details of his sources of *Sanchay Patras* and *Amanat Patras* (fixed deposits) on p. 3, item 4 of his first asset statement mentioning *inter alia* that he had opted to take all his pension benefits at one go (1998), (ii) annualized (at 8%) rental income of Tk. 87.97 lacs (8.797 million) between 1992 and 2006 in his second statement of assets submitted on April 28, 2007; (iii) estimate of savings of his regular salaried income (15% savings of monthly salary annualized at 8%) between 1963 and 2001 of Tk. 76.46 lacs (7.646 million); (iv) estimated yield of Tk. 65.63 lacs

(6.563 million) of his investable funds (total of sub-items from (Ka) through (Ha) of item 4 of the first statement of assets with annualized 8% return totaling Tk. 574 lacs (57.4 million), all in accordance with internationally accepted good accounting practices. He said that Defense Witness, Dr. Forrest Cookson, a recognized financial analyst of the Asian Development Bank and the World Bank testified about the correctness of these estimates and figures. These estimates of his savings and investment funds generated over 38 years or so, Advocate Syed Rezaur Rahman asserted, proved that all of Dr. Alamgir's assets were in full conformity with his known and legitimate sources of income. This coupled with the Prosecution's failure and inability to find out that the accused acquired any asset in a dishonest way proved, beyond all reasonable doubt, that Section 27 of the ACC Act could not be applied against him the way it was done by the Prosecution.

Then Advocate Syed Rezaur Rahman pointed out that in his statement of assets, constrained as he was by lack of time, access to relevant records and consultation with income tax advisor and lawyer and a medical condition originating in aging, as required by the notice, he described his immovable and movable assets earned over a lifetime with sources/incomes from memory and stated, amongst other facts, that (i) costs/values mentioned against each item of the statement were estimates or approximations; (ii) his wife Sitara Alamgir, a Masters in Economics from Boston University, U.S.A. (the first woman from Bangladesh to get such a degree from the USA) aged 60, his elder son, Dr. Jalal Alamgir, an Assistant Professor in the University of Massachusetts, Boston, U.S.A. and an accredited consultant of UNPF, New York, aged 36 and his younger son, Joy Alamgir, Chief Executive Officer of Consilience, Inc. a software firm in the USA, aged 28 were, insofar as their incomes originating in Bangladesh, separate income taxpayers without their being in any way economically dependent on him. In the letter covering his statement, Dr. Alamgir stated that in the event the ACC required any explanation in respect of any information given in the statement, it would be appropriate for them and conducive of their purpose to see him in the jail where he was detained or at their option, in the ACC's office. This statement was on record with the court of the Special Judge where he was tried summarily.

The Advocate blurted out that without seeing and obtaining any clarification on any item of the statement from him, the ACC froze the bank accounts of Dr. Alamgir, his wife and sons, filed an FIR under the Emergency Powers Ordinance 2007 {rule 15 of sro

15; 15(a) (b) and (c)} and the Anti Corruption Commission Act, 2004 (Sections 26 & 27) and the Prevention of Corruption Act, 1947 {section 5(2)} with Tejgaon P.S. Dhaka on March 6, 2007 alleging that Dr. Alamgir had not mentioned in his statement of assets about (i) six FDRs valued at Tk. 117 lacs (ii) sources/incomes from which these had been obtained and thus had purported to have concealed them and (iii) from the start of his service till date Dr. Alamgir had obtained dishonest income and properties.

In the FIR so filed however, it was not mentioned that in Dr. Alamgir's asset statement in reference he had stated that he had *Sanchay Patras* and *Amanat Patras, i.e.*, FDRs valued approximately or more or less at Tk. 90 lacs and mentioned their proximate sources of funding. Instead it was mentioned in the FIR by way of obfuscating the truth that these FDRs were not mentioned in the wealth statement pertaining to his income tax return for FY 2006 furnished to the Income Tax Department earlier, when it was not so required by the Income Tax law and rules. Under law he was required to submit particulars of these in his wealth statement of the income tax return in 2007. Dr. Alamgir could not therefore be accused of an omission retroactively when in fact there was no such omission. Nor was it mentioned how and when the accused had earned dishonest income in his service life.

(5)

After this Advocate Syed Rezaur Rahman rested and Advocate Ayat Ali Patwary took the floor. He stated that in accordance with Rule 12 of the Emergency Powers Rules, from filing of the complaint or the First Information Report to investigation, to the pre-trial proceedings and the trial, the provisions of the Criminal Procedure Code was to be applied and followed. This warranted the Investigation Officer to undertake and complete investigation independently and without interference from any quarter or body. This was specifically mandated by the High Court Division (in 31 DLR AD 71). During investigation, an Investigation Officer would follow the principle of neutrality and honesty and would not act arbitrarily, predilectively and with unstable mind. This was, in the same vein, mandated by higher courts of this subcontinent as a principle to be followed (in PLD 1967, Pesh 237).

In this case, despite the law and the mandates, Advocate Patwary asserted that the Investigation Officers were subordinate members of the Task Force led by a Major acting outside and beyond the authority of the Army Act. The Emergency Powers Ordinance under its Rules 15 and 16 did not empower a Major to supervise, lead or be associated in any way with the process of investigation. Obviously the investigation, as was pursued by three Investigation Officers in this case, was influenced by extra-legal coercion and motivation. The Major was not produced as a witness by the Prosecution either. Further, disregarding the connotation and intent of the orders of the Special Judge, the Investigation Officer in the supplementary charge-sheet specifically mentioned that he had been mandated and instructed both by the ACC and the Special Judge to submit the supplementary charge-sheet, proving that his investigation was nothing but a colorable and prejudiced exercise of authority violating the principles of neutrality. The mandate was for impartial, honest and dispassionate investigation as it should have been to find out the truth, definitely not to drum up charges irrespective of truth or falsehood.

Advocate Patwary in furtherance of his argument on this line stated that the ACC Act provided and enjoined the Commission to be independent in discharge of its responsibilities given under law. The recent statements and utterances of the Chief Advisor and his colleagues calling for punishing the politicians purported to be corrupt and the activities of the National Coordination Committee to Combat Crime and Corruption, specifically to hand over the best of the political persons purported to be corrupt to the Commission and to authorize their arrests and their prosecutions, thwarted, colored and provided for unfair investigation and improper and legally untenable authorization for prosecution by a member of the Commission only, instead of the entire Commission as required by law, and partisan trial by the Special Court as was the case with Dr. Alamgir, which made the entire process vitiated with illegality. In this context, the government widened the way for a sort of frenzied trial by media instead of trial on facts, merit and law, violating all precepts of a civilized society unblistered by the arm of brute force bereft of reason and logic.

At this point Advocate Ayat Ali Patwary reiterated that the alleged earning of disproportionate assets was in the period between 1963 and 2001, when the accused was a public servant as defined by Section 21 of the Penal Code. For prosecuting a public servant, a formal sanction of the government was required. This sanction was not obtained by the so-called independent ACC. This had vitiated the entire proceedings against Dr. Alamgir.

Finally, Advocate Patwary came up with a subtle legal point that bespoke a certain hard-headedness on the part of the administrators of the State of emergency in the country. Advocate Patway stated that Rule 15 (d) 5 of the Emergency Powers Rules functionally made non-submission of statement of assets or submission of baseless or false statement of assets an offense under the purview of the ACC. This virtually amended the definition of corruption as given in Section 2 of the ACC Act. Such a virtual amendment or amendment in any form of a provision of law, *i.e.*, the ACC Act in this case, could not have been made by enacting and amending a Rule (*i.e.* rule 15 d 5) of another law such as the Emergency Powers Ordinance, 2007. This, Patwary pointed out, had botched the entire legal frame for action by the ACC in this case, giving it an unhealthy smell of making the law-making procedure of the regime a soaked-up construct of conceptual contradiction.

When with this Advocate Patwary rested, Advocate Syed Rezaur Rahman stood up once again and wanted to place his arguments centering on deposition of the defense witnesses as well as on the statement made by me under Section 342 of the Criminal Procedure Code. It was 6:30 in the evening and the Special Judge ruled that he would not hear any more argument that day or thereafter from the defense. Advocate Syed Rezaur Rahman protested saying that without an analysis of these depositions and the accused's statement, the trial would be unfair and incomplete. I also raised my hand and said I would like to state my defense as well. The Special Judge said, come what may, he would not give us further time. He wanted me to give my arguments in writing within three days if I so wished and fixed the date of judgement seven days thereafter. I said in a deep despair that sitting in the jail without paper, not to speak of a typewriter or a laptop, I could not give my arguments that way, Anger gave way to panic as words jumbled up in my head and I said this was but a definite way to deny me the opportunity to defend myself and a denial of fair and impartial trial for both the parties.

The Special Judge did not listen or care; he walked off from his high chair of justice. He was obviously mandated to dispense justice in accordance with the wishes of those in power. Major Kamruzzaman sitting by the side of the Public Prosecutor Mizanur Rahman looked at me and gave a glassy and sly smile. Instantly I knew what the judgement would be seven days from that day.

Before leaving, the Special Judge at the request of Advocate Syed Rezaur Rahman permitted me to sit in the courtroom with my lawyers, brothers and sisters for 30 minutes. Sitting with them, we identified three suffocating implications of the Special

Judge's conduct that afternoon. First, giving an opportunity to submit our arguments in writing on the deposition of the defense witnesses and my statement presented earlier instead of deliberating on them in the open court was nothing else but a ruse to ignore our position and to virtually deny us the opportunity for defense in full. The Special Judge would take at least six full working days to write his judgement if he had not already done that. So, even if we could submit our arguments in writing within three days from that day, he would not have time to consider those while writing his judgement or revising it if already written or giving the verdict.

His assurance was at best ephemeral, loosely rooted on the soil of a false promise and pretension. Secondly, by not giving time to argue in the open, he denied us the opportunity to rebut the construct of the Prosecution, presenting obvious falsehoods on the basis of the depositions made by the defense witnesses. In the courtroom, which would have been open in a limited way, we could have shattered the Prosecution's position publicly, that the depositions of the defense witnesses were insubstantial and unreliable, into a thousand fragments of misrepresentation and misinterpretation of both facts and law.

And finally, the Special Judge's denial stopped our programs that we had drawn up for the presence of a few representatives of foreign missions to observe the Special Judge's conduct and hear the better part of our arguments. This would have allowed outside observers to see the functioning of a kangaroo court designed as a camouflaged tool to wipe out politicians on drummed-up charges of corruption, justifying a needle-point entry of a regime like that they had in Myanmar. The denial thus made us realize all the more that we had come to inhabit a world of hard surface of deceit, hypocrisy and all-pervasive fear, geared up for acculturation of a long-term subjugation of democratic ideals. For a long ten minutes I sat speechless, having a fearsome vision of justice. Then I got up, embraced my brother Dr. Jahangir, took leave of my other brother, sisters, relations and lawyers and indicated to the armed escort of the illegitimate government that I was ready to leave for the jail.

10 In Jail: After Verdict

(1)

It was about 10:00 in the evening by the time I reached our abode in the Kashimpur Jail. The walk from the main iron-clad high gate of the jail, along the paved way lined on one side by coconut trees and guarded by the walls of the jail infirmary on the other, past the wall-less, sordidly roofed square where the Superintendent of the jail gave audience to the ordinary prisoners, and then by the four-storied building interning the lifers to the "division" building in which we the political prisoners were accommodated, seemed to take a very long and tiring time. From the verandah of the third floor where the politicians were accommodated, Salman and Lotus-Kamal kept their eyes on me as I entered the premises of the division building and climbed up.

"What happened?" they asked in unison.

"What did the sons-of-bitches do today?" Kader joined them with the query wrapped in hate.

"It happened the way the sons-of-bitches wanted it to happen," I tried to answer all.

Over bites of our evening meal for which they waited for me, I told them the day's happenings: the mockery of a trial that unfolded from the morning, the shameless conduct of the Special Judge and the menacing role of the spook sitting without guile by the side of the Public Prosecutor.

They listened in silence and without further questions. At the end, Nasim, the former Home Minister, said:

"None of us will get a fair trial by these Special Judges; we were arrested on political grounds and we will be freed on political settlement."

"That will take two years," sighed Lotus-Kamal.

"More likely one year. You see, the situation is not tenable; they cannot last this way," said Salman.

"It will be sooner. The whole country is reeling under the unbearable weight of their audacity and stupidity," I said, in support of Salman.

I retired to my cell. Hearing mosquitoes singing around, I drew the mosquito net over the bed and crept in. But sleep would not come easily. Awake, I thought of the filth, the noise, the excesses and the insults hurled by the regime on us trying to build this country for which the founders dreamed and fought. "In our efforts to build, did we all put in our best, cooperate collectively and rise above personal considerations and group interests?" I asked myself. I did not find a resounding affirmation. The dawn was breaking in a haze. It was an empty sky, slate-like in solitude that seemed to hang above us with the burden of failures and unfulfillment, leaving space for the menacing aliens and usurpers.

(2)

Late in the morning next day, I got hold of the two-volume collection of memorial articles on Bangabandhu Sheikh Mujibur Rahman edited by Nazrul Islam, now living in Vienna, Austria. In these two volumes, amongst the writings of others were three, one each of my brother Dr. Jahangir, my nephew Dr. Muntasir Mamun and myself were included. There were messages and writings from Nobel Laureate Amartya Sen, West Bengal's fabled Chief Minister Joyti Basu and India's senior Congress Leader Pranab Mukherji. Contributions of a very good number of authors of Bangladesh who had written about Bangabandhu were included in these volumes. A piece each by Sheikh Hasina and Sheikh Rehana of their personal memories, as the daughters of the father of the Bangali nation, were also there. Their memories resounded with the affection of their father for his daughters and the simple life that he lived. All the pieces reflected quiet reverence for the great man that he was. His greatness did not shift shape over time.

Despite living abroad, Nazrul did a wonderful job by collecting these writings on Bangabandhu and publishing them. It reflected his allegiance to the ideals of freedom and human values pursued and left behind by Bangabandhu. I started reading right from the beginning. Reading these kept me out of the gloom left by the conduct of the Special Judge and gave me refined amiability, reticent inspiration and somewhat evanescent confidence.

While reading these memoirs about Bangabandhu one of these days, I sat with Nasim, Salman and Lotus-Kamal in the verandah late in the afternoon. The sun on its way down was spreading its golden rays through cracks of white clouds floating idly in the blue span of the sky. The scene reminded me of our earth and the country, bountiful and beautiful despite plundering of resources and human values by a hypocritical power in the darkness of our loosened vigilance.

"Will you tell me what distinguished Bangabandhu from his colleagues and contemporary politicians?" I asked them.

"Bangabandhu was the poet among the politicians; he was the poet of politics," said Lotus-Kamal. He described how *Newsweek* distinguished Bangabandhu in 1972.

"Bangabandhu loved his people, us, more than anyone else. No one loved the Bangalis the way he did," Nasim, son of Bangabandhu's dear colleague Captain Mansur Ali who was killed after him, stated gravely.

Salman tried to say something, but then kept mum. He was a very close friend of Kamal, Bangabandhu's son, who was killed immediately before Bangabandhu on that fateful night of August 15, 1975. Sorrow and grief were evident in his face, reflecting very many years behind him.

"I don't agree with what you say," I said aloud. "To me, there were two prime qualities which made Bangabandhu different from and distinguished among his contemporary politicians and colleagues; first, unwavering determination and second, indomitable courage. None of his colleagues and contemporaries had these."

Then I cited some events of his life that I witnessed and found on record. I told them Bangabandhu never wavered from his determination to win freedom for Bangladesh. Right from his protest against Jinnah's proclamation about Urdu as the only State language of Pakistan in 1948, till his death in 1975, this determination was reflected in his speeches and utterances, movements and maneuverings. I cited his insistence in 1972 on withdrawal of the Indian army from Bangladesh, despite Indira Gandhi's warning that such withdrawal would endanger his life. I recalled his courage in launching and spearheading movements, in negotiations with Ayub, Yahya and Bhutto and while facing death in Layalpur (Faisalabad) prison right by the side of the grave ostensibly dug for him by Yahya's goons in 1971.

These were not unheard of events. Everyone around knew about these. But these interpretations that I made, in terms of determination and courage, gave everyone around two stark, simple, and at the same time dazzling truths of his life. No one said anything. They agreed in respectful silence and silhouetted embodiment of their own memories. These meanings of Bangabandhu's life as we realized that afternoon wafted in a renewed sense of direction, strengthened our resolve to tide over imprisonment, immorally and illegally imposed on us, and to defeat the persecution that was schemed up to make us suffer and bow down to hail some brat as the captain of the ship.

With my wife Sitara I had visited Vienna in the summer of 2002. Nazrul, Rubel, Murad and about a hundred more Bangalis living in Vienna at that time met us, took us to various places of interest and a wine village, where free and famously independent men and women gather in the evenings to enjoy the bounties of earth and the gift of freedom. Then they took us on a drive to Mauthausen, the second Auschwitz of the Second World War. Preserved across Linz city on the Danube, Mauthausen with its relics of suppression and oppression and cold-blooded killing of the Jews by the Nazis before and during the Second World War, tied us into a knot of realization of the deathly turn to which undemocratic elements could take civilization. That was a proof of unbridled power of a few to break across achievements of a country in fields of science and technology, to be sullied into a despicable destruction in less than a decade.

Bitter in my solitude, I thought about Nazrul and others, their hopes and aspirations that I had come to know. This made me shudder perceiving the possibility of human disaster originating in Nazi-like governance looming large in our country. This was the gash that was created in our hearts by happenings and events, manufactured by raw power in our country since January 11, 2007. Under a cover of conquering corruption by physical force alone, the applicators wanted to conquer their own motherland. Brooding over these matters in the confines and constrictions of the jail, I realized the same were the elements of the thought, sentiments, desperation and also hope of Nazrul and others in Vienna. Amidst destruction of the societal frame and the demolition of values we dreamed about together, memories and ideals of Bangabandhu lingered in our minds here and abroad not to lose hope and to take leave of our dreams.

Seven days to judgement went by almost in a daze of solitude and thought, smudged with the ragged air of degradation of values broken through with hopes based on memories and ideals of the father of the nation. The hope was not audacious; it was a daring conduit for survival and freedom. July 26, 2007 was fixed for announcing the judgement on my trial. On July 25, my friends in the jail, some drawn from the common convicts, assembled and prayed for me: Oh God save him from injustice, do not let him suffer more at the hands of the persecutors of the present. On July 26, 2007 the hope and the well-wishes of my friends empowered me to reach the court of the Special Judge in a relatively unagitated frame of mind, without fear or dread.

From 10;00 in the morning to 2:30 in the afternoon, I was made to wait in the prison cell adjacent to the courtroom. Around 12 noon I began to writhe in anxiety. A little after 2:30, I was taken to the courtroom and made to stand in the dock, surrounded by a team of not-so-friendly policemen. They wanted me to take off my shoes. Earlier in one of the kangaroo courts, the victim of a trial in dazed anger had thrown his shoes at the Judge. I refused to take off my shoes. Surprisingly Major Kamruzzaman was not present. Instinct told me the Major had already known what would be the verdict.

Around 3:00, the black-robed Special Judge, with an aura of intimidation entered the courtroom and perched himself on the high chair of justice. He took three minutes to read out the operative part of his judgement. He announced that the Prosecution had proved all charges against me beyond reasonable doubt and he convicted and sentenced me to suffer simple imprisonment for three years under Section 26(2) of the ACC Act and rigorous imprisonment for ten years under Section 27(1) of the same Act and to pay a fine of Tk. 10 lacs, in default to suffer imprisonment for another year and forfeit all properties of myself and my dependents, which was disproportionate to my legal/valid sources of income.

He also announced that the imprisonment would be in consecutive terms, meaning the total imprisonment would be at least thirteen years. Announcing the verdict and the sentence, he left hurriedly, like a person without any grip on his own authority. He did not read out or give us the entire judgement. Asked about this he said it would be made available in due time. It billowed wide and high the apparent truth that he had not as yet written the entire judgement. In accordance with the diktat received and obeyed, he would go about the business of finding out and put in writing a paralegal cover to justify his announcement of the verdict and the sentence.

I looked hard at him for a while, tried to grasp the graphic difference between truth and falsehood hewed out by a person bereft of values and courage. Then I stepped down, embraced my brothers Drs. Jahangir and Arefin, held the hands of my sisters Kohinoor and Nilufar, thanked my lawyers for their attempt to obliterate injustice and walked back to the prison cell adjacent to the courtroom. My relations were in tears, as were my friends. The journalists covering the trial ranted openly against small minds and swathing egos and about allegiance that could be bought or traded in course of trial in these courts sponsored by the military. I was silent, speechless, choking tightness in my throat. Fortunately an urge to shout alluded me, for I wanted to stay focused on what I would do now at the age of 67 to get myself adjudged innocent to the future generation after I leave this world.

The police on a tip from the cohorts of the military were apprehensive that on my way to the jail, my supporters, the Awami League workers might block the road and snatch me from their clutches. So they arranged three more contingents of forces to accompany me on the rutted road and arranged for guarding the crossing points by other security forces. When all arrangements were made, it was about 8:00 in the evening. We started, the guards hooting on sirens, flexing their muscles in front as well as in the rear and reached the Kashimpur Jail after 10:30 in the night. I found all other inmates, Salman, Lotus-Kamal, Kader, Kamal, Mosharraf waiting on the third floor of that division building, resembling flickering lamps in a desolate landscape in the dark. They embraced me in anguish and tears, not yet fully immune from the absurdities that had taken hold of our society.

(3)

Till late hours of the night, I was locked in my own thoughts. Thirteen years of jail was a damned disgrace for me. I did not expect to live thirteen more years and get out of the jail in one piece at 81 when the current average life expectancy in this country was no more than 62. Since I was a student, there was always much to do for me. I studied hard, tried to excel in debates, actively participated in games, remained always eager to help my parents and relations, tried to lead a happy and productive life with my wife, busied myself with the progress of my children in school and colleges, actively participated in development and welfare activities of the local area, took my wife out for variety whenever and wherever I could. I always dreamed of a world as I wished it to be without looking away from things as they were. With sweat trickling over my skin, I asked myself now within the four high walls of the jail, darkened at times with meaningless rumors of exasperation and fear drifting from outside, what I would do? I would be a helpless bystander when the evil, falsehood and almost unbridled personal ambition of a few usurpers of power would go on parading their victory with heavy boots.

In the pre-dawn hours, I felt a gentle and cool swirl of wind. Feeling a patter of rain that followed, I fell into a dream that kept me awakened in conscience if not in body quite often in the last 37 years. It was about what happened in Dhaka on the night of March 25, 1971. My elder son Shuvo was a little over two months old, hardly capable of recognizing anybody other than his parents. It was around 11:30 in the night when the Pakistan Occupation Army started entering Dhaka city from the cantonment with full fire-power in their hands. Just back from Karachi on transfer, we lived with Sitara's parents near Rath Khola intersection of the Nawabpur Road. When the Pakistanis, firing rifles and stenguns from the trucks from the Nawabpur Road billowed up smoke around our old and dilapidated shelter, I along with Sitara and our first-born infant Shuvo, found a narrow alley to the north not wide enough for a truck to enter, and ran out into it in the dark. After running for about 300 yards, we found a door to a house open, entered with about ten more families.

In the morning, we located ourselves in a government apartment in Eskaton where Mohammad Ali, a senior colleague of mine lived. I went out and reconnoitered the area to observe the savage killings and damage wrought upon the Bangalis, and then relocated ourselves in my sister Nilufar's house in a narrow alley in the middle of the old city. Then for nine months, in a ceaseless war of liberation spearheaded by sweat, blood and tears, with the belief that there was nowhere else to go but forward, we saw actions, deaths and survival in Noakhali, Feni, Chittagong, Mymensingh and finally victory in Dhaka on December 16. Our son grew up and became a toddler during the war amidst sacrifices of our people on the blood-soaked soil of the country, crouching through the low bushes of the plain to avoid death, but always in the hope and enthusiasm for a ceaseless motion towards dawn, light and freedom.

As a family, the experience through the fire of this fight for freedom hardened our resolve to contribute our might to build up this country, make everybody share and enjoy the fruit of independence. Now 37 years after the victory, some people who never experienced this glorious history, nor felt the urge to be free, and on the contrary at times connived with the foe or remained shamelessly indifferent to the cause, have come to label us with raucous glee as corrupt and betrayer to the very cause for which we fought. I got up from my bed and, with hands clasped behind my back, walked out to the verandah being hit with hard sheets of rain. I said to myself, I would not give up. I would not be defeated; the unbridled persecution and intimidation in its damned crime would not be able to make the cause of justice cry and wither us up as incapable, untrying and silent bystanders. We had to defeat injustice, achieve our rights and uphold our dignity.

The other inmates did not expect me to rise up from bed so early after the disaster, the ruinous catastrophe of injustice meted out to me yesterday. As the sun came up over the jail's high walls they huddled around me in glum silence. I said we had no time to dawdle, to allow pessimism and frustration to yank us off from the path of survival we had to follow. I told them we could not as yet return sacrifices made by common people for freedom and I stood up and quoted from Shamsur Rahman:

"Freedom, you are an arbor in the garden, the Koel's song, glistening leaves on the banyan trees, my notebook of poetry, for scribbling as I wish."

Everyone looked at me with pleasant surprise. I looked down on the open country to the southeast, its undulating ground and small clusters of trees, and then sitting down on those dilapidated chairs, I told them, I was yet to return the sacrifice of a family, quite unknown and definitely unsung for our freedom.

It was the beginning of November 1971. The guerrillas of the *Mukti Bahini* had entered into Dhaka by then. I was one of their points of contact and supply.

On the evening of November 9, some of them came to me. After they were fed with whatever I could arrange, without making noise they wanted some money for their movement, living and operation. I did not have any more money with me. Asking them to see me after an hour, I trudged into an alley called Abdul Hadi Lane, in about the middle of old Dhaka. Under the cover of darkness, I jumped over the boundary wall of a house I knew and knocked at a mangled door. It was opened by a woman I hardly knew, since the husband was my only acquaintance in the family. She must have heard about me and my followers from her husband. She let me in quickly and closed the door.

"What is it brother? Why are you here at this hour? Don't you realize it is dangerous to be out and here with the Pakis around?" She asked me in a whisper.

"Is your husband in?" I wanted to know.

"No, He has gone to the village to bring some rice. Will be back tomorrow."

"Then . . . then . . .," I hesitated.

"Please tell me what you want." She knew about my contacts with the guerrillas and my activities. She had seen me talking to her husband earlier in their house.

"We need some money for them," I said matter of factly.

"Here, take it," She took the golden chain off her neck and handed it over to me. There were no words coming out of me. Holding the chain in my hand I just looked at her, an innocent face radiating in warmth and love for the country. It was difficult controlling tears welling up in my eyes.

"Wait. I will be back in five minutes," she said and left me in the sitting room.

I thought she would bring tea. I felt thirsty, feeling a little shy even admitting such to myself.

In about five minutes, a girl of about 10, probably her daughter, came with a cup of tea and a toast biscuit and then stood at the inner-door, arranging her unruly girlish hair with her fingers. And after about another five minutes the woman entered with a small wooden box, sat by my side and opened the lid.

"These are our family ornaments, some that I have kept for my daughter's wedding," she said and pointed her fingers at the girl standing at the inner door, clutching the worn out knob.

"Take all these. You and your boys well need them."

"No I can't. I will not take these; your chain should be enough for now."

"Don't say no; freedom has to be won; my daughter will be wed in freedom. We all have to do something at this hour to get that freedom. It's getting late. Take these and use these. Hurry."

She insisted, touching my hands.

I took the box under my chaddar. The chain was already in my pocket. I met the boys at the appointed place and gave them the chain and the box, told them to go to one goldsmith I knew at Tantibazar hurriedly and get the money to meet their need. They did. The fight within Dhaka in that part rolled, lurched, swerved and was finally won throughout the country on December 16.

In the heat of joy, enthusiasm and work, I could not make time to see the woman till December 24. When I arrived, no one was in the house; nothing was left there except telltale signs of blood and loot. I never found them. I had not asked for their home village. I am yet to give her something in return for the sacrifice she made without tears and hesitation, for the life she and her family gave. To me, her sacrifice was the glimmer of faith and hope in freedom. Her's was one of millions of lives that embraced death placing unwavered confidence in the future. No amount of tirade based on falsehood could loosen our march to the end of making ourselves worthy of this confidence. Emotion overwhelmed me in the fresh scent that wafted from the southeast over the high walls in our direction.

Everyone around looked down in feeling and emotion. Kader tried to speak, but a dry crust in his throat did not make his voice audible. I looked out, saw smoke billowing up from the kitchen below in the south. It seemed everybody thought we could not accept our captivity, be denied justice, and tolerate humiliation in quiet stoicism. We had to overcome the depraved dream; we might writhe in agony but could not wail and cower down.

I kept mum for quite a while as everyone around did.

Then I said, "You will have pre-written judgement in your cases also. Take it from me, whatever evidences and arguments you produce in your defense, the pliant Judges will ignore. I am told these Judges got slush fund from the intelligence agencies to legally maim and murder innocence and honesty. But even then, try to get recorded as much evidence and arguments as you can. That will be helpful in the High Court when your appeal will be heard. Even if these will be ignored there, these will remain as records of your innocence and honesty to your posterity of the deliberate injustice done to you."

Everyone agreed. An itching of dread was replaced by an aura of confidence.

(4)

As the morning wound into the evening passing through a morose summer noon with sporadic pattering of humid rain, I thought about my father. Unlike me or my other brothers, he was named Asheq Ali Kahn by his parents. He was tall and broad-shouldered and fairly well-complexioned. Graduating as the first Muslim of Chandpur district in 1922, he devoted his whole life to teaching. He built up a school and college in his home village where our ancestral home was, and after his retirement nursed it to become the best institution of the local area, before he died in 1974. We were a family of four brothers and four sisters with our mother and father. In addition, a number of cousins lived with us and my father saw that they were also educated the way he was.

With so many mouths to feed, bodies to clothe, books to be bought and fees to be paid when we were students, it was not a very solvent and want-free life. At times, my mother did not have rice in her earthen vessel for feeding us the next day. Nothing else than an assured stock of rice and *dal* for an entire month gave her more contentment those days. At a time like this, whenever a student came to my father for help, he used to give him whatever he needed. When he did not have enough money, which was more often the case, he unhesitatingly borrowed from others to help out the student in need. One evening sitting over a meal of rice and dal, amongst brothers and sisters, I mustered courage to ask him,

"Dad, why do you have to help a student with money when we do not have enough even for the next day? Will it not be prudent if you wait three or four years when most of us will be able to stand on our own feet and help you a little in your charity?"

My mother, almost always given to silent service to all of us, choked. She was afraid dad would not respond or worse ask me to shut up, as the hard-charging disciplinarian that he was. After a stunning silence for a few minutes, dad opened up.

"My children, I don't help students as you see, I just try to repay the debt I owe to them," he said with tenacious seriousness.

"How can you owe people, students who are not even known to you?" we asked almost in unison.

"Then listen," said our father.

As we listened, we came to know what we had not known till then. It was 1911 when our father readied himself to sit for the Entrance (*i.e.* Matriculation or Secondary School Certificate) Examination from Baburhat High School located near Chandpur. The school had no road link to our Police station or village. One had to walk in the dry season and wade through chest-high floodwater during the wet season all the way to the school. Father used to stay at the house of a middle class farmer, in exchange for teaching his children in the morning and the evening.

When the time for payment of examination fees of about Tk. 14 in those days came, Father waded through floodwater and came to his village home to take money from our grandfather who was himself a poor farmer. He did not have any money at that time. So our grandmother took out the silver band from her neck, the only ornament that she had and gave it to our father and told him to sell it and pay the fees. Controlling an urge to cry, Father waded back to Baburhat at dead of night. The next morning he went to Baburhat Bazaar, found out a goldsmith and produced the silver band from under his chaddar. The goldsmith, a Hindu Brahmin, thought at first that the boy had stolen this from somebody and wanted to sell it for merrymaking.

"Why do you want to sell this? Whose silver band is this?" the goldsmith asked.

"It's my mother's. She gave it to me to sell it," replied our father.

"Why?"

"For I have to pay the fees for my Entrance Examination," explained Father.

Hearing this, the goldsmith took him inside where he and his wife resided, made him sit and take two pieces of *sandesh*[33] with a glass of water as was the custom and then asked his wife to give him 14 Takas.

"You don't have to sell the silver band. Keep it with you as a memento, a token of good fortune from your mother. Pay the fees, pass the examination and stand on your feet."

"Sir, you are very kind. I will take your money on one condition. It will be a debt for me from your good self and I will return it whenever I will be able to do it."

"You don't have to return this."

"Sir, I insist, I will. Please permit me to do that."

"Are you sure you would do it?" Asked the goldsmith.

"Yes sir, I will do that. Please permit me."

"My boy, I am old, so is your aunty. We don't have any child. Even then if you insist that you will return, you can do so in only one way."

"Please tell me how."

"Well, whenever any student in need will come to you for help, you will help him the way I did. That is the only way you will return the debt if you want to. Is it okay with you?"

"I will do that, Sir. Please pray for me."

"So you see," Father told me and my brothers and sisters present, "I owe a perennial debt. I have to repay as I have been repaying since I started earning. For me it is not charity, it is repayment of debt."

And so he did through the rest of his life. In pursuit of the ideal, he built up a school and college on his homestead, donated all his lands for the institution, and left us just one parcel to the north of the school in order to build our house. We built a twin house as a common property of all brothers and sisters in two stages over a period of fifteen to sixteen years.

In that backdrop, despite reporting so in my asset statement and explaining at length in my written statement presented to the court, I had this house as an element of corruption adjudged against me by Special Judge Shahed Nuruddin. The Major leading the Task Force, obviously born after the War of Liberation, had a hearty laugh. He did not have a long stretch of wakeful time to pass; he could prove on his turf that power flowing

---

[33] A confection of flour, milk, and sugar.

through the barrel of the gun was honesty and dedication to the cause of society.

I looked beyond the thickets of short trees spread out from the base of the jail building to its high walls to the southeast. With hate rising and twisting inside me, I entered my cell and hit my rock-like bed with my sandals on. Anguish was haunting me.

Much later, after my graduation I read *Freedom at Midnight* by Lapierre and Collins. There I found a similar story of repayment of debt throughout life by helping the poor and the needy. Menon, who started his life as a stenographer under the British in the 1930s and then by the dint of his merit and hard work rose to be a secretary to the government of India under Lord Mountbatten, had been given railway fare at Delhi rail station by an old Sikh to enable him to go to Simla, the summer capital of India in those days to get his first job as a stenographer. And acceding to his insistence that he would repay the fare taken, the Sikh gentleman enjoined him to pay back by helping all and everyone coming to his door for help in need. And Menon paid back his debt even when he was on his death-bed. I thought that was a generation imbued with such ideas of fraternity, fellow feeling and honesty of purpose and deed. That was some sort of self-fortification to develop everyone of the generation to be able to shoulder the responsibility of impending freedom from the Raj.

Next day I was awakened by Omar. The sun was quite far up; it was past 9:00. It must have rained throughout the whole night. I came out on the verandah, took a deep breath and felt the calmness of the cool air. Salman, Lotus-Kamal and Nasim walked from the western most corner of the long verandah and sat by my side. They must have anticipated gut-churning gloom covering me. They were relieved to see that the gloominess could not slog over me. But I saw in their faces and eyes glimpses of hell. I recalled Winston Churchill of 1943. Expressing his determination and exuding confidence in his colleagues, Churchill had said to the cheers of millions of his countrymen: “We shall not fail or falter; we shall not weaken or tire.” I did not repeat Churchill that morning. But seeing them, I, as a matter of fact, all of us living in mutual bond and friendship, got grips back on our minds. We would not be ruled by intimidation; we would neither fail nor falter in our will and determination.

I thought over the lay of the land we were in: two generals and their eleven shoeshine boys desperately and dishonestly trying to hold rein on all our people. They thought people respected power, that even its victims did. History told us it was nothing else but an outrageous act of stupidity. I said unconsciously to the shoe-shine boys led by Dr. Fakhruddin: "The generals will fail; on the way they will spit you out when they are done with you." I did not know whether anybody heard me.

(5)

Evening over, I pushed myself into my room, sliced a wedge from the wretched bin of injustice already thrown out at me. I thought about my soft-spoken mother, recalled the sacrifice she made to rear us up, pushing us gently but firmly and without any deviation into the world of possibility and hope she dreamed about for her children.

I recalled, before sitting for the Matriculation Examination in 1956, I went home in our village to study with intensity not thought possible by my eldest brother Misbahuddin Khan at Dhaka, with whom and whose wife I lived as a student in the city. My father was away from home on some business, which I did not remember. The other brothers and sisters, all studying, at that time were not in the village home either. Mother took care of me, giving me good meals on time and making sure I was not disturbed in my studies in any way.

One noon, while coming inside from the outer house, I saw my mother walking up from the pond. She went to the pond for a bath and a cleanup of some utensils. When she came up on the bank of the pond, I noticed the *sari* that she wore was wet. I asked her where the dry *sari* was that she should put on after the bath. She told me with all the affection in the world, "Oh, it is alright. It is hot today and the *sari* will dry up soon." Then I realized, she did not have another *sari* to put on. The demands for making all her children study to go up the ladder of success in this world were so much that she had to put on a single *sari* and go about in it even when it was wet after bath. This was the portrait of a mother bent upon making her children climb the ladder of life. That was the portrait of honest effort and honor of motherhood.

Then, following that, I remembered my mother's one dinner taken in solitude observed by me. It was 1959. I was then a student of Dhaka University. On a vacation, along with other brothers, sisters and cousins we were in our village home. Our parents even in those days used to take care of the education of our cousins. After eating a happy evening meal of rice, chicken and fish, served by my mother, everyone else went out of the kitchen for walks in the warm moonlit night around the house, with dream-like aura created by the leaf-laden trees and shrubberies. I waited on my mother, thinking about how she could manage all the chores. She was hesitant taking her meal out of the pots around her.

"Will you not go out?" she asked me.

"No, I will sit for a while. I am not feeling well. I think I overate. Food was so delicious," I said and then pretended to be absorbed in drawing something on the hardened mud floor. As soon as she took a portion of rice out of the cooking pot on her tinplate, I asked her to start with the chicken.

"It was so delicious, I said. "You may not like to eat the fish."

She sat silent and motionless.

I got up and said, "What is delaying you? Please eat, Mom," and then I removed the bin from the pot supposed to hold some chicken or fish for her dinner in solitude. The fish pot was empty; there was a little gravy in the chicken pot, without even a piece of meat.

"So you gave us everything. Did not keep even a small piece for you," I said angrily.

She smiled with all the affection in the world, and said, "It's alright. I am not hungry. And don't tell the others."

That was my mother. That was her sacrifice for rearing us up. She died in 1961, a month before my final graduation examination. Reaching home with my brother Jahangir and sister Nilufar, we saw her lying silently and in peace in her grave under the shade of a coconut tree she had planted herself. Tethered to the tree, the age-old, deep gray milching cow that she lovingly took care of for years was shedding tears for her. I had never seen a cow grieving for her mistress that deeply.

Compared to Father, Mother was not very well known in the local area. Father was outspoken, vibrant, always pulsating with the gift of life. He set up the school and college, the mosque, the post office, the library and a host of institutions in our village and outside. Mother was the person behind to make us grow, get proper education and to ensure that wordly needs and wants did not stand in our way to get established in life. She was soft-spoken, bordering on almost being silent despite her steadfastness to principles of honesty and hard work and sense of honor and dignity. Since no institution was set up till the 1980s in her name, it was my sister Nilufar's idea that we should do something to carry forward her principles and memory. Till then, since the late 1960s, I used to distribute *saris* to poor and destitute women, out of our own savings and contributions from other family members — always remembering that for our sake Mother smilingly suffered the hardship of putting on a wet *sari* even, every year in the last week of Ramzan.

Initially, it was 200 or so *saris* that would suffice to give one to each of the poor women who used to come on an appointed day in the month of Ramzan. By the late 1980s, I could collect over 2,000 *saris* so that no one coming for a *sari* to the house left to us by our mother would go empty-handed. That was one way I could, I thought, honor the hardship that we as children caused her while growing up and settling on our own feet, and show respect to a woman who never deviated from her principles of honesty and hard work and sense of dignity and fellow feeling.

In the late 1980s, I do not remember the exact date, sister Nilufar proposed that we should jointly set up a trust, the Sultana Foundation named after Mother and institutionally arrange to help the poor, especially the students in need then and in years to come. An agreement was drawn up and signed on August 10, 1988 to set up the Sultana Foundation with an authorized capital of Tk. 100 lacs and to register it under the Trust Act after the subscribed capital amounted to Tk. 50 lacs at the minimum. To start with, Tk. 27 lacs was contributed by all her children and grandchildren.

It was decided that the paid-up capital of the Foundation would be kept in my custody to invest in securities, shares or business to provide educational support and economic assistance every year in a limited way in accordance with the objectives of the Foundation, till the paid-up capital was raised up to its authorized level. The Sultana Foundation thus was an organized step by us children to provide clothes to destitute women and needy students since 1988. Despite pursuing its objectives to provide this assistance every year since 1988, the capital fund of the Foundation in my custody stood at Tk. 31 lacs in 2006.

All these, along with the agreement on the establishment of the Foundation duly notarized by an authorized public notary, were produced before the Special Court, in sequel to an explanation to the Task Force. But they were so enraptured by the diktat from above to prove my guilt that they proved themselves incapable of seeing the truth. In place of appreciation for coming up with aid for the destitute women and students in need, and for spreading and preaching the principles of honesty and hard work and sense of dignity and honor to be emulated, they came to parade their arrogance and parochial interests with heavy boots of the diktat they had received. For them, power became not only knowledge, but also honesty. For them, those who pursued knowledge as power and honesty as a cherished value of life needed to be proved corrupt in a raucous, enthusiastic and unfettered display of arrogance. Facing such dismal absence of values, I felt I did a good thing in outlining how we tried to keep Mother's memory alive. I did not mention that my wife Sitara, in addition, had set up and operated an orphanage named Sultana Shishu Niloy (Sultana Children's Home) out of her savings and earnings in our village home. She had not seen her mother-in-law. We were married seven years after mother died. She heard about her conduct and contribution from other women of the village when they sat by her side gossiping and conversing when she was at home.

(6)

A week passed by. Dusty swirling air, with sporadic spattering of rain, kept me mostly confined to my cell in the jail. My brother Dr. Jahangir visited me once a week at the jail gate. I was awaiting the full judgment written and delivered by Special Judge Shahed Nuruddin. It was not received, despite payment of the required fees and filing of application. We were told the Special Judge could not complete writing the judgment in full in those many days, even after the pronouncement of the punishment for me. This was the judge who did not allow me to produce my important witness through adjournment of the trial for a day and now taking weeks to deliver the judgment after announcing the verdict. I realized, he was trying hard to give a legal cover to the unjust act done and pronouncement made. I clenched my fists, wanted to scream at anything, hit everything to control the anger that rose and burned inside me. The other inmates, through exasperated words and gestures tried to put up a distance between what burned inside me and what went by the name of sanity. It was a stubborn fight not to lose a dream that seemed to be disappearing in a wisp of gray smoke of frustration and grim dismay. And I found in despair a certain strength and resolve not to lose and slither back into holes of defeat.

Then on one night, I recalled how Sitara and I built our house brick by brick and hand by hand in Banani model town Dhaka. It was 1977 and I was Deputy Commissioner, head of the civil administration of Jessore, an administrative district in the southwestern corner of the country. The country was under military rule led by General Ziaur Rahman. By showing an example as to how, by organizing local people, infrastructural facilities like irrigation and drainage canals and roads could be built, I had, without my being conscious of it, earned some sort of recognition. At that time RAJUK, *i.e.*, the Capital Development Authority of Dhaka, invited applications for allotment of some residential plots in Banani. We did not have a plot or a house at Dhaka.

Anticipating that we would need one to live in after retirement from the civil service, I applied with an initial deposit of Tk. 40,000/= or so. As I was fairly well known as a Deputy Commissioner, RAJUK allotted me a plot in Banani measuring more or less 10 *kathas*.[34] It was usual for a civil servant to get allotment of a residential plot of such a size. We had deposited Tk. 40,000/= out of tobacco and rice that we had grown on 40 *bighas* of land around the bungalow of the Deputy Commissioner and recorded as part of the garden-residence inherited from the days of the Raj. The full price of a 10 katha plot at Banani was fixed at Tk. 200,000/=. I sat with Sitara and found out we could not pay an additional Tk. 160,000/= out of savings from salary income. By selling the car that I had earlier bought after completing higher studies in the U.S., we could arrange to pay Tk. 60,000/= and no more. So I wrote to RAJUK to give me a plot of 5 kathas in place of 10, which RAJUK promptly agreed. We made the payment and became the owners of by far the smallest plot ever owned in the model town by a civil servant of that status and age.

Then after transfer to Dhaka, I borrowed about Tk. 3 lacs from the House Building Finance Corporation and started building the first two stories of our house of a planned four-storied one. At that time we were allotted a government house on road 12, about three-quarters of a mile from the plot that we had come to own on road 25. We found a labor contractor to build the house with construction materials to be personally bought or procured by me. To keep us within the budget, I personally went to the godown[35] of TCB (Trading Corporation of Bangladesh) to buy cement, to the brickfield on the bank of the Buriganga River to procure bricks and to Chittagong to buy timber. To avoid pilferage of cement and to ensure proper mixing of mortar, every morning at about 6:00, with a flask full of tea, I walked down to the construction site and with an umbrella over my head perched myself on a load of bricks on a corner of the plot and watched the house going up brick by brick. Around 9:00, my wife with our firstborn son Shuvo came

---

[34] A variable unit of land measurement; in a city like Dhaka, approximately 0.025 acre.

[35] A warehouse or other storage place.

with breakfast in a basket; I ate that with them, and then took leave of them to go to my office. I returned around 2:30 in the afternoon to relieve her. She went back to the house and brought lunch in a hot pot and then together we ate and watched the construction work and prevented possible pilferage of materials till the work stopped at sundown. Despite all these efforts, at the end when the roof was slated to be put on, we fell short of money. Sitara took out her wedding necklace and gave it to me to sell it and finish the work. Full of shame, I did that. We had a house and the happiest time of our life as a couple.

"Are you happy?" I asked my wife.

"Yes, my dear, I am the happiest," she said clasping her hands around our two sons.

That was how we built our house. The cost of construction and sources of funds were all scrutinized and accepted by the Income Tax Department in that year. Living in the house allotted by the government, we rented out our house to a governmental body at a monthly rent of Tk. 40,000/, repaid the loan of the House Building Finance Corporation ahead of time and then with the balance of Tk. 6 lacs or so, took up construction of the 3rd and 4th stories and completed them in 1991-1992. Costs and fundings were reported and accounted for to the Income Tax Department in accordance with law. Then we moved to the 3rd and 4th floors and lived there since then keeping the first two stories for renting out.

That was how we constructed our abode; that was how we lived. And now, in 2007 an arrogant Major of the Task Force said that the house was built in a corrupt way and an inept and incompetent Special Judge, in an unstoppable course of dispensing selective justice, readily concurred. "How could a judge hammer this insult into an outrage caused by a disgraceful bully?" I asked myself and passed the night without sleep and swathed in mute blackness. "These brutes and henchmen want to rule the country by intimidation," I said aloud to myself gritting my teeth.

(7)

Three weeks passed by but still the Special Judge could not give his judgment in full. The draconian law prescribed that I had to file an appeal, if I so wanted, within thirty days of pronouncing the verdict or the judgment, deducting the time taken for giving the certified true copy of the same. And the draconian law did not provide an avenue for me to be posted on bail even if the Special Judge took an eternity to hand over the judgment in full.

Some people, friends and party workers from my electoral constituency, came to Kashimpur to see me on these days. It was a lot of trouble for them, first to travel to Dhaka, obtain permission from the iron-clad authority of the prison inspectorate and then travel to Kashimpur and take further consent of the Superintendent of jail to see me for 30 minutes under the vigil of a deputy jailor and a spook of the Police. I was pleasantly surprised to see Hatem, Khaleq, Shaheed B.Sc. Shikdar, Pran Krishna Swapan and others. All of them were in tears. With difficulty I controlled mine. I told them I was well. Through a hole in the sealed-up window of a room in the jailor's office, I showed them the cell on the third floor of the building where I lived. I wanted them to believe that I lived in reasonable comfort. I asked them to give my regards to all my party leaders and workers. Some of them brought fruit — oranges and bananas, which the jail guards allowed in after eating more than half of them themselves. They were hungry like locusts for anything they could grab or lay their hands on.

I got, in a clandestine way, two notes from my American friend, Forrest Cookson. He said, the economy was at a standstill, inflation galloping, investment going down and the advisors at the helm of affairs lying about the actual state of affairs. He felt genuinely for this poor country. I recalled how when I was free we made time at least once in a month to have breakfast in Dhaka's American Club and exchanged notes on the economic situation and political turn of events. He sent me a few books through my brother Dr. Jahangir. The Superintendent of the jail kept the books with him for a week. Since he or those working under him were not very conversant with English, he ultimately gave me the books thinking probably that what they could not read could not influence them, or the government they served or me in their custody. Ignorance was indeed bliss. Forrest by his kindness and affection touched my heart; made me determined not to yield a yard of ground to the adversary in filth. It was indeed a formidable fortress against meanness and persecution in a man's difficult and somewhat frightened existence.

As the weeks wound on, I thought about the moronic incapability of the Prosecution and the Special Judge to understand the estimates and calculations of my assets that I produced in course of the trial. Three annexures contained these calculations and estimates. In one annexure, I gave them an estimate of my savings from regular salaried income. I stated that I received Tk. 500 per month as salary in 1963 when I entered the job and then in

2000 when I ended earning such income the monthly salary was Tk. 22,000, yielding an average of Tk. 11,250 per month. I estimated that I saved 15% of this average monthly salary. This was a very conservative estimate inasmuch as the nationwide household survey of income and savings made in 2004 revealed that on average a household in our country saved 25% of its income. On such a very conservative assumption, estimate of my average annual savings figured at Tk. 20,250 per year. Between 1963 and 2001, I worked for 38 years. On the reasonable assumption that my annual savings yielded a return of 8% per year, total savings worked out at Tk. 48,18,310. Starting from 1963 through 2001, for every year my savings coupled with annual return was cumulated in another annexure.

This process of estimation was in accordance with the internationally recognized good accounting practice and I reiterated this in the statement to the court that I made in my defense in accordance with Section 342 of the Criminal Procedure Code. The Prosecution and the Special Judge did not raise any question about these calculations and estimates. Sitting in the jail without any access to records and within the constraints of a ridiculously unreasonable time limit could anyone give a more reasonable or accurate estimate of one's savings from regular salary income? Could a tenuous look backdoor for diktat make a person with reasonable education to his credit ignore these simple and acknowledged tools of calculation and the most reasonable estimate yielded by them? I had gone to enormous lengths to explain these calculations and the estimate. With rain falling in hard sheets on that July night, I could not reconcile myself with such a blister on reasonableness and rationality that mocked our judicial system. With a stifling sigh I fought to hold back the embarrassment of emotion with an attempt to sleep, but could not close my eyes even in the deep darkness around me.

Next afternoon, I recalled the calculation and estimate that I made of my extra-salary savings or savings from incidental income as was annexed to my statement made under Section 342 of the Criminal Procedure Code. In my first asset statement, on the day I wrote the statement in about one hour sitting in the jail without access to records and in presence of the jailor and government's spook, I had mentioned 25 sources from which I funded fixed deposits that I had. In these 25 items were included income earned abroad while on higher training and deputed service, sale proceeds of tax-free cars brought from abroad in accordance with the law in force, royalties from more than a dozen books that I authored, the pension, provident fund and gratuity that I received at one go when I retired and other income, excluding regular salary and rental income from the first two stories of the house at Banani that I and Sitara built brick by brick with sweat of perseverance and tears of hope. In nominal terms this amounted to Tk. 65.638 lacs (6.5638 million). Following the internationally recognized accounting practice, assuming reasonably that I had invested this amount in 44 years between 1963 and 2006, the average annual investment figured at Tk. 149,000 (Tk. 65.63 lacs divided by 44). Holding this constant, I annualized it for 44 years at 8%, assuming the latter to be the minimum rate of return that a reasonable person in this country, through investment of his savings or assets, would obtain in order to save it from erosion of value caused by the average annual rate of inflation experienced over years. These figured at Tk. 574 lacs (57.4 million) as the reasonably acceptable savings on this count alone.

I had asked Sitara to fax these calculations and estimates to my elder son Jalal, Assistant Professor, University of Massachusetts, Boston, for his scrutiny and comments. After about three days he faxed back saying these calculations and estimates were usual and correct. At the same time, as faxed back by him, I found a weighted calculation scheme that applied a simple weighting to the money invested over 44 years. In this process, the amount of money invested in later years was assumed to be linearly more than the former years. This was a more realistic assumption because a person was expected to earn more as he progressed in his career. In order to weight it linearly, arithmetic progression was used to find the denominator. The denominator in this case was the sum of 1 through 44 representing years from 1 through 44 equal to 990. The total amount of money invested remaining the same, *i.e.*, Tk. 65.63 lacs the amount of money invested; it was Tk. 7,161 in year 1 and over years raised itself Tk. 3,056 lacs in the 44th year. The calculations spelled out yearly for 44 years, giving an estimate of savings/investment of Tk. 3,056 lacs (Tk. 305.6 million), could not be questioned.

I showed these calculations and estimates to Lotus-Kamal, a chartered accountant by training and he certified them to be correct and unassailable under any scrutiny. In this backdrop, I found the Prosecution and the Special Judge totally immune to both expertise and realities with unbridled intent to punish the innocent irrespective of facts and figures. For them I was a sacrificial animal to be slaughtered for the satisfaction of their masters. Rechecking my calculations this way, I hit my ramshackle of a bed in utter exhaustion, in darkness thick and heavy around me. The monsoon wind turned louder, became a gale hissing over the high walls of the jail, leaving me in dark anguish, staring at distant shadows of unearthly things and praying for the dawn of the day.

Late in the next day, I thought how the Special Judge as well as the Prosecution metastasized entirely my account of rental income that I had given in my second or supplementary asset statement. I had stated that starting from 1992, I received as house rent at a rate of Tk. 30,000 a month, *i.e.*, Tk. 360,000 a year. Deducting one month's rent on account of annual maintenance and another month's rent on account of city corporation taxes, annual rental income amounted to Tk. 300,000/. In an annexure appended to my statement made before the court under Section 342 of the Criminal Procedure Code, I spelled out that on this basis between 1992 and 2006, assuming an annual return of 8% on this rental income, my saving/investment figured at Tk. 87.97 lacs (8.797 million). The Income Tax Department had records of the rental income that I had received. But for malfeasance, corruption and moral turpitude, the Prosecution and the Special Judge could not take these amounts into consideration, while they specified my legitimate asset-building capacity.

Adding up my estimated savings/investment as spelled out in detail, the total figured at Tk.710 lacs, *i.e.*, 71 million. In other words, the reasonable savings/investment capacity from my legitimate income far exceeded even the inflated value of assets as quoted with a no-holds-barred malfeasance by the Prosecution and accepted by the Special Judge without any question. The Special Judge even treated the pension amount that I had earned in course of 31 years of my service with the government as illegitimate. The calculation and estimates made in all these details were testified as correct and in full conformity with the recognized international principle and practice of fair accounting by the internationally acknowledged financial expert Dr. Forrest Cookson. His testimony to this effect was ignored with a sly smile by the Special Judge, making the trial as was done in this case a business instead of a mission. This was tantamount to a foreclosure not only of simple arithmetic but also of justice and fair play under the law. Duties and responsibilities of public service were thrown off in preference to the evil that stood up-for-grabs, glorifying servitude, selfishness and greed, devastating the very vitals of an independent country.

(8)

In the week that followed, I came to know of another stark instance of degeneration in the process of public prosecution and trial in our country, almost to the point of perfection of the art for a malicious cause. One Joj Mia was imprisoned both as an undertrial prisoner and a convict in the Kashimpur Jail. On August 21, 2004, at a public meeting on Bangabandhu Avenue in Dhaka, addressed by Sheikh Hasina the Leader of the Opposition at that time, as many as twelve grenades were thrown in an attempt to kill her and other leaders of the Awami League. Standing right behind Sheikh Hasina on the deck of an open truck, I was myself a witness to this heinous act done without question under the blessing and guidance of those who were in power at the time. As many as twenty-four leaders and activists of the Awami League were killed. Of those killed, Ivy Rahman was President of the Mohila Awami League and wife of Zillur Rahman, the senior most member of the Party's Presidium.

The Police Commissioner of Dhaka did not visit the place where the attack occured. The Inspector-General of Police did not find time to come. None from the Ministry of Home, located at a distance of 310 yards from the scene of this ghastly crime, thought it necessary to visit the place of occurrence either. To top it all, the police at first refused to receive the First Information Report on the incident and the killing, which was taken to the Police Station by Abdul Jalil, the General Secretary of the Awami League. In the face of countrywide protests and aggrievement, the police found one Joj Mia, a poor man of a remote village Birkot within Senbag Police Station of Noakhali district and made him confess to this crime. This was reportedly done on orders of the then-State Minister for Home Affairs Lutfuzzaman Babar, carried out under the supervision of Special Superintendent, Criminal Investigation Department of the Police, Ruhul Amin, with Assistant Superintendents Abdur Rashid and Munshi Atiqur Rahman, doing the actual mischief. On June 9, 2005, Joj Mia was picked up by the police, taken into remand or custody of the police for fifteen days, tortured and then made to confess on June 26 before a magistrate that he knew that the crime was committed by a top terrorist Subrata Bain, a fundamentalist Mollah Masud, a miscreant Tanvirul Islam and a few others. All these criminals, at that time were either out of the country or not traceable. This, to the conspiring police seemed to be the perfect scheme to shift the culpability on a few who were not at the scene, but more important, could be publicized as untraceable despite best efforts made by the police.

Meanwhile, the Ministry of Home, declared a prize of Tk. 10 million for anyone catching or giving clues leading to the arrest of the culprit. As the story went, the conspiracy to obstruct justice in this way also included distribution of Tk. 10 million amongst themselves, with a minuscule amount going to Julekha Begum, mother of Joj Mia. Julekha Begum was given Tk. 3,000/ a month and was told that her son would be released and rehabilitated with money and honor very soon. In the statement extracted by the police from Joj Mia before the Magistrate in Dhaka, in the heat of an imminent victory, they overlooked the fact that Joj Mia, brought in as the accused, mentioned specifically in an answer to a question put by the Magistrate that he had never seen a grenade, had no idea about what it was or what it looked like. As a result, the confessional statement of Joj Mia in this sinister attempt to hide the real culprits sitting on high chairs of the government in power, turned out to be a cruel joke and an example of handcrafted case of malfeasance, corruption, obstruction of justice and injustice in every conceivable form.

The story did not end here. After some time, the conspirators thought that Julekha Begum was no longer required to be sanitized with money. They stopped payment to her. In her anguish at last, she gave out the betrayal to a group of journalists. The story was published and the police officers concerned were put in a tight corner. To take revenge, they hatched up a conspiracy once again and showed Joj Mia as an arrested accused in a criminal case involving use of explosives in Sutrapur Police Station of Dhaka city much earlier than December 27, 1998. In that case previously the police had charge-sheeted or arraigned one Shamsul Islam. A supplementary charge-sheet was handcrafted to implicate Joj Mia in that case. The judge, as the record has it, did not object and readily succumbed to the pressure of the police. After the caretaker government took over from Khaleda and her cohorts, on public demand, the crime of August 21, 2004, was re-investigated and Abdus Salam Pintu, a deputy minister in Khaleda's government, his brother terrorist Tajuddin and a few others were found culpable and Joj Mia uninvolved and innocent. The court accepted the charge-sheet against Abdus Salam Pintu, Tajuddin and others and ordered for the release of Joj Mia. His mother was relieved to hear about the impending release. But Joj Mia could not be released as he was shown arrested under that case of explosives of 1998 vintage. And so Joj Mia remained incarcerated in the Kashimpur Jail as a living testimony of injustice and shame of society.

As I learned from Joj Mia and others, Tk. 10 million was distributed as prize money amongst three officers of the Criminal Investigation Department. The Additional Inspector of Police of the Criminal Investigation Department of the time, one Khuda Baksh had masterminded Joj Mia's arrest and hiding of the actual criminals. As the story had it, he also had a share of the booty. Not only that, being subservient and loyal and making Joj Mia quickly accept the role of victim as the sacrificial goat, he asserted his entitlement based on easy shedding of responsibility and morality and was promoted as the Chief of the Police of the country by State Minister Babar and his mentors of the time.

As I listened, Joj Mia and other inmates sympathetic to him sobbed and cried. I controlled my urge to cry, to smash the canopy under which the Superintendent of the jail sat, heard and mitigated grievances of inmates every day. Their tears have forfeited the moral language that would have helped infuse even this Fakhruddin government's action with a larger meaning of governance and protection of people's rights. But here also, as doubts persisted in the minds of inmates of the jail and of people living under intimidation outside, a number of real culprits, some much above the level of those accused through reinvestigation remained, unscathed and free. Money spoke in their support and favor at similarly high levels, leaving the message of justice sufficient space to weep in silence and remoteness in the backdrop of its helplessness in the face of the yet unchallenged power that was.

Another two weeks passed by. The Special Judge did not hand over the judgment in full. In frustration and under compulsion, I started drafting my appeal against the judgment yet to be received. I had noted depositions of all the witnesses and the law points raised and debated in course of the trial. Assuming that the Special Judge would deliberate on most of them, I thought my draft would not be out of context and missing the main points of the appeal. I decided, along with the copies of the relevant documents I would send the draft appeal to Barrister Rafiqul Huq for his perusal, examination, correction ahead of time and finally filing with the concerned division bench of the High Court.

(9)

In this period, as gleaned through newspapers given and information from outside brought to us, I along with other inmates in the "division" building of the jail came to form a dismal view of the role of the Appellate Division of the Supreme Court, the last refuge of citizens wronged or aggrieved by the system of governance and societal administration. In the first place, to our utter amazement, we observed the Chief Justice changing benches of the High Court Division before time and with such composition so as to support the government's action not based on or following the constitution and the law of the land. Whichever division bench issued rules on the government asking them to show reasons for seemingly obvious excesses, was changed to be composed with pliable judges lacking in courage to uphold the constitution and act in accordance with the oath they had taken to dispense justice as per law without fear or favor. In one instance, composition of a bench of the High Court Division was changed an hour before it was slated to announce its judgment on an important issue of constitutionality. Secondly, we found an element of dangerous moral relativism in the action of the Appellate Division when it, led by the Chief Justice, pigeonholed almost all decisions of the High Court Division to release political detainees arrested under the Emergency Powers Rules coupled with the Special Powers Act. This was tantamount to functionally upholding the practice of the government based on intimidation, encompassing human sacrifice in broad daylight under the cover of legal procedures.

Thirdly, the Emergency Powers Rules denied detainees even the right to apply for bail. Since Pakistan days the High Court had been upholding a position that such a draconian curtailment of the fundamental rights of a citizen under the cover of emergency or defense (of Pakistan) rules was applicable only in case of lower courts. The High Court or the Supreme Court set up specifically under the constitution and mandated to uphold the same, rain or shine, was not bound by the emergency restriction preventing the provision of a right to bail. The higher courts had unbridled power as well as responsibility to consider and grant bail in such cases also.

In the absence of such power at the level of higher courts (i) the supremacy of the constitution (ii) the principle of assuming everybody innocent unless and until proved otherwise (iii) the requirement to produce an arrestee before the competent magistrate within 24 hours and (iv) the mandate of equal treatment of all under law, were all in jeopardy. The dictum that in interpreting and application of lawful power, no other authority in a State could push the Supreme Court was violated in the event the aforesaid four principles of the Anglo-Saxon framework of law were not followed. The Supreme Court of the time, as it turned out, in their actions and pronouncements threw off these principles and diktat given by law and developed over decades, down the Ganga-Meghna. To us, it appeared as the shoddy product of lawyering also inasmuch as most of the top lawyers of the country excepting two, namely, Barristers Rafiqul Huq and Shafiq Ahmed, did not come forward to defend these principles. The conscious community of lawyers, who had played glorious roles in the fight for liberation, rule of law and separation of the judiciary from the clutches of the executive seemed to have gone into a moronic calm.

Lastly, the Appellate Division led by Chief Justice M. Ruhul Amin in one of its latest rulings said that under the Emergency Powers Rules effective January 11, 2007, the government could prosecute and the court could take cognizance, try and punish people for offenses committed and law violated before that date also. The constitution specifically debarred the Parliament from enacting law, the executive from proceeding with and the judiciary for taking cognizance of offenses with retro-active effect. How the Appellate Division of the Supreme Court could violate the constitutional dictum in its full sense was beyond our comprehension. To us, it was an impingement on most of the values with which the nation would have proceeded towards a just, stable, and progressive society with everyone having a stake in terms of principles. Never in the history of the subcontinent, so few men in the garb of Justices of the Republic could allow such an ostensible drift of the constitutional dictum and legal values acquired over centuries to stifle the rights of so many in so little span of time. It was a monstrosity of enormous proportion, transformation of judicial independence into license for a stifling arbitrariness, encompassing human sacrifices under the influence of greed, selfishness and cowardice in the face of illegitimate intimidation. To our chagrin the Chief Justice of the day, M. Ruhul Amin, came to be jeered and sneered at as Major Ruhul Amin, as if he was but an important nail in the coffin of the judiciary at that level.

On about the third day we had been talking about this monstrosity at the highest legal levels, around 3:00 in the afternoon. The sun forced itself through the monsoon clouds, making all around bright and clear. From the verandah on the third floor of our "division" jail, Salman, Lotus-Kamal, Kader and I looked south over the high jail walls and found a dozen barefooted youngster cricketers. From the winding alleys surrounding an abandoned dry paddy field, they had emerged with a ball, a bat and three stumps and started playing. Salman and Lotus-Kamal were cricket fans, both members of the Abahani Club set up by Sheikh Kamal, Bangabandhu's eldest son. Kader was the State Minister in charge of Sports and Culture during Sheikh Hasina's government. In still quietness, dreaming perhaps about the future of cricket in Bangladesh, the three of them admired the way these barefooted half-clad cricketers were bowling, fielding and batting. Their response to both bowling and batting reflected ragged reflexes of the young and budding, raising rhythm of our hearts in sync with the possibility of giving the benefit of opportunity to everyone everywhere to bloom. Our dreams, without any specific expression we felt, grew spacious with the young in the center of our life on that glittering afternoon. After a while, observing that they were playing with one bat and three stumps smattered with flecks of mud, Salman announced he would present the youngsters with a brand new cricket set. They must be able to resolutely cast themselves upwards, said Salman. We all felt, sitting in the jail with all creative actions thrown to a standstill, closer to the needs and requirements of the picturesque summer plains of the country we loved and to which we owed our lifetime of work.

It rained throughout the night. In the morning, I found the sun blotted out by the grey mass of clouds floating low in the horizon. A while later, thick sheets of water started pouring heavily from the sky. After a meager but leisurely breakfast, I sat on the verandah with Jeff Shaara's *The Rising Tide.* The novel was based on deep research on the Allies assault against the Germans in North Africa in preparation for the invasion of France in the Second World War. The great players, Churchill, Roosevelt, Eisenhower, Montgomery, Patton, Rommel, Kesselring and others came alive in their resolves and fights. I read for an hour, then walked on the long verandah looking at sheets of rain and a sky full of clouds for half an hour and then read again. I skipped the lunch as I was feeling queasy because of much raw tea I had taken, facing and walking in rain, touching me with lingering drops and cool moisture. In the late afternoon the rain stopped for a while, the sun turned crimson over the western horizon. I came down on the ground in front of the division building, tried to breathe in the swelling smell of the soil wafting from the two sides of the paved walkway and felt the life in the shrubs glistening with limitless possibility of growth. Then from behind, Nasim joined and whispered into my ear: "Thank God, she has crossed over and is now in Kolkata."

His words chimed with a hard thump of relief in my chest. For about a month, I had been telling him to send Mrs. Nasim, our *Bhabi*,[36] out of the country. There was no sense, I had told him, for her to stay within the country. The regime was bent upon taking vengeance on the detainees by including their wives and children as accomplices in their alleged corruption. This was a lesson that these usurpers, prostituting themselves to power, brought from Musharraf's Pakistan. As he told it, the escape was difficult; in the rain, by a boat laden with jute-sticks keeping Bhabi beneath the load and following a meandering canal not navigable by the patrol boats of the border guards of either Bangladesh or India. I congratulated Nasim. I told him with a chauvinistic tone that now as a man he would be able to face the odds, day in and day out, for months and years. Nasim blinked in contentment, murmured a few incantations to protect her from the evil eye. He did not say anything further. I knew he was relieved, now that his nerves would not threaten to overwhelm him as each night would fall.

A few days later, as I was finishing Jeff Shaara's *The Rising Tide*,[37] Kader walked into my cell, sat on the dilapidated wooden chair I had and unusually asked for a cup of tea. I traced out Omar on the verandah, made him boil two cups and sat questioningly before Kader. After a while he told me,

"Your Bhabi has left."

"Good. You have done the right thing. Now you can face the odds boldly and without unbearable worries," I commented.

"I don't know when I will meet her again. She is now in Kolkata, with our friends and co-workers though."

"Well, we are this time bound without choice; the time will change; the political landscape will change," I wanted to touch his sadness and cheer him up out of the quiet pessimism that seemed to swathe him.

He sat for a while, asked for another cup and said, "You were right. I did the right thing," and shrugged despondently.

Anticipating that she would also be made a co-accused in the case being framed up against him, I had been telling Kader to send her out in any way he could. I felt relieved; it was done.

---

[36] Wife of an older brother; sister-in-law.

[37] Jeff Shaara, *The Rising Tide: A Novel of World War II*. New York: Ballantine Books, 2006.

"She was a remarkable woman, a loyal and loving wife." Kader was on memory lane. I let him do so. A bellowing circular wind outside the verandah brought in rain in droplets, which helps in the catching of *hilsha* on the Padma-Meghna confluence by the loin-clothed fishermen of the plains. In leaden silence we sat motionless with a vision of the Bangalis living happily with a never-ending supply of *dal*, fish and rice in peace, safety and plenty.

11 The Judgment: Aftermath

(1)

After an elapse of a full two months from the date of announcement of the verdict, the Special Judge delivered the judgment officially. My brother obtained two certified true copies, one for Barrister Rafiqul Huq and the other for me. We had to file an appeal against the verdict within thirty working days from the date of delivery of the judgment. So I immediately started to examine it sentence by sentence, keeping the initial draft appeal I had started to work on and tried to come out with a final draft for the Barrister. The judgment was a handwritten one of 127 pages. As I examined it, I found it perfunctory, superficial and irrelevant; on the whole it was an attempt to give legal cover to the verdict that was pronounced on July 26, by the Special Judge with the connivance of the Leader of the Task Force, performing a task on diktat from above.

It was perfunctory inasmuch as it did not go deep into an analysis of the depositions made and evidence produced in course of the trial. The first accusation was that I concealed fixed deposits of Tk. 117 lacs in my asset statement and did not show their known or legitimate sources. In this context the Special Judge did not deliberate upon two asset statements that I had submitted, as he did not take into consideration the sources of income I had shown in them. Besides, in the judgment there was no deliberation on the defense's explanation of assets, which was given by the accused in reasonable terms. The judgment did not consider the fact that he was not, in accordance with the income tax law, required to give details of his interest-income accruable in the year following the year for which the asset statement was asked. In this context, the judgment did not refer to the substantial testimony given by the concerned Assistant Commissioner of Income Tax.

The second accusation was in respect to ownership of land in and around my village home. The evidence brought in by the Prosecution in this respect from the police and the registration offices did not provide any assessment of my savings/investment capacity generated from auxiliary, salary, and rental income as were estimated in accordance with the internationally recognized good accounting practice. The estimated savings/investment capacity was adequate enough to justify ownership of land in and around my home village. Besides, I was required by the ACC's notice to describe my assets, in this case land, not give their values, at cost or market price. The judgment did not contain any deliberation or consideration of these matters. The third accusation was that I had two houses in my home village and the judgment accepted this without any question or analysis. The Prosecution could not testify or prove that these two houses were solely mine. From the defense side we had shown land records proving that these houses were common and undemarcated properties of the family of four brothers and four sisters and their heirs and these were mentioned as such in the relevant asset statement. This was totally ignored in the judgment, falsely imputing ownership to me.

The fourth accusation was in respect of ownership of (i) the Sultana Filling Station (ii) a house in the Comilla housing estate and (iii) a set of under-construction shops within the premises of Gulbahar Himagar Ltd., Kachua. The documentary proofs were presented before the court showing that these were not my properties. The judgment did not refer to these; cite any reason for ignoring these proofs. The fifth accusation was that I had concealed value of my house in Banani Model Town, Dhaka. The value at cost that I had mentioned in my asset statement without having any access to records, more or less approximated the value accepted by the Income Tax Department in the income tax returns that I had submitted in the relevant years. The judgment did not consider the fact that once so accepted, revaluation at current prices by the engineers of a division other than the division of the PWD where the house was located, could not be considered as true in substitution of the value so accepted earlier and on which due taxes were paid by me. This was in violation of the principle of estoppel of the Evidence Act itself. Despite this, in the judgment, power of imposing punishment turned out to be the substitute for knowledge on the basis of which law required exercise of such a power.

The sixth accusation was that my figure for approximate balance in my bank accounts given from memory and sitting in the jail without having access to records was lower than the actual balance the Prosecution found in those accounts on and around the date on which I had mentioned my estimate. This accusation was required to be judged mainly in consideration of (i) correctness of statements of accounts obtained from the relevant banks; (ii) reasonableness of a person to give exact figure of his balance in bank accounts on a particular day from memory and (iii) possibility of deposits made into these accounts on behalf of me by my debtors and the caretaker of the home and land in the village without my instant knowledge.

The judgment, as I found it, did not contain any analysis of these relevant facts and considerations. Despite that, these were pointed out by the defense and also testified by the Prosecution Witnesses themselves. The last accusation was about ownership of three motorcycles. As testified by the Prosecution Witnesses themselves, these motorcycles were not registered in my name, nor recovered from my possession, nor seized from anyone in my employ. In the judgment I did not find any consideration of these points. Showing unblinking obedience to those in power, the judgment accepted the accusation, ducking law in the face of obvious truth to the contrary.

And then I found the judgment blatantly superficial. The judgment did not consider the legal points raised *inter alia* in respect of illegality of (i) the notice asking for asset statement; (ii) appointment and functioning of investigation officers; (iii) investigation beyond the scope of the First Information Report; (iv) not providing an opportunity for hearing to the accused; (v) exceeding the time limit for investigation set by the ACC's own Rules; (vi) retroactive application of law; (vii) misjoinder of charges; (viii) non-examination of the accused's statement given in writing under Section 342 of the Criminal Procedure Code and (ix) limiting the defense's right to produce more witnesses and present full arguments. The judgment, if it was a serious exercise, would have contained deliberation on these legal points raised by the defense and the reasons on the basis of which these were not adhered to by the Special Judge. It seemed the judgment was a final breath of dishonesty twisting facts and truths with a vicious disregard of legal education and tradition. It was marred by misuse of both power and responsibility, eroding off trust from the administrative-legal system of the country.

And in my assessment, the judgment in its lusty embrace of falsehood was irrelevant. The facts-in-issue in this were mainly three: (a) whether there was concealment of assets; (b) whether assets as reported by the accused were disproportionate to his legitimate income and (c) if so, what exactly was the amount of assets that was so disproportionate. The judgment did not consider, in terms of facts and figures produced by the Prosecution and the defense, as to concealment of assets beyond reasonable doubt. There was no analysis of the two asset statements and estimates of auxiliary, rental and salary income and savings and yields therefrom as were produced before the court. The judgment did not consider, or analyze the asset statements to point out concealment, if any. No analytical justification was given in the judgment for not considering these estimates in accordance with internationally recognized good accounting practice.

As it turned out, even pension obtained by the accused was adjudged as disproportionate to what should have been the legitimate income and ordered to be confiscated. The judgment did not quantify what was or should be deemed as legitimate income of the accused. Without quantifying the legitimate income/savings, it was ridiculous for the court to quantify the disproportionate amount. As a matter of fact, the judgment accepted whatever the Prosecution stated as disproportionate. The judgment could not differentiate between constant and current value of assets, especially of houses/buildings, and ignored increase in construction cost index compiled and published by the government itself. The position of the Prosecution in this instance was merely whipped high by a servile court. The value of properties not owned by the accused were included by the court in the total value of assets of the accused.

Such a billowing irresponsibility emanating out of legal adjudication was unheard of in the annals of even our not very illustrious judicial system, choked by wands of sporadic military rule, lack of competence, as well as lack of independence of the country's legal system. This was a vicious disregard of legal learning and tradition. The Evidence Act that governed production and application of evidence in our legal system emphasized relevancy of facts in adjudging an issue. In the judgment that I received, the relevant facts were starkly missing, making its author a graphic, startling, hulking monster bent upon obliterating honesty and truthfulness.

(2)

This assessment of the judgment in terms of its stark perfunctory nature, superficiality and irrelevance was more or less in conformity with the draft appeal that I had started writing. I had gone to enormous length to examine the judgment. Its worst falsity was that, despite it being written more than a month after the verdict was announced, it bore the same date as that of the verdict. Shoving off darkness presented by frequent loadshedding, in the dreary and wet nights, I worked on the draft appeal and then within seven days from the date of receipt of the judgment, handed over the same to my brother for passing it to Barrister Huq. From the date of receipt of the judgment, we had thirty days to file the appeal with the High Court Division. I remained quite tense about meeting the deadline. Barrister Rafiq was so overwhelmed with work as he was about the only one taking up the cases of persons under persecution as being corrupt, that I thought he needed prodding. This was done by my brother Dr. Jahangir.

In the meanwhile, when I went to the Bangabandhu Sheikh Mujib Medical University Hospital along with Salman after much persuasion of the jail administration to mend my ailing teeth, Barrister Rafiq managed to meet and assure me that he was aware of the deadline and seized with the fine-tuning of the appeal in the form in which it would be filed. Through discussion with him, I could clarify some of the finer and subtler points, and more important, obtain relief and satisfaction that he was quite attentive to what needed to be done, when and how. Within three days I received a revised draft of the appeal from him and was asked to give my comments within three hours and to suggest addition or deletion of some points, if needed. Mafiz came with the draft and I kept him sitting in the visitor's room at the jail gate and worked on the draft for full three hours; in addition to a few factual corrections, I penciled in some modifications, sighed a breath of relief and sent it back to Barrister Rafiq. After seven days I received back a copy of the appeal that was filed with the High Court Division on November 11, 2007, *i.e.*, about four months after the announcement of the verdict by the trial court. According to interpretation of the Rule to file appeal within thirty days of the receipt of the judgment, I could not even apply for bail. For incompetence and moral corruption of the judge, liberty of a citizen was to be sacrificed. In this intervening period of frustration with the legal procedure as interpreted at will, I had almost nothing else to do but to wait and read a few books that reached me from Sitara.

(3)

Of these books, one I read with almost unstoppable admiration was Barack Obama's *Dreams From My Father*. This was a story of race and inheritance of a mixed American aspiring to be the Democrat's candidate for the American Presidency. Obama's father was a black Kenyan and his mother a white American. Obama described how, after working as a student and a community organizer, he persistently searched for a workable meaning to his life as a black American. He had studied law in Harvard — in my consideration the very best for learning the philosophy of law in the whole world. In the light of his experience of life in Kansas, Hawaii, Indonesia, Kenya, Chicago, Boston and New York (the two parts of world's divide in wealth as well as understanding of the meaning of life), he found law "a sort of glorified accounting that serves to regulate the affairs of those who have power — and that all too often seek to explain to those who do not, the ultimate wisdom and justness of their condition." But that was about the law's loopholes to be closed in a civilized society. Obama's summation of the law's loopholes would have been the severest had he known what was happening in Bangladesh in this first decade of the twenty-first century. As an afterthought, more in hope based on the diagnosis of the current incoherence, Obama concluded: "The law is also memory; the law also records a long-running conversation, a nation arguing with its conscience." With a nod of assent amidst the surrounding darkness on a rainy night in the Kashimpur Jail, I wondered whether my appeal against the mischief of illegitimate power, would be able to provide an element of argument in the nation's conscience.

I found Obama's *Dreams From My Father* very revealing and a profound discovery of one's own strength in confronting varied, at times both painful and wrathful but at the top of all, despite these limitations, a world of unlimited possibility to be realized through individual and collective efforts. At the same time he did not lose his part of a collective consciousness. To him his own brother's face was reflected on all other's, "multiplied across the landscape, across continents — hungry, striving, desperate but all knotted in a brotherhood." I came to like Obama for his feelings as well as insights into the problems that we had been facing across countries and continents.

In his *Dreams From My Father* Obama had given his experience as an unwanted guest along with his sister in Nairobi's New Stanley Hotel. Despite having a wallet full of American dollars, the color of him and his sister did not get attention and service from the colored waiters of the hotel's outdoor cafe. The colored waiters were more intent to serve the white tourists. I recalled I had a similar experience in the same hotel in 1981. On my way to Uganda's Kampala as the UN's consultant, I stayed at the New Stanley a night and, because of the color of my skin, I did not get the same attention and service from black waiters, though I paid the same price in American dollars for my bed and breakfast. To me that appeared to be a cultural barrier, containing common expectation of higher return or remuneration from white men, fed into a common subconscience built over centuries of colonial rule and repression. We see the same lineage of attention and service here in Dhaka, over there in Delhi and Karachi, though in smaller magnitude, even these days. It seemed the poor and the deprived almost never tires of expecting favors from the rich and the fortunate, though the latter at times delight in harassing and mocking the materially weak.

In this book, Obama mentions about Makarere University on the outskirts of Kampala, Uganda, which his father, as Obama indicated, would have been happy to join like some of his age-mates. During my stay in Kampala in 1981, I had occasion to visit the Makarere, located on tree-clad deep green hillocks with its various faculties and residential buildings looking like post-card pictures. It was a good seat of learning to groom up new African leadership for the region left unscathed even by a tyrant like Idi Amin. In my view, there was no substitute for a good university to fount out ideas that change society and mould out leadership as change-agents. I recalled meeting Yoweri Museveni, Uganda's military strongman, in the Micro-Credit Summit in Washington in 1997, He had a tallness unmatched by a well-fed paunch developed in the middle, I had asked him about the Makarere. As we have seen in our own country, the military leader thinking about and acting to secure welfare to his people by himself, was not very sure as to what use that budding beautiful Makarere would be for his society or his espoused objective. No one could question that there was only stagnation that could come out of unbridled power of a few over millions, and shame in the silence that such power produces.

I was impressed by Obama. He wrote and expressed himself well. It was not just words dancing in the hands of a linguist; it was feeling that came out of experience, growing up, understanding oneself as a part of the community to which he belonged. I received his other book, the more celebrated one, *The Audacity of Hope*, also from Sitara. I read hungrily, thought deeply, felt widely and came to admire this man. Towards the end of his *Audacity of Hope*, Obama looking out over the Reflecting Pool of the Vietnam veteran's Memorial in Washington gave out his deepest feelings: ". . . nation's founders, who somehow rose above petty ambitions and narrow calculations to imagine a nation unfurling across a continent and those like Lincoln and King who ultimately laid down their lives in the service of perfecting an imperfect union. And all the faceless, nameless men and women, slaves and soldiers, and tailors and butchers, constructing lives for themselves and their children and grandchildren, brick by brick, rail by rail, calloused hand by calloused hand to fill in the landscape of our collective dreams." And giving out that feeling Obama said, with determination strengthened by humility of a common man, "it is that process I wish to be part of."

I recalled, while visiting Bangabandhu's shrine in Tongipara, in front of the replica of a bountiful waterfall coming down from the sky to sustain and cherish the productivity of farmers and workers of this country, I always thought of making myself worthy of the supreme sacrifice made by the father of the nation and the four national leaders. I wanted to be a part of the sweat, tears and blood of people who worked for making this land as dreamed by our founding fathers. I must say Obama, by his intellect, feeling and love for the country, inspired me out of the gloom of incarceration in Kashimpur.

Then I read David Bornstein's *How to Change the World: Social Entrepreneurs and the Power of New Ideas*. The book was sent to me by my dear old friend, William Christensen, the soul behind the Institute of Integrated Rural Development (IIRD). In this, Bornstein had tried to described how an emerging landscape of innovators were advancing solutions that have the potential to transform life around the world. He focused on the indomitable will of Florence Nightingale transforming nursing from a job into a mission throughout the world, path-breaking idea and work of Fabio Rosa, who electrified rural Brazil, societal consciousness and programs for child protection in India spearheaded by Jeroo Billimoria, ways and means for assisted living as shown by Erzsebet Szekeres of Hungary, down to reforming health care as practiced by Vera Cordeiro in Brazil, wider and more productive access to college education as innovated by J. B. Schramm in the U.S., extension of care for AIDS patients in South Africa by Veronica Khosa, propagation of disability rights in India by Javed Abidi and spearheading child survival revolution throughout by James Grant.

Earlier I had read Bornstein's *The Price of a Dream; the Story of the Grameen Bank*. Bornstein's focus on these social innovators and entrepreneurs reminded me and other inmates with whom I discussed them of the need for encouraging them in our country. I recalled in recent months in our country the development of HYV rice (*haridhan*) in Jenidah, demonstrative production of a highly productive electric generator with almost no fuel in Chittagong by an unknown innovator, and a water-powered irrigation tube-well in Jhikargacha by a poor mechanic. I observed, regretfully, that they were not being recognized and funded. I was convinced, in a country where politics remains a business for the illegitimately ambitious rather than a mission for extending freedom and increasing welfare, such a recognition and funding of ideas that were a fount of power and change, could not take place.

"The illegitimately ambitious could come because the politicians failed in their mission," commented Kamal Majumder, when I sat with the other inmates to discuss Bornstein.

"This situation would not have come if both the Awami League and the BNP went for election," hypothesized Engineer Mosharraf.

"You said the politicians failed because you expected too much from them. Obviously there were pitfalls on the way of the politicians, but to conclude they failed would be wrong — missing entirely the point," said A. K. M. Mosharraf.

"Can we accept that these crooks demonizing the politicians succeeded? Can't you see the misery of choked voice, squalor of intimidation and servitude, these rats and lice eating off our souls, the half-naked barefoot children going about in the streets in the school hours and living with crumbs of the common man?" I asked all of them rather angrily.

I did not get any reply. None commented as if they were finally in agreement with me.

(4)

Of the various newspapers that could be slipped inside, Salman and I found the *New Age* playing an honestly courageous role. Its headlines, emphasis on local events, editorials and sub-editorials depicted the true picture of society despite a sinister attempt to subdue everyone. Specially, editorials by Nurul Kabir and commentaries by N. M. Harun reflected depth of analysis and the shine of courage and at the same time indicated that salvation from the rot would not be too easily won. We dared to hope for survival and freedom, to move beyond the demeaning existence into which we had been thrown.

One of these days, in the early morning from the verandah of the third floor, I observed a procession of about 100 men, women and children going west from east along the road to the south of the jail wall. They were accompanied by a so-called band party making awakening music by drums, flutes and cymbals. From Omar and his friends, I learned that the procession was going to a shrine of a local Muslim saint for collective prayers and offering of respect. On the two sides of the road, I saw assemblage of common people, similarly poor in dress and appearance, but ostensibly of the low-caste Hindus, seeing and at times clapping and welcoming the processioners. Some of the women with red *sindhur* marking their foreheads were bowing to the processioners showing respect to the saint. In the late afternoon, I observed a similar procession, this time composed of the Hindus coming from the west to the east. From somewhat different music that wafted in as well as from the dress worn by the processioners, it was evident they were going to a wedding. On the two sides of the road, I saw men and women, common and poor but ostensibly Muslims observing the procession, smiling and clapping. These two processions, their compositions and the onlookers' appreciation of each other, made me realize once again that amongst our common men there was no communal strife; that they were more united in their doings and aspirations than different in the choice of their faiths. Their stories of life were common, the sweat they shed for decent survival was the same and the blood that flowed through their veins was indistinguishable. As the last procession wound its way to the wedding venue, I vowed to make their tears our tears; we would make this society rise above the demeaning communalism that was always used by the illegitimately ambitious usurpers of power and rights as a weapon to divide the people and rule over them while denying their rights. When I said these things, even Mufti Shahidul Islam, the arch-religious amongst us, agreed. There was no avenue or justification for persecution in religion, he announced. Lotus-Kamal and Salman nodded, as did Ali Asgar Lobi and Kader.

In the dailies we were allowed, more often than not, we read about rallies organized by the government in Dhaka to observe various national and international days. There were days for polio vaccination, vitamin-A swallowing by children, AIDS awareness creation, women's rights, saying no to drugs, protesting corruption, protection of the aged, saving of the rivers, and all other conceivable causes and occasions. The advisors, secretaries, office employees, T-shirted volunteers, taxi and three-wheeler drivers were all in these rallies as it appeared from snapshots published. "Wherefrom they got the money? Was there any appropriate budget provisions for observing these days?" we asked. Then I realized only a caretaker government without any obligation to people's representatives for obtaining sanction for public expenditures, could do these. In a country of soaring prices of food grains, pulses, edible oil, daily necessities and most people still half-clad and going about without rudimentary shoes, such a free hand in spending taxpayer's money appeared to be the height of fiscal irresponsibility and financial corruption.

12 Appeal: Thereafter

(1)

Following the filing of the appeal with the High Court, on November 4, 2007, a procedural delay was to be faced and overcome. A paper book containing all papers of the trial, starting from the FIR to charge-sheets, testimonies, documentary evidences, day-to-day decisions of the trial judge and the final judgment needed to be printed or typewritten and bound chronologically for producing before the High Court Division. This, as per the rules of the High Court Division, was the responsibility of the government. The Registrar of the Supreme Court, *i.e.*, the High Court and the Appellate Divisions, exercised supervision so as to make sure the paper books were prepared on time. In my case, an assessment of the earlier pending work and the sluggish way things were done in the Registrar's office, made us believe that it would take more than two years to prepare the paper book, while the law in my case required filing of the appeal within thirty days of the receipt of the certified true copy of the judgment of the trial court and disposal of the appeal so filed within ninety days thereafter.

In this predicament, guided by Barrister Rafiq, my brother Dr. Jahangir arranged to prepare the paper books by his own efforts outside the sluggish operation of the government printing press. In this process he expected help and support from Registrar Iqtiar Ahmed Chowdhury, a member of the judicial service. Iqtiar was known to me as a son of one of my former colleagues — who had been sub-divisional officer, Pabna Sadar in 1968 when I was an Assistant Commissioner there. Till I was not incarcerated Iqtiar used to come to me, talk about various problems he was facing in the Ministry of Law where he worked and sought advice as to how he should get through the swirling disaffection of his bosses. I helped him, even made a few calls to people who mattered to him.

To my surprise, this time, beyond saying: "Yes, oh, yes," to my brother's request to expedite preparation of the paper book by making available the relevant papers from the trial court, he did not do much. My surprise did not eclipse, however, when I knew the process to be pursued at that level in the Supreme Court. One was required to satisfy almost all, brick by brick, polished hand by polished hand, so that it was not mucked up in front of the Registrar before he could put his approving seal on the paper book. At last, divided in three volumes, containing about 1,500 computer-printed pages, with six copies of each of the volumes, my brother through Barrister Rafiq could formally file in the paper book on April 3, 2008 to steer the appeal within the set course.

Counting from July 26, 2007, when the verdict on me was pronounced in the kangaroo court, it thus took eight months and seven days to file the appeal and cross the threshold of the High Court Division for its consideration. This was a definite violation of the provisions of even the draconian law for filing appeal within thirty days of the judgment of the trial court and disposal of the appeal within ninety days thereafter. To the accompaniment of this poignant insult to justice and wounds inflicted by what went in the name of legal procedure was the blatant violation of my human rights to be posted on bail or assumed innocent till finally proved guilty. The ruddy, ugly and menacing face of trial under the Emergency Powers Rules providing for expeditious disposal thus became nakedly exposed as a convenient conduit for suppressing rights and tearing apart the process of dispensation of justice.

The text of the appeal, excluding appended testimonies, documents, records and judgment of the trial court consisted of 75 computer printed foolscap pages. In line with the arguments that we had earlier placed before the trial court in the appeal it was pointed out and focused upon that:

(1) Secretary, ACC was not authorized to issue notice on the accused to submit asset statement;
(2) The notice was not based on satisfaction of the ACC preceded by an investigation of allegations;
(3) Unauthorized issue of notice by the Secretary, ACC could not be authorized retroactively by amendment of the law subsequently;
(4) The notice required description of assets not their values and did not ask for particulars of assets of others held by the appellant;
(5) The notice did not ask for mentioning valid sources of income nor indicate the assets disproportionate to the income of the appellant;

(6) The statement of assets was forced out of the appellant from the jail without giving him any access to records or lawyer and within severe time constraint; the appellant was not given a personal hearing, which violated the law and the principle of natural justice;
(7) The appellant did not in his statements of assets conceal any of his assets; he had given sources of income including his tax-exempt earnings abroad;
(8) Investigation report on the basis of which the appellant was notified to submit asset statement, was not supplied to him;
(9) The FIR lodged with the Police was incomplete as regards time and place of occurrence of the alleged offense and misleading inasmuch as it did not mention that the appellant had mentioned his Fixed Deposits in approximate terms, under constrained circumstances of being in jail and without access to relevant records;
(10) The Investigation Officers and the Public Prosecutors did not take into account the appellant's revised or second statement of assets, having corrections and additions, specially of Fixed Deposits, and his custody of the capital amount of the Sultana Foundation;
(11) Investigation Officers did not find out or identify the appellant's known or valid sources of income so as to pinpoint the amount of assets not justified by such income;
(12) Lumping Sections 26 and 27 of the ACC Act together for trial was a misjoinder of charges not permitted by the procedural law;
(13) Permitting further investigation beyond the scope of the FIR lodged earlier, as was done by the trial court was illegal and tantamount to abuse of the process of the court;
(14) Investigation was completed beyond the time frame prescribed by the law making its findings untenable;
(15) The trial court framed charges or arraigned the appellant under laws assuming their retroactive effect; this violated the appellant's constitutional rights given under article 35 of the constitution;
(16) None of the 37 Prosecution Witnesses deposed that the appellant had any illegal source of income; testimonies of all these witnesses read together made it clear that the appellant did not conceal any of his assets nor acquired any income beyond any known source, making Sections 26 and 27 the ACC Act not applicable in his case;

(17) The appellant, in his written statement of defense under Section 342 of the Criminal Procedure Code, rebutted all the accusations made against him; neither the Prosecution nor the trial court rebutted his defense; the court violated the law (Sections 265 and 342 of the Criminal Procedure Code) by not examining the appellant giving his statement in writing under Section 342 of the Criminal Procedure Code, vitiating the entire process of trial;

(18) The Prosecution in its attempt to show mismatch of the appellant's income compared his total income shown in income tax returns for 23 years with the value of assets earned in a lifetime work of over 44 years; this was evidently incorrect, deceitful, and thus not legally tenable; and

(19) The deposition six defense witnesses adduced by the appellant testified about his integrity, dedication to work and the country's interest, correctness of his estimates of savings/investment capacity for 38 long working years of life and valuation of his residential house as had been accepted by the income tax authority.

Focusing on these points and others we appealed for setting aside the conviction inflicted on me by the Special Judge on diktat from his lords and mentors.

(2)

After the appeal was formally filed and appended with the Paper Book, we waited for its being taken up for hearing. It was pointed out to the concerned bench of the High Court Division, but it did not expedite its taking up for disposal within the 90-day time limit set by the law. I remained incarcerated in the Kashimpur Jail under the burden of the draconian law of the State of Emergency that did not allow me to apply for bail even during the pendency of the appeal or its delay in disposal for no fault of mine.

I recalled an episode in *Alice in Wonderland*: the outrageously nonsensical trial of the Knave of Hearts. Under the silliest of pretenses, the Knave was falsely accused of stealing some tarts. The accused is brought before the hopelessly inept Judge (who also happened to be the King of Hearts) and an acquiescent jury made up of playing cards and an assortment of beasts and birds. In the middle of a witness' testimony the King ("for the twentieth time that day") announces: "Let the jury consider their verdict." "No, No!" said the Queen [whose mantra is "Off with his head!]. "Sentence first — verdict afterwards." In this case, I was enduring conviction before the trial in its entirety was complete. "Had we returned to that wonderland?" I wondered in exasperation.

While in jail during these days, we witnessed two events happening in the wonderland of ours. First, one evening, through the grapevine of the jail guards, we came to know Khaleda Zia would be leaving the country and before doing so she would come to say goodbye to her son Tareque incarcerated in Kashimpur Jail 2, lying immediately to the north of the Kashimpur Jail 1 where we were interned. Very early in the morning, almost in lyrical tilts, the jail guards informed us of her arrival in a black SUV of the RAB followed by two other similar vehicles. We were told by someone above the guards, through a gliding of an uncomfortable whisper that a plane had already landed in Dhaka airport for taking her to Saudi Arabia to live in exile. That was one part of the so-called minus-2 program hatched by the chair-borne leaders of Bangladesh's armed forces under the Emergency Rule. Khaleda met Tareque for about an hour in private in the Superintendent's office of Kashimpur 2 and then she scampered back to her residence on Moinul Hossain Road of the Dhaka Cantonment.

Also through the grapevine we came to know, on reaching her residence given gratuitously earlier by the Ershad government after her husband's tragic death, she refused to get out once again to board the aircraft brought for her. This she could do, despite being on the edge of the precipice to which she was pushed by the Forces Intelligence, because of the strength to hold back supplied by her brother Saed Iskander through Major General Masud Uddin Chowdhury. Major General Masududdin Chowdhury was wedded to the sister of Saed Iskander's wife. Next day, however, a substitute story wafted in. The Inter-Service Intelligence of Pakistan could convince the Saudi authority in Riyadh not to issue a visa to Khaleda Zia for going to and staying in Saudi Arabia. We did not get, in the swirling blackout of information within the four walls of the jail, what actually was the reason. But as it turned out, Khaleda stayed back in pampered relaxation. The BNP inmates of the division building boastfully claimed that the regime had to bow down to her uncompromising principle and courage. In my assessment, irrespective of the way her exile was averted, Khaleda did a good job of hammering out a makeshift escape from going down the escarpment.

The second event was Sheikh Hasina's sojourn to the U.S. for medical treatment and stay with her son and daughter and the obstruction created thereafter by the regime against her return. Hasina was under the impression that the regime had no other alternative exit route but to lend support to her till such time that she, as the Leader of the Parliament to be elected, ratified their failure to hold election within 90 days and consequent stay in power for more than 120 days and forays into undoable and untouchable policy matters and decisions beyond their constitutional mandates. Appropriate arrangements were made by the regime to make her depart from Dhaka airport for the U.S. Perhaps slightly overwhelmed by the arrangements made for her despite arrests of a number of her party leaders before, more in humor than in seriousness, she said that she and her party would ratify all deeds (misdeeds?) of the unelected caretaker government in the next Parliament. We in jail were dumbfounded and dejected. For us it was a blotch of darkness blacker than the incarcerated surroundings in which we lived.

"Are we cannon fodder in this fight for power?" someone amongst us asked in frustrated fury.

"Don't be charmed by the apparent consent to license misdeeds by the gun bearers. Her comment may be a humorous indication of apartness, definitely not of friendly disposition or admiration," I commented. But not everyone thought the time was right to leave the country, leaving the leaders and workers without the presence of her protection.

In the month that followed, we did not notice any dimple in the flat and dull landscape of prison life. In heat as well as in rain, we attended courts, went to hospitals for treatment, walked the sunwashed walkways within the high walls and at times looked at the life of flowers and vegetables sprouting out of soils mulched by convicts ruled by intimidation and hurling of insults of being called mother and sister fuckers by the guards. And then the bolt came from the blue. The Fakhruddin government asked Sheikh Hasina not to return as scheduled and instructed all airlines not to carry her to Dhaka till decided to the contrary. This was the "one step forward, two steps back" formula of politics for Bangladesh. Hasina, admirably obstinate as she was, landed in London, raised hue and cry about her right to return to the country of her birth and citizenship, drew national and international attention to the ostensible denial of her human rights and then landed at Dhaka amidst a tumultuous reception of thousands of people despite prohibition on assemblage under the Emergency Powers Rules. Watching this in grim discomfort, the regime took a step backward scheming to take two forward later in anger and vengeance.

In about a month's time the two steps forward were taken. As many as three cases of corruption were framed up against Sheikh Hasina. In one case, in a State-to-State deal for setting up a power-generating station from Russia, she was accused of raising subscription through her cousin Sheikh Fazlul Karim Selim. In the second in a similarly State-to-State deal with Russia for procurement of MIG 29 fighters for the Air Force, she along with the Air Force and the Army Chief of the time were framed. In the third she was framed for extortion for the Bangabandhu Memorial Trust from the suppliers/erectors of a barge-mounted, power-generating station. On July 16, 2007 she was arrested by the government at the behest of the ACC in the first case and then shown arrested in the other two and denied bail on grounds of the prevalence of the Emergency Powers Rules. And about a month after she was incarcerated, Khaleda Zia along with her youngest son Arafat Rahman Koko was arrested for approving a container-handling contract negotiated by the Chittagong Port Authority at a cost 30% lower than the previous contract price at which the Port Authority had operated. Thus short of sending the two leaders out of the country under the aegis of the "minus-2" scheme, the military-backed government incarcerated the two ex-prime ministers and heads of the two major political parties to observe how the public would react.

(3)

Over days, we in the Kashimpur Jail discussed the government's immature minus-2 scheme; as it appeared to us, the leaders of the government of the day lacked political maturity in their attempt to balance personal ambition with realism.

"It is the damnedest — gravest mistake that the government has committed," Salman declared.

"This seems to be the beginning of the end," commented A. K. M. Mosharraf.

"As the Bangla saying goes, there is no medicine when one's death time comes," I commented.

"There will not be an immediate protest or uprising; the people in power must have contacted some quislings in both the parties before arresting the two leaders," said Ali Asgar Lobi.

"Let us wait and see," concluded Kader. And we waited, observing events and developments in their attempt to make us and our families cower to them dissolutely.

In this period, four other events were made to happen. Hostility combined with personal ambition was plainly seen in these happenings. First, true to the threat given by him earlier Major Kamruzzaman of the Task Force made Rahela Khatun, Assistant Director, the ACC to lodge a First Information Report (FIR) with the Ramna Police Station, Dhaka against my wife Sitara under Sections 26 and 27 of the ACC Act and Rule 15 (d) 5 of the Emergency Powers Rules for concealment of her assets and its disproportionateness to her known income. The FIR was lodged on December 24, 2007. It was a concoction of mistakes of facts and miscalculations, and amongst other flaws over-ruling of income tax law under which she had paid taxes on purchase of an apartment out of her known or legitimate income. Rule 15 (d) 5 of the Emergency Powers Rules empowered the ACC to arrest her and keep her without bail in jail indefinitely following the filing of the FIR. I thanked Allah that she had left the country before this insult and humiliation could be imposed on her out of vengeance. I took steps to make her income tax payment up-to-date. I did not inform her the details of allegations drummed up against her. In this backdrop, I thought our decision to send her out of the country was an appropriate one. Here, power for persecution was undisguised and naked but not indiscriminate.

Our manager Mafiz obtained a copy of the FIR and gave it to me at the Kashimpur Jail. I had a copy of the asset statement that Sitara had furnished to the ACC before she left the country. I compared the content of the First information Report with her asset statement and found the allegations concocted and baseless beyond reason. In her asset statement, Sitara had shown 11 items of her nominal income in terms of salary, rent, royalties, pension and gratuities received between 1968 and 2007, totaling Tk. 93.50 lacs (9.35 million). She stated that I, as her husband, had borne almost all her living expenses. On a very conservative assumption that between 1968 and 2007, this income of an average of Tk. 2.45 lacs per year had given her an annual return of 5%; she gave yearly calculation of her income totaling Tk. 293.35 lacs (29.335 million) which more than adequately justified holding of all her movable and immovable assets as listed in the asset statement. In addition she had given details of fixed deposits and bank accounts jointly held with her expatriate sons and sisters, holding their money on their behalf. Point by point, against the allegation made in the First information Report, in her absence, I prepared a brief for Barrister Rafiqul Huq for moving to the High Court for stay and quashment of proceedings against her. Barrister Huq advised that we should wait till submission of a charge-sheet and strengthening of the political opposition against the regime. He said, since law had largely been abandoned in our country by the regime, issues like framing innocent people on extra-legal grounds would be decided largely on streets rather than in courts.

Second, apprehending that the High Court Division might accept my appeal on the basis of facts and figures given by us and I might be released, the Leader of the Task Force Major Kamruzzaman acting on orders given from above forced one Abdul Monem, a road construction contractor to lodge an FIR on extortion against me with the Gulshan Police Station on October 10, 2007. In the FIR it was stated that I had extorted Tk. 1 crore (10 million) from Abdul Monem, half in cash and half through a brother-in-law of mine, a U.S. national, in April 2001, a mere three months before Sheikh Hasina's government went out of office. The money was extorted, it was alleged, before a contract for construction of five road bridges, all funded out of foreign aid could be given to Abdul Monem Ltd.

This was a made-up case inasmuch as in the position of State Minister for Planning, I had no authority to award contract, which in this case was done by the Ministry of Communications with the prior approval of the donor. Despite the ludicrously unbelievable nature of the allegation, the Chief Metropolitan Magistrate, ostensibly then discharging his responsibilities with the recently endowed separation from the executive part of the government, took cognizance and I was shown arrested in this case as well, so that in the event I was released by the High Court Division on my appeal against conviction of corruption wrought down through the kangaroo court, I could still be incarcerated in the jail. Later, to interrogate and intimidate me into submission, I was allowed by a Magistrate to be in the custody of the Police in the Cantonment Police Station for one day. I was interrogated there by Major Kamruzzaman; the police officer-in-charge of investigation confided with almost tears in his eyes that he was helpless in this process of mocking justice.

Third, earlier and unknown to us, on March 30 2007, Jiban Krishna Roy, Deputy Director of the ACC and the first Investigation Officer investigating the alleged corruption by me, filed a First Information Report with Comilla Kotwali Police Station that I had acquired a house in the Comilla Housing Estate through criminal conspiracy and false declaration. The alleged offense was not within the purview of the ACC and that was why Investigation Officer Jiban Krishna acting on unusual enthusiasm filed this First Information Report with the Comilla Police. The house was built on a plot that I had purchased in the early 1980s. The

Agrani Bank funded its construction, took it on lease, set up a branch of the bank there. I gifted the house along with the plot to my youngest son following the Islamic principle of *heba* and the lease deed of the building was in his name; he had been receiving rents and paying taxes as a separate individual and taxpayer. The house was earlier shown as mine in the charge-sheet placed before the kangaroo court that tried and convicted me for corruption.

The allegation was false inasmuch as (1) the house was not mine; (2) none of the parties to any conceivable dispute regarding it, the Housing Estate, the Agrani Bank and the Income Tax Department had anything to complain about its ownership, tax payment and management and (3) it was a subject matter of adjudication earlier in the corruption case framed up against me. Despite all these, the allegation was taken into cognizance by the Magistrate concerned and the Ministry of Home gave its consent for it to be tried by the Special Tribunal, Chittagong, treating it as an offense coming under the mischief of Rule 14 of the Emergency Powers Rules. Inclusion of Rule 14 in functional terms meant that in this case also I could not apply to be posted on bail. Later, I moved to the High Court Division for staying all proceedings of the case on grounds of illegality and they accepted my motion, asked the government to show reason why the case would not be quashed *ab initio*. The government did not as yet show any reason, the proceedings of the case in the Special Tribunal remained suspended and I continued to be detained in the jail without any right to apply for bail even. The men with unattainable ambition to subjugate all possible opposition remained satisfied that their machination under the cover of law served their purpose.

The last in this series was another frivolous case filed with Mohammadpur Police Station of Dhaka. On November 27, 2007, a First Information Report was lodged with the Police in Mohammadpur Police Station by Mir Mohammad Jainul Abedin Shibli, Deputy Director, the ACC, alleging that when I was the State Minister for Planning in Sheikh Hasina's government, I had approved a proposal for printing questionnaires for the census of 2001 by a private printing press, though there was a printing press installed in the Bangladesh Bureau of Statistics, the government's arm for conducting the census. It was alleged that the proposal was made by the then Secretary of the Statistics Division of the government in collusion with three other officers of the Division. In approving this proposal, it was alleged I made the government incur an additional expenditure that was presumably misappropriated by me and other accused.

The allegation was utterly baseless and false inasmuch as (i) the printing press of the Bureau of Statistics was not capable of printing all the census questionnaires before the time of census fixed by the cabinet; (ii) the census could not be postponed, as it was designed to cover remote hill tracts and coastal areas and the more than 100 enclaves located within the Indian territory requiring the consent of the government of India to cover them under the census on a specific date already fixed; (iii) the private printer's rate per printing was the lowest and (iv) no other government or semi-government press was capable of printing these machine-readable questionnaires. The case was filed under Sections 409, 418, 420 and 109 of the Penal Code and also under Section 5(c) of the Prevention of Corruption Act, 1948.

I knew this was done at the machination of a discontented officer Syedur Rahman of the Bureau of Statistics, who bore grudge against all of us accused because of a departmental disciplinary action that had been taken against him. As the story went, an officer of the Army working in the ACC was his close relative and both conspired to hew out this case to show their power and invulnerability. Initially I was not shown arrested in this case. But when the Investigation Officer went to the Judicial Magistrate for permission to interrogate me on this case, the police officer assigned to the court, known as the General Register Officer under his own handwriting added a sentence of request showing me alone as arrested and the Judicial Magistrate knowingly or unknowingly of the implication, signed the paper on the margin which showed me arrested in the case file.

For interrogation about this case, on the basis of the order of the Magistrate, Investigation Officer would have gone to the Kashimpur Jail where I was incarcerated. In a show of might, in collaboration with the Inspectorate of Prison, instead he asked me to be present in the Dhaka Central Jail. So in the rattling prison van I was transported to the Dhaka Central Jail one fine morning, made to wait from 10:00 in the morning to 3:30 in the afternoon, when the Investigation Officer arrived to interrogate me. With patience, I explained to him the census operation, formulation of machine-readable questionnaires, time constraint involved in training non-departmental personnel and the constraints about covering the remote areas and enclaves where our people could go only with the consent of the government of India and the lowest cost delivery by the printer in question. He was satisfied with my explanations and said he knew there were no elements in the case to proceed with it, except for pressure exerted by someone from the army.

Sometime in June 2008, a few days after I had undergone a thyroid operation and been recuperating in the Bangabandhu Sheikh Mujib Medical University Hospital in Dhaka, the same Major Kamruzzaman along with Rahela Begum, an Investigation Officer of the ACC saw me in my cabin. The Major told me that they had not accepted the report on the case by the earlier Investigation Officer of the ACC. It was stated in the report of the earlier Investigation Officer of the ACC that there was no incriminating evidence in the case against me and other officers of the Bureau of Statistics. Rahela Khatun was appointed as a new Investigation Officer to reinvestigate into this. Rahela Khatun was also the investigation Officer investigating into the asset statement furnished earlier by Sitara. I saw a scheming connection between Rahela's twin assignments. However, I kept silent and waited for the Major to tell me why they had come to visit me in the hospital.

"I would ask you three questions about the case of the Bureau of Statistics," stated the Major rather ceremonially.

"I hope, you will ask me questions that I can answer easily," I wanted to cut through the discomforting surroundings, wiping some sludge from my eyes.

"Why could not you postpone the census date so that the Bureau's own press could print the questionnaires?"

"I could not, for it was beyond me: first the date of census was fixed by the cabinet on the recommendation of the National Statistical Council. I was not competent to change the decision of the cabinet; second, census work was to be completed through temporary workers drawn from government and non-government teachers, students of colleges and employees of other government departments and non-government organizations. They were trained and assigned to be on thousands of selected spots throughout the country, including remote areas of Chittagong Hill Tracts and the coastal belt and the enclaves within the Indian territory on a date already fixed. Once a particular date was fixed, it was very difficult, almost impossible, to change it and roll back the arrangements. We could not expect to shift the date for covering the enclaves with the government of India very easily." I explained. The Major thought for a moment. Rahela Begum took notes. And then the Major asked,

"From records we have, we see you had given approval of the proposal to print the questionnaires from private printers on the very same day it was put up to you."

"Correct. It was always my aim and attempt to give decisions on files on the very same day these were sent to me. I always believed in expeditious decisions. You may note, when I was in charge of the Planning Ministry, the rate of implementation of the Annual Development Plan was the highest since 1975. Without giving expeditious decisions, this would not have been achieved," I explained, keeping my cool.

The Major stood up, extended his right hand to shake mine and took leave with silent Rahela. A realization rolled through my mind that all these cases, one after another, on frivolously false grounds were being filed not to lose grasp of the terrain to hunt me down. I wondered at the tireless efforts of the young Major to this end. "Could he succeed as an element in the scheme for fulfillment of the unbridled ambition of the few with the barrel of the gun in their hands?" I asked myself and wondered. In the worst example of tyranny of the Nazis, almost till the last, they could go ahead and stand up with the evil design because they could motivate, rightly or wrongly, the young Germans to die for their fatherland and its Fuhrer. Would this Major be willing to die for the power that he was representing and serving? I could not entertain the notion that the vision of a few half-educated brutes with the power of guns in their hands would be able to make their vision of the society prevail and to erase decades of sacrifices, trials and errors on our march to the goals of freedom for the country, individual liberty and other human rights.

(4)

In the meanwhile, unable to control spiraling prices and to resolve shortage of power and fertilizer, the regime came up with a proposal that in our assessment was driving the spear deep into the wounded prey that was our economy. Chief Advisor Fakhruddin announced that to the end of making both milk and honey flow into every home, his government would constitute an advisory body named Better Business Forum and publish Citizen's Charters for every public department and organization. The Better Business Forum would advise the government to better the business environment and to encourage private enterprise to spearhead growth. It would be constituted of businessmen and professionals involved in the field. The Citizen's Charters for all government departments and organizations would list every service to which citizens were entitled from them. This would be a long step forward towards good governance, boasted Fakhruddin and his cronies.

For almost a fortnight every night, in mostly dark corners of the verandah in our prison building, we sat and conversed on Better Business Forum and the Citizen's Charter. The conversation was more or less a runaway, bantering about the benefits to the economy from this government, bound by ignorance as well as inexperience.

"How better will be business with fetters around the businessmen," Salman started the thematic evocation.

"With Salman, me, Hashem, Mintoo and others in jail, with a thousand others trying to defy the hungry onslaught of the Task Force, how does business becomes better?" asked Lotus-Kamal.

"Does not Fakhruddin know that thousands of roadside bazaars and hats where small businessmen used to sit with their wares have been banged out by the Task Force?" I asked.

"If the mother-fuckers dig into bank accounts of anyone who has shone and rose in business, how the hell will business grow?" wondered Hashem.

"Do you know that a Task Force has been deployed to patrol the winding alleys of Khatungonj in Chittagong to force selling of soybean oil and milk powder at prices fixed by them? How can those phonies fix prices without finding out import prices?" Engineer Mosharaf wanted to know.

"Better business means both privatization and deregulation. Both privatization and deregulation imply impediments to aggressive and insinuating actions of the local Task Force — even the government leaders. They cannot do it," commented A. K. M. Mosharraf.

"Does better business mean banning trade unionism, not protecting labor, and increasing unemployment coupled with decreasing wages?" wondered Kader.

"Passing one punishing law after another, arresting people at will, silencing voices that express free will and thinking — are not these enough of a citizen's charter proposed by Fakhruddin and company?" asked Nasim. Nerves threatened to overwhelm Nasim when he tried to add something else.

"God does not love oppressors; God does not tolerate the liars," opined Mufti Shahid.

"Citizen's charter — a smelly hiccup in the political landscape — one cannot fool the people with such gimmicks," Dulu commented.

"When he is talking about better business forum and citizen's charter, Fakhruddin is echoing a low and guttural moan of the World Bank where he worked the better part of his life," I concluded.

As days went by almost nothing came out of the Better Business Forum. Business throughout the country was dull, bearish and fearful. A number of government departments and organizations published their full-page citizen's charters as paid advertisement in national dailies, but these could not halt the steady plunge of public service anywhere. The result was best permeated when the Chief Advisor was reported to have urged his security personnel to plan and implement his movements in ways so as to cause the least disturbance or stoppage of normal vehicular and pedestrian movements on the capital's roads. The sun of prudence of those at the helm of affairs traveled low and dipped beneath the horizon of common man's understanding. Not even paid and loyal columnists of the government came out with half-assed remediation of the themes of Better Business Forum and Citizen's Charter. Specially in the constricting socio-political environment of the emergency rules, the concept of Citizen's Charter sounded like a cruel joke on people's rights and the ruler's responsiveness and accountability.

Another joke that emitted from the regime was the Truth Commission. It was announced with indentations of both pomposity and distasteful munificence that a Truth Commission would be set up to expedite squeezing out the truth from those who had committed dishonesty and corruption. As proposed, anyone arrested or being hounded for such a crime, except those against whom charge-sheets had already been submitted, or trial taken up or who had already been convicted could appear before the Truth Commission, surrender his dishonestly earned assets and seek forgiveness. The Commission if satisfied with his submission could let him go free on the condition that he would not be able to seek election to a public office for the next five years. As the report went, amongst others, Barrister Rokanuddin Mahmud and Advocate Anisul Huq were assigned by the regime to draft the law setting the Truth Commission to realize these objectives. As we could see from the verandah of the third floor of the division building of the jail, the horizon was obstructed by buildings with their muted and still appearance; such was reflective of dull business all around. Truth extractable through the Commission at the behest of merchants of falsehood was an idea turned out dizzy with improbability.

"I did not steal anything; I earned my money in lawful way. Why should I go to the Truth Commission and say that my earnings in part were dishonest?" blared out Ali Asgar Lobi.

"I will go and convince the Commission that all my earnings were honest and tax paid and I will get out of this hell," Lotus-Kamal conjured up truthfully in support of the Truth Commission and announced.

"Do you realize that your admission before the Truth Commission will be an admission of guilt of which you are not liable?" I pointed out in smiling bemusement. "Liberty in that case will be traded for loyalty to the beach-combers of illegitimate power. Will you want this to be on your conscience?" I added and asked.

"Truth Commission — well it is traitorous rubbish. You should not touch it with a barge pole — use your oars to keep far away from it as fast as you can row." Salman said most decisively.

The Truth Commission that was so designed was not like the Truth Commission formed in South Africa for bringing and sustaining national reconciliation. This sounded more like a process of self-criticism forced out before a committee of the partisans to punish and plunder an accused in lieu of jailing or executing him as was practiced in Mao's China during the counter-productive Cultural Revolution. Everyone, at the end of at length deliberations, agreed that the Truth Commission was in fact a trap into which no one in his good senses should step. And everyone wondered how lawyers like Barrister Rokanuddin Mahmud and Advocate Anisul Huq could be associated with the framing of this trap. Was not Barrister Rokanuddin the pivot in finding out, complaining against and finally ousting unceremoniously a judge of the High Court Division for taking bribes? Was not Anisul Huq a worthy son and a successor of Advocate Serajul Huq who was the first person to charge Khandker Mustaq Ahmad publicly in Bangabhaban, why he had killed Bangabandhu? Advocate Anisul Huq was meek and soft-spoken, and yet on a number of occasions, in the electronic media he justified the formation of the Truth Commission by the regime. Barrister Rokanuddin Mahmud with unfailing flair and style, however, did not do so, according to the knowledge of us who were in jail.

13 Life in Kashimpur Jail

(1)

Very promptly the jail administration received the operational part of the judgment on me. Given that I was sentenced for rigorous imprisonment for three years and simple imprisonment for ten years to be administered consecutively in addition to fine and forfeiture of assets adjudged as disproportionate to my known income, the jail administration assigned me labor or rigor as a gardener within the jail. When he received the "ticket" for such assignment the morning after the operational part of the judgment was announced by the more partisan than the illiterate-in-law-and-accounting judge, the jailor gave me the assignment to plant, hoe, water, dress-cut the shrubs and mulch the flower-beds starting and ending with croaking of frogs at sunup and sundown.

When I received the ticket for assignment, I laughed aloud. Here was I, a person trained in Economics, at Ph.D. level in the U.S. and having served as Secretary to the government and the State Minister for Planning assigned to rhyme with croaking of frogs, perpetrating the injury wrought on myself by the degenerated judicial-administrative system of the country. Everything in the system was now run according to the law of terror, never knowing justice or milieu for peace and prosperity. The system celebrated any winner, any strongman no matter who he was or how he won or acquired strength. It was a darkness, menacing and terrifying and yet glowering over the shroud of meanness. I wrote a note to an American friend of mine, observing that an economist trained with aid received from the U.S.A. had now been turned into the most qualified gardener in the jail of the country that received the aid. I managed to get the letter smuggled out under the ruddy, ugly faces of the jail guards. As the administration had never been short of cunning solutions, after a week or so my assignment was changed. I was ticketed to suffer rigorous imprisonment looking after the jail's library containing 69 unreadable, dog-eared books and pamphlets.

Suffering rigorous imprisonment, I had more insights into the lives and livings of the common prisoners. They were huddled in groups of 25 to 30 in a room 20 feet in breadth and 25 feet in length, *i.e.*, in 660 sq. ft. or about 16 sq. ft. of living-space per person on average. Toilets and baths, more often than not, waterless and odorous, were at one end of a floor consisting of 15 such rooms. On one floor thus lived about 450 inmates with facilities for pissing and shitting in two latrines and using four taps without basin or shower. The "chow" at breakfast consisted of one heavy, round leavened bread or *ruti* with two grams of cane-gur or molasses. As the *ruti* was heavy, supposed to be of 30 grams each, it was mostly half-baked. The *ruti* was often made of rotten and odorous flour. The breakfast was brought in large flat wooden baskets and buckets, baskets containing *rutis* and buckets, cane-gur, accompanied by a thousand gloating flies attempting to feast on them. The breakfast "chow" was brought in by selected servile convicts and kept outside at the entrance of the relevant prison building. The inmates lined up before the arrival and took the chow one at a time, exchanging insults and obscenities with each other, probably in their effort to distract their thoughts from the quality and quantity of the nutrients brought for them.

Morning chow over, the prisoners were divided into categories. In the first one, from amongst a total of 2,500, about 50 were chosen on the basis of gratification in one form or other received by the jail guards and the deputy jailors or the prisoners assessed of misconduct the previous day for an audience with the Superintendent or in his absence the Jailor. To the north of the "division" building and at the southern end of the largest vegetable patch within the four walls, there was a covered meeting space without walls; the floor was brick-built, the concrete ceiling posted high on eight concrete pillars. There on the southern end on a cushioned chair with a mid-size veneer-less wooden table in front, sat the Superintendent. On his one side sat a deputy jailor with a register noting punishment and decisions excepting caning. Caning, I was told was not noted, as the law had made it illegal. First he adjudicated on the complaints against the prisoners. With a minute or two of an opportunity to explain his conduct, the prisoner was awarded punishment with caning, push-ups, two hands holding two ears, reduction of diet, solitary confinement for some days, back bashing, slapping on the cheek, deduction of remission of sentences, and very rarely, severe scolding (such as calling names like mother-fucker and sister-fucker). Such obscene name-calling was a common parlance of the jail. Then came the turn of the applications: a letter to go out to home, a transfer to another jail near home or a petition to be forwarded to the court of law, a request for transfer to the jail infirmary, or an appeal to change rooms to avoid the clutches of sodomists. The Superintendent's audience was on average over in less than two hours, as by 9:30 in the morning the heat from the sun became unbearably intense.

In the second category, about 300 were grouped in three or four teams and led to vegetable patches and flower beds. There in groups of three and four, they shoveled and mulched soil, sowed seeds and planted saplings, watered, dressed and harvested and gathered. In these groups, I found the prisoners not very intense in grief, at times happy and laughing while working in quiet, humble and pliant ways under the scowling supervision of havildars and their cronies known as mates. I was amazed to see how efficiently and quickly these groups worked, even under the fierce rays from the clear sky or the rain falling in sheets from the dark clouds above. Rain or shine they persevered in silence, with calloused hands but pleasure of creation right in front of their eyes. I did not hear name-calling in these groups. I found havildars chewing *paan*[38] under shade trees in a relaxed mood and their cronies exchanging laughs and jokes without profane expletives. The reason probably was that most of the prisoners in these groups came from the rural areas with agricultural practice in their flesh and blood. To me it was a colossal wastage of their skills and productivity as farmers and tillers. A system of allowing them to go out on parole after some time would perhaps have been a more socially prudent and productive way to use the talents and sweat of these creative people.

In the third category, were the cleaners, a hundred of them distributed in groups of ten or so, assigned to clean the pathways, drains and the sewers of the jail. These were comparatively dirty jobs for which the less favored or disliked convicts were selected and they used to do their tasks reverting to wise silence to avoid offensive name-calling and even contemptuous beatings by sticks by the havildars. They used to work sullen-faced in the blazing sun or biting sheets of rain, all without shoes, umbrella or raincovers of any sort. The convicts of this category used to work both in the morning and the afternoon.

The fourth category consisted of skilled convicts looking after the maintenance of water supply lines, electric wires and fixtures, repair of bedsteads and other wooden furniture, and serving as

[38] Betel leaf, a mild narcotic, popularly supposed to aid digestion.

attendants to patients in the jail infirmary, cooks and headload carriers. In this group the most sought after job was that of cooks; they had enviable opportunities to feed themselves whenever and whatever quantity they wished. Cooking started at 6:00 in the morning and continued till 5:00 in the afternoon without any break.

The midday "chow" consisting of fatty rice, a hodge-podge of unidentifiable vegetables and lentils in almost unlimited quantity of boiled water was similarly taken to the entrance of each building and distributed into enamel plates and bowls carried by selected convicts. It was served between 11:30 to 12:30 noon. After the midday meal, except the third category of convicts assigned mostly as cleaners, others did not have much to do. They gossiped, loitered, and at times fought amongst themselves within their assigned precincts. The evening meal consisting on most days of two pieces of *ruti* (leavened bread of flour) of medium-size and weight and *dal*, somewhat more visible in the water in which it was mixed when given before sundown. Two times a week, once in midday and the other in the evening, the chow officially consisted of two grams of fish or meat each thrown about in a cauldron of vegetables of the cheapest kind. Either because of smallness in size or over- or under-cooking, neither meat nor fish could be identified in definite shapes or tastes.

Given the bland nature of food, there was always demand for green chilies and onions amongst these convicts. These they used to smuggle in through their visitors; a small quantity from the kitchen of the "division" building, contingent on acquaintance or friendship with cooks and attendants working there found their way out for the convict's consumption. Being food by definition, the guards were lax in preventing their coming in from outside and we the "division" prisoners also looked the other way when we saw some convicts hurrying in and out of our kitchen with something hidden in their *lungis*. Cooked food from the visitors was not officially allowed in; fruit and dry food were. In case of both, however, the guards needed to be gratified. Once in, an inmate used to share the acquisition or the gift with all others living in the same cell.

(2)

Outside the jail premises there was a canteen. This was set up with formal official sanction. The canteen sold edibles, toiletries, medicine and clothes. The inmates were allowed to buy these out of money given to them by their visitors. Prices charged for items sold were about double of the free market shops, but here availability was the matter of consideration. We were told profit earned by the canteen was used for welfare of the jail employees. The jail guards, however, always complained, they did not receive anything from the canteen's profit.

Grief, drudgery, insolence and depression had created a large demand for *ganja* or hashish, and phensidyl,[39] in addition to cheap cigarettes and *bidis*[40] in the jail. These were smuggled in through visitors in connivance with jail guards and at high cost to the convicts. In addition to cash transaction with the jail guards, at times such things passing inside on credit was also practiced. If the credit remained outstanding more than a fortnight then the jail guards used to catch the defaulter "red-handed" on an alleged offense, take him to the audience of the Superintendent or the jailor borne on high chairs and have them punished with caning, short diet, isolated living and also through reduction of remission in the length of sentences already attained on account of good conduct in the past. These punishments were absorbed in silence by the convicts despite their sharp impact in physical terms. Those who could not gratify the guards, in their frenzy to be "high," as habit wanted, devised newer and inconceivable ways to bring their "medicine" and *masala*[41] in. Once a convict of over 50 years in age, stout in appearance and docile in demeanor was found to have brought *ganja* in plastic drug tubes pushed inside his anus.

TV and one-band radio were allowed inside the room of the ordinary convicts as well. I found quite a number of TVs, mostly small ones, in their cells with jutted out antennas. But these could be tuned to only the BTV; connections to other channels through cables or dishes were not allowed. In evenings, when popular soaps were shown at times, there were crowds in front of TVs. Almost never I found the crowd when news was telecast by the BTV; I asked a few about their abhorrence of the BTV's news. They said the BTV's newscasts were mostly false and unappealing. Instead they crowded to listen to news broadcast of the VOA and the BBC. I heard more often than not, convicts booing in unison whenever Dr. Fakhruddin, Barrister Moinul Hossain and General Moin U. Ahmed came alive on the BTV. It was perhaps a reflection of an abominable hatred for and the shame of the ad-

---

[39] Cough syrup. It is often abused as a narcotic.

[40] A type of cheap cigarette common in rural areas, used by both men and women.

[41] Spices and flavorings. Aromatic vegetables such as onions and garlic are also considered "masala."

ministrative-judicial system they represented and of which most of the convicts became victims. Some talked about injustice, false framing, shoddy adjudication, price spirals and other such matters loudly and in the open, without a twinge of fright overpowering the contents of their melancholy memory.

In the jail I found one Zamir who played a flute. I heard his flute one evening after sundown, coming on its melodious sound from the first story of the prison's Padma building. A few days after, in the shade of a coconut grove to the west of the jail's infirmary, I found him sitting with a flute with eyes closed and deep in thought or dream. Carefully avoiding sound of footfall, I went near him and stood by. After about 10 minutes he, a man of about 30, in a *lungi* around his loins and a white *fatua*[42] above, opened his eyes, saw me the convict in charge of library but still living in the division building and tried to stand up hiding his flute. I touched his shoulders, pressed him down to sit in the grove and asked him to play. With some hesitation, he started playing closing his eyes. It was a profound serenity that he created — a true delight to my ears, tenderly touching my sense of a radiant and lovely tune. I now gazed at the sky between him and the coconut branches and found in that cloudy afternoon, the earth mingled with what was sublime and above us. When after about 30 minutes he stopped, I asked him,

"Where did you learn to play flute?"

"I just picked it up from my father," he said.

"Where is your father now?"

"I do not know."

"Why are you here in jail?"

"I do not know."

"What? How did the police and magistrate find you?"

"While playing the flute by the roadside on the bank of the river Bangshi, one evening, I fell asleep. The next thing I knew, I was surrounded by six policemen, taken to the police station and accused of persecution of a woman I never met."

I understood. More than anyone else perhaps, I knew how oppressive the typical policemen were in our society, and how callous, and at times fearful and pliant, our magistrates have allowed themselves to become. I recalled one Captain Aziz of the army who played flute and made out tapes and discs of some of his tunes. Later he left the army, concentrated on playing flute and became known as Ustad or maestro Aziz. I loved Aziz's mu-

[42] A man's garment resembling a sleeveless shirt.

sic. I found another sprouting up as maestro Aziz in the Kashimpur Jail. I decided, I would find out what could be done to let out the musical talent in him, to free him out into a world where a freeman would not feel like dying.

(3)

After being freed from the jail five years back, I had read Kiran Bedi's *It's Always Possible*. Kiran was a well-known police officer of India. For her straightforwardness and honesty, despite merit, she was thrown out of the main ladder of her career and appointed to a dismal position: Deputy Inspector General of Prison, the Tihar Jail of Delhi. Tihar, was infamous as a jail. Bursting with thugs, thieves, political activists, brokers, students, smugglers and prostitutes, with dilapidated buildings dating from the Raj, unbridled corruption of the jailors and frequent infighting amongst the inmates, it was a hell, where one could burn in fire with tears unable or insufficient to put the fire of the forbidden deeds out. Kiran took it as a challenge to reform the system, move the fire out of the hell.

In the light of Kiran's programs and attainments in the Tihar jail, as a convict in the Kashimpur Jail, I thought, to start with, the following should be the elements of an effective reform here:

(1) Participation of inmates in kitchen management through a committee of ten members;
(2) Participation of inmates in management of the infirmary of the jail through a committee of five members;
(3) Implementation of an individual and collective awareness creating and raising initiative; this would arouse a collective consciousness against criminality and in favor of correction; arrangement of lectures by social reformers and religious leaders coupled with teaching of correct religious practices would constitute definite parts of this initiative;
(4) Skill development in fields like carpentry, electric and electronic repairs, tailoring, cooking and kitchen management, para-medicine and medical technology, auto-driving and repair, plant grafting and nursery raising, etc;
(5) Arranging programs with the National University for education beyond SSC [10th Grade] level, in addition to provision of facilities for primary and secondary teaching where needed; and
(6) Discipline management in association with a committee of inmates.

I discussed these reform measures with a member of inmates, both convicts and under-trial prisoners and received enthusiastic support. I deliberated on these before some divisional prisoners and political detainees. They gave their enthusiastic agreement. Then I took it up with the Superintendent and the Jailor. Their response was swathed in mute silence; they thought these measures would be a challenge to the authority they had been exercising on these emaciated mute bodies, with obedience bordering on slavery.

Then one evening I took it up with the DIG Major Shamsul Haider Siddiky. He heard with patience, asked wherefrom he could get a copy of Kiran Bedi's book and said he would look into it. But then perhaps it was forgotten like a flicker of a lantern blown out by a gust of wind of indifference. I arranged to send him a copy of Kiran's book, along with the one that I had written when I was incarcerated in the Dhaka Central Jail in 2002 by the BNP-Jamaat coalition government. But I could not make the shutters of windows of their minds flap or cross the threshold of the gate of their inner administration. Then one evening when I was strolling on walkways by the side of vegetable patches in front of the division building, a havildar walked by and whispered, "Sir, please do not talk about your reform programs."

"Why?" I asked.

"The administration thinks your program will lead to a revolt, a collapse of their system." He answered.

"How do you know?"

"I was in Dhaka yesterday; I heard this eavesdropping into an informal meeting of the officers in the DIG's office. Some of them said you should be transferred to Dinajpur or Khagrachari jail so that these ideas do not spread out."

"I see. Thank you."

As a convict, I could not be firm and unwavering with ardor and expectation. I realized that in prisons the reforms would have to be initiated largely from outside and in the dignity of freedom. Justice does not easily and quickly emanate out of a cesspool where victims of injustice were interned and do not have a say.

(4)

It took me a number of days to brood over the failure in bringing about change in the life of the prisoners. But I thought an initiation of change from outside, once I would be out of these four walls of indignity and inaction, could come through forming and operation of an NGO aimed at the welfare of the prisoners and protection against injustice. In my mind, I made a head start about what needed to be done; the foremost of all that I listed as reform measures to the jail administration would be legal aid to the innocent and the poor and collective watch on corrupt judges and the police. I decided the NGO would be called "Justice," and funded locally. I would ask all inmates now in the division building, incarcerated on grounds of social and political opposition to illegitimate and unbridled ambition of a few with clubs in their hands, to contribute to the initial capital fund, estimated at about Tk. 50 lacs. I would provide the office space downstairs in my Banani residence. As we would take up cases, spread elements of consciousness about the existing injustice and the restlessness with an obsession to justice, prisoner by prisoner and step by step, resources and support would be forthcoming and we would be able to overcome the inevitable resistance to improving our vision, strengthening our capability and broadening our action. That would be our social entrepreneurship to change the kind of society in which we lived.

While jotting down the salient points of "Justice" as an NGO during these days, I read Joseph E. Stiglitz's, *Globalization and Its Discontents*. Stiglitz had won the Nobel Prize in Economics in 2001. He was a renowned Professor in Columbia University; he had served as the Chief Economic Advisor of the World Bank. While in the World Bank, he saw firsthand the devastating effects that globalization, free trade and integration of national economies, had wrought on the least developed countries, especially the poor eking out their living there. After a thorough and thoughtful analysis of various aspects of free trade, Stiglitz concluded quite tersely:

> ". . . for millions of people globalization has not worked. Many have actually been made worse off as they have seen their jobs destroyed and their lives become more insecure. They have felt increasingly powerless against forces beyond their control. They have seen their democracies undermined and their cultures eroded." (Stiglitz, Joseph E., *Globalization and its Discontents, Norton*, 2002, p. 248).

Observing the opening up of our borders in the name of free trade and non-intervention in the market in the face of unabated price spirals, unemployment and withering of investment under the cover of free enterprise, a few shoeshine boys of the regime, who had earlier worked in the World Bank and related organizations, now called "clerks" of international financial organizations by some leaders of the Awami League, seemed to be on a destructive path. This was a path about the danger of which another poverty guru from Columbia University, Jeffrey Sachs, under whose influence the Poverty Reduction Strategy Papers had been prepared and revised here and elsewhere, gave further warning, but to no avail. Earlier in freedom, I had read Sachs' *The End of Poverty,* which in my assessment was a seminal work on the subject.[43]

Sitara had sent me Stiglitz's book. I had read Jeffrey Sachs before I was interned. Now in the jail on three evenings I discussed their diagnosis and therapies with Salman, Lotus-Kamal and A. K. M. Mosharraf all of them having hands-on experience with industrialization and development work in this country. Over the melancholy lowing of cattle outside the jail walls in the dusk, an unanimity in our views emerged, whipping and howling out doubt. The shoeshine boys had already stunted the growth of private enterprise in the country; they did not realize as yet, that their failure lay in their inability to see and hear the reality amidst cheers and trillings resounded by bands of sycophants and hired pseudo-intellectuals.

"How long can these hypocrites last?" I asked in desperation, keeping the looming trouble in sight.

"Not long; this is an untenable, impossible situation," observed Salman in a grave voice.

---

[43] The only thing needed in the work of Sachs and Stiglitz is recognition and advocacy of removing artificial barriers that inhibit or prevent ordinary people from participating fully in the free market as both producers and consumers, and as direct owners of the means of production as well as suppliers of labor. Such are the recommendations of the Center for Economic and Social Justice (CESJ) in Arlington, Virginia, U.S.A, outside the nation's capital, Washington, DC. CESJ has contributed a number of very thoughtful books and papers on the subject of overcoming world poverty. Its treatment of the subject from a natural law perspective makes CESJ's "Just Third Way" adaptable and applicable in any economy that recognizes universal moral principles, as written by God and self-evident to every human heart. For writings on the "Just Third Way," see *Curing World Poverty: The New Role of Property* (1994), John H. Miller, editor; *Capital Homesteading for Every Citizen* (2004), Norman G. Kurland, Dawn K. Brohawn, and Michael D. Greaney; *In Defense of Human Dignity* (2008), Michael D. Greaney. Special note should also be made of two very important books by the late lawyer-economist Louis O. Kelso and Aristotelian philosopher Mortimer J. Adler: *The Capitalist Manifesto* (1958) and *The New Capitalists* (1961), as well as William J. Ferree's pamphlet, *Introduction to Social Justice* (1948). Many of these books are available free in electronic format from www.cesj.org.

"I do not hear receding footfalls of the demons, the sons-of-bitches. No, it will not be easy to drive away the demons, the sons-of-bitches," observed a somewhat despondent Lotus-Kamal.

"They will be mired in their own shit. I had seen Ershad in a hilarious mood even days before his downfall. The trouble with these demons is that they don't, they can't see the writing on the wall," said Mosharraf who had been quite close to the country's former dictator, General Ershad.

"Wait and see. Don't forget, evil never tires of its pleasure," I wanted to shroud my thought in an abstract manner, as the horizon twinkled with lights of neighborhoods still in freedom.

(5)

Of the bands of sycophants, none was more patronized than one Dr. Ferdous Ahmed Qureshi. As the story had it, he had been an ardent activist of the BNP. For his anti-party work, he was earlier expelled from the BNP. Despite being an ardent party worker, he found both time and resources to build up his business in various fields including readymade garments. He was a close relation of Lt. General Masud Uddin Chowdhury, one of the two main architects of the military-controlled government that took over Bangladesh on January 11, 2007. In all probability, he was groomed by his relative General Masud Uddin Chowdhury to found a party styled the Progressive Democratic Party (PDP) to support the caretaker government and its reform programs as pressed in by the military.

Once perched in an office in the middle of the city, Qureshi started calling himself a doctor of philosophy. Where in this world he got this earned or honorific title was not known to us. In support of the military government, the series of punishment laws passed by it, multitudes of extra-legal measures taken to cleanse public properties, areas and lands by the military and all emergency powers exercised by it, Qureshi remained unparalleled. He was after sometime followed by Major General (Ret.) Ibrahim with his Bangladesh Kalyan Party (BKP).

Compared to Qureshi, Ibrahim was a slow traveler but treading the same path. Almost at the same time appeared Shawkat Nilu, an expelled activist of Ershad's Jatiya Party, who thought scavenging behind the military-backed government with sporadic cawing like a crow would yield him something on which to live and thrive. And then there were Dr. Kamal Hossain expecting to be the Prime Minister under a military President and General Ershad lusting for a feast of the Presidency like crows do for locusts when they go on fighting with each other. In our assessment within the Kashimpur Jail, we found Dr. Badruddoza and Dr. (Colonel) Oli Ahmed with their respective cohorts playing at opportunism with bleating of sheep facing the stick or the staff of the olive-uniformed shepherd. And of course there were donkeys running for carrots in the two major political parties, who needed to be corralled and kept in animal folds to prevent their division, as schemed by the military with their shoeshine boys in the front.

Living in jail without access to full information about the rest of society, I was not surprised when I found Fakhruddin's government could not draw up a development plan for the economy. In my assessment a coordinated plan of action for (i) food security ii) education and health care (iii) expansion and maintenance of infrastructural facilities and funding support to private enterprise and (iv) initiation of a social safety net were called for. In action and reactions, pronouncements and utterances, the caretaker government appeared to be innocent of any proactive thought and planning about these matters. With a highly touted "zero tolerance" for corruption, the government of the day was oblivious of a simple truth: toeing the line for fulfillment of personal ambition and interest and doing nothing for development and wellbeing of the people was the worst form of corruption of any government in any society at any time in history.

One morning, as the sun rose over the high walls, sitting on the verandah, we witnessed the signs of a killing or suicide. Outside the southeastern corner of the jail's perimeter, almost by the side of the high walls, in a thatched hut with a small yard full of mango, jackfruit and *shimul* trees and a grove of banana plants, lived a couple. We did not see a child playing at any time in the yard and thought the couple was childless. The husband, in his 30s, went out with a handcart every morning almost immediately after sunup and returned before sundown, washed by the water drawn from a worn out tubewell and then draped himself into a fresh *lungi* held by his wife, standing by with a smile of satisfaction and with her long braids loose and swinging in the gentle breeze. They were poor but in love and happy. As we could see in the dusk their home was quiet and peaceful, twinkled with the light of a lantern, unable to disturb their togetherness beyond a point in the darkness where night gathered around the household.

That morning we saw the cart lying idle on the southwestern corner at the edge of the road, the yard forlorn with a worn out printed *sari* flapping in the wind and a seeming pall of gloom all around. At about 10:00, we found about 10 to 15 people gathered in the yard to the north of the hut, the women among them weeping and wailing. After about an hour, ten policemen in a van arrived, took out a dead body shrouded in a *kantha*[44] and then left the place. Through the grapevine of the jail guards, we heard the wife, after a fight with the husband, committed suicide in the night. When the husband became aware that his wife was no longer, he stealthily left the hut to avoid arrest by the police. Except for neighbors, all poor and hardy, the couple did not have any relations around.

We were told that about five years back they came to this place from some river-eroded village of Faridpur and built their hut on that piece of land owned by an industrialist who came from the same area. It was a case of transient madness of the husband, fueled by the wife's anger about something concerning their life and living. This madness would not have taken such a toll if they were a part of society. A well-knit society is about the best institution to absorb such transient madness or fights that erupted therefrom. Rapid urbanization of the area had eroded the age-old societal fabric capable of absorbing such madness and turning the transient evil into peaceable living in calm and order.

Later we learned the origin of the fight was food; the husband could not get any work during the day. Moving from bazaar to bazaar in search of work and earning, he found his belly growling in hunger. He came back to eat something. His wife was without food from the earlier night when she had given a few morsels to her persevering loving husband. When the hungry husband wanted the starved wife to feed him, she burst out in anger and frustration. Thus unemployment coupled with the price spiral led to the fight and the suicide or murder. "Would the police, the magistrate and the society at large in their march to bury the dead, arrest and imprison the husband care to know what havoc the price spiral and unemployment caused to a loving couple, to the happiness and simple living of common people?" I wondered, feared and dreaded.

I was the Deputy Commissioner — the head of the civil administration — of greater Jessore district in the late 1970s. At that time I came to learn that the incidence of suicide per 100,000 people was highest in Jhenaidah sub-district of Jessore. I had occasion to enquire into this unusual situation. I found there a cul-

[44] A light quilt.

tural construct developed over centuries by the *Bauls*[45], which promoted indifference to worldly cause and possessions. This viewpoint, coupled with abject poverty, was behind this anti-life attitude and the proliferation of suicides that swathed the area. I thought that setting up a pro-life communication with the *Bauls* and a systematic program to lift the people out of poverty would provide the remedy. I mixed with a group of *Bauls*, both men and women, and convinced them to be somewhat more pro-life and appreciative of material things, by saying that in one way or other we had to respect people in life, in terms of material wellbeing, so as to respect them in death or the perpetual hereafter. I encouraged them to compose songs along this line and not to take life and death with indifference as they did.

To an extent, I succeeded. This effort, coupled with regeneration of irrigation from the Ganges-Kabodak canal system, contributed to production of more food grain and vegetables in the area. I found in two years, the reported suicide rate had gone down markedly. I could not keep track of the happenings after a year when I left the area on transfer. I requested that a student of sociology from the area, studying in Rajshahi University, look into this and identify more clearly the elements of change. But his joining the Revenue Service of the Republic took him off the scene. To me it appeared that despite its scarcity, we in this society did not make the best use of whatever knowledge we gather or learn in order to improve our situation.

[45] Mystics/ascetics. Bauls constitute both a religious sect and a musical tradtion used as a vehicle to express Baul thought. Baul thought has mixed elements of Tantra, Sufi Islam, Vaishnavism and Buddhism.

14 In Hospital

(1)

At about the same time the appeal was formally filed with the High Court Division, I fell ill in the Kashimpur Jail. The jail's doctor examined me, gave a number of pills, but my complaints about abdominal pain and dizzy headache throughout the day did not subside. Then on September 23, 2007, the Superintendent, on the advice of the jail physician, sent me for admission into Bangabandhu Sheikh Mujib Medical University Hospital in Dhaka.

Following the cobweb of the procedure of the jail administration, in an ambulance privately arranged and paid for, I reported to Dhaka Central Jail at 10:00 in the morning. The Dhaka Central Jail, reeking of overcrowding and associated indifference took me under its fold, arranged for three jail guards and three policemen in three hours and then sent me to the Hospital at about 1:30 in the afternoon. I reported to Prof. Anwarullah of the Neuromedicine Department, accompanied by Deputy Jailor Rafiq. Prof. Anwarullah tried to admit me, talking to various admission personnel of the Hospital but could not do anything; the admission was the responsibility of the Resident Physician, who demanded that for my admission, a mere "no objection" from the jail administration written on my letter would not do; a formal letter from the Deputy Inspector General of Prison would be required. At 2:30 in the afternoon the office of the Resident Physician would close down for the day so I would have to obtain the letter in about 40 minutes. I asked Prof. Anwarullah to leave for his home as his wife was calling him for lunch quite frequently as his office also closed down at 2:30.

I came down from Prof. Anwarullah's office located on the fifth floor in C Block without knowing what to do. If I could not get admitted that day I would have to go back to Kashimpur. And for this I would have to go to Dhaka Central Jail with the jail guards and the policemen given from there to guard me and then take a new seat and wait for a vehicle to be arranged by the jail administration for going to Kashimpur. That would take at least four hours. The deputy jailor who accompanied me, finding me in this predicament vanished. In his absence, I could talk to Bahar, a person of my area known to the DIG Prison. I asked him to come and meet me at the hospital gate, which he did in about 30 minutes. I gave him my papers and asked him to run to the Deputy Inspector General of Prison to get that precious formal letter. He went there, found the Deputy Inspector General, drafted the letter himself, obtained his approval, but then when it was being processed in the computer, the electricity went off. Then he went to an area where electricity was on, got it processed in a computer, went to the home of the Deputy Inspector General, got the letter signed by him, went to the DIG's office to get the docketing done and inscribing of the number, etc. and reported to me at about 5:00 with the letter. By that time the Resident Physician was gone for the day.

Deciding that I would spend the night on the corridor of the hospital instead of going back, I went to the prison cell of the hospital, where prisoners who fell seriously ill were treated and guarded 24 hours by the jail guards. There I found Kazi Zafarullah, another member of the Awami League's Presidium, waiting for an operation of the gall bladder. When told about my predicament, he suggested to me the way out: "Go to the Emergency which works 24 hours, report your illness with that precious letter of the Deputy Inspector General of Prison and they will admit you either into their Emergency Ward or, if a private cabin is available, into that. Tell them you will pay the rent and bear all costs of treatment."

I did as he said, found a sympathetic young physician there, who found the Resident Physician over the phone and, after a long conversation with him, sent me to the cabin block for admission. I walked back, found one Dr. Kakon in charge of the cabin block who knew about me. He admitted me into a good private cabin, showed me in and before I could settle down, came back to me and said rather regretfully that someone "up" over him wanted that I should be given a second grade cabin instead of what was allotted to me earlier. I laughed aloud: for setting up this medical university and hospital as a State Minister-in-charge, Ministry of Planning, I had given them more than what they had wanted from the government at that time and the very cabin block from which I was being shifted to a second category one was inaugurated by Prime Minister Sheikh Hasina in whose cabinet I served.

Laughing all the way, I walked to the second grade cabin no. 303, which I found quite alright for me. After all I was a prisoner, whose identity could not be erased even with the pumice stone of his earlier doings. I arranged to bring in clean sheets, towels and soap from my house at Banani and hit the bed without dinner, tired and depressed as I was. The hospital charged me for dinner that night but could not give it as the dinner trolley had left by the time I was installed in the cabin of their choice.

Next morning around 8:00 a.m. I got up from bed. A hot bath under a shower for a long 20 minutes soothed my body out of its dizziness and my depression. The attendant from my house brought me breakfast and tea; a taste of the home-cooked *paratha*[46] and egg and hot tea from a flask reminded me of life in freedom. It was like a dream where the present became the past. Around 9:00, Professor Anwarullah with five of his internees came, asked questions and noted my answers concerning symptoms of my ailments. He examined me and then ordered a series of diagnostic tests. I realized I was in good hands and, despite being imprisoned, felt I would recover. The jail administration had posted three jail guards and three policemen right in front of my cabin to guard me from escape or mischief; they came in three shifts 24 hours a day.

After blood was drawn from my neck and skull for tests, I lay down on my bed, in silence heavier than relief. I got hold of Naguib Mahfouz's *Children of the Alley*. Mahfouz, an Egyptian writing in Arabic, was awarded the Nobel Prize for Literature in 1988. *Children of the Alley* was perhaps his most famous novel, first published as early as 1959. It was translated into English by Peter Theroux in the same year. As I read, I found the translator had done a good job, making me feel that the book was originally written in English and not in Arabic. When I was through with the preface, Enayetur Rahman Bappi, Managing Director of the National TV, came and introduced himself. A prisoner like me, getting treatment in a cabin across from mine, Bappi told me how he had been tortured by the concerned Task Force while in confinement in the Dhaka Cantonment, was asked to give cooked-up evidence against himself and Mosadeq Ali Falu and, on refusal, sent to Dhaka Central Jail through the "independent" judicial magistracy. He also told me about the conduct of the jail guards

[46] A flatbread usually made with whole-wheat flour, pan fried in ghee or cooking oil, and often stuffed with vegetables, especially boiled potatoes, radish or cauliflower and/or paneer (Indian cheese).

and the police assigned to each of us and the spooks that came on regular rounds to check on them as well as on us. He advised that, despite unlawful restriction imposed by the jail guards even on our walking in the corridor in between the two lines of cabins, it would be better to comply and to keep cool; if not, there was every possibility that one would be thrown out of the hospital by the jail administration. After about 10 minutes the two jail guards assigned to him came and told him and me that we were not allowed to talk to each other. I almost shouted at them, but recalling Bappi's advice, kept my cool.

Mahfouz's *Children of the Alley* was to a great extent allegorical. Seeing themselves betrayed by regime after regime, yet in the hope of securing the future of their dreams, people bore the outrages steadfastly, taking refuge in patience. They held fast to hope and whenever they were persecuted they said injustice must have an end, as day must follow night. It was their firm belief that they would see the death of tyranny and the dawn of light and miracles. Miracles, as Mahfouz spinned his story, emanated out of understanding, realization and endeavor to keep death at length. As people lived better, Mahfouz wanted us to realize, the pain lessened fatalism, life became more valuable and every happy person wanted to fight death to keep as much of his happy life as possible.

Through one of his heroes, Mahfouz wanted us to understand that death prospered in poverty and misery. I came to like Mahfouz penning this simple but deeply touching allegory of human sufferings and strivings.

It took me a few days to finish Mahfouz's *Children of the Alley.* In between going for tests in the pathological department and enduring visits of the physicians in bands, I read, relaxed, became sorrowful at times and then rejoiced. And on my way through its pages, I recalled the life of Jarina, who had a hand in rearing all us brothers and sisters, assisting our parents.

(2)

I did not know about Jarina's life till I was about 14. Jarina was a member of our household, our family. She used to play with us as toddlers, show us various corners of the garden in our village home, bathed us and fought with anyone standing in our way or, in her assessment, likely to hurt or harm us in any way. My mother used to feed us herself and then the rest was left to Jarina under her watchful eyes. Once, for reasons I did not understand at that age, Father was very angry with her and asked her in fury to leave the house. She wept almost ceaselessly, stopping the singing of life and song in the garden house and I, in that young age, told her that if she went out, I would also go with her. Reverting to profound silence for about 30 minutes or so, she said that she would not go and would remain with us. I ran to my parents and told them so. Visibly they were relieved, their eyes shining with desperate sorrow so deep and intense was our affection. Jarina called our father, "Father" and our mother, "Mother," and persevered rain-or-shine in helping the household feed so many mouths and meet so varied needs, without any complaint or tiredness. With time not moving very quickly, we were all indeed the children of the alley, one household with twittering of birds and ringing of life and song under the unquestioned obedience to our father and silent watchful guardianship of Mother.

"Will you tell me wherefrom you came? How was your village, parents and other relations?" I asked her once, looking at the clear blue sky through the branches of trees over us.

"My home was in a village near Gouripur, near Daudkandi. I don't remember my parents — both of them died before I could understand anything of this world. We were two sisters. I was the elder, Karuna was the younger. We were brought up by my brother Shabbir. All that I remember of our home is water — flood water all around, paddy grown over water and all kinds of fish, both big and small ones swimming in and caught from the water," she reminisced.

"How did you meet my parents? Who brought you to them?"

"You remember that year of big famine? No you can't remember; you were born only the year before that," she was referring to that big famine of 1943 during the period of the Raj.

"That year, my brother could not get rice for us. The family starved for days together. At that time Father (meaning our father) was on a government job at Daudkandi. My brother brought me and Karuna to him and said he couldn't feed us; he said that we would work in Father's household if we were given just food. I was about 9 years old, Karuna was 6. Father took us inside, Mother fed us and we lived with them thereafter."

"Didn't your brother visit you after that?"

"Yes, he did. For the first few months unfailingly at least once a week, he did. Later, frequency of his visits decreased." I understood. Time blown over by the wind of need elsewhere and right before our eyes, also erases affection for near ones.

"Didn't you long for your home? Gouripur was just four miles off from Daudkandi." I wanted to know.

"Well, I cried a lot, but did not go. I did not know how to go. There was no road at that time. Besides, people were starving. Mother (*i.e.* our mother) consoled us, took good care of us, gave us clothes. We started calling her as our mother." I felt proud of my mother.

"Then?"

"Well, Father was transferred from Daudkandi to Gafargaon, Mymensingh. On our way, we went to Chandpur, to the house of the father of Mother. There, her brother's wife took a fancy to Karuna and kept her within her household. I accompanied Father and Mother to Gafargaon."

"Then?"

"Well, one day as I heard, Karuna was scolded by your maternal auntie. In a rage, she left them. I never heard of her after that."

So Jarina stayed with us, reared all of us sisters and brothers. Once of age, she was given in marriage to one Zahed Ali, who served our parents as a cook. In time a son was born to her. After a few months the son died. Zahed Ali went to Mecca for pilgrimage and never returned. We grew up under Jarina's care. Except for food and clothes, a small trunk of hers where she kept all the new *saris* given to her at festivals, she did not receive anything else. She did not need anything either. When my parents died and Jarina became old and infirm, my sister Nilufar took her to Dhaka and looked after her till death. In Nilufar's apartment, I saw her lifting Jarina in her own hands to take her to the toilet and for bath. Till her death she was cheerful, never complained and was always happy whenever she saw me or us around. How could one live a life without one's birth parents, brother and sister, so happily and without any worry? Had the world turned black to her at any time in a household that was not hers? How could a life, persevered in silence serving others, be satisfying? Lying in the hospital bed in chains and longing for my family, I wondered.

I remembered in 1974, when my father was still alive, I took her in my Volkswagen to Daudkandi and Gouripur on our way to our village home. By that time Daudkandi-Gouripur was well connected with the rest of the country by a metaled road. Busy markets replaced desolate water areas; paddy-stalks rising over the water and stretched in a mosaic of green to the horizon were no longer visible. Reaching Daudkandi, I told her where she was. She looked old, with stooped shoulders, a face full of creases. She did not believe it was Daudkandi. When Gouripur came into vision, I told her so. She looked out with disbelief. I refrained from telling her it was her home; we were almost in her home village. Reared up elsewhere, she was not in a position to recognize her own birthplace. But then when I got her near our home village, about 46 miles to the south. I did not have to tell her; she recognized everything, trees, fields, chirping birds, ponds and mosques. It was her village; it seemed that it echoed the tearing and longing going on within her chest. Her look was distinctly silent as I tried not to plumb the depths of either the cruelty or the gift and fragrance of life.

(3)

I had a history of hypertension, diabetes, IBS and mildly enlarged prostate. Following tests, the physicians started their treatment. Over a dozen pills and capsules a day were prescribed. A bland diabetic diet was fixed by the dietician. Professor Anwarullah was the lead physician. His specialty was neuro-medicine. He referred me to an urologist and to a gastroenterologist. Professor Kibria was the urologist and Associate Professor Mujibur Rahman Bhuiyan was the chosen gastroenterologist. They came to see me every morning. Slowly I started to improve. My improvement would have been speedier but for the obstruction of the jail guards. Despite prescription for a bland diabetic diet, which could not be provided by the hospital, at the beginning and thereafter sporadically, they prevented my attendant from bringing food from my house. They raised objection on one ground or other. I did not get my dinner on three nights. They expected some gratification from me. This was something to which I hated to succumb. I thought, if this was given to these minions at my level, then the State would be taking a definite turn towards a failed one. After about a month, these guards reconciled with the reality that they would not get what they expected from me and grudgingly started to abstain from creating much of any such obstruction.

The one main reason for expecting gratification was that they used to receive it from three other political prisoners having cabins on the same floor. One was Lutfuzzaman Babar, the former State Minister for Home Affairs under Khaleda Zia. He joined this floor about five days after I got a cabin on this floor. He was followed by Mosadeq Ali Falu, a former Member of the Parliament from the BNP and a very close associate of Khaleda Zia. And Falu's associate Enayetur Rahman Bappi had been here across from my room before I came. Attendants of all these three persons, moneyed as they were, did draw a schedule of rates for gratification of all jail guards and policemen working in three shifts. Thus they did not have any difficulty in getting their food and visitors inside their cabins. Their attendants knew money spoke and facilitated and they did not bother about the institutional failure as long as they succeeded in getting whatever their bosses wanted. This was an organized deception that I abhorred. At times in utter wonderment I received fruit and delicacies from their cabins without any objection from the jail guards. I hesitated to accept but always ended up not refusing. At times I felt values that I sustained and cherished were squirming out of my grasp. But being a prisoner even in the hospital shrouded my sense down to a fight for nutrition and rapid recovery. It seemed that evil never tired of its pleasure.

And evil, undulating as a charmed snake nourished in its basket, visited me in person twice as I was in the hospital. On the first occasion, as I was rising in the morning from bed with giddiness in my head from lack of sleep, the two entered with pleasant smiles. Youth, confidence and enthusiasm were apparently visible in their chests, wider than those of average Bangalis. Introducing themselves as spooks of the Forces Intelligence, and giving their names (which were not real ones, I believed), they asked me about the treatment I had been receiving and whether I wanted anything to improve and increase my medical attention and care.

"I am alright, they are taking good care of me. Thank you," I replied, matter of factly.

"This life — living in hospital and jail must be very uncomfortable for you," said one of them, who had given his name as Jainul and who smiled rather tenderly.

"It's alright with me. I have got nothing to complain of or ask for," I replied in profound serenity.

"You can do something for us, for yourself and the government, all at the same time," said the other one who had given his name as Harun, looking at me intensely.

"You had my answer earlier. What is it now?" I referred to their meeting with me in the Kashimpur Jail earlier.

"Please see this," Harun handed me a type written paper and said "Just sign this. You will have a secure future."

"I can't read; I cannot find my reading glasses. Why don't you read it aloud for me?"

He read. The text said Sheikh Hasina, when she was the Prime Minister, had asked me to sign the Ganga Water Treaty as the Indians would want it.

"That's not true. I was authorized by her to negotiate the treaty to our advantage as best as I could. Negotiation was done on an authorized brief!"

"Well, the treaty is there. What difference will it make if you sign it?"

"If it will not make any difference; why do you want me to sign this?" I showed him the paper in his hand. Then rather firmly but calmly I said,

"I will not do it. I can't do it. I can't make a false statement."

They sat silent for a while. They were almost convinced I would not succumb to the temptation thrown at me. But then hoping against hope, they said they would come again and that I should think it over for my benefit. Scowling at me with gloomy faces, they extended their hands to shake mine. I feigned looking for my glasses and kept sitting without extending my hands. They left, somewhat banging the soft wooden door of the hospital cabin. I stood up and opened the door to the back verandah. I looked at the sky through the skeins of the clouds floating above between the two high-rise structures, into one of which I was interned. The jail guards entered my cabin with thumping footfalls, found me standing on the back verandah in silence, looking upwards. Bewildered perhaps, they left after a minute or two.

I came out into the corridor in between the two lines of cabins; walked from one end to the other slowly and brooded over the loathsome cowardliness of these spooks. Bappi's wife came out of his cabin and invited me in for a cup of tea with him. I accepted gratefully; the jail guards followed and asked us to keep the door open and kept standing on the threshold. I did not tell them anything about the spooks. His wife, young sweet lady that she was, almost sobbed over Bappi's detention. I consoled her, saying that it would be over soon. In a voice that cut to the depth of her heart, she said she wanted to believe so, but could not stand the wrong done to him, to her and his families by the Task Force — the muscled arm of the illegitimate power that swathed over the land. Bappi smiled a rather pallid smile, which indicated his hope over the frustration in which he was immersed.

(4)

A few days wound by. One evening to my pleasant surprise, I found Prof. Anwar Hossain of Dhaka University and General Secretary of its teachers association in the cabin opposite to mine. He was admitted for sinusitis and infection of his eardrums. I went into his cabin and he was delighted to see me. He wanted a writing table in his cabin, which I could manage to bring in through cooperation of nurse Jahan Ara and cabin-boy Basir already quite known to me. Prof. Anwar Hossain was in prison, for alleged violation of the Emergency Powers Rules within the University area; he had protested against the beating of his students by a contingent of the army posted in the gymnasium of the University. His cabin was guarded by the police and the jail guards in the same way as mine. I talked with him for some time while the jail guards, now double in number, visibly felt uncomfortable. In a maddening calm I came back to my cabin, sat in silence for a while and then sent him some fruit through a jail guard. After some time, he came to my cabin while I was listening to our national anthem on the speaker-attached ipod that my son Joy had sent me from Boston. We stood up in silence as long as the national anthem was played.

The Ipod had over 600 songs — mostly Tagore's whom I liked. In my leisure time, when I did not feel like reading, I listened to Tagore. One of my greatest favorites was "Oh! he does not heed to my saying no, when I turn my eyes away, he says no. Oh! no." Listening to Tagore led me into deep thought. Memories from far back in time rose up with vivid particularity: our life, soil that fed us, water that quenched the thirst for the growth of people, plants and everything around. A sorrowful path in search of the meaning of life became a grand view of the sweetest things and dreams in Tagore's songs and my feelings.

As the sky surrendered to dusk and to a hundred lights of freedom outside the grilled cabin block of the hospital, it made me yearn to be a part of that pulsating mosaic of life. I recalled our visit to Jorasako's Thakur Bari and the Rabindra Bharati University in Kolkata some five years back. With respect echoing from the depth of our hearts, Sitara and I entered the *Thakur Bari*, were led to the room where the poet was born, shown his living quarters and the verandah where he used to rest and write. We were amazed at his lifelong perseverance to modernize our language and develop our culture. Nearby in Rabindra Bharati University, in rhythm with life, we sat in various classes seeing dancing being taught and singing being rehearsed and poetry under recitation in deep-set meaningful and transmitting voices. No other single person, anywhere in the world and at any time, we realized, contributed so much to his language and literature, culture and development of human values as Rabindranath did. We recalled our visits to his garden houses in Patisar and Shahjadpur, both in Bangladesh, with remnants of things with which he lived with and memories of what he took from the rain-fed soil to bloom up all that was beautiful and bounteous in our human existence. Being very conscious of the surroundings, I recited Tagore.

"You have made me endless; that is what is your mysterious art." Sitara smiled.

Beyond Anwar's cabin, a flower-like girl of 12 was the patient in cabin 305. On one mid-evening when I was taking a walk in the long corridor, I heard a girlish footfall and looked back. She came forward with a smiling face.

"My name is Isha. I am in that cabin with my parents, she said

"Where are you from?"

"Gaibandha. Can I call you uncle?"

"Yes, of course. What class do you read in?" I asked.

"Class VIII. I love to read. I think I will be a doctor," she said breathlessly.

As we walked, she told me about her school, the village shrouded in trees and fragrance, the ponds in which she bathed and swam and the twinkling horizons of a youngster's life. I was charmed by her knowledge, understanding of things and her yearning for life. Later, seemingly tired she returned to her cabin. I was joined by her mother looking older than her age, who with tearful eyes told me her daughter was a leukemia patient with very little hope for life.

"Does she know?"

"No. And please do not tell her or make her understand about her ailment."

I nodded, wondering in bewilderment. The sweet breeze of autumn could not soften the queasiness that crept into my stomach. Knowing death coming with certainty in an unbelievably short time to end the life that deserved living in surging waves of knowing and understanding things around was painful, a perilous hospitality of those without ailments and nearness to death. The sky became colorless to me; the thousand lights of freedom outside dimmed down to dismay and despairing memories.

Whenever I found time, in between visits of doctors and going for tests and Isha was out of her cabin, I went out, walked the corridor with her, talked to her, wanted to fill her soul with the warmth of a father and the pain of the knowing that very soon she would wither out, be an all-gone history, droop like petals of a wilted flower wanting to be a joy of life.

(5)

The hospital and the University appeared to me like a jungle of concrete. The University and the hospital were set up centering around the Institute of Post Graduate Medical Research set up by Bangabandhu Sheikh Mujibur Rahman in 1972. In 1998, when the then Minister for Health, Salahuddin Yusuf along with the newly-appointed Vice-Chancellor of this medical university, Prof. Quadri, met me in my capacity as the State Minister for Planning, having control over allocation for development work of the government, I gave them the money they wanted along with an additional Tk. 500 million for training their best and brightest young doctors in the West European and the North American medical schools and requested them to employ the very best architects of the country to build up their physical facilities in the prime location of the city that was theirs.

Being a prisoner patient now, seeing the structures that have gone up since then in the campus, I found they have succeeded in transforming the site into a jungle of concrete. And talking to the young doctors, I found most of them frustrated, bereft of appropriate training facilities either within the university at home or abroad. I was told, fund earmarked for higher training was mostly utilized in attending seminars abroad by the Professors, without presenting any scientific paper in most cases. The young doctors said that the University should be administered firmly by the Ministry. I said that would go against the very concept and the sprit of setting up a university for teaching and research in an unfettered environment. The responsibility of the government in this respect would be of a master facilitator of the university's activities and objectives. And the activities and the objectives would always remain the responsibility of the university's teachers and managers. They have to, therefore, assess their performance and delineate their mission and programs themselves.

Of the young doctors, I became familiar and close with amongst others, Kakon, Jafar, Shantu, Shireen, Kaneez, Shamema and Farzana. Quite often, at their leisure at late night I used to sit in the doctor's room, drink tea with them and converse about the country's situation in general and the university's problems in particular. All of them along with nurses, Jahanara, Parveen, Beauty, Mayabini and others were very attentive to my treatment and care and also keeping the jail guards at bay while food, books, papers and magazines were brought to me by my relatives.

Dr. Kakon on occasion invited me to take dinner with him, sent from his home and cooked by his mother and wife. A well-furnished cabin earmarked for VVIP patients, but remaining vacant almost all the time on the ground of its being important, was the venue where Dr. Kakon and I used to converge along with some of his friends. We gossiped and ate leisurely meals while the guards slept, closing the main entry to the floor under lock and key. On occasion arrangements were made to talk to dear and near ones home and abroad over the phone through some simple and quick technological improvisation, which the improvisers said could not easily be taped or traced to origin or destination by the government's spooks. These improvisations looked similar in ways to what I observed to have been occasionally pressed into service in Kashimpur. The caretaker government by law could wiretap all phone lines without judicial authorization and they did so as if they were administering a police State.

The improvisers talked freely with their friends overseas, placing the improvised jigs by their sets. They said, their improvisation enabled free service even from the operators abroad. But I marveled at the innovation that these young people made to beat the system they abhorred. As in the U.S., private innovators here were way ahead of the government's clustered ability to impose control and surveillance over free communication and expression. A decade back in the U.S., to control speeding on the interstate highways, the police patrol remained in ambush to pounce on the violators while the would-be-violator attached some electronic jig over his car roof to warn him about the presence of the patrol lying in concealment.

Once flagged down for slow driving and causing a jam on a fast lane by the police patrol, I was asked to drive faster without any comment on the jig that was fixed on the car roof to warn me about their presence. I was told that the jigs available freely in the open market were legal contraptions that could be used even to beat the police patrol. But that was a land of the free and the brave that practiced freedom as a self-evident truth for all persons created equal by God.

(6)

Early in the morning one day, those two Intelligence Forces spooks knocked at my door. I rose from my bed, opened the door and found them smiling politely.

"Won't you ask us to come in?" one of them asked.

"Surely," I said wiping the sleep off my eyes. They sat, putting some papers on the tea table, which I looked over.

"So you will not cooperate with us," Jainul commented.

"You know I do not cooperate with falsehood," I said.

"Cases are being prepared against your sons and wife."

"I know. Still the answer is no."

"Won't you look after the bright future of your sons?"

"They are well-educated. In our time we fought with the Pakistanis to secure our rights — rights that you enjoy and even abuse. In their time, if there be need they will fight for theirs," I replied.

"Will you give us tea?"

"I can't. I have only one cup with me as allowed by your guards," I said.

They got up and went out, banging my door shut.

One night after Ramadan, Sitara told me, when I was connected to her through the improvisation of our young folks at whom I marveled, that she would like to go for Haj from the States. I said yes and she gave me the time and day of her departure from Boston to Jeddah. On the day of her departure, around 10:00 in the morning our time, I told the two jail guards present that I would like to make a call before my wife boards the plane for Haj. I said if they did not object, I would use the mobile set of my attendant. All these days I had seen, by buying consent of the guards, other co-prisoners on this floor using phones in their rooms. My guards agreed, I made the call, wished her god speed, thanked the guards and returned the set to my attendant.

After 30 minutes, the senior of the guards entered my room without a knock and whispered that some spooks had seen me talking over the phone and they needed to be gratified. I felt insulted. I thought if at my level, I became a party to this process, I would be losing a moral right to be in politics. I said, I used the phone with their consent and I would not go for gratification. The guard went out with a gloomy face. At about 2:00 in the afternoon when I was eating my lunch, six of them entered and searched my room; they said it was on orders from above and finally brought out a mobile set from above the false ceiling of the attached bathroom. Holding the set before me, one in civvies amongst them said very politely that I should give them in writing that it was found in my room. I took a piece of paper from my table, wrote that the guards showed me a mobile set which they said they had found over the false ceiling in my bathroom, and that it was not mine and not recovered in my presence. I asked them to take the set with them with the piece of paper on which I wrote this. They went out gloating.

In the late evening, Deputy Inspector General of Prison, Major Shamsul Haider Siddiky visited me. Without being asked, I told him everything about what happened. I told him, in addition that, in the Jail Code as I knew it, there was no mention of telephone or its use by the prisoners and the place where it was found by his guards was hospital, not the jail or the prison cell within the hospital which could be considered as the jail, and I supposed it was brought by the guards themselves for my refusal to gratify them for the call I had made with their consent to my wife before she left for Haj. I said I was sorry if I caused any embarrassment to him and added at the same time, I thought I did not violate any of the provisions of the Jail Code. Major Siddiky listened with attention and left saying that he would look into it and that it should not have happened the way it did.

As days wound by, through the grapevine of the deputy jailors and guards, I came to know that those up in the prison inspectorate, after sitting and eating in a series of meetings over this, decided to send a complaint about unauthorized use of phone by me and few others to the district magistrate, Dhaka. The district magistrate reportedly did not find any provision in the Jail Code relating to use of phone by inmates, sat over it for two months or so and then sent it back to the Inspectorate to take appropriate steps as permissible under the Code. I thought that was the end of it and gave attention to treatment and prognosis of my ailments. Feebleness and sickness did not leave me, making me feel like lying on my bed during the daytime, which I had almost never done in my life. I looked at the mirror and found myself looking older than my long years — beyond the average life expectancy in Bangladesh — should have made me.

(7)

In time not given to treatment, doctor's consultation and nurse's care, I read quite slowly Tahmima Anam's first novel, *A Golden Age*. Tahmima was the daughter of Mahfuz Anam, the editor of the *Daily Star* and a Ph.D. in Social Anthropology from Harvard University. In simple and closer to the soil language, Tahmima's Golden Age was our liberation war, of its passion and revolution, of hope, faith and profound heroism. In this she spun a tale of a widow, who at the end of a shimmering soft fight for her children and the country, on December 16, 1971, in the backdrop of a pale and iridescent sky, tasted victory and determined to clutch her country's flag, hold her breath and wait for the return of her son who fought for liberation. While the earth below her shook with memories of love, affection, a little waywardness and at the top of all, glistening patriotism, she thought her journey through the fire of suffering and struggle was at its end and emblazoned contentment and satisfaction was now hers. The war that had taken so many sons had spared hers, burned so many daughters, but not hers; she did not let them die and be burnt. Remembering those days of 1971, days of persecution, determined revolt and relentless fight, of sacrifices in sweat, tears and blood, I felt proud of my inheritance. In *A Golden Age* as the freedom fighters, after winning the war, were home-bound singing Tagore, I also sang out in a deep dark night in fetters and in spite of everything, "Oh! My Golden Bengal, My love is for thee." Tahmima touched my heart. I thanked Forrest my friend for sending the novel to me.

A number of visitors came to see me in the hospital, despite the bounds of the Jail Code and its administration. My brother Dr. Jahangir visited me every Friday without fail. He cared for me in a manner the like of which I have not seen anywhere and in anybody else's case. Along with him came my two sisters, Kohinoor and Nilufar and Ishaq Sikdar, a devoted activist of the Awami League, Kachua. Most of the time they were accompanied by Dr. Shamsul Haq Bhuiyan, President of the Awami League, Chandpur. Often my nephews, Farid, Shameem and Irfan, came. Another nephew of mine, Dr. Omar Faruq, who was in charge of the Critical Management Department of BIRDEM, came twice. Dr. Arefin, my youngest brother came often. In addition a host of political activists, Shahjahan Shishir, G. M. Atiq, Shaheed B.S.C. and his wife, Bahar and his wife, Kamal Bhuiyan and his wife, Rafiq, General Secretary of the Jubo League, Kachua, Shahjahan, Shujit and others visited me. Advocates Mobarak Hossain and Fazlul Haq Sarker from Chandpur came once or twice.

More often than not, they were not well treated by the jail guards posted at my doors. Almost all of them came with fruit, soft drinks, specially made food at home as tokens of their love and respect for me. Some of them wept and said the regime colluded with the truly corrupt and harassed innocent and honest persons like me. One of the female visitors — an activist from Dhaka's Mohammadpur area — gave vent to her anguish by pulling frenziedly at her hair, almost tearing wisp after wisp.

As I came to know later, a number of visitors were not allowed to see me; I was not informed when they were coming and I was inside my cabin. Many activists wet with tears, raised questions: "Why all these miseries? Where have our dreams gone?" I always tried to console and cheer them up. But most of the time, it seemed, more than merely my being in incarceration, they did not see justice around them, experience mercy, observe dignity and never heard of honesty and sincerity of those who had imposed themselves as the rulers.

While going to various departments of the hospital for consultation, at times I could meet Salman, Lotus-Kamal, Nasim, Mufti Shahidul, Engineer Mosharraf and Kader coming for outdoor treatment from the Kashimpur Jail. The jail guards did not like these meetings, and hovered over us when we talked. As their way of sending us a message of disciplined conduct, they misbehaved with other patients we did not even know. In these meetings we exchanged notes about what was being done in the legal and political fronts for our release. But more than that, these were reunions among similar minds, intermingling of feelings, encouraging each other to fight the darkness that swathed like death over the pulsating, throbbing, creative and productive life.

Both in mid-morning and late afternoon, I, Babar and Bappi used to walk along the long corridors in between two lines of cabins in our block. While walking, we conversed with each other, exchanged information that came to us from various sources. Walking in the late afternoon usually ended with exchange of fruit and homemade food that we in fetters received from our homes and relatives. The jail guards, stationed at two ends of the corridor while we walked, did not like such an exchange, but restrained themselves by flaring their nostrils and shouting gloatingly at low-grade hospital staff, since they received a portion of surplus from us.

As the jail guards did not like and allow us to meet in our cabins, at times we used to converge at the nurses station in between the two lines of cabins, sat there for 10 to 15 minutes as if to look into our respective files on diagnosis and prognosis, and talked with each other. Bappi's wife came quite often and joined us. She was a beauty of a young woman, very affectionate and respectful to me. One day she presented me with a beautiful T-shirt, like the very same one she brought for Bappi. I kidded Bappi saying that she gave me the better one. Bappi gave his wife an artificial scowl and asked: "Is that so?" She smiled at him lovingly. It seemed that I heard her singing an indistinct melody with Bappi, with ardor and expectation to live a life in freedom.

At the end of my walk, quite often I stood on the eastern end of the corridor and facing the central office of the Bangladesh Betar across the wide Kazi Nazrul Islam Avenue. I looked at the vehicular and pedestrian traffic, all hurrying to reach places of their work or rest. I longed for the freedom that the pulsating avenue represented before me. I saw peddlers peddling their wares, auto-rickshaw drivers bargaining over fares, teenage boys and girls crossing the avenue hand-in-hand ignoring the over-bridge in their defiant youth, and the going out of patients visibly cured and happy. At times to the south past the turn-about circle, I found throngs of university students chanting slogans, hotly debating issues unknown to me and patting each other's shoulders.

I recalled that further to the east was Dhaka Club where I used to play a set or two of tennis in evenings, take my sons for lessons in swimming or enjoy a late evening with my wife. We would be sitting on chairs under the trees looming overhead, reaching towards a starlit sky and dropping dewdrops as if diffusing scattered and unmindful thoughts in a breeze-laden atmosphere with the fresh scent of leaves. How different life was in contrast to the grilled floor where we were now interned, with claws in every hand and poison on every tongue of the jail guards, guarding to deny us our rights to move, create, produce, contribute and breathe freely.

Sometime in November, we had a spell of five consecutive days of rain with a blotch of darkness all around. And then on the night of the 15th, in the wind that we felt whipped over the hospital, cyclone Sidr struck the southwestern coastal belt. Looking at the dark sky pierced by lightning from time to time and the fallen big tree at the opening of the hospital, I knew these were days of disaster. The newspapers that I received in the morning carried some details about Sharonkhola and Southkhali Unions of Bagerhat that writhed and wailed in agony. With about one-seventh of the country seriously affected by Sidr, the government relief efforts took time to trudge south, with inadequate response to people's needs and spread-out responsiveness. In my experience, despite pitfalls, a democratic government beats an undemocratic, intimidation-based set-up. A democratic set-up does not crave power and riches; its responsibility and accountability to people makes it responsive to people's need. With relief at the end of the cyclone Sidr, I remembered how in 1998 Sheikh Hasina's government responded to the worst flood of the decade. I recalled how Motia Chowdhury, the Minister of Agriculture jumped into the waist-deep water of drowned paddy fields out of a boat she was riding with me and then waded through waist-deep water to the nearest not-yet-sunk road, walked barefoot to join Sheikh

Hasina, taking a firsthand measure of the devastation caused and relief and rehabilitation needed.

With Sidr gone, the winter crept in. My sister Nilufar gave me a warm new woolen blanket that she had brought from abroad. She had seen and assessed that the thin-layered red hospital issue was not enough to keep me warm in the night. In an eerie still quietness of my cabin, all the delights of Bangladeshi winter floated before my eyes. The cloudless blue sky, hundreds of wild flowers on roads leading to our village home, competition in catching fish from ponds, the sweet dessert made of "*gur*," assemblage of people under *chandni* (moonlight) to listen to mystic folksongs and view football and cricket tournaments, drawing half-clad barefooted spectators from remote village fields from far and wide and hundreds of lantern lamps fighting darkness like twinkling stars in village markets — all these memories made me wish I were again a part of that guileless throbbing life. I yearned to be with my wife and children on walks through the city's parks or along the village roads with birds twittering overhead in the tree branches shrouding our existence from the mundane. I felt these were our inalienable rights that our founding fathers won and bequeathed to us with strength and action and we lost the same through intolerance, cowardice and lack of foresight.

At the end of December, one morning, I had a pleasant surprise. Nowara, daughter of my sister-in-law Rita, came with her mother to see me. Nowara, a chemical engineer from Birmingham University lived and worked in New York. I had watched her growing up since she was a toddler and really loved her as if she was my own daughter. Under the glowering eyes of the guards, she and her mother could not enter my cabin and sit for a while. I went out and walked with them in the long corridor, talked to them for about 10 minutes while walking. Rita wanted to take a photo of Nowara and me in her digital camera, but the guards did not allow it. I prayed to Allah for Nowara's long and happy life and bade them goodbye. I stood on the little open space in the middle of the corridor and looked at them till they waved back and boarded their car.

15 In Kashimpur Again

(1)

As December 2007 wound into January 2008, I could feel a pressure was being built up by the Inspectorate General of Prison to make us leave the hospital. Through the grapevine of young doctors and nurses, I learned that the Inspector General of Prison, a Brigadier drawn from the army, had seen the Vice-Chancellor of the Medical University exerting pressure to discharge us, treatment completed or incomplete. Vice-Chancellor Dr. Taher in his turn asked the Professors, under whom we the prisoners were being treated in cabins at our own cost, to discharge us accordingly. Professor Anwarullah, on January 1, came to see me in my cabin and told me what he had been told by his boss Dr. Taher. I did not want to embarrass him on my account. I agreed to leave the hospital in three days without completing the treatment that was underway. So on January 4 in the afternoon, bidding goodbye to Doctors Kakon, Jafar, Shanto, Rifat, Hasan and Kaniz and nurses Jahanara, Parveen and others, wishing all the best to Isha and other patients and thanking Dolly, Shikha and other helping hands, with a trace of exasperation, I boarded that rattling, smoke-emitting prison van on my way to the Kashimpur Jail. Hossain, my loyal attendant, ran with the prison van up to the hospital gate and then failing in the race to keep up, stood back wiping his eyes.

It was about 10:00 at night when I reached the Kashimpur Jail gate. With a raking motion of wrist and forearm, I shifted out of the vertiginous confinement of the rattling prison van and stepped out. The jail with its dark and high main gate appeared to be a rude reflection of a world gone wrong. Denial of rights and values was its purpose. A gangly havildar along with Deputy Jailor Shahadat searched my bags and belongings. They found everything — packets of biscuits and fruit, bag of medicines, briefcase of papers and daily notes that I wrote, and my clothes fit for entry — along with me. But they kept the ipod, the songs and music that helped me tide over loneliness and remain in touch with the rhythm of life, saying that they would not allow it inside. I told them it had been inside before I went to the hospital. They said that permission had been withdrawn; ipods of other inmates had been taken out and the new Jailor and the Superintendent would not allow these in. I argued that the ipod in my case would be used as a radio through which we listened to song and music, which was allowed in the revised Jail Code.

But no amount of logic would shift him from his position of calibrated sarcasm. Considering that these were deeply degenerate times, I walked in, leaving the ipod behind. Passing another havildar, pissing on the walls of the infirmary with trousers unbuttoned, as he could not perhaps leave the post of his duty for this bodily function, I struggled through the loadshedded night and climbed the stairs to the second floor of the division building. I was greeted at that point by Mufti Shahidul Islam, who took my hands and led me to the improvised dining room. I found everyone with plates in front and hands washed waiting to take their meal with me. Through the grapevine they had been informed about my arrival and all of them waited to take their dinner together with me. To me they appeared to be as good as people could be.

It was going on midnight by the time we ate our dinner and I told them about my life in the hospital, the malevolent universe and the etiquette fraught with arbitrariness of power shown to me at the jail gate.

"You haven't seen their benevolences. They took our freezers where we kept our insulin and medicines needing cool temperature," Engineer Mosharraf said getting up from his chair.

"They have stopped entry of cooked meals for us, for everyone from outside," complained Nasim

"They have stopped rigging in fixtures for heating water at our own cost that they had agreed to earlier," said Salman.

"They searched our cells, took off two or three irons that we used and heaters that heated water for our tea," complained Ali Asgar Lobi.

I listened in silence, wondered whether we would now be living in confused state of law or suffering from withered senility of the jail administration. Then I asked,

"Did they take the blue reed mats from the floor of Lotus-Kamal and the green ones from Salman's?"

"No, not yet," said Giasuddin from Narayangonj. I stood up and took the stairs to the third floor to my cell. This was occupied in my absence by Chittagong's Mayor Mohiuddin Chowdhury, who had shifted himself down to the eastern portion of the second floor that evening, hearing that I would be coming. I walked back to his cell and told him, he did not have to do that, he could have stayed in my cell. With a face all scored with age and frustration of being in fetters, the agile freedom fighter that he was, smiled and took hold of my hands in silence. I was touched. Nothing was spoken between us. Our feelings became eloquent in silence.

Sleep was a sorrowful path for me in the night. I lay flat on my back in the dark with arms on my chest. I could not sleep till the small hours of the morning when fatigue overtook my anxiety. When I got up from bed, the slanted light of the morning sun fell in sliced beams on the verandah through the high grills. My attendant, or rather Man Friday (I vividly recollected from reading *Robinson Crusoe*), was ready with tea, breakfast and a bucket of warm water for a bath. With effort I went through the chores of the morning and then sat on my dilapidated plastic chair on the verandah. Others with teacups in their hands came and sat around. I rubbed my hands down my face to compose myself for wakefulness and attention.

"Well, you remember when we brought those freezers, the Superintendent told us, once brought inside the jail, we won't be able to take things out?" asked Ali Asgar Lobi.

"That was not a commandment — a half-joke at best," I recollected.

"Well, the Superintendent was about to retire out. He thought taking these freezers and heaters now will give him an opportunity to take one or two when he goes out."

"Why didn't he ask for one? We could have all contributed to meeting his yearning for cool water and fresh vegetables and fish," I commented, raking my fingers through my thinning hair.

"That would not have formed a sharp edge of the present-day national policy of zero-tolerance for corruption," said Mayor Mohiuddin with a tinge of sarcasm. I understood jail was a world where every opportunity presented to the jailors to assault the chained and weak was taken to their advantage. We lived in a never-ending uncertainty if not fear. Denial in every form was the purpose of the jail.

(2)

For about a week, in the afternoon and till late in the night when others slept or rested in their cells, I concentrated on reading. A number of books were sent by my friend William Christensen. I read Robert Harris's *Pompeii*, a novel depicting destruction of Pompeii by the eruption of Vesuvius on August 24 AD 79 (releasing thermal energy about 100,000 times that of the Hiroshima atomic bomb), and of the Romans' yearning for life, living and love.

I recollected how in 2003 Sitara and I visited Rome, the Vatican City, the ancient Roman resort on the hilltop and its recreation site nearby. We had marveled at the Roman ingenuity for constructing aqueducts, fountains, recessed places for relaxation and well-laid-out terraced cooling gardens even in those days. Visiting the Vatican, we saw the priceless paintings in the Basilica, the amphitheatre and other architectural marvels outside. Recalling the sweat of the slaves, the blood of the brave, and the pretence of leadership leading to merciless and senseless killings and wars, I wondered, "Could not humankind avoid these follies and miseries and take civilization through peace and tolerance to heights greater than where it was now?"

I read Dava Sobel's *Galileo's Daughter*, a historical memoir of science, faith and love. Galileo's daughter was born out of his illicit liaisons with beautiful Marina Gamba of Venice on August 13, 1600, in the very same year astronomer-scientist Giordano Bruno was burned at the stake in Rome for insisting that the earth revolved around the sun instead of remaining motionless at the center of the universe. Galileo christened his daughter Virginia after his sister, but she adopted the name Maria Celeste after becoming a nun professing a life of prayer and penance. Serving as a Professor of Mathematics in 1609, when Maria Celeste was no more than 9, Galileo had set a self-made telescope in his house, set it skyward and observed the nebulous Milky Way of densely packed stars, mountains and valleys that were on the moon and the four moons revolving around Jupiter — the marvels of creation hidden in obscurity till then. All his observations lent credence to the scientific sun-centered universe of Copernicus. In 1616 the Papal authority ordered Galileo to abandon and not to hold, teach or defend by word or in writing the opinion that the sun was the center of the universe and the earth moved around it. In 1633, Galileo stood trial for violation of this order by the papal inquisitors, who put him into semi-confinement and prohibited his scientific work *Dialogue*. Galileo died in 1642, after discovering lunar hibernation and losing his eyesight. In 1835, after over 200 years of prohibition, Galileo's *Dialogue* was dropped from the index of Prohibited Books and in 1966 the Index of Prohibited Books was abolished by the Second Vatican Council, a triumph for the right of expression and spread of scientific knowledge. In 1971 Apollo 15's Commander David R. Scott dropped a falcon feather and a hammer on the lunar surface, found them falling together and said that proved Galileo was correct. In 1995 NASA's spacecraft to Jupiter was named Galileo and reached Jupiter, the crown of honor to Galileo's findings as early as 1609.

Galileo's life, as seen by his daughter, made a number of important impressions on me while living in the jail. In the first place, I came to realize how important it was for society to encourage, sustain and cherish advanced thinking and creativity. Quite a number of us here in this prison both in the division building and outside as ordinary prisoners were incarcerated for expressing our thoughts and demanding our rights. We demanded democratic government, the right to unfettered votes without being cowered by physical force, and we were struck with the hailstones of corruption. In other buildings there were trade unionists and day laborers and sharecroppers demanding a rightful share of the produce, a living wage and treatment as free citizens, and they were charged with violation of law and order, disorderly conduct and subversion of discipline and even of State interest. And so they were accused in the eyes of the inquisitors of raw power, who administered deprivation and injustice.

I asked a poorly clad barefoot prisoner, "Why are you here?"

"I demanded that the owner of the rickshaw that I pulled for a living should not make us pullers bear the repair charges. Furious, he brought a charge against me for destroying his property."

"Did you have any witness to defend you?"

"No, I came from Sureshwar, Faridpur, as the Padma eroded my land and homestead. I did not have anyone in Tongi to defend me as a witness. I could not pay for the lawyer."

"Where are your wife and children? How do they live?"

"I do not know. Maybe they are now begging and living on streets."

Galileo was a non-conformist and scientist. In his country and his days they could to a great extent twist the malevolence out of their lives. In this country at this time, greed for power and control gnaws at life and liberty, which continues in retrograde steps.

In the second place, Galileo's emphasis on practical application and value of science and scientific knowledge in preference to metaphysical consideration of causes was vitally ignored in our penal system. Largely based on metaphysical considerations, we defined obedience and offenses, prescribed punishment for their violations but never ever inquired scientifically, say through the prism of social anthropology, why offenses were committed. At the time of near-famine conditions, widespread unemployment, total absence of social security, persistence of hunger and want, victims of these situations were led to theft or robbery. Once caught in the act, the hungry and those in want were tried and punished. In the process their families were also punished. But no one inquired to find out why, in a supposedly democratic and egalitarian society, the offender incarcerated in the jail had not been given equal opportunity to grow and be productive.

In the third place, even about 400 years back, Galileo valued love over the paperwork of a wedding, in living with Marina and siring three children. Galileo recognized his illegitimate children as the heirs of his lineage and their mother as his mate. In the context of transient mortgage of conjugal love (under the aegis of *"hila"* marriage amongst the Muslim fundamentalists in our country) and the inapplicability of the law to combat it, Galileo carried the flag of love, unencumbered by an exogenous compulsion of agreement on paper, reflecting the equality of the sexes without devaluing it in exchange for life's security.

Seeing some instances of *hila* marriage — forcing a loving wife into consummation by a third person, if deemed divorced by the husband in a transient rage before she could be united with him again — I felt that social leaders had taken our society deep into the Middle Ages. Law, lawyering, and adjudication had been turned into helpless, powerless and valueless social instruments. I wished a person like Galileo, with intelligence and courage, were born here. He would show the value and sublimity of love as yearning and desire, persisting and persevering beyond mere flesh and paper. I met a number of convicts who had, before being convicted, lost their dear wives through the obscene custom of *hila* marriage. For them, as it appeared the society was pitch-dark having not much attraction for them to return.

Finally, Galileo showed how, in the face of blind ignorance, one had to spearhead knowledge to new frontiers and cross them with innate strength. I recalled how stupidly the public prosecutor in my case argued that statistics as a discipline was not credible as evidence, and that computer-generated data, irrespective of the realistic nature of its parameters, could not be accepted as true unless signed by the computer user. I remembered also how ironically the Special Judge in his beggared understanding remained foolish beyond belief in giving credence to him.

An acquaintance with the life of a change-agent like Galileo could have given these morons some elements of ability to live meaningfully and blaze through this fast-changing world. Around me outside the jail, the green patches seemed to be singing the victory of life, all in time's winged chariot to happy and meaningful living. Contrasted with all these realities in my vision, Sitara became all the more beauteous; she had been awfully pretty. Our two toddlers were the brightest stars amongst all others spread across the sky.

Reminiscing about that golden time, I recalled a tear-stained deep ache that still roiled inside me. One evening, in a toddler's shop opposite the departmental store Columbus, on Sepulveda Boulevard in Los Angeles, our toddler Shuvo saw a toy motorcycle, sat on it while we sipped coffee outside and would not leave it without taking it home. The price tag showed about 10 dollars, which I thought at that time quite expensive and that we could go without spending it on a child's thing of joy. I took the toddler in my arms with Sitara following gloomily. Shuvo cried all the way home, got tired and slept, skipping his dinner.

Whenever my mind floats back to that, I feel a distant and painful regret and become wistful. I have no way to know if our toddler of yesteryear, now a teacher in the University of Massachusetts, Boston, remembers his father's inability to give him that simple plaything on which to ride. Was denial of a thing to someone you love so much an inevitable consequence of living, the waning of the moon without a prospect of its waxing in full?

(3)

Our golden days in Los Angeles after they passed did not shift their shape or meaning for us over time. Confined within the four walls of the jail, other memories from deep in the past floated vividly before my eyes. With so many years and events behind me, I recalled deep in the nights, sleepless but wistful, three more heart-felt consonant feelings of life with our two children. One was in a crowded street in Hong Kong in 1974 when Sitara, Shuvo our firstborn toddler, and I were laid up for a day by PanAm on our way to Los Angeles. Far into the afternoon we were enjoying the mild moist breeze coming from the bay, the crowd of colorful attires from almost all over the world and the shapes and colors of skyscrapers. Feeling life pulsating and seeing the progress made in Hong Kong, despite being an economist, I thought that getting what one wanted was largely a matter of claiming what one wanted.

At that point our toddler Shuvo refused to walk, wanted to climb on my shoulders to be carried onwards. I was annoyed, tried to make him understand that everyone over there walks freely and independently and that he should not act as a cry-baby. But he refused to move. Anger overtook me and I slapped him harshly, asking him to be a part of the hard and wondrous flurry of life. Holding my hand that was coming down for another slap on him, he told me with tears in his eyes and yet firmness "Dad, don't beat me. I will walk. I will not want to ride on your shoulders ever." I thought it was a kind of statement of selfhood that hardened a child to be out of the ambit of affection and love of parents as he grew in age. After some time rain started falling at a slant from the sky and I wanted to take him in my arms. He would not let me do it and walked defiantly ahead of me. I recalled General Patton's slapping a crying American private in Europe in the Second World War that turned his troops into defiant victors all the way. It took me, as I recalled, almost a year before I could take our toddler on my shoulder again and give him a giggling ride in a park, looking across the luminous arc of sky that the moon rode on an early evening.

Then I reminisced about the loss of a camera while driving from State College PA to St. Lawrence NY via Cornell sometime in 1989. Somewhere in between State College and Cornell we took a country road, skirting hills, with beautiful trees on both sides with the autumn's colored leaves. At a scenic point I stopped the car. Joy our younger son, then about 12, was with myself and Sitara. We were going to see our firstborn Shuvo doing his undergraduate work at St. Lawrence University in upstate NY. We came out of the car with the camera that we had bought earlier for about a hundred dollars, took a few shots of God's beauteous creation around and then, keeping the camera on the cover of the car's boot, went down the deep incline to touch a bush of rhododendrons. About 30 minutes thereafter we came up, hurriedly got into the car and drove ahead forgetting about the camera. After about 15 minutes I remembered about the camera, turned back looking down on the road, came to the spot where we had stopped, but did not find it.

I was annoyed and irrationally angry with Joy. I told him we bought the camera for him at his insistence, and he should have looked after it if he had really deserved it. Our son of 12 did not utter a single word, looking down towards the floor of the car, sitting in the back seat. After a while Sitara told me it was our responsibility also to place the camera inside the car and we did not do it. I realized she was right, stopped and patted our son affectionately on the back. He looked at me with a melancholy but forgiving smile. Remembering always that once I slapped our first-born, I never raised my hand on our second born: he grew up slightly stubborn but remarkably confident and outspoken, which satisfied me as a parent. But as it seemed, I lost to an extent also. When age-induced softening made me mellower towards my children, I found them somewhat too distant to take them under my arms and cuddle them as I wished.

Then I recalled Joy's love for a tiny bird. When he was a little over 4, one summer after a hard rain settled into a slow drizzle, he found a little *doyel*[47] falling on our verandah in a wounded state at our house in Banani on Road no. 12 where we lived at that time. He took the little bird under his care, made Sitara treat its wounded wings with disinfectants and kept it almost always in a cage he would hold in his hand. He fed the bird himself with rice and wheat grains. In the night, he kept the cage open right under his cot. The bird stayed below the cot but never left him. After a few days we found the little bird following Joy wherever he walked within the house. Joy even gave the bird an occasional bath by dripping water from a mug held in his little hand. We were all amazed by the bird's unfailing fealty to him. We also noticed the bird following one or two simple commands like "sit here," "don't move." These configurations of simple words, we observed, carried a freight of emotion for both the tiny bird and our little son.

Then one day when Sitara was twisting water out of her freshly washed hair and Shuvo was fiddling with the TV, an attendant running full speed on an errand trampled the little bird and it died. We were all overwhelmed with sorrow. With some sense of consonance between our moods and the sheets of rain falling outside, we realized how a careless and irresponsible footfall of the big and strong could bring a senseless end to the life of the small and beautiful. I took Joy in my arms and told him he would get a new bird and all of us should always be careful not to trample things small and beautiful for there was space for everything and everybody on God's earth. Then we sat over our midday meal and nobody said much of anything, probably resolving to always push back the darkness to arm's length, while watching through the window the rain falling white against the coconut leaves outside.

Nights passed into days. March, with a scent of warmth and the disappearance of morning dews, was coming to an end. On the

---

[47] An insectivorous bird found in open woodland, the oriental magpie robin (Copsychus saularis) is the national bird of Bangladesh.

night of the 25th, recalling events of 1971 on that night, I sat on the verandah till late in the night. The sky was studded with a thousand stars and moth wings hissed in the dim light in the cell behind. The future that waited for us in 1971 seemed to be pressing down on us in 2008 with all its weight. When I opened my eyes in the first sunlight, with booming guns that saluted Independence Day striking my eardrums, I found myself on the same chair in the verandah that I sat on late in the night.

I went inside the cell and suddenly found myself looking at me from the stained mirror fitted over the cracked basin of the toilet. The mirror reflected my succumbing to the passage of time. My hair, though persisting across most of its usual territory, was turning increasingly grey. My eyes were deeply socketed with loose patches down below; cheeks had lost their youthful tautness. I was past the odious middle passage of life. I wondered how many days were left for me in this world. At the same time I resolved, as long as I would live, I would serve my country and the people in the best way I could.

Like all prisoners I lived on memories and hope. Like all prisoners I wanted to make the impossible very reasonable. This made us live despite a hundred deaths a day, a solid dream crashing down into a thousand pieces every year without fulfillment. And all these reflections resonated in my mind time and again, as I beat down the possible metamorphosis of myself into a looming dismay and a depressed state.

16 Solitary Confinement

(1)

It was the morning of March 26, 2008. Coming out on the verandah, I found all others congratulating each other for the Independence that we had achieved 37 years before. Though we were in chains, our thoughts despite being unspoken centered on a light, a base for life, liberty and individual happiness for all of our citizens. We knew that we had a tryst with the future of which we all dreamed when we were young. Then, with a well-earned belly rising plump under a safari shirt, the Jailor along with the leaner Deputy Jailor came and announced that the Inspector General of Prisons had punished me for using a mobile phone while I had been in the hospital and the punishment condemned me for detention as an ordinary convict in isolation for three months forthwith.

Everyone around roared in protest and disgust. They pointed out that my division status in the jail as an ex-State Minister was given to me under the amended Jail Code, and the status so given could not be withdrawn by an executive order. They said before reaching the decision to punish me as such, an enquiry should have been held to find out whether that mobile was actually found with me and whether I had used it. "Is there any mention about a phone or a mobile in the Jail Code?" they wanted to know. The Jailor said he was obeying orders and had nothing more to do in this regard. The jailor also said that similar punishments were given to ex-Ministers Moudud Ahmed and Nazmul Huda by transferring them to the Narayangonj jail from Dhaka Central. The other inmates threatened to go on a hunger strike if I were taken away from them. After a while, in grudging concession to the protests made, the Jailor agreed that on the first floor of the same building where other ordinary prisoners were accommodated, I would be given a place to sleep on the floor, without any book or writing materials and a mosquito net.

All through I had kept mum. Only at this point, I asked whether they would take me to suffer this punishment on Independence Day? Could they not wait till tomorrow? The Jailor did not answer, but went back to arrange accommodation for me on the first floor. But after about 30 minutes, he came back and told us that he had discussed the matter with Deputy Inspector General Major Shamsul Haider Siddiky who was adamant on executing the punishment right from the Independence Day and would not permit my staying in the division building in any way. So around noon I was taken to the condemned cell attached to the jail infirmary where terrorist Shaokh Abdur Rahman had been interned before his execution a few months earlier. The Jailor made one concession: he allowed me to take a few books and my writing materials down to the depth of that hellish refuge.

The refuge was a dark cell of 15 feet by 10 feet with an open toilet located in one corner, with a knee-high, 15-inch wall on two sides to protect one's modesty when one needed to shit or piss. There was one window to the east of the toilet, but it was permanently sealed, leaving no means for cross ventilation to remove the odor of defecation coming from the unflushable, seatless toilet. A narrow door served as the entrance from a verandah running the short length of the cell from west to east, all grilled up to the ceiling. I was to sleep and sit on the bare floor by the side of the toilet. No mosquito net was provided; fleas and mosquitoes were nourished in the dark and on the almost open sewage outside to the north of the cell, while they found a ready feast in me. Countless cobwebs hanging from the four corners of the ceiling were obviously no match for thousands of singing insects and fleas that inhabited the cell. I would get my food three times a day from the kitchen of ordinary prisoners, doled out in battered aluminum pots that very badly needed cleaning. The inmates of the division-prison wanted to send food from their kitchen but the jailor would not allow it under the indescribable shroud of "orders from above."

My attendant Omar, loyal as he was, volunteered to come with me to look after me in the isolation cell and found a sleeping space on the floor in the next cell; the guards were placed there to keep me under constant vigilance. Out of the division, I was not entitled to an attendant. I asked Omar to go back and stay in the division building with the other attendants, but he refused. Conniving with an attendant of the infirmary who had borrowed a book from me earlier, Omar procured a dilapidated wooden chair from somewhere, most probably from the doctor's room, and placed it on the verandah. While I was turbulent in my thoughts and anger shadowed me all the while, Omar arranged sheets for me to sleep on and cover me against insects and mosquitoes, cleaned my clothes and eating pots and managed to bring some "bottled" water from the division building. In that cold-blooded dungeon dug out to suppress me in mind and body, Omar's silent service sustained me against possible insanity. I always felt like thanking him, pausing at artful intervals of his mopping and washing, but never did. It was a flaw of character in me, I realized.

(2)

Unable to sleep, in the dim light spewed by a 30-watt bulb fitted down the ceiling, I wrote a brief for Barrister Rafiqul Huq to challenge the punishment given to me by the Inspector General of Prisons. In the afternoon, my brother Dr. Jahangir along with Ishaq Sikdar came to the jail gate to see me. Before they came, I scrubbed myself very carefully in a bucket of water to erase the biting marks of insects on my body so that they would not see those and be more agitated and anguished. I conversed with them without gloom and handed over the brief to take it to Barrister Rafiq. I said that a writ for quashment of the action taken by the Inspector General should be preceded by a lawyer's notice that very evening. My voice, I noticed, was mild and companionable. They had brought some fruit and bread for me. After they had left, I trudged back very slowly, step by step from the jail gate to my isolated cell in the remnants of the light of the late afternoon. Deputy Jailor Shahadat did not allow me to take the fruit and bread that my visitors had brought. This was an act that exactly matched the cruelty of his superiors, I thought.

Late in the night, around 12:00 I believe, when I lay shrouded in sheets as a protection against stinging and biting insects, Jailor Saeed came in with two additional guards. He asked the guards to wait outside and said very politely,

"Sir, I want to talk to you."

"Evidently," I said in consonance with as much brevity as possible. By that time at least five mosquitoes had bitten him as I could count from the thumps of his one hand on the other.

"Oh, you don't have a mosquito net."

"I had one. You did not allow me to bring it in." I restrained myself from flaring up in anger.

"I will send in the mosquito net right now." I did not say anything in reply, looked the other way in disgust, trying to fathom the reason for his generosity.

"Sir, I have good news for you." I looked up and at him, but did not comment.

"Your punishment of living in isolation and out of the division has been changed. It will be for just seven days."

"Oh," I said. I realized that it must have been the outcome of the lawyer's notice dispatched to the Inspector-General that evening. He along with his cunning advisors must have understood that their position was not legally tenable and by the time I went to the High Court, five more days would have passed. That way, courageous and honorable as they were, they would be able to show courage of their manufacture and save their egoist sense of honor, restoring my status as a division prisoner without incurring the wrath of the High Court. Finding me uncommunicative, the Jailor scissored a *salaam,* called his guards and left. In 10 minutes after he left, the havildar along with two other guards came with my mosquito net, drove four nails in four corners of the cell, fitted it and left it in an antique and disarrayed manner.

(3)

Next morning Omar managed to bring in two *parathas*,[48] one omelet and a mug of tea from the division building. These were sent by Mufti Shahidul Islam in connivance with Salman. I ate wistfully despite the growling of phlegmic coughing from the infirmary of which my cell was a part. A packet of lunch was brought from the division building in the same way. I thought, despite odds, we would be able to shape a new ground on which all of us might stand together with a common resolve and in a renewed fight. I gave a blank rebellious glare toward the black uniformed jail guards gossiping and chewing betel nuts under the coconut trees outside the infirmary gate.

In the afternoon I had a pleasant surprise. Brother William Christensen came to visit me at the jail gate. William was an ordained priest, a man of God, dedicated to His service through organizing help and support for the poor under the aegis of a non-governmental organization, the Institute of Integrated Rural Development. Sitara was once Chairperson of this Institute. He was persistent in his attempt to visit me and finally the Ministry of Home allowed him to come to Kashimpur. It was refreshing talking to him about our country, the fate and the injustice meted out to the poor by man-made laws and customs and to renew faith in our possibilities. William was willing to stay longer but remembering that he was always busy in his work I bade him goodbye. I did not tell him about the brutal solitary confinement I was

---

[48] Round flat bread, fried in oil or butter.

pushed into. He assured me, God has his own way of doing things for the benefit of every deserving one. Through the judas gate of the jail, I kept looking at him till he disappeared in his little jeep.

I was wrung out by the third night, twisted down to a most miserable condition. I was intolerably lonely, thirsty and hungry. Because of stricter surveillance, Omar could not bring any food from the division kitchen. The gruesome paste of rice and watery lentils, brought from the common kitchen of the ordinary prisoners, spewed out smell almost similar to that emitted by the open sewage lying to the north of the cell. Unabated loadshedding in the moonless night made the time stand still like hatchet-heads hanging overhead. The biting and stinging of the insects seemed to tell me of my falling away in history. What was the meaning of life if it could not stand against one's own misery or contribute to the wellbeing of others? In the wakeful nights, I questioned and thought in the grim aftermath of the brutal treatment through which I reckoned, I might not live. To me death that way had no meaning. I could die without realizing how death looked or sounded, whether it was senseless or heroic or one could die without knowing that one was dead.

When the fourth day of the isolated confinement dawned, I did not find enough strength to get up from the bundle of sheets on the floor that was my bed. Around 9:00, Omar sneaked in with a mug of tea and two toasts that he smuggled in from the "division" kitchen. I gratefully drank the tea and ate the toasts and then with blister-like bite-marks of insects, walked bowed out into the verandah and sat on the dilapidated chair. Mufti Shahidul Islam was at that time walking to the jail gate on his way to the court. Ignoring the raised eyebrows of the jail guards, he veered towards me. Seeing me smiling with blister-like marks on my hands, neck, throat and face, he sighed and said he would bring it to the notice of the Superintendent.

"What matters is that I am alive and *inshallah* I will survive," I tried to comfort Mufti.

"These are not human beings, these people administering the jails. They will meet their own fate in time," growled Mufti, flapping his flowing robes.

"I will myself bring you food this evening," he said and left me at the prodding of the guards. I sat on the verandah looking at the green and fresh leaves and dark smoothing shadows of trees stretched long across the grey concrete walkways of the jail. I then drew out Anne Enright's *The Gathering*, and flipped through its pages. The book was sent to me by Sitara from Boston. In *The*

Gathering, Enright portrayed an evocative and touching tale of a large Irish family haunted by the past. Did the memory of the past help people to get into a future of their liking, a fate they would cherish? It was far into the afternoon when I found myself on the floor of the verandah, where most of the flurry of life did not mean much to me.

In the light falling at a low angle over the coconut grove outside the western walls of the infirmary, I found Omar with another mug of tea and one toast, which I accepted gratefully. He told me I did not have anything for lunch and he did not wake me out of my sleep on the bare floor. I asked for a bucket of water for a bath. He brought a dented bucket full of cool but brackish water and I used the tea-mug to pour water on my head and body. And then drying my body with a sheet, I sat once again in the deeper darkness falling throughout the jail.

The deep darkness made me reminisce about a still darker event that for a long time I had tried to erase from my memory. When I was about 8 and living in our home village, one of our childless aunties, Anu, liked me a lot. She was the wife of Anwar uncle who worked in sea-going vessels as a sailor. He had three more brothers. They used to live together as a joint family with their wives, children and a mother. Anwar uncle sent them money for their subsistence, constructing tin-roofed houses and buying sizeable cultivable lands. Infected with tuberculosis, Anwar came home and after a few months died.

Anu, an auntie, was quite close to my mother and used to visit us almost every day. She looked towards my father as a guardian. After Anwar's death, one day when my father was absent from home, the other brothers, forced Anu into a palanquin and made her leave her dear dead husband's house to find shelter if she could with her brothers living in Kalachor, a far-off village. This was done by the three brothers to occupy all the lands of her late husband, who had bought them all. Wailing and with tears falling down her cheeks, our auntie left our home and village.

This was done, I was told, in accordance with the Muslim law of inheritance. Later, I found such interpretation of the Muslim law of inheritance false, morally wrong and legally untenable in such a case. I also found the three other beneficiary brothers praying five times a day as devout Muslims. And I also found their mother sullen but not able or willing to utter a single word against such an inhuman treatment meted out to her daughter-in-law.

Reminiscing, I felt a crushing guilt about the material winners in our society. Watching late in the night the stars transit through the tree limbs in cloud breaks, I wondered whether my auntie had received the same treatment from her own brothers, or if she survived this societal homicide. Things had not changed much since then. In the silence of the night I spat at social leaders of our society purporting to maintain peace, order and fairness.

Very late in the night, Dr. Rathin, the jail doctor pushed a packet of dinner through the grill of the cell. True to his words, Mufti Shahidul Islam sent me two *parathas* and few pieces of well-cooked kabab, which I presumed came from his home.

(4)

In the morning of the sixth day, I jostled myself out of the cell around 9:00 a.m. with a splitting headache. A mug of tea brought in by Omar made me wheeze in my efforts to be steady. Living brought suffering for me. My whole body disagreed with my sitting or lying on the bare floor. And anxiety coupled with anguish streaked through me. Way out, I could hear cackling conversation of the jail guards. I seemed to have developed a temperature. My forehead burned as if I was facing a fire of straw and dried wood. I tried to walk the length of the verandah and I felt no better. Later I found myself wrapped in a sheet on the bare floor. Omar told me I had fainted and then said something in a guttural voice that he did not understand. I remembered I had a dream of falling and gave out a yell for help. I asked Omar not to tell anybody that I had fainted. My tormentors in that case would think that they had weakened and subdued me. I lay down on the bare floor of the verandah once again. Omar tried to shoo crows off from the nearby mango tree to let me sleep. I let out a low and guttural moan before darkness swallowed me again.

In the late evening the hospital's pharmacist Nuruzzaman came with a dinner packet from the division kitchen, made me sit reclining on the wall of the verandah, took my blood pressure, felt my pulse and then urged me to eat some food that he had brought. I ate a few morsels, drank a full glass of water and retreated to the cell behind. The stench of the sewage coupled with free biting of the insects cast a tired mustard halo around me. Around 12:00, I started belching and burping followed by almost incessant vomiting. Omar was locked up in the next cell along with the snoring guards. I could not call for any help. Living a few more hours till the dawn became most gruesome. While the mango tree outside glistened in a mild drizzle, I felt an hysterical urge to leave and run out, forgetting that the cell was locked from outside. I collided with the hard grills and then collapsed. In the morning, when as sunlight broke over the horizon and the guards unlocked the cell, I found Omar hovering over me in pained anxiety.

That was the morning of the seventh day of my confinement in that solitary cell as an ordinary prisoner under unlawful punishment. I thought my ordeal would be over by 10:00, when I would be taken back to the "division" building and my status as a division prisoner would be restored. I asked the havilder-in-charge to let the Jailor be informed about the expiry of my time of confinement. After two hours he came back and told me with a cryptic smile that I would have to be confined in the cell till sundown. This was nothing but an extended persecution by a sadist bereft of anything called conscience.

Fortunately for me, around 2:00 in the afternoon, Mufti broke through the barricade, found me in that miserable plight and then went to the Jailor and the Superintendent. He made them count seven days in terms of 24 hours each, proved that I should have been sent to the division earlier at 12 noon and said that everyone else in the division was waiting for me to take lunch together. He made it clear that he would not leave their office unless I was released and none in the division would take their food till I reached their table to partake the same. At about 3:00 the Superintendent and the Jailor relented and I walked back in agony and fatigue, holding the Mufti's extended hand, to the division building.

Washing my hands, I took two morsels of rice and curry and fell sick. I was helped to my cell upstairs in the division building by Lotus-Kamal and Omar. I threw up in the bathroom, blacked out and fell on the wet floor with a big thump. After about 30 minutes, I found myself lying on the bed with bleeding head injuries. The Jail Doctor was called, the Superintendent and the Jailor came running, and my head began to spin with the thought of things that might have been different with a little sympathetic treatment by the sons-of-bitches around. Salman, through the Superintendent, called for his company's ambulance and at about sunset with a note on my illness shoved into my pocket, I was put on a stretcher and carried to the ambulance for my journey to the Bangabandhu Sheikh Mujib University Hospital. That was the night of April 5, 2008.

17 In Hospital Again

(1)

The ambulance reached Bangabandhu Sheikh Mujib Medical University Hospital (BSMMU) around 10:00 in the evening. In the emergency section of the hospital, I found my brother Dr. Jahangir, nephews Dr. Muntassir Mamun and Farid, party activists Iqbal, Ahad, Mafiz and others waiting for me. The news about my blacking out in the jail was leaked out somehow and telecast earlier. The emergency section of BSMMU was not well-equipped. It was located in a tin shed without much equipment and facilities needed for critical management. The doctor-in-charge seeing me bleeding from the head rushed me for a CT scan to a nearby building.

There was no one from the jail administration present at the time, though they had been informed by the Superintendent of the Kashimpur Jail over phone. As it seemed, it took time for them to make a move for treatment of a prisoner. For them, even impending death was not a good enough reason for expeditiousness. We as prisoners were not allowed to keep or carry any cash. Despite that, through the good office of Dr. Pervez Reza Kakon, who had come with my brother, the CT scan was completed. My brother, the bank being closed, kept Tk. 2,100 with the doctor-in-charge, a bald-headed young man in shabby dress and with an annoyed appearance. He took a look at the scan and said it was not serious, but at the same time, wiping his eyebrows, advised that I should immediately be hospitalized. When I was limping out of the CT-scan examination room, with my head like an empty pot of ringing noise and incomprehensible sounds, I found Deputy Inspector General Prison, Major Shamsul Haider Siddiky rushing towards me. He said he had been informed over phone about my blacking out and he had come to see me and arrange for my admission; I felt a sense of relief that I was not yet primed for death by them.

The admitting physician, however, told us there was no bed available, but if the jail administration agreed, he could admit me into a cabin to which I was entitled as a retired Secretary to the Government. The Deputy Inspector General furrowed his creased face in obvious disagreement at this stage. Instead he took leave of me saying that he would go to the cabin block and the prison cell within the hospital and arrange for my admission wherever possible. With my brothers and others, I waited for one hour at the emergency entrance and then was told that the Deputy Inspector General had left on an urgent business elsewhere. It must have entered into him that the material world, in all its nuances, was about who owed what to whom. For a powerless prisoner patient, the muting of available service was the best way to serve and satisfy the powerful.

Then as things took course in confusion, I was taken to the prison cell within the hospital. It was crammed with ailing prisoners. In one single room where a former Chairman of the Chittagong Port Authority, Shahadat Hossain, was accommodated, the prison guards shoved in another bedstead and told me that was the place in which I had to lie and live. They could not arrange pillows, sheets and a mosquito net. From the other room Selim Bhuiyan, President of the Dhaka Club, of which I was also a member, sent me a sheet and a pillow. Shahadat Hossain did everything within his bounds to make my stay bearable. He even offered his own bed to me. I thanked him and said I would make do with whatever had been arranged. With severe pain in the abdomen and bleeding head, bandaged at places, I lay down amidst the singing of thousand mosquitoes and insects. I could not buy medicines prescribed by the emergency duty doctor, since I was told these would be provided by the jail administration. I was not allowed to take or carry any money from my brothers even to buy the prescribed medicines.

The night was gruesome. My pain in the abdomen increased; I felt like urinating but could not. Sleep eluded me throughout the night. With the first light streaking through the space over the high-drawn screen across the corridor, I got up and rattled the grilled door that was locked from outside. When the guards came grumbling, I threw the doctor's prescription at them and asked them to bring the antibiotic from the hospital's medicine shop down below. My loyal attendant Hossain was downstairs with a food carrier in his hand. I told the guards that they should take the money from him and pay for the medicines. They hesitated; they had been told I would get the medicines from the Dhaka

Central Jail. In agony and desperation I shouted. Other inmates came running and shouting, and then the guards relented. In 10 minutes I got the prescribed antibiotic, swallowed the dose with a full glass of water and turned back into my room holding Shahadat's hands. In about 30 minutes I felt relief. I took a bite of bland breakfast brought by Hossain from my house at Banani and also a cup of tea made by Shahadat and then collapsed on my makeshift bed. The world, unkind and pitiless, hard and slate-grey, stopped sliding around in my head.

Around 12:00 I rolled on my bed, opened my eyes and saw Shahadat Hossain, Selim Bhuiyan, Amjad and Ghalib sitting around me. They sighed breaths of relief and said Prof. Kanak Kanti Barua of the Neurosurgery department was on his way to see me in the prison cell. Prof. Barua came a little after 12:30, examined me with three of his associates, ordered a series of blood tests, urine analysis and ultrasonograms of the prostate.

He was a good man, smiling all the while and assuring me I would be alright. Examining the injury along with CT scan, he said it was not that serious and would heal by itself. In addition to a plethora of new drugs and medicines, he prescribed liquid, soft and bland food for me. All the while Dr. Barua and his associates were examining me, the jail guards, most of them half-literate, surrounded him as if they also considered him, in addition to me, a suspect and threat to State security. When they left, I observed their mobile phones were handed over to them by the jail guards. That meant they were not allowed into the prison cell with their mobile phones. In a military-controlled government, the half-literate, gun-toting sentries had become more loyal and trustworthy than Professors of the medical university. The arrogance of usurped power, I thought, was destined to bring about the end of John Tylers in this country as well.

After Prof. Kanak Kanti Barua left, I remembered that he was the younger brother of Dilip Kanti Barua, General Secretary of a minor political party of the country allied with the Awami League. I had known Dilip for a long time. Dilip was older than Kanak, but Kanak looked older than Dilip. In his talks Prof. Barua exuded both courage and assurance. Now I was confident that even in this accursed hospital, I would not get cowered down before the black-robed illiterate jail guards, representing the arrogant power around and above.

I had difficulty bringing om drugs and medicines prescribed by Prof. Barua. The jail guards insisted that the prescription be handed over to them for bringing the medicines from the pharmacist of the Dhaka Central Jail. I told them the antibiotic prescribed a day before did not arrive from them till then. So to save myself, I would buy the medicines at my cost through my attendant. After a bout of shouting they relented and I could bring in the prescribed medicines from the shop below.

(2)

The prison cell was in a three-storied old building with two rooms on each floor, with attached dilapidated work-at-will bathrooms. This was a part of the old Shahbagh Hotel that was built by the government in the 1950s. In 1972, the Shahbagh Hotel was turned into the Institute of Post-Graduate Medicine and Research (with an attached hospital) at the behest of Bangabandhu. Prof. Nurul Islam was the first director of this Institute. He was now a National Professor having a lot of influence over the serving Professors, most of whom were his former students.

In 1974, a wing of this Institute's hospital, its best part, was designated as a prison cell to accommodate ailing political detainees. At that time, political prisoners were treated with honor and respect. As a Deputy Secretary of the Ministry of Finance at that time, I was associated with this decision. Little did I realize at the time that one day I would be interned in this cell for treatment as a "division" prisoner of the government of independent Bangladesh. Despite later being classified as a prison cell, as it was the best part, persons like Maulana Bhashani and Mizanur Rahman Chowdhury were treated here in 1974. Before that, Bangabandhu's father Sheikh Lutfur Rahman was also hospitalized in this wing in 1972. At that time, it was not classified as the prison cell.

I found that the then the best wing of the premier hospital of the country had fallen into a dilapidated condition. The hospital administration thought it was a part of the Inspectorate General of Prisons; the Inspectorate thought it was a part of the hospital and should be maintained by them. As a result of being a no-man's property, I found the grills rusted, door-knobs displaced, shower trays broken, toilet covers absent, wash basins almost falling down but for scaffolding pieces of timber, the lockers with peeled-off paint and paint on the walls and the ceiling peeling off freely. Only at two ends did the jail administration fit in new, strong and well-painted grills with glittering bank-locks to keep the inmates securely in. The ground floor was occupied by the jail guards, about 30 of them, under a havildar. The passage down, whenever we went out, reeked of freshly excreted human waste of all sorts.

On the first floor, in the first room, Shahadat Hossain, a former Chairman of the Chittagong Port Authority, now falsely accused of giving irregularly a contract for container-handling to a private operator, was accommodated along with me. Shahadat Hossain was recruited by my eldest brother, now deceased, a former member of the Parliament and Secretary of the Chittagong Port Authority. Shahadat was a nice, simple and helpful person. Outside our room to the east there was a corridor in which two prisoners — one, a student leader of Barisal Broja Mohan College, Sumon by name, and another Mohiuddin, a member of an Union Parishad, Savar, Dhaka — were given two bedsteads, leaving almost no space for walking in or out. When Sumon left after about a month, his place was given to Prof. Rafiqul Islam, a State Minister of Energy in Sheikh Hasina's government, now falsely framed up for corruption. To the west of our room there was an adjacent verandah with a dilapidated wooden table and two worn-out plastic chairs that we used for taking our meals in two shifts, first by Shahadat Hossain and myself and then by the lodgers of the corridor. As the verandah was west-faced, the slanting afternoon sun blistered us off from sitting or reading there.

In the next room lived Selim Bhuiyan, President of the elite Dhaka Club, and Amjad, a former member of the Parliament from Syedpur. Selim Bhuiyan was a freedom fighter, businessman of repute and gentleman of perfection. He was brought in for refusing to be a false witness against Khaleda Zia. Amjad was there for helping donate a few C.I. sheets to some educational institutions in his local area and committing corruption, as they claimed, through this process. In the corridor to the east of their room lived Syed Ghalib Ahmad, a young and ailing person of about 25, imprisoned for obtaining a contract for container-handling of the Chittagong Port at a cost lower by 30% than the cost of the earlier contract.

Ghalib was known to me through his younger brother Tanvir who was a friend of my son Shuvo. Tanvir was in Dhaka Central Jail. I had known Selim Bhuiyan for many years. The Dhaka Club of which he was the elected President was the Club of Dhaka's elite. As a member, I knew most of the other members. By arresting Selim Bhuiyan, the military-controlled government made it clear to the people who mattered in the society that they had a hidden agendum beyond and under the cover of the drummed-up fight against corruption.

In the afternoon, finding an opportunity I went up to the second floor. There in a room, I found Lutfuzzaman Babar and Tariqul Islam engaged in an insignificant quibble. My presence, with a smattering of rebuke, calmed both of them. Tariqul Islam was the Minister in charge of Forest and Environment from 2001 through 2005 under Khaleda Zia. I knew him since I was the Deputy Commissioner, Jessore from 1976 through 1979. Tariq was at that time the Chairman of the Jessore Municipality. He was an amiable and at the same time spirited young politician. I recalled that I had introduced him to General Zia, on one of his visits to Jessore. Tariq was severely ill with diabetes, asthma and high blood pressure, and needed to take oxygen at least twice a day.

Lutfuzzaman Babar was a State Minister for Home Affairs under Khaleda Zia. With a history of villainy in applying the police of the country against the political opposition, he had a debatable reputation. I was not well acquainted with him. Besides in 2002 when I returned from the U.S., Babar and his cohorts arrested me right at the airport on the false charge of activities subversive to the State interest. Seeing him suffering from delirious fever, I was polite with him, asked about his prognosis and wellbeing and even shook hands with him when he extended his. After drinking a cup of stale tea made by Tariq, I returned to my abode under the annoying glare of the guards. I could not go to the third floor where Barrister Sigma Huda, Khusnod Lobi and other female prisoners were accommodated. As per the Jail Code, the female ward, even in the hospital's prison cell, was always off-limit for the male prisoners.

Besides the deplorable living conditions, all of our rooms lacked space; we could hardly walk a few paces. In fact we were caged, comforting the afflicted and afflicting the seemingly comfortable. The other pitiable condition centered around food. We were supposed to take half-cooked food of the ordinary prisoners supplied from the hospital kitchen. In the morning two pieces of bread with a pinch of sugar came as breakfast. Around 12:00 a few morsels of rice were given, lumped on a stainless steel tray hollowed at four places with some vegetables strewn with two microscopic pieces of fish or meat and two tablespoonfuls of watery lentils occupying the other two hollowed spaces around the rice.

In the night, the same quantity and quality of withered food given at lunch was provided as dinner, with an occasional piece of overly green and moldy lemon to squeeze in some smell, if not juice, in order to repel the repugnant stale morsels of rice. I arranged for a supply of food from home, as did Selim Bhuiyan and

Ghalib. Amjad, Sumon and Mohiuddin, not having homes in Dhaka, used to make do with the hospital food. On the first day despite the doctor's orders to give me liquid and bland food, the guards returned my food carrier while allowing Selim's and Ghalib's. Next day, I was told by Ghalib that they had an arrangement with the jail guards. Receiving Tk. 350 from each per week, the guards allowed them cooked food from home. I thought this was both insulting and disgusting.

"But uncle, this is the custom going on over here for a long time," Ghalib said.

"If we have to gratify jail guards at these positions of our lives, what will become of this country?" I protested.

"The jail guards say that their superiors get their share from supplies brought into the jail and won't give them any share. They also say most of the high-ups, who had been sent to the jail administration on deputation from other services, have also started taking money from big-shots as protection against their re-arrests or maltreatment after arrest. So what they will do?" Ghalib explained. Selim and Amjad had smug smiles on their faces.

"Well, if it is an arrangement that you have already made on per head basis, I will not stand in the way here under the circumstances. But I will not talk to the guards on this; I will give my share to you to throw into whatever cesspool you will choose."

"You don't have to talk to them, uncle. I will do the talking and making the arrangement," Ghalib assured. And I started to get my food from home along with fruit and snacks.

(3)

Jao-bhat (soft cooked rice) brought from home, coupled with the antibiotics bought belatedly against the instructions of the jail authority at my cost, eased my pain considerably. After breakfast, when the sun was not yet high, I sat on the western verandah with Craig Nelson's *Thomas Paine*. Paine was one of the greatest minds of the 18th century; his writings were a fundamental source for the European and the American ideas of society and government. He was the best representative of the age of enlightenment, carrying and spreading beliefs across countries and over time. He asserted that the government should be based on consent of citizens; that such citizens were born with certain natural rights; that none were born superior to anyone else; that all would be treated equally and with dignity under the law and that the State had a duty to help the poor and the needy. And at the top of all, Paine and his contemporaries inspired people in general to accept that for humankind, knowledge was power. This was a remarkable transformation of thought in human history and civilization, bringing about a staggering upheaval in technology, science, society and politics.

In the same age, two other revolutionary changes — repulsive to the plutocracy and dictatorial rule ever since, were marked for triumph over time. One was the cornerstone of Martin Luther's doctrine: everyone had a right to communicate with God directly by reading and learning his scriptures. So reading and writing were religion and should be taken up, spread and cultured as religious duties. The second was primed by Philosopher Immanuel Kant, who said loudly and clearly through an essay read by the religiously literate the world over, that the requirement for enlightenment was freedom, providing scope and ability to make public use of reason in all matters and for all to use their minds securely.

I read, paused and pondered: were our dictators and their henchmen retrograde to enlightenment and freedom, the very basis of progress of a human society? Most certainly they were and most certainly, like their predecessors drunk with absolute power and self-assumed guardianship in various countries and ages, they would fail. They would throw us into an abyss of darkness and anarchy from all their opposing and obstructing of creativity, hard work, fortitude, thrift, patience, prudence, tolerance, sobriety and self-improvement, the ingredients that propel progress.

Brooding over these matters, suddenly I looked out through the small opening of the corridor and found my sisters Kohinoor and Nilufar squatting unashamedly and with fortitude on the hospital's concrete walkway to the east of the prison cell. I waved at them. With satisfaction spread over their faces they waved back. I asked the guards how long they had been squatting on the pavement the way they did. The guards replied that they were sitting over there for more than two hours. Since they did not have permission to see me, the guards did not allow them to come in. Shouting, I told them I was well and that they should leave this place of squalor and insult. They waved back, shouting that they were relieved to see me in one piece and walked back.

I recalled, for building this hospital along with the Medical University, I as the State Minister for Planning allocated Tk. 250 crores (Tk. 2,500 million) for the asking and now my own sisters had to squat on its pavement for more than two hours just to have a glimpse of me and to know that I was alive. This was what resulted from the dictatorial rules of those who, I was sure, never heard of Thomas Paine or Immanuel Kant. They were the vestiges of the dark ages, corrupted wholesale by power, trying to darken the light of whatever civility still remained in our society. But I knew at the same time that hell was not easily conquered.

The next day I was examined by Cardiologist Sajal Banarjee and Urologist S. A. M. Golam Kibria. I underwent ECG and then sat with Banarjee with the plate to find out any aberration in the functioning of the heart. Banarjee looked grim and then realizing my presence, came out of impassiveness.

"If they take my ECG, they will find these grayish spots — they are nothing serious," Banarjee said in stylish simplicity in a reassuring tone.

"I understand, Doctor. Tell me frankly, is this that serious — is this the thing that made me black out?"

"No," said Banarjee with impulsive optimism. My anxiety was dimmed to an extent.

Kibria was more forthcoming and jovial. He said, seeing the ultrasonogram report on the lower abdomen:

"Your prostate is enlarged — a common thing for men of your age."

"Do you think a surgical intervention will be needed?" How is PSA?"

"No, not now. We will observe how it behaves, increases or remains as it is; if it does not increase, you will live with it. As of now PSA is ok."

"But I have pain in abdomen — difficulty in urination at times."

"The medication that I gave you will take care of that. Besides, please remember for 68 years of your life it functioned normally. Now like other organs, it calls for a little rest," he tried to joke.

When they were leaving, I observed that they were being searched by the lowly jail guards. Their mobile phones were returned to them, meaning they had not been allowed to enter the prison cell with their mobiles. In terms of patriotism, the jail guards were considered more loyal and superior to full medical Professors. I felt insulted, unlearning the perils of being reasonable. "Was violence more effective as a means of protest and protection of honor than mute non-violence? Did submission to insult lead anyone over the filth of meanness towards others?" I wondered.

(4)

Amongst us in the hospital prison cells, Amjad was a former member of Parliament from Syedpur area. He was a member of the Jamaat-i-Islam, the religio-political party of the country. To me, exploiting religion for political objectives was a full-throttle reversal of secular ideals and values that nourished liberal political attitude and learning. At the beginning, I was therefore reserved, impassive and unforthcoming towards him. But in a few days, I found him companionable and jovial. Quite often he used to be pensive and sorrowful remembering his wife and children.

At times, when he did not receive a response from his wife, either through letters or messengers, he used to become pensive, even choking back tears. I along with Selim Bhuiyan consoled him. And he was a person who could easily be consoled. In his good mood he used to joke about the peculiar habits of the stranded Pakistanis of Syedpur — their dialect, continuous chewing of betel nuts, unabated fondness for kebab and "*gul*" (a chunk of spicy tobacco put under the tongue), and their abhorrence for regular bath and even general cleanliness. As he said, these people took pride in taking brides from the Bangali families but did not like giving their own girls in marriage to the Bangalis. He was all praise for their ingenuity as mechanics and fabricators.

Sumon was a middle-ranking student leader of the Broja Mohan College, Barisal. After the military-controlled government took over, he was arrested and mercilessly beaten by the police. From Barisal prison he was sent to Dhaka's hospital for treatment. He could walk very slowly and holding a crutch. He was an amiable as a well as a spirited young man. Quite often I used to give him a banana, a piece or two of bread, a mango, which he accepted gratefully. Living in the corridor, he used to keep close watch on the pavement down below and inform me about my brothers or sisters who wanted to visit me or see me from a distance. I told him, as the future belonged to the young like him, he must, along with his associates, seek redress of grievances and end of persecution shaking off any propensity or willingness to compromise.

When his mother from Barisal and sister living in Dhaka, both very simple and affectionate women, came to visit him, he introduced me to them as his elder brother. I hope that some day I would be able to share the ideals and the traits of the young generation that Sumon represented. A few days before I left the prison cell, much to my relief, Sumon was posted on bail and taken out by his mother and sister. His career as a student and a productive member of society remained at peril because of his record of arrest, irrespective of reason. In the space between dark and dawn in life, the operation of the police in our society did not change very much since Independence. As the saying in Bangla went: "If one was attacked by a tiger, one was injured once; but if one was chased by the police, one was destined to get as many as eighteen wounds. Because of unbridled exercise of power under an autocratic government, Sumon's interruption in life and studies, I apprehended, would either make him a rebel without any stake in society or a loser in the fight for a good and productive life.

Selim Bhuiyan was a freedom fighter. Since Independence, he concentrated on business and through hard work and amiable nature he rose up. A year before, he was elected the President of the Dhaka Club, an assemblage of Dhaka's elite. He was arrested on a fabricated charge of receiving a bribe from an international oil company, NICO, headquartered in Canada, since he refused to be a false witness against Khaleda Zia, the immediate past Prime Minister. Arresting the President of the Dhaka Club was at best foolhardy: the Club was a sort of invisible collage of top businessmen, bureaucrats and social leaders to whom arrest of Selim made it clear that the government of the day was not a facilitator of good or better business as espoused by Chief Advisor Fakhruddin. And, more importantly, governance was neither aimed at nor based on the principle of rule of law or its due process. In our daily living in the prison cell, we became quite close exchanging books, snacks and fruit. Whenever Selim's brother, wife and son came to visit him on every Friday afternoon, they used to come and talk to me. Mrs. Selim invariably brought some homemade delicacies for me as well.

Prof. Rafiqul Islam, State Minister for Energy in Sheikh Hasina's government, was a simple, honest and straightforward person. I knew him since long ago, from the days I was the Deputy Commissioner, Jessore, from where he came. Corruption of any kind was beyond him. Honesty of purpose was his hallmark as a teacher. He was incarcerated for refusing to be a witness against Sheikh Hasina. Most of the time, he was morose and sorrowful. Selim and I used to sit with him in his pensive mood and tried to raise his spirits. Allegations were made also against his wife and sons who were completely apolitical. As in other cases, vengeance had come to bemoan justice in prosecuting him and his family under this regime.

Syed Ghalib Ahmed was a young entrepreneur. He got a contract for container-handling of the Chittagong Port as the lowest bidder, the bid being 30% less than the previous contract. Being a businessman looking after his interest and applying his own enterprise and acumen, I could not find any element of offense committed by him. In desperation, he said that once freed he would move his business out of the country. To me it appeared this was how the idiotic establishment of the country thwarted entrepreneurship. To spearhead growth the process was to facilitate, not to control, to pursue rule of law, not to fall on arbitrariness. But these appeared not to be strong points with this government. Being placed at the top, rightly or wrongly, they had been forcing people who could create wealth into inaction and morbidity.

While thinking about Ghalib's case, I recollected an incident while I was the Managing Director, Bangladesh Shilpa Bank. It was 1989 and there was widespread default in repayment of industrial loans, threatening the very existence of the bank. There were two reasons: firstly, depreciation of the Taka against the dollar in the case of loans disbursed in dollars; and secondly, sanction of loans on political considerations during the rules of Generals Ziaur Rahman and Ershad to non-entrepreneur party stalwarts, stood on the way of repayment.

In this predicament, the public perception was that the majority of the loanees did not pay back, as they thought they could escape repayment using political clout. This was not true in most cases. Many an entrepreneur tried their utmost to operate and repay, to show to the rest of the world perseverance and honest performance. Against this backdrop, to ascertain the truth in one case of default, I sent two of my female officers to the house of a big defaulting loanee, living in Gulshan to find out how he and his family lived. The officers came back after spending about three hours with the wife and the children of the loanee. They reported that the wife cooked with her own hands, the children did not go to school for non-payment of fees. Privation and poverty were evident throughout the household.

The loanee had said earlier that he could not operate his factory due to labor trouble and shrinkage in export market, which were beyond his control, and could not repay because the repayment liability had gone up due to high appreciation of the dollar against the Taka. He said he himself at times worked on his machine in his factory. I was ashamed. He was a true entrepreneur; for him setting up and operating a business was an obsession.

Instead of recalling, I rephased and restructured his loan and over time he was able to overcome his difficulties and turned out to be a model loanee. I recalled that Henry Ford, before coming out with his famous Model-T in the U.S., could not buy a Christmas dress for his wife, as he needed the money to build the prototype. I recalled the same kind of obsession of Tata as described in his biography *Beyond the Blue Mountain*. I realized that, in order to progress, society needed to encourage these bands of entrepreneurs. As against this need, these arrogant usurpers have been confining them in jails on fabricated charges. Imposed poverty on the creative class, in defiance of principles, begot meanness that stooped low to morbidity. I recalled that Thomas Paine had said this in England as early as in 1774 before he left for the country of the free and the brave.

My roommate Shahadat Hossain was an amiable gentleman. In my assessment, he possessed truthfulness that went beyond words. He was incarcerated on a false and fabricated charge of giving a contract on container-handling, while as a matter of fact, the contract was approved by a committee of the cabinet and signed by someone other than him. Filing a false and fabricated charge was like perpetrating a lie on our administrative-judicial system and also on our future generations. During his time as the Chairman of the Chittagong Port Authority, the Port operated smoothly and underwent much-needed expansion. But as he found out, honesty and hard work were not rewarded in the current system, where individual rights and societal justice as it turned out were almost entirely subject to the self-restraint or whims of the power-hungry military.

Almost every time he took tea he used to make an additional cup for me. It was embarrassing for me to see a man of his age and civility heating the water, mixing tea and gently handing over the cup to me, but I could not restrain him from doing so. We used to take our lunch and dinner together sharing my home-cooked things with his hospital-issue edibles. His daughter was wedded to a Major in the army and when he came to visit, I could gather the extent of dissension and power-mongering that were going on in the cantonments, the degeneration of the armed forces as an institution.

(5)

Medical care in the prison cell was almost non-existent. Besides vexatious restrictions on doctors' entry, equally vexatious was our visit to them with two jail guards and two policemen escorting each of us. Rooms were not cleaned and sanitized regularly; bed sheets were rarely changed, water supply more often than not did not work and a nauseating smell from the cooking shed down below, which was attached to the hospital canteen, made our nostrils furious with doggish sensation. Cats moved freely, with occasional undisturbed accompaniment of big rodents.

There were three nurses. Two junior ones were under the supervision of a senior one, named Rashida, who came only once in the evening clasping her hands tightly below her sagging breasts, but doing nothing. I never saw her taking the temperature of any of the inmates. I was told that when asked to take the temperature of a fevered inmate, she said it was the duty of the doctor and not hers. I figured that Rashida and her like never heard of someone by the name of Florence Nightingale, the embodiment of womanly self-abnegation and smoothing sweetness of nursing. The other two nurses came twice a day, filled in charts of temperatures and blood pressures of inmates without actually checking them and at times, on request, felt our pulses and measured temperatures with visible reluctance.

With the medicines bought at my cost and despite pilfering of my personal cash in an organized way, under the cover of a search of inmate's rooms and belongings, I recovered pretty well. Professor Barua of Neurosurgery, Professor Banarjee of Cardiology and Professor Kibria of Urology took good care of me. My wounds in the head almost healed, pain in the abdomen lessened, cardiogram and ultrasonogram reported favorably and blood sugar count went down within a controlled limit. So, I thought to leave the prison cell of the hospital for Kashimpur Jail, where food was somewhat better and more importantly there was sufficient space for companionable conversation and walking.

At this time probably on April 8, by chance, Endocrinologist Farid Uddin Ahmed came to the prison cell to examine Selim Bhuiyan. On his way out, he met me. I was long known to him. He told me, the Institute of Nuclear Science and Ultrasound that I had sanctioned as a development project when I was the State Minister of Planning, had come up well and it would be a good idea to visit the place. The Institute was located within the premises of the University.

On June 12 Dr. Faridul Alam, Deputy Director of the Institute came to see me. Tall and well-groomed, he insisted that I go with him to the Institute. So I went. While showing me various machines set up to provide hitherto unavailable services, he explained their service procedure. I was impressed. I found quite a number of patients waiting in various departments. Observing my hoarse voice, Dr. Faridul said,

"Why don't you take a Doppler study of your carotid arteries?"

"Will that unnecessarily expose me to harmful radiation?" I asked.

"Not at all. These modern machineries that you gave us are marvels of technological development," he answered me.

So he took me to Dr. Nasrin Sultana for a test. Nasrin made me lie on the table, without forgetting to place a clean sheet underneath. Then she played a Rabindra Sangeet song on her computer and prepared for the test. I was touched to the depth of my heart. Myself an ardent lover of Rabindra Sangeet, I said:

"It is so pleasing listening to these songs while undergoing tests. I wish my wife were here. She loves Rabindra Sangeet more than I do."

"I love Rabindranath. Occasionally I sing. But while at work, I listen to Rabindranath. That does away with my tiredness, gives a new meaning every time I work," she said. I was pleasantly surprised.

"Medicine and Rabindra Sangeet are a strange but delightful combination. Please keep it up," I commented.

The test over, she diagnosed me with an enlarged thyroid gland and recommended treatment in a specialized institute. She got out an additional disc from the computer depicting my affliction of the thyroid gland, so that over time I could find out whether it further enlarged. I did not have any money to pay for it. Two days later when I went to her to pay for it, she did not accept. She said she gave it to me as a token of her respect for me. I was surprised; I had never met her before. I reflected that the world had not as yet gone entirely wrong.

A biopsy of the thyroid suggested a benign state, but requiring surgical intervention to be certain of any possible malignant prognosis. Consulting amongst them, they referred me to Surgeon Syed Serajul Karim. He examined me and said he would operate on me two weeks from then, only if I was moved out of the hellish prison cell to a clean environment in a cabin. Taking the Doppler image and the recommendation of the Surgeon, I went to Brigadier General (Ret.) Zahir, Superintendent of the Hospital to request Brigadier Zakir, Inspector General of Prison to allow me to move to a cabin at my cost. Brigadier Zakir wanted me to put the request in writing, with the recommendation of the Superintendent, indicating this was a difficult proposition for him. I did that;

the Superintendent put his laundry mark of endorsement and it went off to his office.

After about seven days and as many as three telephonic proddings from the Superintendent, the permission came. I could move to a cabin, but on the condition that I would move out, recuperated or not, within four days after the operation. The raw authority based on the barrel of the gun set a limit to my recuperation time, usurping the expertise of the Surgeon. When I showed it to the Surgeon, he smiled and said, "Move to the cabin and then we will see after the operation." I moved that evening with the help of Dr. Kakon and his young colleagues to cabin 301 of the Cabin Block to get myself sanitized for the slated surgical procedure. I observed how existence of authority and the application of the same were two very different things.

Earlier, a day before on June 11, Sheikh Hasina was released by the military-controlled government to enable her to undergo medical treatment in the U.S. Her eyesight and hearing capacity were afflicted in a grenade attack on her in a meeting on August 21, 2004, during Khaleda Zia's administration. Her fixed determination with an indomitable will to serve the country kept her alive and active, protesting against this State-sponsored terrorism and police persecution. I was right behind her on an open truck in the Bangabandhu Avenue when the grenades, as many as twelve, were hurled at her and people who had assembled to hear her speak. Nothing was done to investigate this ghastly crime, which killed as many as twenty-four people.

She was arrested by the military-controlled government on July 16, 2007. For eleven months she was incarcerated on a series of false and fabricated charges of corruption that could not be proved. Her release was unconditional and bore testimony to the government's sordid inability to prove any charge against her. The government committed its greatest folly by arresting her, missing an insight that, in these days following usurpation of power, ethics was grounded not on rules but in empathy. Both in her arrest and release, Hasina gained empathy of the people, who realized that the government of the day was seeking to perpetuate their own awful, unlawful and boastful power under the cover of combating corruption. The people clearly saw that the unrepresentative government had not been treating people equally and with dignity. It had lost its much-touted claim of clean and fair treatment, in contrast to the responsive administration of the politicians elected as people's representatives.

My surgery was slated for May 20. Between then and May 20, I had a few tests to undergo in the pathology and anesthesiology departments of the hospital. Moving with two jail guards and four policemen through the corridors for these tests was quite a spectacle for members of the public. To make my identity ostentatious, to the chagrin of the police and the jail guards, I put on a Mujib coat that blended my existence into a philosophic epiphany. Hundreds of people, doctors and nurses included, raised their hands in greetings when I moved from one building to the other and then amongst various floors. Despite the guards, it seemed I could seize the days; in spite of the imprisonment, I felt I could live a life of inspiring my fellow beings following the principle of *carpe diem*, if not Aristotle's dictum of *eudaimonia*.

In between visits to doctors and laboratories, I found time to read a few books: notables among them were *Madhannaya,* a Bangla novel by Humayun Ahmed and the remaining chapters of Craig Nelson's *Thomas Paine*. Humayun Ahmed had a facile pen; his prose was simple, uncluttered and touching. But materially, I found most of his books generally lacking in depth. I recalled reading one of his first novels *Nandita Narak* (*Idyllic Inferno*) in 1974 in Boston; in my assessment, it remains till now his best work. I found quite appealing his *Janani O Josner Golpa* (*A Tale of Mother and Moonshine*), describing trials and tribulations of a Bangali family during the liberation wars.

While describing Thomas Paine as a representative of enlightenment of the 18th century, Craig outlined very succinctly some of the painful episodes of the American Revolution about which I did not know for certain till then. That quite a number of the Red Indian tribes like Mohawk, Tuscarawas Onondaga, Oneida, Cayuga, and Janice aided the revolutionaries against the English was not known to me. The concept of equality of men enshrined in the American constitution, I learned, was largely borrowed from these Indians and their social customs.[49] Later, especially during the years of Jackson, these helping tribes were pushed to the dustbowl of the Wild West by the Americans themselves.[50] I was fascinated by the contents of *Common Sense* and the series of *Crisis* penned by Paine to keep the revolutionary torch lit and fol-

[49] Other authorities trace the concept of natural equality to the reliance of America's founders on the writings of Algernon Sidney and John Locke.

[50] The tribes named here inhabited America's northeast. It was the Cherokee in the south who, during the presidency of Andrew Jackson, were forced to relocate to the "Indian Territory" (Oklahoma) which a century later became the "Dust Bowl" of the 1930s.

lowed. In his *Crisis IV*, Paine announced, "we fight not to enslave but to set a country free and to make it upon the earth for honest men to live in." I doubted whether Fakhruddin and his cohorts had ever heard of this principle that enkindled the hearts of all people yearning for freedom all over the world.

In *Common Sense*, which helped spark the American Revolution, Paine declared that in America law would be the king and that following Independence the Americans would have every opportunity and every encouragement before them to form the noblest and purest constitution on the earth. When the population stood at 3 million, 250,000 copies of Paine's *Common Sense* were sold, enflaming the population for the self-evident truths of right to life, liberty and pursuit of happiness for all citizens. For the onlookers and at times discouraged people, the summer soldiers and the sunshine patriots who mushroomed around those in power, even in our country, the American Revolution had made it eloquently clear, hell was not easily conquerable. This realization brought consolation and patience to me under these trying circumstances. I thanked Craig Nelson for making me understand Thomas Paine, the mastermind of the time.

(6)

One morning while walking to the dentistry from the prison cell, seeing the telltale marks of a big hall room to the south of the Radiology Department, I recalled that it was the banquet room of the former Hotel Shahbagh. On March 7 in 1968, my father had given the wedding reception for Sitara and me in this hall. We were wedded just two days earlier on March 5. There were about 200 guests, mostly relations and friends. Sitara, clad in a grey *banarasi sari*, was looking exquisitely beautiful at the center of the ladies corner. I had put on a black suit and a red tie. The former Headmaster of Armenitola High School Shamsuddin Ahmed, my teacher who commanded enormous respect, was present. So was Sitara's Headmaster Kazi Ambar Ali, with his flowing beard and encouraging smile. Both of them were former colleagues of my father. After a while, when all the guests seemed to have arrived, my sister-in-law Mrs. Jahangir and my brother Dr. Jahangir took hold of us and made us move amongst the guests seeking their blessings and best wishes. Reception over, my father sat on his prayer mat and offered his *Mughreb* prayer there.

All these memories vividly came back to me when I passed by the former banquet hall. For 40 years we lived as a couple, blessed with two somewhat obstinate but on the whole wonderful sons. Since then a number of dear and near ones died. My mother had died seven years before we wed. My father died in 1974, my eldest sister in 1989, eldest brother in 2006, and the elder sister in 2007. Sitara's father died in 1990; her mother in 2001. There was something scary about death, which painfully shuts down things about which one knew. The bustle of life and existence became distant, more distant than memory could maintain.

Married with joyful dreams and endless expectations, I now found myself in the same place of my wedding, held in chains by an evil band who wanted us not to dream, not to breathe freely, and not to question the profanity of their physical force. Reminiscing and seeing people around, in spite of that, I felt the throb of life, resolved not to immerse in distant darkness and be scared of the silence of inaction, not to desist from questioning of power and incipient State corruption.

Living in cabin no. 301 of the hospital's cabin block was quite a relief from the hell of the prison cell. Entering the cabin, the first thing I did was to go under a long warm shower to rid myself of the filth and worries of the prison cell. The shower in the prison cell did not work. A bucket full of water needed to be carried from downstairs and that too was not available most of the time. The warm shower of the cabin gave me a fresh breath of life and reinforced my idea that I would not allow myself to rot while I would still be alive. My bath over, I ate hot *jao-bhat* with two pieces of chicken brought from my house by Hossain. I ate leisurely, brooding over days to come or not, brooding that gave Hossain time to cut out two pieces of delicious *himsager* mango. And then I hit the bed and slept like a log cut neglectfully in our forest area, till 4:00 in the morning. Awakened, I forgot that very soon I would be under the surgeon's knife and started reading Charles Frazier's *Thirteen Moons*, sent by Sitara from Boston. I continued reading Frazier throughout the whole day.

Next morning, I rose up fresh and in a good mood. After a breakfast brought from my house, Prof Barua and his associates came and checked me; he ordered tests of blood, urine and ultrasound probes. I did not have money to pay for these tests. In their stupendous stupidity the jail authority did not allow us to keep any cash, though they ruled unlawfully that we prisoners would have to pay for our room and medical costs. I asked my attendant to bring the required amount from my brother Dr. Jahangir next morning. Super-abundance of power, coupled with rabidity in execution, deprived the jail administration of the desired effectiveness; they were living and acting outside of reality. What mattered to them was the exercise of power and not the result that would be expected out of such an exercise. The approach was impetuous and conceited to the point where virtue was suffocated.

Left to myself, I sat with the remainder of Charles Frazier's *Thirteen Moons*. Earlier I had read Frazier's *Cold Mountain*. In *Cold Mountain* Frazier portrayed a wounded civil war veteran Inman who through his journey home realized the meaning of nature, of its creation and of the life of fellow beings. He faced a time when his courage, compassion and humanity were tried, when he killed the ruffians who, in his presence, threw a child right out into the cold to die from exposure, while looting and ravishing a helpless widow. Through his struggle and his life, he proved that the tyranny and meanness of hell was not easily conquerable; but certainly the harder the fight for right, the more satisfying and glorious was the victory.

I recalled how, in the vicinity of Ellery Street in Cambridge Massachusetts, where our son Joy lived, there was an Inman Street intersecting Harvard Street. I did not know for sure whether the Inman memorialized in this street was an illustrious descendent of the Inman that Frazier so stoutly and yet so gently portrayed as a man of both courage and heart.

In *Thirteen Moons*, Frazier portrayed one Will Cooper, a young white man discovering the uncharted and enchanted wilderness of the Cherokee nation, which was living in the southern Appalachian Mountains, before they were pushed into the western wilderness by the "Americans" during Jackson's time. Meeting in his middle years the Indian woman whom he loved but did not live with in his youth, "he looked her in the eye and argued all muddled and desperate wisdom of the middle years against her gloom." He realized they were not made strong enough to stand up against endless grief; and yet to him pain was the constant drone of life. In the backdrop of wild and passionate love in mountains, valleys, by rivers, under moonlight and sunshine — as assessed by someone from outside — he accepted that, if a man lacked something for which to fight, he was truly bankrupt. For Cooper the Indians with whom he lived after he was cast out by his own people, were his true family and their home and lands were his home and lands to love, enjoy and protect. Frazier in *Thirteen Moons* made me look back on my life that, with its many gifts and occasional denials, pressed down on me with all its weight. For a very long time on the verandah, in the falling autumn night, I remained looking at stars spread across the unreachable sky.

(7)

While visiting doctors on appointment in these days, I met at times fellow prisoners Nasim, Salman, Lotus-Kamal, Mufti Shahidul and Kader. They came from the Kashimpur Jail to treat their various ailments. Despite long days in the jail, I found them having the spirit of conviviality and the fight not yet beat out of them. With a tinge of retrospection, we talked about the sharp edge of the national policy pursued by our summer boys; we were confident, rule by intimidation would not last, they could not make our people live in a never-ending fear. We discussed about courts turning into a toothless institution with a bunch of sagging old men unable to protect the Constitution and the rule of law, with some honorable exceptions. These talks encouraged us to stand against the forces of evil that took over the country. We assessed the roles of Americans and Indians in helping democratic rule to strike its roots deep into our soil. We became confident: living was not always suffering and sacrifice and not at all unrewarding; certainly we were not there to fall through life's abyss into the darkness of servitude.

During these days I came to know more closely Isha, a girl of 14, afflicted with leukemia. She was intelligent, with bright eyes. She called me uncle and while walking along the corridors, told me about her school, the books that she had read and the dreams she had about days to come. Against the spread of a metal-colored sky seen through the grill-bound corridor, I heard her dreaming fascinating, vivid and powerful dreams about the society in which she would like to live. Her talks snapped me into wakefulness and at times swirling conversation. She had dreams, without knowing perhaps that death was trying to crawl to her. Dreams helped all of us to live longer, with purpose and meaning.

The hospital did not have a proper Oncology Department. There was no arrangement for bone marrow transplantation, which her doctor said could cure her. On our advice, thorough e-mail contacts were made with the Christian Missionary Hospital at Vellore, India, where such transplantation was a specialty. The literature that they sent by e-mail gave a cost estimate of Tk. 12 lacs. I asked Lutfuzzaman Babar, a former State Minister under Khaleda Zia and a fellow prisoner, to contribute Tk. 2.5 lacs; over a clandestine phone I asked my son Joy to send $3,000, which to my pride and satisfaction he did. The rest I asked her parents to arrange in any way — selling lands and other assets and then to take Isha to Vellore. With great effort they did this, went to Vellore, but could not arrange for transplantation as the Missionary

Hospital came up, contrary to their earlier information, with an estimate of Tk. 50 lacs (Tk. 5 million) or more as the cost for bone marrow transplantation.

They came back with Isha, found a cabin on our floor once again and started on a conservative treatment under the hospital's only oncologist Dr. Murshed. Moral outrage overtook me, but I could do very little, besides seeing her twice a day and at times holding her hands in silence, referencing the past and demanding a future over the contours of our lives and living, with a feeling of a distant and almost pain-inured inability to do anything else. Life was so precious and yet so wistfully brittle.

Babar as the State Minister for Home Affairs was responsible for arresting me on political grounds in March 2002. He acted in connivance with my local political opponent. In administration of law and order during his time, the reputation that he had earned was not enviable. Here in the hospital in changes he sported a beard, always kept worry-beads in his hands, prayed five times a day and behaved as a *sufi*.

One afternoon his wife and children came to see him and the jail guards kept them waiting and standing for about 30 minutes. Getting out of my room I found them, the wife and children of a former State Minister for Home Affairs, standing helplessly. I took the guards to task, arranged for them to sit in the nurses station till the permission for visit came over the mobile phone held by the guards, and helped them enter Babar's room with as much courtesy and honor as I was capable of showing under the circumstances.

This perhaps made Babar think that, after all, I was not as bad a person as he and his cohorts had thought earlier. He became companionable and after some time quite friendly. He was ill and fast losing weight. While walking in the corridors we conversed about how the political leadership of the country threw us into the doldrums in which we were. The Special Court in the meanwhile convicted and sentenced Babar with rigorous imprisonment for 18 years for possessing an allegedly illegal sidearm.

Babar told me that the army-controlled government of the day was the brainchild of the then British High Commissioner Anwar Chowdhury with support from the U.S. Ambassador Butenis.

"Four days before the army clamped down the emergency, at Anwar's house at Baridhara, both Anwar and Butenis had called me, told me about the army's plan unless the Awami League and the BNP came to an understanding about holding an impartial and peaceful election. They urged me to take the message to

Khaleda Zia. Butenis herself took the message to Sheikh Hasina. But both of them refused to listen or budge. They blamed each other," he said.

"Did you try to argue and convince Khaleda?" I wanted to know.

"I did. But I could not do anything due to the influence and interference of Salahuddin Quader Chowdhury, Major Kamrul, Falu and of course Tareque," he explained. Tareque was Khaleda's elder son and Senior Joint Secretary of the BNP — the actual power broker.

"Who do you think influenced Hasina in this episode?" I asked.

"You must know better," he replied.

"Perhaps. But still I want to know your version."

"Hasina was influenced by Zafarullah and Salman. And also by some agents of the Forces intelligence," he replied.

"Forces intelligence?" I feigned surprise.

"Yes. They told Hasina the country will be hers. And at the same time they urged Khaleda to hold fast, for victory was around the corner."

I walked in silence. He busied himself with his worry-beads.

Quite often he sent me snacks, pizza and burgers. Every Friday he brought in *biryani* from the share he contributed to the devotees and distributed in the *Mazar* of the High Court. Once or twice I sent him some fruit, kiwis and apricots. Every evening we exchanged notes about happenings about which we came to know through radio and friends.

One evening I asked him, "Why did you arrest me in March 2002 and file fabricated charges of corruption?"

"I did not. The Minister, Air Vice Marshal Altaf Chowdhry did," he replied, taken aback.

I did not believe him. He was quite chummy with my local political opponent and had given detailed instructions to the local police to bulldoze down the local Awami League office, arrest my supporters and file fabricated cases against me and them. But from a consonant feeling from my own heart, I kept mum. In the hospital I found him a different man beyond belief; entirely changed from his earlier philosophy that getting something was largely a matter of claiming what one wanted from the pedestal of power. He embraced me saying that, after experiencing the final failing of the ruffians, we should remain friends and brothers together. I nodded more out of civility, than with true response from my heart.

(8)

As prisoners in the hospital we were always under the guard of the jail security personnel and police. In addition, mostly attired in robes of religious persons, there were spooks of various agencies. Some of the guards were rough and mean, while most of them were civil and sympathetic. The rough and mean ones wanted to be gratified indirectly. They made their wants clear to my attendant Hossain. I forbade him to give them a Taka or even a piece of biscuit. To annoy me, whenever I went out of the room to take a walk in the corridor, they would walk by my side. I ignored them as little, jumbled-up insects, and continued my daily exercise. Whenever I went to another block to see a doctor, they became impatient to get back.

To give them a feeling of raw justice of some kind, I used to climb the stairs, avoiding lifts. Mostly pot-bellied and prone to sitting down and drowsing, they were implacable. With faces scored with annoyance they asked me to ride lifts, to which I always said no. I told them my doctor wanted me to climb the stairs for exercise and I would do so. If they wanted to take the lift they could do so. I knew, as they did, that they could not take lifts without me. My excuse for taking stairs was hardly a palliative for these persons well past the formative stage of an honest and hardworking life.

One of these days early in the morning there was a gentle knock at my door. Opening I found Professor Ashrafunessa of Gynecology with a small box of breakfast for me. Ashrafunessa was the daughter of Prof. Sharif Hossain of Jessore, one of the most dedicated educators I ever had the opportunity to know and work with. She was wedded to Prof. Mesbah Kamal of Dhaka University. As a gynecologist she had a famous name in the hospital. I was deeply touched by her gesture, carrying breakfast for me all the way from home. She told me she would bring me breakfast every morning. I told her it would not be necessary for I got breakfast from my house. She was at that moment, with her compassion and sympathy, as beautiful as people could be.

On her way out she was confronted by two mean jail guards asking her who she was and what she brought for me. I got out of my room in a rage, shouted at those withered specimens of rudeness bent down to their own gratification. They cowered like patched-up stray street dogs. After this incident, Prof. Ashrafunessa came on three more mornings with breakfast baskets. Then, at my pleading about the precious nature of her time and attention, she stopped coming.

Every Friday my brother Dr. Jahangir, despite being ill, came to my cabin and sat with me for about an hour. He was usually accompanied by Ishaq Sikder of our area and Shamsul Huq Bhuiyan, President of Chandpur Awami League. Occasionally my brother Dr. Arefin came as did my nephews Farid, Shamim, Dr. Mamun and Yameen. My sisters, Kohinoor and Nilufar, used to come every mid-week. We talked about the framed-up cases, lawyer's performances and our past, walking the memory lanes right through what appeared to be the last glorious expression of a dying world of close community and joint family. I told them as the operation day approached, that it would be a minor procedure and I would be out and walking in a day or two. Everyone realized that my assurance was but a forced desire to survive against all depredations of time, but certainly not a reminder that life always failed us.

Some said disease was nature's revenge for our destructiveness. This was not a good enough reason to forget death, but I did. The dominant nodule in the right lobe of my thyroid gland that needed to be removed required application of general anesthesia. General anesthesia in effect made one's senses lost and limbs inoperative; it was like a journey through death. And general anesthesia needed certification of the cardiologist for its application.

All preliminary steps taken, on the 20th around 10:00 am, I was taken to the surgery where Prof. Syed Sirajul Karim was waiting with his knives and scissors. I was made to put on a green robe by a sympathetic nurse surrounded by her juniors. Then I was made to lie on the operation table under a set of very bright and blinding operation lights. My brothers and sisters came up to the operation room and took their vigilant positions right outside the door. Before I entered, I passed a note to Ahad for my wife and children telling them they should know that I loved them with all my heart. I asked Ahad to fax the note to them as soon as possible. He looked at me in startled amazement, but obeyed.

Anesthesia was injected. I became almost unconscious and saw the surgeon coming up towards me with a smiling face. He exchanged various calls and signals with the anesthesiologist and junior surgeons and then adjusted the yellow circle of the operating lights over me. Then he applied his knife on my throat as if he intended to ceremoniously slaughter a bull. I felt his work with the knife but did not feel any pain. He completed, as I came to know later, his hemithyroidectomy in about 30 minutes and then sent the specimen for frozen section biopsy. The biopsy reported absence of any malignancy. The wound was sewn up, keeping a conduit for letting out the oozing blood. Then I was wheeled into the ICU and with an injection was made to drop down into a deep sleep, almost like falling away into history. I had gone past stupor back to lack of lucidity. I did not wake until the mid-morning next day, swinging back by the hasp of my conscious existence into a live world.

The surgeon came with his juniors, tapped various parts of my body, examined the bandages that wrapped my neck and declared that I was doing well. He allowed me to take a bowl of soup and asked the nurses to put me on sedatives afterwards. I slept, or rather fell back on my bed, with a darkness weighing heavily on me. I was moving in a dense fog, where near things resisted shape and color and far things escaped vision. Compared to the situation in the jail it was bliss, which brought a strong desire not to die in this beaut of a world. It was a sort of reflowing expressiveness, without being able to express in full. Memories from deep in the past came gently flowing through me, making me an endless part of the mystical work of God.

A day after, following another in-depth examination by Prof. Sirajul Karim and his associates, measurement of blood sugar and pressure, I was wheeled out of the ICU in a chair and taken to my cabin to the relief of my brothers, sisters, and friends. I chatted with them for a while and then lay down and slept. I dreamed of a blue day under the canopy in which on a hazy and cozy hilltop I was picnicking with Sitara and my sons. I dreamed of that beautiful Route 17 that I once drove along from Binghamton to New York over hills and valleys, in rain and sunshine, stopping on the way to eat hamburgers made at home by an old lady whose children were away from her in other states.

Waiting for the appeal to be heard by the High Court, I continued my treatment. Prof. Barua visited me almost everyday. Prof. Sajal Banarjee was also a frequent visitor. I went to Prof. Sirajul Karim and Prof. Pran Gopal Datta. Prof. Sirajul Karim assessed my prognosis of the thyroid operation as satisfactory. Prof. Pran Gopal gave medication for sinusitis. In addition, for root canalling of two teeth I became a frequent visitor to Prof. Howladar of Dentistry. For waning eyesight, I visited the department of optometry. Prof. Shariful Islam prescribed a bifocal with high-powered reading glasses for me. But my abdominal pain coupled with IBS continued almost unabated. Change in medication and diet could not bring any seeming improvement.

In between visits of or to doctors, lying down on my bed, I thought of death. Rabindranath Tagore, thinking about death in 1941, wanted to pay his respects before his departure for the next world to those who had spread the light of life along his way. To me the departure he so cherished was rather slow, braked with hesitation, for he never wanted to die in this beaut of a world. My idea of death was somewhat similar to the forest-lore heard from the Red Indians living in the Appalachian mountains. Identify the enemy, ride your favorite horse, take the hatchets that had killed so many bears far into their midst, strike down as many as you could, and then embrace a death to be glorified by the children, the next generation. The world would not be gloomy; the stars spread in the sky on the night of death would memorialize the dead in terms of their desire, bravery, accomplishments and compassion.

In the course of my stay in this cabin block, I observed three deaths, all spreading pales of gloom and shrouded under covers of sorrowful un-fulfillment. Gerontology had not as yet made its learning or understanding very popular in this medical university and hospital. In passing I thought that our jailors would be happiest in the pale of gloom and sorrow of our dear and near ones if we were to die, if all our tales like fully bloomed flowers with unremovable silence of leaves all around, shrouded our existence in anonymity.

During these days I found time to read James Michener's *The Caravan*. Michener in this novel depicted the clash of modern with pristine ways of life, and the happiness and coherence in the ways primitive gypsies went from place to place, in rags and hardship but having close bonds with animals. It included love between a modern American diplomat and a charming *Pawindah* girl, all in arid and borderless Afghanistan. Sitara and I had been to Afghanistan sometime late in the 1960s and the terrain described by Michener appeared too familiar, with traits of men and women very true to a society that remained behind what we might call modern.

In cruelty and generosity, enmity and hospitality, simplicity and cunning, the story as it was unfolded over a desert terrain by Michener appealed to me. It made me wonder, what exactly was life? What was that life to which we humans should aspire by misty veneration of the past? Did such veneration carry a tinge of retrospection about what life was all about? I could see groups of people in shadows around me — none very familiar, all too distant and out of material mindfulness. As it was apparent while writing the *The Caravan*, Michener researched extensively into the ways of lives of the Afghan gypsies. In novels or writings in Bangla in general I found such research and hard work lacking. Leaving out emotive content of one's own language, this difference had taken the English novels far above ours, the sixth richest language of the world.

(9)

In the meanwhile, with pauses at artful intervals, the harassment continued. The ACC all of a sudden hung two notices at our Banani house on our two sons, Jalal and Joy, living and working in the States for more than 17 years, to file a statement of their assets within seven days. The ACC knew that our sons were non-resident; they had their overseas addresses with them as well. On my instructions, our people following hanging of the notices this way informed them once again about their addresses overseas.

I informed our two sons about these notices and asked them to furnish their asset statements. But both of them, as young as they were, refused. They told me they would not do a thing unless they received notices at their respective living addresses and they would seek legal protection against such an arbitrary onslaught of the Bangladesh's ACC under the law of the U.S. I was not very happy about their response. For I knew these ruffians turn-coated into "honest hands" of the ACC much more than my sons did. Even then I felt proud at the stand that my sons took.

I told Sitara over a clandestine phone connection contrived by my friends that during our time we fought against Pakistan's armed rulers to protect our rights; during their time they would fight with Pakistan's Bangladeshi embodiments to secure theirs. In the process, temporarily, they might be dispossessed of some of their properties or assets in Bangladesh. But honor, ability to live in freedom and courage to face palpable injustice, were far more valuable than cranking out usual grievances for some lowly worldly possessions.

Almost every afternoon I along with Babar walked the entire length of the corridor of the cabin block for about an hour. One afternoon while walking somewhat belatedly, we saw a commotion on the road between the hospital buildings. A thousand or more attired in flowing long robes and prayer caps thronged and chanted slogans. After some time, we saw similarly attired Matiur Rahman Nizami, Chief of the Jamaat-i-Islam, the religio-political party of the country, coming out of the prison cell, getting into a new black SUV with sun-roof and getting out of the hospital compound in a triumphant way.

Nizami was arrested about a month back on alleged involvement in approving the container-handling contract of the Chittagong Port, kept in the Dhaka Central Jail for a few days and then transferred to the hospital on the pretext of an ailment. We knew nothing would happen to him; all usurper-rulers in our part of the world found the fundamentalist religio-political hands close allies in their governance. Nizami's triumphant release, despite his being a known enemy of the Liberation War in 1971 and keeping us behind in chains in Independent Bangladesh, was sorrowful to us but not unanticipated. Watching Nizami going out into freedom from the corridors of the hospital into which we were dumped, both Babar and myself became, without knowing, more morose than remorseful. In our state of mind, we remained incommunicative, maintaining perhaps the etiquette of grown-up men urinating together at a darkish tree on which a scavenging bird nestled its home.

Illiteracy and half-cooked training, joined with guns in hand, could easily turn people into beasts. Usually I read and wrote until late in the night. Time at that hour was so quiet, so facilitative of thinking about everything around one, so profound in visualizing everything one loved in life. One night around 2:30, I heard rather unusual footfalls past the nurses station near about the doctor's room. Slightly annoyed, I went out of my room, and to my horror, saw four guards with guns posted to guard Babar and myself. With satanic smiles they loitered on two sides of the doctor's room, where two female doctors I knew were on duty. The doctors were conversing with each other, keeping the door to their room ajar.

Obviously the guards, with the strength of guns in their hands, were about to succumb to their lust and were gearing up to do something awful. Only two nights back, two hospital security guards had raped a woman patient late at night down under the attic of the D block building. Boldly and loudly I told these gun-toting, betel nut-chewing guards that they should return to their place of duty in front of Babar's and my rooms at once, and that they did not have any business going near the doctor's room at that hour of the night. Morally weak as these people always are in such circumstances, they retreated.

Next day I told Khalifa, Additional Superintendent of the hospital about this and asked him to rearrange the duty-roster of female doctors in the night shift. I also told a female doctor about the incident and asked all her colleagues, through her, to keep the door to their room always locked after 10:00 in the night and not to open unless a known hospital staff or an attendant of a patient asked them to come out in aid of the afflicted. The jail guards, chewing betel nuts and falling into disarray of impropriety were withdrawn from the duty-roster the day after. Most probably the Additional Superintendent of the hospital, a freedom fighter of repute, took up the unspeakable matter with the Deputy Inspector General of Prison to hammer home some civility into the heads of their henchmen from their end also.

A number of young doctors, constrained with the gridlock of being medical officers, became quite friendly with me. During breaks from their duties they used to drop into my cabin or I would go to the doctor's room. Over tea, biscuits and *samosas*,[51] we conversed on various matters, the problems and prospects of the university and its hospital and the always-fascinating dreams of young people. Of them, Kakon, Rifat, Hasan, Jafar, Shanto, Mithu, Nigar, Shirin, and Shiplu were quite companionable and helpful. One of their friends was O.G. Khan who, although being a qualified doctor, traded in the stock exchange. After the day's brisk business he used to come over with chocolate and coffee. He was quite companionable. One night, following a conversation on Arundhati Roy, he presented me her latest book, *An Ordinary Person's Guide to Empire*. Dr. Jafar presented me with Maurice Bucailles' *The Bible, The Quran and Science*. I was really touched by their good wishes for me.

These medical officers were working in a blind alley without any avenue for being enrolled in higher courses. The authority, they said, told them they had been recruited as medical officers and would remain so. Without any avenue for higher training, working in a blind alley would destroy their zeal for work and yearning for learning. I told them they should take the matter up collectively with their authority and tell them that keeping a blind alley irrespective of merit did not do any good to any institution. It would make the institution moribund and kill off all elements of dynamism so very essential for developing into a world-class institution.

I myself took up the matter with some Professors and then with the Additional Superintendent. The Vice-Chancellor, Dr. Taher avoided seeing me. I told them when in 1998, in my capacity as the State Minister for Planning, I had a hand in approving this

[51] A small fried bread made of flour, potato, and spices.

University and hospital as a project. I had allocated an additional Tk. 50 crores (Tk. 500 million) for sending the thirty best and brightest young doctors to North American and European medical schools for undergoing higher and specialized courses. That not yet being done, trapping the medical officers in the blind alley would further hamper desired excellence.

They accepted the essence of the argument. Coupled with this acceptance, the demand by these medical officers provided a little shove that made the authorities open up the blind alley. This provided for taking in about 20% or so of them in various departments for higher courses every year. The authority at least subconsciously realized that an intelligent application of pruning shears could snip dead brown petals, yielding a place for new blooms right from the seemingly barren stems.

A number of young doctors almost always complained about their low salary and hard work. I told them that in our society given their scope for practicing privately in contrast to other public sector employees, they were better off. Then I told them a grievance of a successful lawyer. When he was young and working hard he craved good and delicious food but could not afford it. But when he established himself in his profession and all his pockets were full with wads of notes he could not eat them either; he did not have time for such delicacies served in a multiple course dinner.

Having passed mid-life, I had the advantage of speaking like a guru: when everything one wanted was available immediately and infinitely reproducible, nothing remained valuable. And then in a lighter vein, before both male and female doctors, I told them: despite their efforts and medication, statistics still showed that almost all men died of heartbreak while women survived to leave this world out of old age. The males looked slantingly at the females, while the females pinched each other with girlish giggles. I drained my coffee cup in poignant indifference.

(10)

On the evening of October 16, through Radio Today, I heard that the ACC had submitted charge-sheet, *i.e.*, arraigned my wife Sitara, two sons Jalal and Joy and my youngest brother-in-law Tafiq and his wife Ipshita and another sister-in-law Shireen Mansur, all permanent residents of the U.S., for corruption. The next morning the newspapers carried these matters in detail. Sitara had furnished her asset statement before she left for the U.S. Jalal and Joy, residents in the U.S. for the last sixteen to nineteen years, were not served with notices to provide their asset statements. Shireen Mansur lived her entire working life in Australia and Singapore.

These arraignments were done out of vengeance by Major Kamruzzaman, leader of the so-called Task Force let loose against me. The last time he and ACC's Investigation Officer Rahela Khatun saw me in the hospital, he told me all of my family in the U.S. were earning handsomely and they should share some of their earnings with them so that everything could be managed and taken care of. I had ignored his heinous suggestion, and now they came charging with all their might under the cover of law.

I thought we would fight their leaders and the perpetrators of corruption to secure a good future for the next generation. At worst they would seize my family members' properties in Bangladesh and would not allow them to come back to their own country. But the perpetrators of corruption would not be able to wheel the stars across the sky of freedom out of their lust for other's hard-earned money. They would only be allowed to acquire their own filth and falsehood.

Earlier on July 9, 2007, on grounds of delay for no fault of mine on disposing my appeal against conviction for corruption given by the kangaroo court, an application was made to the High Court Division of the Supreme Court to grant me bail as I was seriously ill and in the hospital. All medical records were submitted along with the application. The High Court Division took about a month to bring the application under consideration.

On July 25 a division bench comprising Justice Md. Mozammel Hossain and Justice Syed A. B. Mahmudul Huq, in conformity with an earlier decision of the Appellate Division of the Supreme Court in respect to bail in such cases of delay past the time limit given by the law, ordered the Inspector General of Prisons to have me examined by a duly constituted medical board and reported upon by August 25.

At the request of the Inspector General, the University Hospital on August 13 constituted a nine-member medical board led by Prof. Kanak Kanti Barua of the Department of Neurosurgery. The other members of the Board were Prof. S. A. M. Golam Kibria of Urology, Prof. Pran Gopal Datta of Otolaryngology and Neck Surgery, Prof. Anwarullah of Neuromedicine, Prof. S. Sirajul Karim of Surgery, Prof. Projesh Kumar Roy of Medicine, Prof. Sajal Banarjee of Cardiology, Dr. A. B. M. Abdullah of Medicine and Dr. Md. Farid Uddin of Endocrinology.

The Board examined me at length for three hours on August 14. It reported that, in consideration of multifarious serious ailments and prognosis of their treatment in the hospital, my life at an advanced age of 68 was in danger; I needed specialized, continuous and supervised treatment in a stressless condition. In consideration of the opinion of the Board and in the context of merit of the relevant case, the High Court Bench composed of Justice Md. Mozammel Hossain and Justice Syed A. B. Mahmudul Huq on August 28 granted me bail, despite vehement opposition from the counsel of the ACC.

The ACC not surprisingly was represented by Advocate Khan Saifur Rahman who had earlier defended the killers of Bangabandhu in the trial court. On my side, Barrister Rafiqul Huq moved the petition with unassailable argument and fervor. The same bench of the High Court on the same day stayed the proceedings of the case pertaining to the framed-up charge of approving an alleged overpriced printing of questionnaires for census and granted bail to me, while another bench composed of Justice Sharifuddin Chakladar and Justice Md. Emdadul Haque Azad granted bail for another framed-up charge of extortion.

My brother Dr. Jahangir and ardent loyalist Sikdar were in the court premises all the while, freighted with efforts and hope and running from courtroom to courtroom. Though granted bail, I could not be released immediately as in another framed-up charge in respect of alleged concealment of ownership of a house in the Comilla Housing Estate, despite the stay of all proceedings ordered much earlier by the High Court Division, I had to be posted on a formal bail. I reckoned that would take, from the start to the end, at least seven days from August 28.

As the High Court Division took a strong stand, detainees were being bailed out one after another. The most sensational one was of Tareque Rahman, accused in as many as thirteen cases. In the last one he was bailed out on August I and then finally released, in the midst of a jubilant crowd and supporters on September 3. On this day at least two of the BNP's second-ranking leaders reported to have been working hand-in-hand with the government — namely Barkatullah Bulu and Ehsanul Huq Milon — were booed, slapped with sandals and shoes and disrobed by the party's supporters when they came to see Tareque and to jump onto the bandwagon.

On September 4, Prof Rafiqul Islam, State Minister for Energy under Sheikh Hasina, was released on bail. Khaleda Zia was also released on bail on September 11, ostensibly under an understanding of conduct acceptable to the regime. The High Court Division also played a laudable role in exerting its authority in this regard. Following her release Khaleda escorted by two police contingents came to see Tareque in the Bangabandhu Medical University Hospital where he was staying, despite his release earlier on bail and program for going abroad for medical treatment. Through the window I could see about 1,000 activists of the BNP following Khaleda and chanting slogans. After about two hours Khaleda left Tareque in a visible attempt to wipe out the past with tears.

Next morning Tareque was allowed to board a flight that took him to London. But before that he signed an undertaking not to participate in active politics for three years. Reading the news in the print media next morning, it seemed to me that Tareque now lived a life of lie and unbelief. Walking in the corridor later, I heard murmurs of people about the end of acting all-macho by Tareque and his company. Before Prof. Rafiqul Islam was released; on August 31, Kamal Majumder of Awami League and stalwart in Mirpur was released on bail from the Kashimpur Jail.

On September 5, Obaidul Kader, the ranking Joint Secretary of the Awami League, was released. He was given a cabin on the same floor as mine on grounds of illness and need for intensive treatment. When I went to see him, he could hardly talk or walk and open his eyes. A large number of party leaders and activists thronged to welcome a free Obaidul Kader. I was guarded by the police and overseen by the spooks when I pushed my way to see him in his cabin.

About ten days after I was operated upon, the Inspectorate General of Prison wanted to take me back to the Kashimpur Jail. One night around 10:00 a deputy jailor came to see me. After exchanging clumsy pleasantries, he said a decision had been made to take me back to the jail and said if I wanted I could go to the Dhaka Central Jail instead of Kashimpur. Keeping my cool, I told him that duration of my stay in the hospital would be a matter to be decided by my physicians and I could not be pushed out without their consent. So for closing me behind the rusty padlock of the jail either at Dhaka or Kashimpur, he should swing the hasp and open the door of the doctor's office first.

Snorting disappointment from his nostrils, the deputy jailor departed for the night without saying goodbye. I could see him looking at his amulets tied in thongs in his right hand over elbow wishing that they would give him power to have his way. As I heard later from Prof. Barua, he went to him next morning and had the Inspector-General Prison talk to him over phone. Prof. Barua in his integrity and courage before the raw force and its gesticulations, made it clear that I would be released only when the doctors would find me fully recuperated. The Inspectorate-General of Prison damped down in its enthusiasm and retreated startled. I thought of an old adage: illness was nature's revenge for human destructiveness and an intrepid act of defiance was the only cure against human meanness.

In the course of my stay over months in the hospital, a number of nurses, Jahanara, Beauty Sutar, Dorothy, Mayabini, Nahreen and others became quite friendly and helpful to me beyond the normal call of duty. Jahanara was quite tall and stout. But beyond that, while dealing with the patronizing and obstructive conduct of the jail guards and the police assigned to guard me, she was very firm and assertive. She knew her work well and at times even the doctors consulted her about blood transfusion, pushing unusual intravenous injections, etc. From others I came to know, she had struggled and won over head-slamming obstructions to take her brothers and sisters out of an abysmal life, defeating the forepaws of poverty. She was ever-smiling and free of the mutinous weariness of over-worked nurses.

Dorothy was middle-aged and plump but quite active and very sympathetic. Almost every night she used to ask me whether I had taken my meals and was feeling well. Beauty Sutar was soft-spoken, but quite skillful in getting work properly done by the cleaning assistants. Almost at the end of my stay in the hospital, she went for higher training at her own expense. I found it quite strange and backward that the university did not open up avenues for higher training of Beauty and other nurses like her. It seemed not many in this administration bothered to remedy the boredom, desperation and depressed feelings of the nurses that accompanied their work-life here.

On September 4, Salahuddin Quader Chowdhury, Khaleda Zia's Advisor on Parliamentary Affairs was released from the Kashimpur Jail-2 on bail. To some of us, this reeked of tacit understanding or even collusion with the government. To me, the important thing in life was how it should be lived and from that point of view freedom surpassed in importance all other elements of life. The government filed as many as ten cases against him, a few ludicrous even by the standards of this government — he was even accused of cattle-rustling. These were clear cases of harassment and I was happy he was out of incarceration. On a number of issues we differed, but despite that I liked him for his courage and out-spokenness. We both agreed, degeneration prospers in misery and in individual and collective cowardice to confront it.

Coming out of jail, Quader came out with a statement that to solve the continuing political crisis, an effective understanding about the working of democracy should be reached between the Awami League and the BNP, instead of one or the other of them with the government of the day, which was not representative of the people. I found his statement hopeful and indicative of a change of heart, capable of providing an element for change stronger than mere patience against the outrage of tyranny and despotism based on the barrels of guns.

Following Salahuddin Quader's release, Salman F. Rahman was also released after a tough legal battle fought by Barrister Rafiqul Huq. In my assessment Salman was the best and the brightest entrepreneur of the country. Keeping him in jail without much of a charge for twenty months was a sordid damper to the growth of entrepreneurship in this country. From the confinement of the hospital-prison, I sent him through a party loyalist a note of congratulations. Receiving that, the good soul that he was, he came to the hospital's cabin block. Through the help of a doctor, I met him, both of us choking back tears.

We talked about the legal fight needed for release of Mufti Shahidul Islam and myself and charted the course of actions. Both of us agreed that under the circumstances for the citizenry, freedom was the war and the war had to be won. We also agreed that the night of the Generals and their shoeshine boys would be over soon and the victory would be of the people yearning for freedom and progress. The same night he boarded a flight for Jeddah to perform *Umra* and *Ziarat* at Mecca and Madina respectively. Both to my regret and relief he, the entrepreneur of our time, had turned himself into a *sufi*.

As already stated, the ranking Joint Secretary of the Awami League, Obaidul Kader was released on bail on September 5. In that grenade attack on August 21, 2004 on Sheikh Hasina and other Awami League leaders, Kader was wounded. There were still 96 splinters in his body that could not be operated out. One of his hands and both his thighs were getting thinner. In addition, he suffered from depression because his wife was out of the country, as she had been prosecuted in a fabricated case of income tax evasion. Released, he was admitted into a cabin across from mine on the same floor. Hundreds of party leaders and activists came to see him, quite often with garlands, wishing him early recovery. When, disregarding jail guards deployed in front of my cabin I went to see him, I found his face clouded like a glass of water made turbid by swirling sediment. I sat by him, took one of his hands in mine and told him injustice must have an end and soon.

When the last light of the afternoon was shimmering through the soft shadows of a cool September, I took leave of him and came out. With Kader I had so many memories of movement with people, speaking in public meetings and being charged by the police batons, the past sufferings and fight against subservience. Kader was one of the few amongst us who could call for the will and daring of the party activists.

On September 7 Barrister Rafiqul Huq was too busy with Khaleda Zia's bail application. When moved to one bench, it refused to hear the application on the plea that it was not given any power of such hearing. Barrister Huq then took it to the Appellate Division of the Supreme Court and obtained an order for its hearing by a different bench. In this running about from court to court he did not find an opportunity to take up my case for bail. The court that was empowered to hear Khaleda's petition for bail was presumably empowered to hear all such applications. Barrister Huq therefore, decided to take up my petition in the same bench after disposal of Khaleda's petition. That meant he would place the petition on September 9.

As a citizen I was somewhat baffled by the empowerment of various vacation benches of the High Court Division by the Chief Justice. As I went through the cause list — *i.e.*, the schedules of twelve vacation benches constituted for hearing important matters from August 29 to October 11 (during the autumn vacation of the court) — I could see none of the benches were given specific powers under Sections 498 and 561 of the Criminal Procedure Code for bail and quashment respectively. The unbridled power of the High Court Division given by law under these two sections could not be lawfully limited or taken off by administrative orders defining jurisdiction of various vacation benches.

Long before in the 18th century, Thomas Paine had said "rights of man" would come to mean not just civil and natural rights, but a re-engineering of the government to provide for the greater good, a State designed for the happiness of the largest number of citizens instead of its elite ruling class. In all democracies, in one way or other, this interpretation was accepted and practiced. In the case of work distribution of the vacation benches of the High Court Division of the time, I found it noticeably absent. So much so that only two days before, while moving a bail petition for erstwhile Justice Fazlul Haq accused of financial corruption, two benches refused to consider his petition until one particular bench was specially authorized by the Chief Justice to hear and dispose of it.

To me this amounted to a sliding of the system into degeneration through manipulation of meaningless procedures drawn from antiquity. As the protector of the Constitution and citizens' rights given by it, the Supreme Court was not expected to be a party in perpetuating the most wretched of lives in miserable prisons, as imposed on society by undemocratic forces based on the barrels of guns. The applicators of these forces conveniently and disdainfully forgot that throughout the world, since the days of the American and French Revolutions, the only legitimate source of State power was the citizens. This was nothing but a wounding betrayal of the very cause of our fight for freedom.

An understanding of the cause and meaning of our freedom was most lacking in the jail guards. Except for a few, most of them would stand in my way to walk, get my food, greet an acquaintance passing by chance and even talk to doctors. They expected gratification, to which I always refused to succumb. On a number of occasions I had told them, but for Independence presented to all of us by Bangabandhu, most of them would not have the jobs they were doing, would have served under foreign elements and would have been treated like slaves. They should therefore treat people with dignity and show us respect and honor, and must not abuse doctors or any hospital staff. Just because they were now given the duty of guarding others in chains, this did not give them the position to abuse and mistreat others.

Once very reluctantly, I had to tell a brute that one word from me or another political prisoner would be enough to beat him down to the bone once he was out on the street; so he should not regard himself as a "satrap." Living and working in jails or on jail duty was miserable as well as demeaning. As days went by, most of these people succumbed to the demeaning of values and misery of life as normal human beings. A number of them complained that during Khaleda's administration from 2001 through 2006 they had to bribe political masters to enter into their respective jobs. They had to borrow, sell their lands or other properties to get these government jobs and now they had to get back at least what was extorted out of them.

To this I did not have much of an answer that could satisfy them. I told them, despite their wants, if they bear the need out, they would raise good children; only that way could they get back what the system forced out of them. At times I told them about various events of the Liberation War, of successful struggles of poor men's sons and daughters to establish themselves in life, and of the American and the French Revolutions. The story of the fall of the Bastille in France inspired in them awe as well as hope in the people's power.

I told them they had to choose whether they would be an element in the people's power with pride and glory, or work to obstruct this power and against the common man's interest, and leave nothing for their posterity to be proud of in them and their life. If one guard, through his personal example of behavior and work could reform one convict, then his work would be a mission instead of a mere mercenary job of cruel and gruesome force. A few listened attentively, became pensive and I could observe a marginal change in their conduct. During Eid, as a result, despite absence of their superiors and unavailability of permission from them, these guards allowed our friends and relations to meet us almost freely. This confirmed my belief that one needed to know that what was worth dying for was also worth living for.

(11)

Some time in the middle of September, I developed a serious and persistent back pain. This coupled with insomnia made my daily walking laborious. Examining me thoroughly, Prof. Barua referred me to the Department of Physical Medicine. Avoiding the wheelchair, I went there, shuffling my legs with a raking motion. I was examined by Dr. Shamsunnahar and her assistant Therapist Azad who made me undergo microwave heat on the lower back and shoulders/arms and advised complete bed rest. Undergoing the treatment everyday for one hour I felt better, but the pain did not leave me entirely. I was told that at this age, with so many complications, getting rid of the ailment altogether was beyond the range of treatment available in this country.

On September 28, while going for my usual heat-treatment, I found that all the walkways within the hospital had been blocked by the personnel of the President's Guard Regiment, Special Security Force, the police and the spooks of various agencies. A stoppage of movement by ambulances as well as patients was imposed, due to President Iazuddin's visit to the hospital to examine his minor hearing problem.

A pregnant woman wailing with pain was made to stand still for about thirty minutes. But for a lady doctor, running courageously to the woman and shouting at the guards to make way for the gurney she had brought for the patient, the woman would perhaps have broken her water on the pavement.

I admired the courage of the lady doctor who said loudly and clearly that under the circumstances she did not think it was in public interest to stop people's movement like this for the seeming convenience of the President. She also said such a savagery was not seen anywhere in the world except in mid-Africa. I did not know if Yazuddin had some realization filling the empty space of his mind that his visit to the hospital, as the President of a People's Republic, could bring to the very people he was supposed to serve another dose of misery in their afflictions.

During this period, I was also referred to Dr. A. B. M. Abdullah of Medicine Department to examine my digestive system. Examining me thoroughly, he diagnosed the affliction once again as irritable bowel syndrome resulting from anxiety, stress and unwholesome food, for which no remedy was available in the hospital. Accordingly he did not prescribe any medicine. Dr. Abdullah was a charming personality and exuded confidence from his face and eyes.

Early one morning, two days after Dr. Abdullah's visit, Vice-Chancellor Prof. Taher along with Superintendent Brigadier Zahir visited me, surprisingly and without any sordidness. I did not expect the Vice-Chancellor in my cabin, since it was not his habit to come and sit by a victim of the system. He asked about my wellbeing and requirements and said that to him all patients (meaning political victims like us) were of equal importance.

I recalled while facing difficulty in getting admission into the hospital earlier, I had wanted to talk to him over the phone of Dr. Anwarullah at his request but he had refused to receive my call. Since in his system everything was said to have its motives, pretexts and special circumstances, very soon I came to know why he visited me. He was seeking yet another extension of his term as the Vice-Chancellor. His visit was an instinctive act of leaving no stone unturned for personal advancement, which was not perhaps a banality of evil in this regime.

Visiting various departments of the hospital and observing the general conduct of its personnel, I came to conclude that this premier institution of health service was not configured to provide help and treatment for the poor. For one thing not many of the poor, either through hearsay or referral by government doctors working in the rural areas, knew it as a center of excellence. Second, the admission procedure was cumbersome and lengthy unless facilitated through the strength of acquaintance or extra money. Third, the hospital employees at points of actual service, including most of the medical technicians and nurses, were not very helpful. They neglected, even ignored, those in tattered clothes and worn out shoes and with disheveled appearance. Dedication to people whose taxes in one way or other operated this hospital was an irritation to them. Fourth, the food was despicable, almost vile and bereft of attention by nutritionists. The chronic patients told me food was better in the neighboring BIRDEM hospital. Fifth, cleanliness had much room for improvement, specially in areas where the poor patients were quartered. The task of cleaning was out-sourced, leaving a sizeable scope for middlemen to make money at the cost of the poor and helpless personnel. Under direct administration of the hospital this money could have gone to them, which would have helped combat the main disease of the country — hunger at the low income level. Sixth, maintenance of machines was deplorable. I found very many valuable machines in a very poor state of maintenance and repair. The professors were very good both in knowledge and skill and diagnostic ability, but the treatment at levels where service was embodied as physical delivery was beyond them. Their commandments were always made favorable to the affluent at points of delivery. I hope some day people who would matter would have at least some insight into these afflictions of the hospital itself.

During these days, the High Court Division's vacation benches did a remarkable job. Showing courage as well as fairness, they bailed out quite a number of persons with drummed-up corruption cases and even put on hold punishment of at least four politicians sentenced by the kangaroo courts or the special tribunals. Misapplication of law, non-adherence to lawful procedure and even lack of appreciation for facts while giving verdicts were discovered by the High Court Division. It called for an explanation of the conduct of some of the spring-time judges who had taken leave of their judicial senses in looking at the carrot hung before them by those in power.

Open criticism of the kangaroo courts was heard amongst members of the public, on electronic talk shows, and even in the print-media. Violation of human rights under the cover of combating corruption and extra-judicial killings were pointed out by the national as well as international human rights bodies. A number of prominent lawyers like Barristers Amirul Islam, Rokanuddin Mahmud, Advocate Abul Baset Majumder could almost wrest themselves out of the clutches of the ACC in this period.

Deplorably, military personnel were reported to be occupying some space of the Supreme Court itself, determining its cause list or schedule for disposal of cases. Only Dr. Kamal Hossain and Advocate Anisul Huq remained unnerved and unmoved in their opportunistic rhetoric and acts in combating corruption with unbridled power of the ACC irrespective of law and human rights. Dr. Kamal went as far down as to openly criticize enlargement of persons accused of corruption on bail. There was seemingly no one to educate him even at this stage of his lawyering that one fundamental principle of law was to treat all accused as innocent till proven guilty beyond all reasonable doubt.

Sometime in mid-September in the cabin block I was joined by erstwhile Law Minister Moudud Ahmed and Communication Minister Nazmul Huda, in addition to Lutfuzzaman Babar as prisoner patients. As a result, the number of prison guards and the policemen were doubled to scare off visitors to other cabins. Visitors to the newcomer prisoners were mostly known to me and as a result I found it difficult to walk on the corridor as between two rows of cabins. When alone, I thought it was perhaps not a good idea to live too long. If not in play, it was better to retreat into oblivion without resisting the pull of the nether-ward forces, and lamenting the lack of fairness ruling our lives.

Death of conscience at times appeared to be a clinical reality, for our consciences as it turned out were totally different. I could not forget the high-handedness of Nazmul Huda, the twisting of the legal system by Moudud and his cohorts and the partisan application of law by Lutfuzzaman Babar when they were ministers in Khaleda's government. That the country became the prey of the beastly ambition of those with the barrel of the gun, forcing the people to suffer deception of life, was largely a contribution of these ministers of the erstwhile government. I came to despise, irrationally though, all positions of responsibility in government of such a character.

Personally, I did not succumb to tribulation. Huda treated me to tea and *samosas,* which came to him almost in an endless stream. At times his wife Barrister Sigma joined and gave us a lowdown on the outer world. Moudud was very well-behaved, mostly busy with writing two books, so he said. He explained well the legal positions and prospects, some with despair and some with hope. Babar became all the more religious. He walked with me regularly with his worry-beads in his hands and chanting religious *suras*[52] almost all the while. He showed a sideways interest in my well-being.

One morning, rather unmindfully, I introduced my nephew Dr. Muntassir Mamun to him. Dr. Mamun, young as he was, spoke with unbounded hatred, in a torrent sweeping everything in its path: "Yes, I know him. He is the person who jailed me unlawfully in 2003." It was a fact and I did not try to shush him. I could not swallow the rotten potatoes that stuck to the roof of my mouth, as though I was going to suffocate in the fight between the stubborn truth and hypocritical opportunism based on brute physical force. I let Mamun's words slide past without making any attempt at mediation or to apply the palliative of seeming civility. Neither had I looked at Dr. Mamun in reproach. I felt that persecution of Babar now was not a good enough reason to forget; one could not be a martyr without dying.

---

[52] Religious prayers and chants.

18 Bail and Freedom

(1)

The bail granted to me on August 28, was deliberately delayed by the Registrar of the Supreme Court through sluggish processing — by the lower courts signing the bail bonds through slow handling on orders of those in power, as well as by the Inspectorate General of Prisons under the cover of scrutiny and verification, reportedly as desired by the intelligence agencies. The delay in execution for about seven days allowed the Attorney General to file an appeal with the Chamber Judge Justice Jainul Abedin of the Appellate Division against the orders for bail and frame yet another criminal charge against me under the Income Tax Ordinance, 1984, in the court of the Senior Special Judge, Dhaka, *i.e.*, the lower court. Justice Jainul Abedin toyed with one appeal on two dates and then fixed October 6 for hearing of the ACC's appeal against the decision of the High Court Division granting me bail on the framed-up charge on irregular printing of census questionnaires. All these things were done to keep me in chains, since their tongues could not form words of obvious betrayal of the form and spirit of the remnants of law that still existed under the regime.

On the first day of appeal to the Chamber Judge of the Appellate Division. Advocate Khan Saifur Rahman appearing on behalf of the ACC said that he needed time to see the relevant papers. To enable him to see the relevant papers, the Chamber Judge allowed him a fortnight, a lengthy procedural asphyxiation for the accused already in incarceration but ordered to be free by the High Court. On the date fixed for the hearing after this fortnight given to Advocate Khan Saifur Rahman, another Advocate of the ACC, one Wing Commander Aziz, settled in for more mischief. He stated that he needed time to scrutinize the report of the duly constituted medical board on my ailments. So another incredible fortnight was allowed.

Unfortunately on that date Barrister Rafiq was out of the country and his juniors representing me could not convince the Chamber Judge for an immediate decision. He fixed a date at the beginning of the next week, October 6 as fixed earlier, and then left for London in the midweek. It was time that crept in to kill the incarcerated, while the procedures imposed a pretension that it was the other way around. Symbolism of honesty and fairness, pretentiously squeezed out of an allegiance to truth, left limited scope for me to frankly believe that the judicial process, in its broken bits and pieces, had not solidified into an unwarranted agony.

The case framed under the Income Tax Ordinance was obviously stupid to anyone with a marginal acquaintance with the relevant law and procedure. It was alleged by an Additional Assistant Commissioner (Tax) that I did not pay some due taxes for three years starting 2002 on assets that I was wrongfully adjudged by the kangaroo court to have amassed beyond my known income.

The allegation could not stand on five main grounds. In the first place, for the alleged amount of amassed assets beyond known source of income, I was already punished by the kangaroo court on July 26, 2007. Even if the punishment was taken as legitimate, under our Constitution one could not be prosecuted twice for the same offense. Besides the punishment so awarded had become the subject matter of appeal already admitted by the High Court Division. What remained to be decided by the higher court could not be adjudicated by the lower court. Secondly, the prosecution for non-payment of taxes could not be instituted as per S-161 of the Income Tax Ordinance unless sanctioned by the National Board of Revenue. In this case no such formal and legally tenable sanction for prosecution was accorded by the Board. Therefore institution of the prosecution was unauthorized and illegal. Thirdly, the concerned Special Judge for trying such cases could not, in accordance with S-171(2) of the Income Tax Ordinance, 1984 take cognizance of such an offense unless a complaint in writing was filed by the concerned Deputy Commissioner of Taxes. In this case the complaint was filed by the Additional Assistant Commissioner of Tax, making it legally untenable. Fourthly, cognizance of such a case could not be taken in the absence of the accused. In this case, the court of the Senior Special Judge took cognizance of the case in my absence and transferred the same for trial by the Special Judge. On grounds of illness I could not attend the court of the Senior Special Judge on the designated date. The impugned cognizance was irregular and vitiative of justice.

Finally, in this case the Prosecution invoked Rule 15(d) 5 of the Emergency Powers Rules as a basis for the offense I allegedly committed. As per Rule 15, the Additional Assistant Commissioner of the NBR was not given any competence and authority to lodge such a complaint of short payment of taxes. The action of the Additional Assistant Commissioner, in this case, was a trite reflection of willful transgression of lawful authority. On all these grounds, though distraught, I requested my brother Dr. Jahangir to ask Barrister Rafiq to file an application with the High Court for quashment of all proceedings of this case. I told him we needed to point out where the blame for violating the law was due, or we would become more its victims and make the law a burden on society instead of a propelling force for sustaining its dynamism.

In my assessment and from my point of view, the most difficult case to overturn was that of my conviction for corruption by the kangaroo court. In accordance with Rule 11 (3) of the draconian Emergency Powers Rules, a convict of such an offense even after filing appeal in the High Court Division against conviction, the appellate court was debarred from posting him on bail or staying his punishment during pending of the appeal. At the same, time Rule 11 (c) required disposal of appeal within ninety days from the date of filing the appeal. In my case about eight months had expired from the date of admission of appeal by the High Court Division. The Prosecution was inclined to believe that no posting on bail during pending of the appeal was non-violable or mandatory, while disposal of the appeal was directory or contingent on the will of the concerned court.

Earlier the Appellate Division had decided that for sentence not exceeding three years, when the appeal could not be disposed of within ninety working days for no fault of the appellant and/or in case of serious illness endangering life of the accused, in appropriate cases bail might be granted in an appeal. In consideration of my being in hospital for the second time since April 4, 2008, for serious ailments endangering my life as certified by a medical board duly constituted by the University Hospital on the direction of the High Court, the same Court in a bench composed of Justice Md. Mozammel Hossain and Justice Syed A. B. Mahmudul Huq on September 28 posted me on bail for four months.

Later when, on behalf of the ACC an appeal against this decision was made, the Chamber Judge of the Appellate Division, on October 6 upheld the decision of the High Court Division. On the same day, as per the appeal of the ACC against the decision of the

High Court Division composed of Justice Md. Mozammel Hossain and Justice Syed A. B. Mahmudul Huq to post me on bail in the drummed-up case centering around the ludicrous allegation of printing of census questionnaires at high cost, Justice Jainul Abedin of the Appellate Division upheld the decision granting me bail but rejected the decision for stay of all proceedings of the case till disposal of the rule already issued by the High Court. This was a slight disappointment for me, but then again upholding the decision on bail gave me relief and reassurance that I would soon be out of jail.

On October 6, the jail administration along with those in power, almost forced me to attend the Special Tribunal 8 where the Senior Special Judge Dhaka unlawfully transferred the alleged tax evasion case. I was having pain in my back and undergoing heat treatment in the Physical Medicine Department of the Hospital. After applying heat on my back, the concerned physician Dr. Shamsunnahar advised in writing that I should be on bed rest. DIG Prison Major Shamsul Haider Siddiky insisted on the phone to Dr. Nahar that, as per orders of the court, I had to attend, even if I had to take an ambulance. Dr. Nahar took a strong position as a physician. Over the phone, she said to the DIG, in front me:

"As his physician I have prescribed absolute bed rest for Dr. Alamgir. If despite that you want to move him, responsibility will be yours."

"You are unnecessarily protecting him," retorted the DIG.

"No. I am doing my duty as a physician," replied Dr. Nahar very firmly.

"Well, he will take an ambulance to the court."

"That will be your decision, not mine."

Seeing things going out of the ordinary, I asked Dr. Nahar not to argue more. Deputy Jailor Naser arranged an ambulance and I went to the Special Court 8 at my expense. Reaching the court premises, I was told my mere presence in the ambulance on the porch of the court would suffice for attendance. I did not have to go to the judge's chamber. I said, since I had come I would go, and I went. The judge, a sickly fellow with an aura of annoyance all over his face, came, perched himself on a high-borne chair and looked questioningly at me. I found Air Vice Marshall (Rtd.) Altaf Hossain Chowdhury who, as the Home Minister during Khaleda's regime, had arrested me unlawfully in February 2002 sitting with a glum face, for he was accused in a corruption case under trial in the same court.

Ignoring his smile and extended hand for shaking, I took the accused's dock and told the judge and the assembled lawyers and the onlookers that there was no cogent reason for arresting and taking me before his court. The objections were four: First, no notice as per law was issued on me that there had been short payment in my income tax from 2002 through 2007; in the event the notice was issued, the matter would have been settled in the normal course in accordance with the relevant law. Second, the National Board of Revenue did not, as required by law sanction my prosecution. Third, the law required I could be arraigned only on the basis of a complaint lodged with the Board's sanction by the concerned Deputy Commissioner of Tax. In my case the complaint was lodged by an additional assistant commissioner and therefore was not actionable. Fourth, the case was not actionable under Rule 15 inasmuch as the Additional Assistant Commissioner (Tax) was not authorized to lodge any complaint under this Rule. On all these grounds I urged the judge to discharge me from the accusation. In the event he could not, he should, I pointed out, post me on bail as further detention of me, on grounds already mentioned would be unlawful.

The judge sitting like an owl, heard, saw the relevant sections of law, and fixed October 20 for the next hearing. My lawyer Advocate Patwary said the judge could not do anything else despite my arguments. He was under instruction of the brute force above him. Later I came to know that I was taken to his court almost forcibly so that the Appellate Division of the Supreme Court could not order for my production on that day before them for release.

Not surprisingly, I did not see anyone representing the National Board of Revenue, either through a lawyer or the complainant officer, in the court of the Special Judge. I pointed this out to the judge and requested him to note this in his case file. It seemed he made some notes. I asked my lawyer Advocate Patwary to obtain a certified true copy of the complaint against me and other relevant papers so that, in between then and October 20, I could make a move to the High Court Division to see what a so-called independent judiciary down below them had been dispensing as lawful orders and justice.

"Yes, of course," said Advocate Patwary forcing a sardonic smile of acquiescence.

"Decisions of these courts these days do not depend on papers and records," commented a young lawyer I could not identify.

With that I left the cramped and squalid courtroom for an ambulatory ride back to the hospital.

(2)

Reaching the hospital, I came to know that Tariqul Islam of Jessore, having obtained bail in all cases, would be released from the hospital's prison cell that day. I was happy and relieved for Tariq. He had been suffering from all sorts of ailments. He had been tortured like a beast earlier when General Ershad had seized power. He was not spared this time either. I also heard that finally Mayor Mohiuddin Chowdhury of Chittagong was granted bail by the High Court on the 6th. He would be released as soon as the relevant orders were received through the official channel.

We had been friendly since the early 1990s when we had fought against the misrule of General Ershad. Mohiuddin Chowdhury had cardiologic problems. He was quite eager to see his only daughter Tumpa, who was undergoing treatment for cancer in Bangkok. Our shared distaste and opposition to rule by intimidation united us solidly and permanently. Around his cell in the hospital, from hundreds of supporters, I could hear the daunting sound of freedom. His supporters radiated confidence and youthful aspiration as free citizens.

Hearing about my imminent release, a number of summer patriots from our party came to see me. When I went out in the corridor for my daily walk, avoiding the watchful eyes of the guards, they veered in from four corners, shook hands and told me in so many words how anxious they had been for me and how daring were their fictitious deeds in local areas in my support. I walked and listened in silence.

Leaving aside these summer patriots; some genuine party activists also saw me in the corridor. G. M. Atiq, Iqbal, Ayub Ali Patwary, Shahjahan Shishir and his wife Nahar, Shaheed, Sattar, Matin and others came, embraced, shed tears. I consoled them and asked them to be ready for strenuous struggle to secure the future from the enemies of freedom. Besides Tofail Ahmed, Matia Chowdhury, Suranjit Sengupta and Amir Hossain Amu appeared through the crowd avoiding the spooks and the jail guards. Tofail Ahmed embraced me, pecked my cheek and told me the crisis was coming to an end.

Amir Hossain Amu told me he was crying himself hoarse demanding my release at every opportunity. I looked at him with all the surprise as from the slosh of a sudden rainfall. In my careful assessment, I found the BNP leaders had been more vocal in their demand for release of their political leaders and workers. Sheikh Hasina and Zillur Rahman demanded release of the party's leaders and activists from time to time. The voice of others in this respect was feeble, hesitant and overly opportunistic. I told such to Asaduzzaman Noor and Nuh-e-Alam Lenin who came to see me later. Mukul Bose also came one day, but I was too busy with my thoughts to talk to him on this or about his pretexts and motives.

While in the Special Court, I came to know that the ACC had started trial *in absentia* of Sitara, my two sons, two sisters-in-law and one brother-in-law, all living and working in the U.S. as permanent residents. The alleged offense was having assets disproportionate to their income, the usual weapon used to make the politicians bow down to the rogues of the State. They had by the 6th examined seven witnesses with nobody to cross-examine them.

The next date was slated for October 12, when they would produce twelve more witnesses, keeping twenty-two more in the pipeline. The charge in specific terms was fictitious; Sitara had assets disproportionate to her known income and her two sons, two sisters and one brother-in-law abetted her in acquiring this, inasmuch as they had a few joint saving accounts with Sitara. Since Sitara stayed in Bangladesh most of the time for meeting their needs and helping their relations, these accounts were jointly in their names. But without enquiry or even notice to them to explain their positions, vendetta was reflected in prosecution involving the so-called independent ACC, partisan investigation officers, a pliable judge and a dishonest public prosecutor — all appointed or paid for at public cost.

All these were the results of our refusal to satisfy Major Kamruzzaman and his cohorts, who proceeded to give us a bundle of wounds under the cover of honesty and judicial process. Getting this information from our lawyers, I decided to move to the High Court Division for quashment of all proceedings against them on October 12 — the date the High Court would come to invoke its power to the end of justice after the long summer vacation.

Two good news items invoked with the help of God awaited me in the hospital in the afternoon. My brother Dr. Jahangir came and told me that the Appellate Division, despite renewed attempts by the ACC, had affirmed my enlargement on bail in cases of alleged corruption pertaining to disproportionateness of assets with known income and irregular printing of census questionnaires earlier sanctioned by the High Court Division. The Appellate Division, however, kept the modification in respect of the case on census questionnaires, by killing the stay order on all further proceedings as had been decided by the High Court Division.

This meant investigation of the case would continue. Since the charge-sheet in this case could not as yet be finalized and submitted to the court, it was not much of a worry. Fabrication of falsehood for wrong punishment under the steely cover of law would take time, I thought. Since I was fighting against a distasteful attempt at wrongdoing by a batch of rogues, I knew that I, along with others involved in the case, would fight well.

Along with these news items, I got a copy of a letter written by Joy and Shuvo's lawyer Steven R. Long from Boston addressed to the Chief Advisor, the Advisor of Law, the Attorney General and Chairman of the ACC that they could not legally proceed against my sons in Bangladesh without proper notice and following the legal procedure of the U.S. and Massachusetts, where they had been living and working as permanent residents.

Attorney Long stated clearly to them, that as the government of Bangladesh does not abide by the "principle of due process of law" and its definition of the term "corruption" was "creative, suspect and void for vagueness," their action against his clients would be completely without merit in Bangladesh, the U.S., Massachusetts as well as under international law and treaties thereto. The Attorney further stated that their apparent abuse of the legal system to achieve political ends was "nothing less than a rogue attempt to retain a suspect system of government."

The Attorney warned that failure to respond to his letter would prompt seeking redress to the fullest extent provided under the laws of the U.S. I was happy to receive this letter as the first specimen of specific international protest against using "combat against corruption" here in Bangladesh by the illegitimate regime as a tool for their political business.

About proceedings in the court of the Chamber Judge Justice Jainul Abedin of the Appellate Division on October 6 in respect to affirmation of bail for me, my brother Dr. Jahangir let a word slide past his usual serious manner. When Barrister Rafiqul Huq was presenting his arguments on my behalf, that miserable wretch of a Major in civvies was trying to fly words from his mouth to the ears of one Wing Commander Aziz Khan, representing the ACC in the newly acquired black attire of a lawyer, over the head of the Barrister.

The Barrister ignored it at first, looking at him in reproach; but when it did not stop and the Major went ahead with his "heroic" advice over his shoulder, the Barrister lost his patience and with 75 years of life on the shoulders of his slender body shouted "stop this swinging, you bastard." The Judge asked the Barrister to calm down, but refrained from turning out the Major from the court.

Even in civvies the Major was not authorized to be in the court of the Justice of the Appellate Division of the Supreme Court. Or he should have realized that being a bastard was something more than a birth out of wedlock; a bastard was a perpetrator, protector and supporter of illegitimacy and immorality. Self-aggrandizement at the cost of service, fairness, civility and hypocrisy were ingredients that reflected bastardly origin and conduct of a person. I felt proud of Barrister Rafiqul Huq.

The Major was undaunted despite this and deluded in thinking that he could score a return on his way out to a wrought-out victory of ego. While exiting from the courtroom, in an unabashedly smiling tone he asked my brother Dr. Jahangir,

"How are you, sir?"

"Well, very well," answered my brother.

The major's attempt to transform himself into an amiable person capable of empathy, flipped upside-down. He went out distraught, with a furrowed crease in his dark face. My brother never had a streak of feebleness in his character to bow down to any hypocritical brute force.

(3)

The 7th and 8th of October in the hospital was dismal. Like other prisoners I tried to live on memories: good things that were done and could be done; sincere friendships and heroic deeds; selfishness and betrayal of some; meaning of death in prison and dying within it without realizing the realism of truth or its subjugation into mere convenience pursued by past generations. I thought over and over and then decided that one must not pity oneself; for if he does, he was doomed to hopelessness and fears.

In these two days while taking my evening walks in the corridor, I was joined by Barrister Moudud Ahmed and Nazmul Huda, both powerful ministers of the erstwhile government of Khaleda Zia. Our discussion centered around past pitfalls and mistakes, hypocritical maneuverings of the regime in power and some illogical steps taken by both the Awami League and the BNP. They suggested with active support from Lutfuzzaman Babar that both these parties should now take an united position against not holding or participating in election with the sword of emergency hanging on heads of politicians and forge amity between the two party chiefs. I agreed with them and told them that they should take the initiative. As the Awami League leaders and activists suffered persecution for five years at their hands, the offer of amity and understanding should come first from their side. For making the victim sit next to the perpetrator, the latter had to extend hand of friendship. They understood but, for reasons known to them only, kept mum.

On one of these days Moudud complained about the abnormal greed of the jail guards. He said he had observed that one of his nieces had to open her handbag to pay Tk. 100/= to the guard as the price for seeing her uncle Moudud. I told Moudud, the guard was recruited during their days in the government and at a high price to the political masters. So it was their defeat. I said that I recalled an old saying: "No one in this world was defeated from outside; every defeat came from inside." Never lacking in instant intelligence, he laughed out his complaint.

In days left for me in the hospital, I started reading Elias Khoury's *Gate of the Sun* sent to me by Sitara from Boston. It was a touching description of the sufferings and sacrifices of the Palestinians to get a place they could call their home. The *New York Times Book Review* called this a genuine masterwork. Going through the book, along with Khoury I understood and agreed that at times coming to the grave of one's ancestors, one needs to mourn the brave lost one, weep for the loss of one's love and be inconsolable in the midst of collective yearning for freedom. I recalled Poet Shamsur Rahman: "The child who could not understand hovered over your dead body in the hope that you would come, oh freedom!" Khoury sought to evoke the full sweep of Palestinian history since 1948 and he was eminently successful.

On October 12, the case on alleged corruption on printing of questionnaires came for a hearing in the court of Justice Md. Mozammel Hossain and Syed A. B. Mahmudul Huq. Barrister Ehsanul Karim, Barrister Rafiqul Huq being busy before the Appellate Division, presented my case and pleaded for stay of proceedings as well as bail. Wing Commander Aziz Khan opposed on behalf of the ACC. After a long hearing the Justice asked the Wing Commander to study the relevant law carefully and announced that they would give their decision on the next Sunday, four days thereafter. In the meanwhile on the following day, Justices Tarikul Hakim and Sheikh Abdul Awal granted *ad interim* bail for six months to Lutfuzzaman Babar, who had been convicted and sentenced to rigorous imprisonment for eighteen years under the Arms Act. All of us prisoners in the hospital were surprised and at the same time relieved that finally one avenue out from the conviction of the kangaroo court was opened up. Babar himself came to my room and gave me the news.

On October 15, my brother Dr. Jahangir along with my ardent supporters Sikdar and Mannan and my nephew Yameen came to see me. One of my former students and colleagues Dr. Saadat Hossain, Chairman of the Public Service Commission, and his wife passed by. My greeting to Saadat and his wife perhaps reflected a meaning beyond a mere formality. For a long time with my brother and others, we analyzed the case against me, my wife and children drummed-up by the regime. Our analysis, somewhat representative of a neo-liberal hope for organized resistance against repression, led us to believe that I would be getting a just treatment come Sunday and be released on bail two days thereafter. That was a dream of freedom.

On October 16, the High Court Bench composed of Justices Syed Mohammed Dastagir Hossain and Farid Ahmed stayed a corruption case against former Prime Minister Khaleda Zia and sixteen others. In a lower court on the same day, Khaleda stated that the regime should know that for prosecution of one member of the elected government at least three of the unelected government would be prosecuted. The news was blacked out in the media but spread from mouth to mouth like wildfire. On the same day, Justices Sheikh Rezwan Ali and Md. Raisuddin extended former Prime Minister Sheikh Hasina's freedom of movement home and abroad till November 4. Acting Awami League President Zillur Rahman announced that there would be no election without freeing Hasina from the false charges framed-up by the regime.

These two decisions in their fairness and independence were steps in the direction of the cause of rule of law. I became all the more hopeful that I would be posted on bail on October 19. To that end, I prepared an additional brief and sent that to Barrister Rafiqul Huq. For me apprehension was not good enough reason not to do what I was capable of doing on the basis of my acquaintance with the relevant law. I found it difficult to clear my thoughts and words to prevent them from disappearing within myself. I hated the idea of standing in the dock in the trial court and putting my hands on the bars like an animal in a cage. Each bail granted to me by the High Court Division was confirmed by the Chamber Judge of the Appellate Division when taken there by the ACC.

I was expected to be out on bail on the 20th, when the ACC once again took that ludicrous census questionnaire case to the Chamber Judge for review. The Chamber Judge rejected the review petition of the ACC and as a result I was out of the jail-in hospital on the 20th at 5:00 in the afternoon. Till 5:00 in the afternoon, the Inspectorate of Prison, kept the order on hold discussing things with the intelligence outfits. When we let it be known that we would lodge complaint for contempt with the High Court Division on the 22nd if I was not released by the 21st, they relented, sent their Deputy Jailor with papers to sign and then let me out of incarceration.

From February 3, 2007, I was incarcerated until October 21, 2008, a long period of one year ten months. This was definitely a punishment. The 19th century prison reformer Elizabeth Fry posited that punishment was not for revenge but to lessen crime and reform the criminal. However, my incarceration for about two years served the purpose of revenge and for preventing potential opposition to dictatorial abuse of society that I represented to those brutes with the barrels of guns in their hands and of their shoeshine boys. I felt satisfied that among so many of us caught in the process, I realized that the work of a civilized society resided in its capacity to defend the rights of its citizens, to protect them from dishonest and arbitrary treatment, harm and persecution from the State or ambitious illegitimate individuals.

As I passed out through the gate of the Bangabandhu Medical University and Hospital, with my brother Dr. Jahangir and sisters on my two sides, hundreds of party activists raised slogans for freedom. As the air of freedom invigorated my body on Nazrul Islam Avenue outside the hospital and the clutches of vegetable fertility of confinement and looming death, I at first felt forlorn and unspiritual and disconsolate in my thoughts about freedom; but then after a time, its concept turned out to be dauntingly clear, a feeling more compelling than breathing the free air that displaced the eddies of dust which rose in rebelling spirals in the afternoon sun.

Freedom originated in being born free and equal. Being born free meant absence of discrimination on grounds of color, race, faith and location of birth and locus of ancestry. Being equal called for equal treatment and nourishment for growing up and getting equal opportunity to go up the social, political and economic ladder on the strength of merit and perseverance. Freedom in this context meant free education till adulthood and medical care throughout life. Freedom meant right to life, liberty and pursuit of individual happiness without limiting the same for others. Freedom meant right of organization, assembly, movement and communication. Freedom meant guarantee against arbitrary arrest and harassment by the State or the government. Freedom did not consist of providing improved diet to persons imprisoned unlawfully. Freedom meant equal and fair treatment under law. Freedom pursued due process and rule of law. Freedom meant dismounting of summer patriots and their shoeshine boys. Freedom warranted the guards of the State not to occupy their own motherland, not to treat their masters, *i.e.*, the people, as their subjects. Freedom meant inviolable safeguards against booted kicks from the country's military and their civilian batsmen. Freedom meant guarantee for helping the disabled and handicapped. Freedom meant end of hunger, pestilence and poverty, for poverty killed. Freedom meant free choice of government by people through unfettered election. Freedom called for independent judiciary, administration neutral in provision of services as between people of differing political and regional affinities. Freedom meant fostering of enterprise and creativity. And freedom meant a life of shared bounties, deprivation and hardships. Freedom required dignity of all, willpower to sustain and cherish values that enrich life and its ways, liberation in the soul of feelings that were locked up in one's heart, in fear and tribulations. Freedom sustained and cherished creativity *sans* bigotry and inquisition. Freedom implied reasoned conclusion about personal, social, political and economic issues. And freedom does not always require crossing a river of blood, but does demand constant vigilance of an individual and recognition of collective rights.

As the procession of people took me out of the prison-hospital, I counted not many of these freedoms we have attained thus far. Loss of freedom, backwardness, feudal conduct, lordly mannerism and, above all, ignoring others for one's self, stood in our way. Encouraged by the chanted slogans of thousands, I committed myself to freedom for whatever years of life were left for me.

I recalled that while I was in jail, propelled more by affection than by reason my son Shuvo in one of his letters entreated me to get out of incarceration any way I could, considering myself as a prisoner of war. I could not, for I could not consider myself as responsible for my interest alone, or as an easy beast of prey for a bunch of hoodlums and traitors. At the same time, I felt relieved and delighted that I did not. If I did, I would not have realized these meanings and implications of freedom; I could not have resolved to fight the unfreedom, to assure my progeny that I would strive the most, contribute the utmost and bestow the best I could to make this world livable for the child that was born last night, announcing its arrival with a sharp cry for securing its rights.

Index